— THE —
COMMISSION

The **Uncensored** History of

the 9/11 Investigation

Philip Shenon

TWELVE

New York   Boston

Twelve
Hachette Book Group USA
237 Park Avenue
New York, NY 10017

Visit our Web site at www.HachetteBookGroupUSA.com.

Twelve is an imprint of Grand Central Publishing.
The Twelve name and logo is a trademark of Hachette Book Group USA, Inc.

Book design by Fearn Cutler de Vicq
Printed in the United States of America

First Edition: February 2008
10 9 8 7 6 5 4 3 2 1

Library of Congress Cataloging-in-Publication Data
Shenon, Philip.
The Commission : the uncensored history of the 9/11 investigation /
Philip Shenon.
p. cm.
Includes index.
ISBN-13: 978-0-446-58075-5
ISBN-10: 0-446-58075-9
1. National Commission on Terrorist Attacks upon the United States.
2. September 11 Terrorist Attacks, 2001. 3. Terrorism investigation—United
States. 4. Governmental investigations—United States. I. Title.
HV6432.7.S496 2008
973.931—dc22
2007039659

To the memory of the people who died that day
And to their families, who are still trying to get the full truth told

NATIONAL ARCHIVES
Washington, D.C.
MAY 30, 2002

Sandy Berger walked down Pennsylvania Avenue toward the row of massive Corinthian columns that were the most notable architectural feature of the National Archives. The public entrance to the archives was around the corner on Constitution Avenue, and it would normally be jammed with throngs of boisterous tourists on such a bright spring morning, eager to gaze upon the great documents of American democracy. But on the day of Berger's first visit, the few out-of-town visitors who did not have special permission to enter the archives were turned away. The building had been closed to the public for months, undergoing a $125 million renovation. The pair of 6.5-ton bronze doors at the public entrance were locked tight. The archives' most precious documents—the Declaration of Independence, the Constitution, and the Bill of Rights—had been removed from their display cases in July 2001 and placed in storage at a secret location as part of the renovation. After the terrorist attacks on September 11, 2001, the archives was in no hurry to return them to public view, since the building was considered a potential target if al-Qaeda carried out a second wave of attacks. The new goldplated titanium display cases being built for the documents would seal the Declaration, the Constitution, and the Bill of Rights in argon gas beneath layers of bulletproof, bombproof glass, protecting them from anything that Osama bin Laden's terrorist followers might have in mind.

It was May 30, 2002, eight months after the terrorist attacks, and Berger walked unnoticed into a separate entrance on Pennsylvania Avenue that was used by the archives staff, who had continued to work in the building during the renovations. Berger had special permission to visit the archives that day, although he was hardly pleased to be there. The archives employees who encountered Berger that morning would remember that he made little effort to hide his annoyance with the assignment he had been given there by his old friend and boss Bill Clinton.

Samuel R. Berger, "Sandy" to almost everyone, had a right to be annoyed. It was the Thursday after Memorial Day, and Washington seemed finally to be catching its breath in the aftermath of 9/11. Finally it was almost summer again. Many in official Washington, especially those who had any role in responding to 9/11, could actually think about leaving the city for a few days' rest. But here was Berger, preparing to spend the entire day inside the vaultlike archives. Thousands of documents? Tens of thousands? Berger had no way of knowing. What he knew was that this was the first of what might be several days of poring over bankers boxes stuffed with secret documents about the Clinton administration's struggles against al-Qaeda. Specifically, about Berger's performance as Clinton's national security adviser in dealing with the threat from Osama bin Laden's terrorist network.

Berger, an international trade lawyer before joining the Clinton White House, figured he had not done a document search like this in thirty years; it was the sort of laborious research work he would normally have left to a paralegal at his old law firm or to one of his army of young assistants at the White House.

But there was no other option for Berger, who ran Clinton's National Security Council from 1997 to 2001 and was easily Clinton's most trusted adviser on foreign policy. Berger had to do this research himself. The documents were so highly classified that he was one of only a handful of people apart from Clinton who had authority to see them. The classification on many of the files was "SAP"—special access program, higher than top-secret, with many files stamped in red with code words that limited their distribution even further.

From his new home in New York, Clinton had named Berger as his representative from the NSC in dealing with the special congressional committee that had been set up in early 2002 to investigate intelligence failures before September 11. Berger assumed he would later fill the same liaison role for Clinton if the 9/11 families overcame fierce opposition from the Bush White House and managed to pressure Congress to establish an independent commission to investigate the attacks. Before

Berger talked with any outside investigators, he needed to remind him-self what was in his files and in the files of the rest of his NSC staff.

Berger thought it was just so typical that he would be left with the assignment. He brought it on himself, he knew. "Just leave it to Sandy" had been a mantra in the Clinton White House, and Berger had never protested enough when he heard it.

Since 9/11, he had been forced to become the Clinton administra-tion's de facto spokesman again, responding to all of the reporters who wanted to know whether Clinton and his White House team felt they bore any responsibility for the attacks, whether Clinton had done every-thing he could during his eight years in office to kill bin Laden. Many of Berger's former colleagues in the administration had ducked the report-ers' calls—"Everyone else stepped back from the questions," he said—but not Berger. He guessed he had spent hundreds of hours answering reporters' calls since 9/11; that work was all unpaid, of course.

But if annoyance was his first reaction to the assignment in the archives, his second was fear. And that, too, was typical of Sandy Berger. Beneath his gruff amiability, there was deep insecurity that, even he admitted, bordered on paranoia.

Was there something in the White House documents that might embarrass Berger? Was there some e-mail that would give his enemies a chance to argue that Berger and his NSC staff had left the nation vulner-able to attack by al-Qaeda? If he found embarrassing documents in the files, what would he do?

Was this the day he first considered smuggling classified documents out of the archives—in his pockets, in his socks—to try to protect himself?

Berger entered the lobby of the archives, passed through the magne-tometer, and was ushered into the comfortable private office of Nancy Kegan Smith, a senior archivist responsible for White House docu-ments. Berger carried his cell phone and a leather portfolio that had a notepad inside. His use of Smith's office to review the documents was a violation of several government rules on the handling of classified doc-uments. He should have been placed in a secure reading room, where he might have been monitored by a guard or a surveillance camera. He should have been forced to leave his cell phone behind. But the archives had long made exceptions for former senior officials like Berger. He might be out of government now, but the archives staff knew that in Washington's revolving door, Berger was likely to be back in power in a future Democrat administration—Hillary Clinton's secretary of state, some thought—and able to make trouble for the archives and its budget requests. Keep him comfortable. Keep him happy.

Berger took a seat next to a coffee table in Smith's office. For his first day of the review, five boxes had been placed on a metal cart that was wheeled up next to him. The boxes contained documents taken from the "W" library; the 153 boxes that made up the "W" library held some of Clinton's most secret White House intelligence files. The archives staff said Berger made a special request to see one of the boxes, W-049, that contained Richard A. Clarke's personal office files. Clarke had been the NSC's counterterrorism director since early in the Clinton presidency— a job he continued to hold in the Bush administration. Berger knew that Clarke's files would be the definitive record of how the Clinton White House had dealt with the al-Qaeda threat.

Whatever the headaches of spending so much time in the archives, friends thought that Berger should have taken comfort from the assignment. He was being reunited with paperwork that, they believed, showed that Berger had mostly done his job at the White House when it came to al-Qaeda. Certainly he had a lot less explaining to do than others. During the Clinton presidency, Berger had been as obsessed with bin Laden and the terrorist network as anyone in the administration. As obsessed as Clarke, the White House's "Chicken Little" on al-Qaeda. As obsessed as George Tenet, the director of central intelligence, who liked to say that his "hair was on fire" when it came to bin Laden.

It had been Berger who helped convince Clinton in the mid-1990s, at a time when bin Laden and his terrorist training camps barely registered with the Washington press corps and not at all with the public, of the danger posed by al-Qaeda. It was Berger who requested that the CIA prepare a daily report for the White House with all of the agency's overnight intelligence on bin Laden. It was Berger who made Clarke a member of the White House Principals Committee when it met to discuss terrorist threats, allowing an otherwise middle-ranking NSC bureaucrat to treat Tenet and Secretary of State Madeleine Albright as equals (which the empire-building Clarke was pleased to do). Berger had worked through Christmas Day 1999 and the following New Year's Eve, waiting to respond to the al-Qaeda attack that had been predicted for the millennium.

At 3:00 a.m. on January 1, 2000, Berger called Clarke. "Can I breathe now?" he asked. Clarke believed the fact that there was no attack probably had something to do with Berger's hard work.

"Sandy got it," Tenet would say of Berger, his sometime friend, sometime adversary, on the question of al-Qaeda. It occurred to more than a few people at Tenet's CIA that the world would be different if Berger had still been national security adviser in the spring and summer of 2001—and not Condoleezza Rice, Berger's successor, who had seemed so astonishingly incurious about the agency's drumbeat of warnings in the months before 9/11.

But Berger was not a man to take comfort from the facts. Facts could be spun, he knew; they always were. He had always been a worrier. Friends said it was a trait that dated from childhood; his father died suddenly when Berger was only eight, leaving his widowed mother to struggle to run the family's small department store in upstate New York. In Bill Clinton's frenetic White House, Berger's worrying became obsessive; he had become a catastrophizer.

Even by the standards of Washington workaholics, Berger was exceptional. His fifteen-hour workdays at the NSC alarmed his staff. They worried that his perennial weight problems mixed with exhaustion would one day end up with him clutching his chest in a heart attack; Berger hid his paunch beneath well-tailored, dark business suits. He seemed to think that if he went home, if he was away from the White House even for a few hours, something would go terribly wrong, and he would be left to take the blame. Reputations could be destroyed in a single news cycle. He had seen it again and again.

Investigators believed Berger had wanted to review box W-049 for a special reason, although he certainly did share that reason with Nancy Smith and the other archivists. He wanted to find a copy of a highly classified fifteen-page report that he had asked Clarke to prepare in early 2000; it reviewed what had gone right and wrong in the government's efforts to respond to millennium threats. It was clear that major attacks by al-Qaeda and its sympathizers had been thwarted in December 1999, including the bombing of Los Angeles International Airport. The Algerian-born terrorist who intended to carry out the bombing, Ahmed

Ressam, was arrested by an alert customs agent as he tried to cross the border from Canada.

Berger's assignment to Clarke to write the "after-action report," which included a list of twenty-nine recommendations for overhauling government antiterrorism programs, might have been seen as one more bit of evidence of Berger's admirable focus on the threat.

But in his paranoia, Berger could see that the report might be read differently—*would* be read differently—if it became public. Certainly it would be read differently at the Bush White House and among congressional Republicans eager to find a Democratic scapegoat for 9/11. Since several of Clarke's recommendations had not been acted on before Clinton left office, Berger had reason to fear it would be seized upon as proof that he had not done all he could to prevent a terrorist attack. All of his hard work at the White House, all of his obsession with bin Laden, would be beside the point.

Berger's first day at the archives ended in frustration. He feared he would have to come back. He had seen only a small fraction of the documents in the files. He had not found a copy of Clarke's 2000 after-action report. Eight years of e-mails and paperwork! How could he possibly get through it all, even if he devoted several more days to the task? It was doubly frustrating because the archives' rules required Berger to leave behind the pages of handwritten notes he had taken that day. Since the notes were based on classified documents, they, too, were classified.

It was during the second and third visits that, Berger later confessed, he decided to begin to break the law.

His second visit, on July 18, 2003, came more than a year after his first. He had returned to the archives to prepare himself to answer questions from the newly created independent commission—the 9/11 commission, as it was being called—and to review the NSC files before they were turned over to the commission's staff. The special congressional 9/11 committee had been blocked from seeing NSC files, on separation-of-powers grounds. But the White House had reluctantly agreed to make them available to the 9/11 commission.

During this visit, Berger decided that whatever the archives' rules, he would take his notes with him. It seemed crazy to return to his office empty-handed, as if he could have otherwise remembered what was in the thousands of pages of documents he had reviewed. Removing the notes seemed innocent enough. It wasn't as if he were stealing the documents themselves, he argued to himself. And most of the documents were from his own files, so this was secret information he had already seen.

He needed to create a distraction and asked Smith, who sat at her desk working on her computer, if he could have a few minutes of privacy to make a phone call. His secretary at his newly opened consulting firm had called him about six times that day with messages from clients. He needed to call them back. He still had a business to run. Smith agreed, leaving Berger alone in her office.

He moved quickly. He ripped off the top fifteen pages of his handwritten notes from the pad, folded them into thirds, and placed them in one of the inner pockets of his jacket. He left two other pages behind in hopes that would throw the archivist off the trail. He hated to leave any notes behind, but he was pleased to have something he could review in his office. Some notes were better than none, he thought.

It was on his third visit, on September 2, 2003, that Berger began to steal the documents themselves. He had finally found a copy of Clarke's 2000 after-action report; it had been faxed to the archives a few weeks earlier from Clinton's presidential library in Little Rock, Arkansas.

He created the same distraction with Smith, claiming he needed to make a phone call for business. She obliged. But Berger turned out to be a lousy thief, and he was detected almost immediately. Another archivist, John Laster, bumped into him on his way to the men's room. "Okay, I know this is odd," Laster wrote to Smith in an e-mail later that day. He explained that when he passed Berger in the hallway, he saw him "fiddling with something white, which appeared to be a piece of paper or multiple pieces of paper" that had been "rolled around his ankle and underneath his pant leg, with a portion of the paper sticking out underneath."

Smith was alarmed. She tried to convince herself there was an innocent explanation. In a return e-mail, she speculated that Laster had seen something else—maybe a white compression sock, the sort used for phlebitis and other circulatory problems; maybe the sock had the same color as white paper. Berger was overweight. He had seemed agitated. Maybe there was some health problem.

Surely Berger wasn't stealing classified documents, she thought. She prayed. For an archivist responsible for classified documents—and few documents were as highly classified as the ones Berger was reviewing—the idea was almost too much for Smith to bear. Taking secret documents was a crime, of course. Surely it would ruin Berger, ending his hopes for another important government job; he might even be sent to jail. And there was every reason to think the archives staff would be punished—fired?—for having allowed it to happen.

It was too late to try to reconstruct the files Berger had already gone through; they had never been fully cataloged, so it was impossible to know exactly what he might have stolen.

Much as she dreaded the idea, Smith decided that she would have to test Berger on his next visit to the archives. He was due to return on October 2. Smith and her staff gathered the files that Berger had asked to see on the next visit and carefully numbered each document on the back in a light pencil. If he took something, Smith could detect it instantly.

350 PARK AVENUE
New York, N.Y.
DECEMBER 12, 2002

The boxy glass-and-steel building at 350 Park Avenue in Manhattan had no sign in the lobby listing its tenants. Visitors entered the thirty-story building between East 51st and East 52nd streets by invitation only. The burly, unsmiling security guards saw to that. One of the tenants, former secretary of state Henry Kissinger, had more stringent security measures. Clients entered the offices of Kissinger Associates, his consulting firm, only if they could prove their identity to a receptionist who sat behind a thick sheet of security glass set in a wall near the elevator lobby on the twenty-sixth floor. The quality of the security was not matched by the decor. Kissinger had nothing to prove to his clients, so while tenants at 350 Park Avenue enjoyed a fine view of the Seagram Building and an especially tony stretch of Manhattan's East side, Kissinger's offices were otherwise remarkably shabby, with worn carpets and dying plants.

Lorie Van Auken of East Brunswick, New Jersey, had an invitation to meet with Kissinger at 11:30 a.m. on Thursday, December 12, 2002. It was cold, and she walked in off Park Avenue in a heavy wool coat. Her husband, Ken, had also worked in Manhattan, about four miles south of Kissinger's office, with what Lorie knew had been a much more dramatic view out his office window. Ken Van Auken was a bond trader at the investment firm of Cantor Fitzgerald, and he had been at work at the firm's office on the 105th floor of the North Tower of the World Trade Center when an American Airlines Boeing 767 plunged into the building at 8:46 a.m. on September 11, 2001. Lorie heard her husband's voice one last time when she returned home from grocery shopping on that warm, cloudless morning to find a voice message from Ken: "I love you. I'm in the World Trade Center. And the building was hit by something. I don't know if I'm going to get out."

Lorie was part of a delegation of about a dozen 9/11 widows, widowers, and other family activists who had come to see Kissinger to hear him justify why he should lead the independent federal commission that had been created to investigate the attacks. The commission's official name was a mouthful ("the National Commission on Terrorist Attacks upon the United States"), but it was already being referred to as, simply, the Kissinger Commission. When she heard that for the first time, Lorie flinched. The Kissinger Commission? She was convinced that Kissinger, whose selection as chairman had been announced two weeks earlier by President Bush, had been a terrible choice to run the investigation. It was hard for her to imagine a worse choice.

The group was buzzed into the offices of Kissinger Associates and escorted into what appeared to be his personal conference room. The room was crazily, unbearably warm—maybe eighty-five degrees, maybe more. Even as they threw off their coats and sweaters, Lorie and the others could feel themselves begin to sweat. It would not occur to Lorie until later that Kissinger might have done this on purpose; his old colleagues at the State Department could have told her it was an old and obvious diplomatic trick to overheat a meeting room if the goal was a short negotiation—or drowsy negotiators.

Lorie quickly scouted the framed photographs on the wall, which showed Kissinger with government leaders from around the world and celebrity friends from New York and Hollywood. She was looking for Arabs, in particular anyone from Saudi Arabia, the birthplace of Osama bin Laden and fifteen of the nineteen hijackers on 9/11. Was there a photograph of King Fahd? Prince Abdullah? She had some idea what they looked like. It's amazing the things I know now, Lorie said to herself. From her research, she knew bin Laden's family continued to control a multibillion-dollar Saudi construction firm that had been close to the royal family for decades. The company, the Bin Laden Group, was just the sort of well-connected foreign outfit that might have sought Kissinger's help over the years—especially after 9/11, when it might have needed to distance itself in the West from any connection to the disowned Osama. Was there a photo of Kissinger with Muhammed bin Laden, the company's patriarch and the terrorist's father? She didn't see any Arab faces in the photographs, at least none that she could identify.

Kissinger was already in the room. He looked much older and more fragile than his visitors had expected. Kissinger was seventy-nine and had not been in good health; he stooped noticeably. Lorie certainly did not want to make the comparison, but she thought instantly of Grandpa Edward, her kindly, very short, Russian-born grandfather. Kissinger just doesn't look like a bad guy, she thought.

Age had not diminished Kissinger's mind or ability to charm. And he impressed Lorie with the warmth of his welcome to the families. As chairman of the 9/11 commission, he said, he had been given the most important assignment of his life. Forget his years as secretary of state, as Richard Nixon's national security adviser in the White House. Forget the Nobel Peace Prize. His new job was the one that "truly humbled" him. "I have never been given a greater honor than leading this inquiry," Kissinger said, his trademark Germanic basso profundo reverberating around the room. He lowered himself onto the sofa, with his visitors in seats in a semicircle around him. He offered them coffee from a pot that had been brought into the conference room.

Hot coffee had no appeal in Kissinger's overheated office. "Dr. Kissinger, do you suppose we might crack open one of the windows?" asked another of the widows, Patty Casazza. "It's very warm in here."

"Is it?" Kissinger answered, seemingly oblivious to the fact that some of his guests were wiping perspiration from their foreheads. Kissinger was in a coat and tie. He agreed, reluctantly, to open a window. The room began to cool.

For the next several minutes, Kissinger was mostly silent, listening—attentively, it seemed—as the family activists went around the room, introducing themselves and describing their long struggle in Washington to create the commission. No one doubted that it was the families' unrelenting lobbying that had forced President Bush to reverse himself and agree to an independent investigation of 9/11. When Kissinger did interrupt his visitors, it was only to salute the families for their commitment to honoring the memory of their victims. Lorie could see she was falling for Kissinger, and she didn't like it. "He is so smooth, so diplomatic," she said.

She tried to force the image of her grandfather out of her head. She needed to remind herself why she was here and what she had learned about Kissinger in her days and nights of digging on the Internet. She needed to think about Ken. This is Henry Kissinger, and he's going to conduct maybe the only investigation of the event that caused my husband's death, she thought to herself. If I don't ask the tough questions now, I'll never ask them.

Since the announcement of Kissinger's appointment, Lorie and a trio of other 9/11 widows from New Jersey—they called themselves "the Jersey Girls," after the Bruce Springsteen song—had been at work, learning everything they could about Kissinger Associates; Kissinger had set up the firm in 1982. A simple Google search showed the widows that Kissinger's conflicts of interest at his consulting firm were obvious—and everywhere. Kissinger had refused to make the client list public. But it was reported to include dozens of Fortune 500 companies, including several oil giants with reason to fear an investigation that might implicate Saudi Arabia and other oil-rich Arab countries in bin Laden's fund-raising.

Lorie was in her mid-forties, older than many of the other widows, and her suspicions about Kissinger went well beyond his consulting firm. She remembered him from his years in power in Washington in the 1970s. Nixon, Vietnam, the secret bombing of Cambodia, Watergate. This was a man so paranoid about keeping secrets that he had some of his colleagues in the Nixon White House wiretapped. It was laughable, Lorie thought, to think of Kissinger as a man eager to expose the truth about anything, especially 9/11. Almost certainly why Bush had picked him, she figured.

The introductions over, Kissinger opened himself up to questions. At first, Lorie and the other Jersey Girls wanted to be diplomatic. But they had come to the meeting with an agenda—and a demand. They wanted to see Kissinger's client list. They wanted it made public. They believed they had the law on their side. Although Kissinger had clearly not understood it when he accepted the job, federal ethics law appeared to require him and the other nine members of the commission to divulge their roster of business partners and clients.

Kissinger did not flinch at the widows' questions, at least not at first. He explained—slowly, patiently—that clients retained Kissinger Associates with the understanding their identities would never be made public. "It is not fair to my clients," he said. "This request for privacy is very common for consulting firms."

The widows' questions about the client list kept coming, and they grew more insistent. Lorie could see that Kissinger was becoming annoyed at the families' effort—less subtle by the minute—to suggest he had a serious ethical conflict in leading the commission. "He got testy," she said. "You could see he was getting a little exasperated." He tried to deflect their questions. Was there some other way to convince the families that there was no conflict of interest? "Surely there is some way of satisfying your concerns," he said. He suggested—hypothetically—that his client list might be shared with an outside lawyer who could vet it for conflicts but keep the list secret from the public.

"Kristen is a lawyer," Lorie said, nodding to Kristen Breitweiser, another of the Jersey Girls at the meeting. "Kristen could do it."

Kissinger frowned; handing over his client list to one of the media-savvy 9/11 widows was not what he had in mind. "I think you should just trust me," he explained.

It was Lorie who then asked the question directly. "With all due respect, Dr. Kissinger," she said, trying to look him in the eye, "I have to ask you: Do you have any Saudi clients? Do you have any clients named bin Laden?"

The room went dead quiet. Kissinger, who had been pouring himself a cup of coffee, was clearly startled by Lorie's questions. He fumbled with the pot, spilling coffee onto the table. He seemed to lose his balance from the sofa at the same moment, nearly falling to the floor. Lorie and the other Jersey Girls rushed forward—like good suburban moms, Lorie thought—and grabbed napkins to soak up the spilled coffee.

"It's my bad eye," Kissinger explained, trying to steady himself on the sofa. He said it affected his depth perception. The widows looked at one another. It was obvious to them that Lorie's questions had thrown Kissinger off balance, not a problem with his vision.

Lorie recalled that another of the widows tried to put the client question more delicately: "Dr. Kissinger, we would certainly hope that no one like that is on your client list. Can you understand our concern?"

Kissinger smiled slightly and looked at his watch. He was not in a mood to answer any more questions. He drew the meeting to a close; he excused himself, saying he had another appointment. He was not going to budge on the client list.

As the widows drove into the Lincoln Tunnel and headed under the Hudson River home to New Jersey that afternoon, Lorie was satisfied that at least Kissinger had been put on notice. The Jersey Girls had demonstrated to Kissinger that the families would scrutinize his every move on the commission. Lorie was prepared to ask many more embarrassing questions of Kissinger, and maybe next time she would ask the questions in front of a television camera.

The next morning, Kissinger called the White House to announce that he was resigning from the 9/11 commission. In a two-page letter to President Bush faxed to the White House, Kissinger said he had "never refused to respond to the call from a president, nor have I ever put my personal interests ahead of the country's interest." But the dispute over his client list would do damage to the "consulting firm I have built and own." He said that "to liquidate Kissinger Associates cannot be accomplished without significantly delaying the beginning" of the investigation.

In the White House offices of Andy Card, Bush's chief of staff, Kissinger's letter was read with annoyance, anger—and a little relief. Typical Kissinger. The White House had never suggested that he shut down the firm; the request was only that he consider complying with an ethics law that seemed to apply to everyone else on the commission. The resignation letter made no reference to Kissinger's awkward meeting with the victims' families the day before, and the former secretary of state has since declined repeated interview requests to discuss the circumstances of his departure.

Card began to think that maybe Kissinger's departure was for the best. To Card, the abrupt resignation was "an embarrassment," of course. But it also ended the debate over Kissinger and the consulting business—"he had a web of involvements that we were probably glad not to be stuck with"—that had seemed unlikely to go away. The White House now had a chance to find a new, less controversial choice to lead the 9/11 commission. Card hoped the new chairman might show as much respect for Bush and for the presidency as had been expected of Kissinger. But without all of Kissinger's baggage.

It was Friday afternoon, and Card wanted to announce a replacement for Kissinger as quickly as possible, preferably by the start of the new week. The dispute over Kissinger's selection had been a distraction to the White House press office at a time when it wanted news coverage to focus on the Bush administration's justification for what appeared to be an imminent invasion of Iraq. Card knew that Bush might be only a few weeks away from ordering a war to overthrow Saddam Hussein.

Of course, Card needed to talk to Karl Rove, Bush's top political aide, before any decision was made. Rove had been involved in the initial decision to select Kissinger, and he would want to weigh in on the names of candidates presented to Bush for a replacement. Rove was worried about the commission. Although Rove would never say it to anyone outside of the White House, he and Card had little doubt that—in the wrong hands—the independent federal commission investigating the September 11 attacks could cost President Bush a second term.

BEDMINSTER, N.J.

DECEMBER 14, 2002

It was a quiet Saturday afternoon for Tom Kean, just as he and his wife, Debbie, liked it. Kean was at home in the leafy, affluent northern New Jersey town of Bedminster when the phone rang. Odd that anyone would be calling at this hour on the weekend, he thought. He picked up the receiver and was shocked to discover who was on the line. It was from Washington. It was the White House.

"Governor Kean, this is Karl Rove."

The White House? Rove? Kean thought he had met Rove over the years, probably shook his hand once or twice at GOP gatherings. But he could not imagine why the architect of George W. Bush's improbable rise to the White House—"Bush's Brain"—would be calling. Kean had mostly disappeared from national politics after stepping down as New Jersey's wildly popular Republican governor in 1990 to begin a second career as a university president. The fact that the White House had tracked him down at his unlisted home phone number on a Saturday afternoon made it all the stranger that Rove was on the line.

Given his reputation as the most ruthless political operative in America, Rove often surprised strangers with his graciousness, or at least his ability to sound gracious. One of Rove's press spokesmen used to explain it to new reporters on the White House beat by pointing out that "if Karl doesn't have to knife you, why should he be rude to you?" So Rove began the conversation by apologizing profusely to Kean for interrupting his weekend.

Then he got to the point.

"Governor, you've probably heard about Henry Kissinger's resignation yesterday from the commission investigating the September 11 attacks," he said. "President Bush is looking for a new chairman, and your name has been mentioned."

There was no guarantee that Bush would select Kean, Rove explained. But would he be interested in the job if the offer came?

Kean surprised himself a little with a quick answer. "Yes," he said. "I would be honored to be considered."

He did not pledge to accept the job. He would want time to think about it and talk to Debbie, who craved privacy. But he told Rove he was certainly pleased to be considered for such an important assignment from the president. Kean did not have to remind Rove, he said, of the trauma that 9/11 had brought to his beloved New Jersey, where many of the victims in the World Trade Center had their homes and families.

"Thank you, Governor," Rove said. "We may be getting back to you."

Rove had forgotten what Kean's almost comically patrician accent sounded like. Old money and croquet mallets. Princeton. FDR-lite. Certainly not Rove's type of Republican. Rove had spent years trying to beat the last remnants of the country club Yalie out of George W. Bush, and he had mostly succeeded. (Kean's accent was actually considered a selling point in a popular television ad campaign for New Jersey tourism in the 1980s that ended with then governor Kean flashing his gap-toothed smile and uttering the campaign's slogan as only he could: "New Juuuuusey and you, puuuufect together.")

Kean hung up the phone after his conversation with Rove, wondering what he had gotten himself into. Following his election as governor in 1981, and before that as a New Jersey state assemblyman, Kean used the same phrase with friends to describe his daunting new responsibilities in government. He would say he felt as though a "ton of bricks had fallen on me."

But after Rove's call, there was almost a physical sensation, his shoulders slumping—brick by brick—at the thought of returning to the political stage like this. For Kean, the September 11 terrorist attacks were not just some faraway horror that he had witnessed on a television screen with the rest of the country. He had lost many, many friends and colleagues on 9/11. Like every suburb in northern New Jersey, Bedminster was devastated by the attacks. These were well-off commuter towns. More than a year after the attacks, there were still faded yellow ribbons tacked on community bulletin boards in Essex and Union and Somerset counties to represent neighbors who had taken the train into Manhattan early on the morning of September 11 and headed to desks on high floors of the World Trade Center and were never seen again.

The afternoon after Rove's call, the phone rang again in Bedminster. This time the voice was familiar to Kean: It was Andy Card, Bush's chief of staff. Kean and Card had known and liked each other for years; they'd first met in the 1980s, when Card was Ronald Reagan's White House liaison to state governments. Card explained to Kean that he was calling on behalf of the president and that Bush had selected Kean to lead the 9/11 commission as its chairman. The president would call shortly, assuming Kean was still interested. Yes, Kean said, thanking Card. He accepted the job.

Kean was genuinely honored by this assignment, although as he talked to Card, he recognized a wariness in his voice that had not been there when he talked to Rove the day before. The more he had thought about it overnight, the more Kean realized that he was probably taking on an impossible job. "I wondered if this was a terrible mistake," he said.

To begin with, he knew he was hindered by ignorance—"zero knowledge"—of most of the issues before the 9/11 commission. "I was an outsider," he said later. "I knew nothing about these subjects—national security, intelligence, and so forth." He knew nothing about terrorism. Nothing about Islamic extremism. He had never seen a classified document before.

More worrisome to Kean was the poisonous partisan atmosphere of Washington, a city he loathed. The ten-member commission was evenly divided between Democrats and Republicans who had been chosen by the most partisan leaders of their parties. The panel was expected to deliver its final report at the worst possible time—in the middle of a presidential election campaign. How could Kean hope to bring together five Democrats and five Republicans to agree on anything, much less whether someone deserved blame for leaving the United States vulnerable to a terrorist attack?

The finger-pointing was well under way by the time Kean joined the commission. The bipartisan congressional investigation of intelligence failures before 9/11 was nearly finished; its final report was expected to show that the Bush administration had brushed aside warnings in the spring and summer of 2001 of an imminent terrorist strike. Democrats saw an opening to blame Bush for September 11; Republicans responded by accusing Bill Clinton of having bungled opportunities throughout the 1990s to kill Osama bin Laden and his henchmen, probably because

Clinton had been so distracted by sexual scandals. How could Kean hope to get past the politics to the truth about 9/11? "I thought the commission was destined to fail," he said.

President Bush called Kean on Monday, December 16, and thanked him for agreeing to lead the investigation. Kean considered himself a friend of Bush's father, but he barely knew the incumbent president. The conversation lasted a few minutes. It was very quick, very polite, Kean remembered. Bush pledged his cooperation to the commission; there was no time for a detailed discussion of how wide-ranging that cooperation might be. Two days had passed since Kean's conversation with Rove. It would occur to Kean later that it had been odd that the first call he received from the White House about the 9/11 commission had come from Rove. Why had membership on the panel been shopped around by Bush's political guru? Kean understood later that it had been a sign of the political struggles to come.

KEAN SAID that he accepted the job, finally, because of his obligation to so many dead friends. For months after 9/11, his calendar had been filled with funerals or, more often, memorial services. Because so few intact bodies and body parts were recovered from the rubble and ash at ground zero, funerals had often not been an option.

The victims of the attacks included one of his best friends, Don Peterson, the former president of Continental Electric Company and Kean's weekly doubles tennis partner for almost twenty-five years. Peterson and his wife, Jean, had been traveling from Newark to San Francisco aboard United Airlines Flight 93 to attend a family reunion at Yosemite National Park. Kean liked to assume that Don Peterson was one of the heroes of Flight 93, which crashed in a lonely field in western Pennsylvania after a struggle between the hijackers and passengers; the passengers' uprising appeared to have prevented the Boeing 757 from reaching its intended target in Washington, probably the Capitol dome.

Kean did not know if Peterson was a Republican or a Democrat. It was typical of Kean, famous in the state capital of Trenton for his ability to reach across the aisle to work with Democrats, that he did not know the political affiliation of one of his closest friends.

"All I know is that Don supported me," Kean said. "He wasn't political at all." In Kean's early races for the statehouse, Peterson had gone door-to-door to round up votes.

Kean had given eulogies at several memorial services for 9/11 victims. He had been a member of the board of directors of the Fiduciary Trust Company, an investment firm that had its headquarters in the World Trade Center; it lost eighty-seven people in the attacks. At a service for one of the Fiduciary executives, Kean urged survivors to find comfort in their memories of their loved ones, not to dwell on the terrible way they had died. He offered a quotation from a favorite writer, J. M. Barrie, creator of *Peter Pan*: "God gave us memory that we might have roses in December."

His quick, positive response to Rove's offer was out of character for the sixty-seven-year-old Kean. He had perplexed and infuriated the Republican Party throughout the 1990s with his refusal to consider running again for office or taking on other roles for the party. Kean had turned down several entreaties—six times, by his count—to run for the U.S. Senate.

Kean had considered reviving his political career. Even a decade out of office, opinion polls showed that he remained one of the state's most popular politicians, nearly as popular with Democrats as with Republicans. GOP strategists promised him a cakewalk if he sought a Senate seat. But finally, each time, Kean said no.

He loved the life he had created for himself after politics. He had bolstered the academic reputation and finances of Drew University, the small liberal arts school that he had led as president since 1990, doubling its applicant pool and almost tripling its endowment. He loved his home in Bedminster, a converted farmhouse on a winding dirt road surrounded by thick woodlands. He had moved to Bedminster after stepping down as governor.

Kean was a passionate environmentalist—one more reason he had found himself unwelcome in the new Republican Party—and he cherished the thought that stretches of the rolling hills around Bedminster looked little different from colonial days, when his celebrated ancestors arrived to help settle New Jersey. Kean was from one of the oldest and most distinguished families in the United States; his ancestors included Peter Stuyvesant and William Livingston, New Jersey's first governor; the Roosevelts were cousins. Kean's father had served in the House for twenty years. His grandfather had been a United States senator.

Above all else, Kean turned down the Senate races because he knew it would require him to live and work in Washington. The city represented all that Kean had come to hate in politics—the vicious partisanship, the endless chase for campaign money, the pleasure that the capital's most powerful residents took in character assassination.

In deciding against a run to replace retiring Democratic senator Bill Bradley in 1995, Kean startled Republican Party strategists by suggesting that they would waste their time asking him to consider another congressional race. There was a "meanness" and "lack of civility" in Washington that he wanted no part of. In a revealing interview that September with *The Washington Post,* Kean said he was offended by the "eyeshade mentality" of the modern Republican Party and the growing influence of "right-wing radicals" in the GOP eager to sacrifice the environment and public education in the name of budget cuts. "If the whole point is just reducing the budget, you're just crunching numbers," he said. "That's not governing." Kean figured that if he got elected to the Senate, he would be instantly marginalized. He was almost certainly right.

He was that rarity in American politics: a man whose ambitions were curbed—ended, really—by his unwillingness to bend on principle. As governor, he supported a woman's right to an abortion, gay rights, strong environmental protection laws, gun control, and well-funded public schools. And he was not going to abandon those convictions even as the GOP seemed to move against them—and him.

His wife, Debbie, clearly hated politics, everything about it, and Kean was not going to lose her or his children in pursuit of a political career. While governor, Kean was repeatedly pressed to consider a White House bid, and he had thought about it. But later he realized it had probably always been out of the question. Among the couple's friends, it was assumed that Debbie would never have agreed to it.

"You have to give up everything, your family, any hobbies or interests, just focus on that and nothing else, and then you have to make all sorts of compromises if you want a national constituency," Kean said. "I was just never that interested."

Kean was comforted by Card's suggestion in the phone call that the job of chairman of the 9/11 commission would be only part-time. He would not need to live in Washington. He could continue in his duties as president of Drew and commute down to Washington one or two days a week for commission meetings. If he memorized the Amtrak schedule and timed his day properly, he could get home to Bedminster most nights. It was a relief to Kean to think that he could escape the "snake pit" of Washington by sunset.

— 4 —

OFFICE OF THE CHIEF OF STAFF
The White House
DECEMBER 15, 2002

Andy Card figured it was his job to worry about everything, and he began to worry about Tom Kean from the moment he put down the phone after offering Kean the job.

Card would have worried in his sleep, too, but there was never much of that. Sleep was a luxury that Andy Card mostly denied himself. George Bush's amiable, hyperdisciplined chief of staff was typically the first to arrive in the West Wing in the morning; he rose from bed in his home in the capital's Virginia suburbs at 4:20 a.m. and often did not return home until after midnight. His waking hours had a single focus: keeping Bush on schedule, on focus, and happy. Card had huge authority, if only because he controlled Bush's schedule and determined who got into the Oval Office and how long they stayed. But no one accused Andy Card of lusting for power. He seemed to find it a genuine thrill to be at the president's side, to witness history. It was Card who walked into the elementary school classroom in Florida on the morning of September 11 and whispered into Bush's ear that a second plane had hit the World Trade Center and that "America is under attack." The photos of Card leaning over to deliver the news to a startled Bush had become one of the iconic images of that day.

Mostly, though, Card's job was one of logistics. It was not nearly as glamorous as all the television shows and movies set in the West Wing wanted to suggest. He joked that the second part of his title—"of staff"—captured the job better than "chief." Former senator Howard Baker, Reagan's chief of staff, told Card the job was the "worst in Washington." The White House chief of staff was responsible for everything. If someone needed firing, the job was often given to Card; it was Card who later broke the news to Secretary of State Colin Powell that his services would not be needed in Bush's second term. If Bush decided suddenly that he wanted a cheeseburger for lunch, Card would handle that, too. If something went wrong, it was Card's fault. If something went right, the president got credit.

There was no time to relax and reflect. "There was always another crisis pounding away," Card said. He had so much to remember during the course of the day that he depended on a memory technique to keep track of it all—imagining Bush's day like a kitchen stove, with the most important tasks on the front burner, the rest simmering at the back.

Card obviously admired Kean—who didn't like Tom Kean? "I think he's a pretty straight shooter, and he is smart, and he's got good political instincts," Card said. The two men had represented the same liberal-to-moderate wing of the Republican Party—Card had been a state legislator in Massachusetts and, like Kean, had supported abortion and gay rights. Card had learned to suppress those views in the service of the far more conservative George W. Bush.

But no matter how much he liked Kean, Card understood that putting him in charge of the 9/11 commission was a risk. Henry Kissinger was the safer choice, certainly politically. Card knew that Bush and Vice President Dick Cheney had regularly, if quietly, sought Kissinger's advice after 9/11, especially as the nation prepared to go to war in Afghanistan and Iraq.

Card knew that Kean had been close to Bush's father; the elder Bush had courted Kean to join his cabinet. President George Herbert Walker Bush and Kean had much in common. Their bloodlines could not have been bluer, with prep school and Ivy League educations to match. Their fathers had served together in Congress. But Card had no reason to believe that Kean had any special loyalty to the new president. To Kean, President George W. Bush seemed so much more rough-and-tumble than his father.

After Kissinger's abrupt resignation as chairman of the 9/11 commission, there was a feeling that a Republican replacement with name recognition—and many fewer conflicts of interest—needed to be found in a hurry. Kissinger's departure was being portrayed in the headlines as a White House blunder. Card wanted the subject changed fast. "In the White House, you don't have the luxury of dwelling on yesterday, so we moved on," Card recalled. That explained why Rove had made the first call to Kean only hours after Kissinger's decision to quit.

Kean had been on a short list of candidates for chairman from the beginning of the search, along with Kissinger and former secretary of state James A. Baker, the longtime consigliere to the Bush family. Rove told colleagues in the White House that he thought he had been the first person to propose Kean for the commission—"to my eternal regret," he said, given Kean's later battles with the White House. Card thought *he* was responsible. "We went through a lot of names of potential Republican figures who would have passed some test of statesmanship, and I honestly believe I was the first one to bring up Kean's name."

Part of Kean's appeal to the White House was the belief that he would be more sensitive than other candidates to the needs of the executive branch. With his encyclopedic knowledge of American politics, Rove knew that New Jersey's governor was arguably the most powerful in the country. It was the only statewide elected office in the Garden State. There was no lieutenant governor; New Jersey's attorney general was appointed by the governor. So maybe, Card thought, Kean would be more understanding than others of the concept of executive privilege and the need for Bush and the White House to keep secrets. "Kean had been an executive," Card said. "Naively on my part, I thought he would come at this from the perspective of a governor who would be concerned about excessive intrusion."

Until it was forced to bow to political realities, the White House had done its best to block the creation of a commission, arguing that the inquiry would distract the government from its mission of preventing new attacks by al-Qaeda. Card had believed that argument wholeheartedly; the commission, he thought, would be a terrible distraction at a time when spy agencies were warning almost daily of the possibility of new attacks.

But Card knew the White House's opposition to an independent investigation was more complicated than that. There was a real political fear of an independent commission. Rove began rewriting the strategy for Bush's 2004 reelection campaign literally the day after 9/11. He knew that Bush's reelection effort centered on his performance on terrorism; almost nothing else would matter to voters. If the commission did anything to undermine Bush's antiterrorism credentials—worst of all, if it claimed that Bush had somehow bungled intelligence in 2001 that might have prevented the attacks—his reelection might well be sunk.

"Absolutely," Card said when asked later if there had been political fears about the commission. "Significant, significant concerns."

As chairman, Kean was the only member of the commission named directly by the White House. Under the law creating the panel, the other four Republican commissioners were chosen by the party's congressional leaders, and Card was not comforted by the rest of the GOP lineup.

Two of the Republicans, former senator Slade Gorton of Washington and former navy secretary John Lehman, were anything but Bush loyalists. Gorton's appointment to the commission was a final act by Senator Trent Lott of Mississippi in his role as Republican minority leader. Lott, one of Gorton's best friends, was never a White House favorite; he was seen as too independent. He was stripped of the leader's job after Bush joined in criticizing Lott over a racially insensitive speech he had given at a one hundredth birthday celebration for Senator Strom Thurmond. (Lott suggested, apparently sincerely, that the nation would have been better off had Thurmond won his campaign for White House in 1948, when the South Carolina Dixiecrat was the nation's best-known segregationist.)

Apparently because he was close to Lott, Gorton had been offered no job in the Bush administration after his defeat for reelection in 2000—no cabinet job, no ambassadorship, nothing. That was grating to Gorton, especially since another Republican senator defeated that year, John Ashcroft of Missouri, had joined Bush's cabinet as attorney general, a move seen as a concession to the far-right wing of the Republican Party. Among Senate Republicans, Ashcroft was considered an intellectual lightweight, especially compared with a lawmaker like Gorton, one of the finest legislative tacticians in Congress.

If Gorton was uncertain in his loyalties, the White House had reason to suspect that Lehman might actually be in the enemy camp. In the thinking of the Bush White House, Lehman had committed the ultimate unforgivable act of disloyalty to the new president: He had supported Senator John McCain over Bush in the race for the GOP nomination in 2000. (Kean was impressed when Lehman came up to him early in the investigation and said that he had been given instructions by McCain: "If it comes down to a party line vote and I think the Republicans are wrong, McCain has told me that I should vote with the Democrats." Kean replied, "In that case, I probably would, too.")

The names of the other two Republican commissioners were only slightly reassuring to the White House. Former Illinois governor Jim Thompson was put on the commission by his old friend House Speaker Dennis Hastert, but Thompson had been out of politics for a dozen years and had no special tie to Bush. The other Republican, Fred Fielding, Reagan's White House counsel, had been loyal to the Bush family over the years and had helped out on the transition in 2001. But Fielding appeared timid on the public stage. (And there were still the persistent rumors, dating from Fielding's work in the White House counsel's office in the Nixon administration, that he was the government's most famous leaker—"Deep Throat" of Watergate fame. The rumors would only be disproved in 2005 with the acknowledgment by a former FBI official, Mark Felt, that he was Deep Throat.)

Card looked over the list of Republican commissioners and "didn't see anybody on the Republican side I would have called willing participants in partisanship"—no one who seemed eager to step in a political fight to defend Bush. That left only one option. Was it possible, Card wondered, that his old friend Kean might fill the role? Could Kean be convinced to take on the job of defending the White House if the Democrats tried to hijack the commission? In offering Kean the job on the 9/11 commission, Card had invited him down to Washington in December to meet with Bush's other senior aides. It would be a chance for Card to gauge Kean's loyalty to the White House, to find out whether he would help protect the president.

— 5 —

OFFICE OF THE MAJORITY LEADER
The Capitol
NOVEMBER 2002

S enate majority leader Tom Daschle was in his office in the Capitol a few days before Thanksgiving, looking over the list of Democratic candidates for the 9/11 commission one last time. It had been such a long, tortured fight to get the commission created that Daschle was determined to get the Democratic membership right. The panel's five Democrats appeared to represent their party's last hope of getting to the bottom of the mysteries of 9/11. Daschle figured it might be the public's last hope, too.

The choice of the commissioners would be among Daschle's last duties as majority leader. The soft-spoken South Dakotan had reason to be angry—and heartbroken—about the November 2002 elections. The Democrats had lost control of the Senate, in part because of what Daschle saw as a craven effort by the White House to portray Democrats during the campaign as weak on terrorism. The White House had gone on the attack even though the Democrats had given George Bush virtually every tool and every dollar he had requested in the so-called war on terror after 9/11, including authority to go to war in Afghanistan and Iraq. An invasion of Iraq appeared imminent, even though the evidence of an Iraqi link to al-Qaeda was still in question. The criticism of Daschle from within the party was that he had been too weak-kneed in dealing with Bush after 9/11.

The most tragic victim of the GOP campaign that fall was Daschle's friend Senator Max Cleland of Georgia. Cleland had lost three limbs as a soldier in the Vietnam War. Yet the wheelchair-bound senator found himself portrayed in a Republican television attack ad as unpatriotic because he had questioned labor provisions of a bill to create a new Homeland Security Department. The ad was considered an instant classic in the black arts of negative campaigning. It juxtaposed images of Osama bin Laden, Saddam Hussein—and Cleland. Cleland's victorious opponent, Saxby Chambliss, a little-known House Republican, managed to avoid service in the Vietnam War thanks to at least four student deferments. Chambliss would later claim the ads were not meant to question Cleland's patriotism.

Daschle would be out of his job as majority leader in January, when the new Republicans would be sworn in. The GOP already controlled the House. Daschle figured that with Republicans in full control on Capitol Hill, Congress would be out of the business of oversight, especially when it came to September 11 and the performance of the Bush White House in dealing with the threat of al-Qaeda before and after the attacks.

It had become clearer and clearer to Daschle and other Democrats— and to the Washington press corps and even some Republicans—that the White House was hiding something, perhaps many things, about what Bush knew about al-Qaeda threats before 9/11.

To Daschle, that explained why Bush and Cheney had taken such a personal role in the campaign to try to block any outside review of September 11, especially the creation of the commission. Daschle had heard through Trent Lott, his Republican counterpart, that Karl Rove and the White House political office had orchestrated the behind-the-scenes effort to block legislation to create the commission. "It's all Rove," Lott told Daschle.

In January 2002, before Congress had scheduled its first public hearings on pre-9/11 intelligence failures, Cheney called Daschle personally to complain about any public airing of the issues. Cheney's tone with Daschle was polite but threatening. Daschle, who was being interviewed by a *Newsweek* reporter when the vice president's call came through, was smart enough to allow the reporter to remain in the office to listen to Daschle's end of the conversation. Daschle wanted a witness.

The vice president urged Daschle to shut down any additional public hearings on 9/11, warning him that a public discussion of intelligence errors before the attacks would do damage to the struggle to capture bin Laden and destroy al-Qaeda—and would do political damage to the Democrats as well.

"Mr. Majority Leader, this would be a very dangerous and time-consuming diversion for those of us who are on the front lines of our response today," Cheney said. "We just can't be tied down with the problems that this would present for us. We've got our hands full." Daschle remembered the tone as vintage Cheney: "muffled, kind of under the breath, quiet, measured, very deliberate."

If the Democrats went forward anyway, Cheney said, the White House would portray the Democrats—by daring to investigate what went wrong on 9/11—as undermining the war against terror. That was a potent political threat at a time, four months after the attacks, when Bush was riding as high in opinion polls as he ever would and Democrats were facing a difficult midterm election in November 2002 as a result.

"I respectfully disagree with your position, Mr. Vice President," Daschle replied. "It is imperative that we try to find out what happened on September 11 and why."

To Daschle, it was preposterous for the White House to argue that 9/11 should go uninvestigated. He knew that modern American history offered plenty of support for an independent investigation. From Pearl Harbor to the Kennedy assassination to the 1986 *Challenger* space shuttle disaster, "there's been a review of what happened after every tragedy this nation has experienced," Daschle said.

Historical precedent was one thing; political muscle was another. And the Democrats' most powerful ally in establishing the 9/11 commission was Senator John McCain, the Arizona Republican. His colleagues said the worst-kept secret in the Senate in 2001 and 2002, if it was a secret at all, was that McCain despised George Bush and the people who worked for him, especially Rove. McCain blamed "dirty tricks" by Rove's political operation for costing him the GOP presidential nomination in 2000. Rove denied any involvement, but the tricks were vintage Rove, and they could not have been dirtier, including a well-organized whisper campaign during the critical South Carolina primary that McCain was the father of an illegitimate "black baby" who now lived with his family. The "black baby" was a Bangladeshi orphan girl who had been adopted by McCain and his wife, Cindy.

With Bush's election, McCain told Daschle in early 2001 that he was still so angry about the presidential campaign that he was considering bolting from the Republican Party, and the two men talked over several weeks about the possibility. Daschle said the talks were so far along that they had discussed the logistics of the news conference at which McCain would make the announcement. "We came very close," Daschle would say later. McCain backed away from the idea in the summer of 2001, after another Republican, Jim Jeffords of Vermont, abandoned the GOP and declared himself an independent; that gave Democrats a de facto one-vote majority in the Senate. McCain told Daschle, "Look, somebody else has given you the majority—you don't need me anymore."

McCain found other ways to take his revenge on Bush. After 9/11, McCain had been among the first in Congress, Democrat or Republican, to insist that the government set up an independent commission to investigate the attacks. The more bitterly the Bush administration opposed the idea, the more impassioned McCain became in advocating for it. His Senate office became a meeting place for the 9/11 families to plot strategy to demand the commission's creation. Bush's closest aides seethed about McCain, but the White House could not ignore him; McCain enjoyed too much credibility within the party as a result of the 2000 campaign. He was beloved by too many independent-minded Republicans, as well as by Washington reporters enamored of his eagerness to confront Bush.

McCain's demand for creation of a 9/11 commission had given cover to other Republicans. Daschle began to hear privately from other GOP senators that they would buck the White House and support the commission if it came to a vote. Daschle could see that Republicans were as uneasy as he was about news reports that spring that Bush had received—and apparently ignored—an explicit warning in August 2001 from the CIA. According to the reports, the agency had told Bush that al-Qaeda was considering terrorist attacks, including hijackings, within American borders.

On November 27, 2002, thanks mostly to pressure on the White House from the 9/11 families and McCain, Bush reluctantly signed the bill creating the 9/11 commission. The bill was not what Daschle, McCain, and the families had wanted. It provided the commission with an insultingly small budget—$3 million over eighteen months, compared with more than $40 million for the federal commission that investigated the *Challenger* disaster. "The budget was a joke," Daschle said. And the bill imposed strict limits on the commission's powers to subpoena documents and witnesses.

Daschle was besieged by Democrats eager for appointment to the commission. Daschle and the House Democratic leader, Dick Gephardt of Missouri, agreed to choose the five Democratic commissioners jointly.

Some of the choices were easy, including the decision of who should serve as the panel's ranking Democrat and would hold the title of vice chairman. Daschle thought instantly of his predecessor as Senate majority leader, George Mitchell of Maine. There was little doubt among other Democrats that he was an ideal choice. *The* ideal choice.

Mitchell had credentials as a statesman—after leaving the Senate, he had been nominated for the Nobel Peace Prize after helping hammer out a peace settlement in Northern Ireland as Clinton's emissary. Mitchell had been a federal prosecutor in Maine; he knew all about subpoenas and document searches. And he was, without question, a strong-willed, sharply partisan Democrat.

Daschle knew the Democrats had made the right decision with Mitchell when he learned that the White House had selected Kissinger as the commission's chairman. Daschle figured that among Democrats, Mitchell would be seen as Kissinger's equal; Mitchell would not allow himself to be seen as anything less. It would be the Kissinger-Mitchell Commission, not the Kissinger Commission. "Kissinger was going to have his hands full," Daschle believed. "It would have been the perfect balance."

There were obvious candidates for the other Democratic slots, including Lee Hamilton, a former congressman from Indiana. It was hard to find anyone in Washington who had a bad word for Hamilton, who retired in 1999 after thirty-four years in the House. Like Mitchell, Hamilton was considered one of the wise men of the Democratic Party, especially on foreign policy. He had been chairman of both the House Foreign Affairs Committee and the House Intelligence Committee. Steady, solid, as consistent as the unfashionable flattop haircut that Hamilton had worn since his first days in Congress.

There had been discussion of naming Hamilton instead of Mitchell to the job of vice chairman. But Daschle and his colleagues knew that Hamilton lacked a taste for partisan fights. In the best tradition of his native rural Indiana, there was little that was cynical about Hamilton. He seemed always to assume the best about people, Republicans included.

That explained why his circle of friends from his days in the House included former congressmen Dick Cheney and Don Rumsfeld. Cheney and Hamilton formed a close bond when Hamilton led the House investigation of Iran-Contra after the arms-for-hostages affair was exposed. Cheney was the ranking Republican. Hamilton had known Rumsfeld even longer. Rumsfeld served in the House from neighboring Illinois from 1962 to 1969. While he might disagree with Cheney and Rumsfeld on policy, Hamilton trusted both men always to tell the truth. They were still close friends when Cheney and Rumsfeld returned to power in Washington in 2001. To Hamilton, they were "Dick" and "Don." Hamilton also had a good relationship with Cheney's powerful White House counsel, David Addington, who had worked for Cheney in Congress.

There was another downside to Hamilton: He was not considered much of an investigator in Congress, at least when it came to ferreting out evidence of a scandal. "I don't go for the jugular," he acknowledged. He was embarrassed in the mid-1980s when, as chairman of the House Intelligence Committee, he did not aggressively follow up on news reports suggesting that the Reagan administration was illegally funneling weapons and money to the anti-Communist Nicaraguan Contras. He took Reagan and his White House aides at their word that there was nothing to the allegations. When the reports about the Iran-Contra affair proved true, Hamilton acknowledged he had been gullible.

Daschle wanted Max Cleland on the commission. After his defeat in November, his friends could see that Cleland had fallen into a serious depression and was in need of a job that would keep him in Washington and might provide him with a staff. Cleland had prided himself on having no income other than his congressional salary, and when he lost the Senate race, there were no savings to fall back on. The commission was ideal for Cleland, since it would keep him in the public eye on military and intelligence issues, always his focus in the Senate. It would give him new purpose, Daschle hoped. Daschle and Gephardt agreed on appointing another Hill Democrat to the commission: Representative Timothy Roemer of Indiana, who was retiring from the House, possibly in hopes of a Senate bid; he had been an author of the bill that created the commission and was close to many of the 9/11 victims' families.

Daschle wanted other commissioners who, like Mitchell, had backgrounds as investigators and prosecutors. He found candidates in

Richard Ben-Veniste, the hard-nosed former Watergate prosecutor, and Jamie Gorelick, who had been deputy attorney general in the Clinton administration. Kean and Hamilton were told later that Gorelick, now a partner at one of Washington's most prestigious law firms, won herself a place on the commission over former New York governor Mario Cuomo by arguing that the panel needed at least one woman member. (Gorelick said later she had no reason to believe that she and Cuomo were in competition for the slot.)

Mitchell had joined the commission reluctantly and with the understanding that the work would be part-time, allowing him to continue his law practice. But within days of his appointment, he could see that this was no part-time job. He found himself in the same ethical swirl as Kissinger, with demands from the 9/11 families that he reveal the names of his clients, maybe even cut his ties to his firm. Mitchell told Daschle that he simply could not afford to go without his regular income. "Because I must work to support my family, I cannot comply," Mitchell said in his resignation letter on December 11.

Daschle was in a bind. It had been difficult to convince Mitchell to take the assignment in the first place; his sudden departure had probably poisoned the well in finding a replacement of equal stature. His best choice, he figured, was Hamilton, who had already accepted a position on the commission, had the background in national security, and appeared eager for the work. Daschle knew he was taking a chance, and he worried. When the time came for the commission to confront the Bush White House to get at the truth about 9/11, would Hamilton be willing to put aside his reputation "for being very bipartisan and very cautious" and fight? As he picked up the phone to offer Hamilton the job as the commission's top Democrat, Daschle wished he knew the answer.

OFFICE OF THE CHIEF OF STAFF
The White House
DECEMBER 2002

Only a dozen years earlier, Tom Kean's friends and political strategists would have predicted that he would march into the White House someday as the man who lived there.

Kean was one of the GOP's golden boys in the late 1980s, a hugely popular Republican governor in a state that normally leaned to the Democrats. New Jersey's economy boomed under Kean, and he made measurable progress in improving the schools and the environment. He brought African-Americans and union workers into the Republican Party, winning 60 percent of the black vote and the support of two-thirds of union households in his landslide victory for a second term in 1985. Kean appointed more blacks to state jobs than all of his predecessors combined. Another part of his legacy was harder to measure but might have been just as important: Under Kean, New Jersey had stopped being the butt of every late night comedian's jokes.

The elder George Bush had encouraged Kean to think beyond New Jersey, inviting him to make the keynote address at the 1988 Republican convention in New Orleans. Just before the convention, Kean published his memoirs, *The Politics of Inclusion*, and it was the work of a man who was clearly thinking about a run for national office; his political handlers made sure every convention delegate got a copy.

But that seemed a lifetime ago, certainly a political lifetime ago, as Kean passed through the White House security gates in December 2002 and headed into the West Wing in his new role as chairman of the 9/11 commission.

A new, much more conservative George Bush was president, and his Republican Party had little room for moderates like Kean.

Kean had come to the White House now as a visitor, and a wary one at that. He had traveled to Washington at Andy Card's invitation, there to meet with Card and Bush's other top aides to discuss Kean's plans for the commission.

Kean had no idea what reception he would face. He was beginning to understand just how fiercely the White House had opposed the investigation that Kean was now being asked to lead. He was keenly aware of the fact that he was Bush's second choice as chairman. "The substitute," he called himself.

Kean had certainly heard all about the "message discipline" of the White House of George W. Bush. The president had surrounded himself with a small circle of aides—Card, Karl Rove, Condoleezza Rice, White House counsel Alberto Gonzales, press secretary Ari Fleischer, communications director Karen Hughes—who demonstrated unquestioned loyalty to Bush and his family.

This White House seemed unwilling to tolerate public dissent, so it was almost never heard, even if Kean thought it left Bush's aides sounding robotic and unthinking in their public appearances. After he came to know them better, Kean would later refer to Bush's White House aides as "the control freaks."

When Kean made that first visit in December 2002, Washington was in a war fever. Bush seemed intent on invading Iraq; it was being described as the next logical chapter in the war on terrorism that began on September 11. Given the administration's repeated claims of a link between Iraq and al-Qaeda, maybe even between Iraq and the 9/11 attacks, Kean wondered how a war in Iraq might affect his investigation.

Rice and the others were being fanned out to the morning television shows almost every day by the end of 2002, mouthing literally the same words, the same script, to defend an attack on Iraq. How many times had he heard the line from Rice and others about how the "smoking gun" of an Iraqi nuclear weapons program might be "a mushroom cloud"?

Kean hoped that things would be different with Card—more straightforward, certainly less scripted behind closed doors. He knew that Card's connection was more to the elder Bush than to the incumbent president. Card was not part of the "Texas mafia" that had come to Washington with Bush from Austin—Card had spent his years out of power as a Washington lobbyist for General Motors and other carmakers—so Kean hoped that meant Card might be more forthcoming.

But as he moved from office to office in the West Wing that day to introduce or sometimes reintroduce himself, Kean began to realize that the "message discipline" extended even to this sort of courtesy call from a fellow Republican.

Clearly Card, Rice, and the others had been given talking points before they met with Kean—were they reading from the same three-by-five card? Just as they stuck to a script with the cantankerous White House press corps, Kean realized they were going to stick to a script with him in talking about the 9/11 commission. Bush's aides were trying to deliver a political message to Kean, although he would not fully understand it until later.

When he sat in one of their offices, it was only a few minutes before Kean began to hear the same phrases—almost word for word—from Card, Rice, and the others in describing their hopes for Kean's leadership of the commission:

"We want you to stand up. You've got to stand up."

"You've got to have courage."

"We don't want a runaway commission."

They did not really explain what they meant by any of it—stand up to whom? courage about what?—and Kean found himself baffled by what he was hearing in the White House meetings. Was this some sort of code? Was he supposed to ask for the context? What did they mean by "runaway" commission?

"I don't want a runaway commission, either," he told them, chuckling nervously when he heard them use the phrase over and over.

As he left the West Wing that afternoon and passed back through the security gates, Kean decided to hope for the best. He wanted to assume that he was being told by the White House to "stand up" for the truth and to show "courage" in following the trail of evidence about 9/11, wherever it might lead.

Kean would realize later how naive he had been. After months of tense negotiations with the White House as it tried to block the commission's access to secret documents and interviews, he would think back to those first meetings at the White House in 2002. He realized that he was not being told by the White House to stand up for what was right.

"I decided that as the process went on, that's not what they meant at all," Kean said in an interview much later, an uncharacteristic trace of anger and cynicism in his voice.

When Bush's aides told him to "stand up," what they meant was that Kean and the commission needed to "stand up for the president," not necessarily for the truth. The truth was secondary. "You've got to stand up for the president, and you've got to protect him in the process. That's what they meant." It appeared that a "runaway commission" was one that issued a final report concluding that Bush and his White House bore some responsibility for 9/11. "That was their nightmare," Kean said later. "I think they never lost that fear."

During that first day of White House meetings, Card and the others also told Kean that they wanted to be "helpful" to him in assembling a staff, especially in the selection of an executive director to run the investigation. They had a couple of candidates for him to consider, including a retired general and a former State Department official.

Kean took down the names and agreed to consider the White House candidates. He was not just being polite; the names were not those of obvious political hacks, at least none that he knew. Maybe these were talented people, he thought. Maybe there was nothing wrong with the White House recommending candidates for the job.

Kean certainly agreed with Card and the others that the choice of executive director was important. It might be the most important decision Kean and Hamilton would make.

It is a polite fiction in Washington that the reports of blue-ribbon federal commissions are written by the commissioners themselves. In truth, most of the reports are written by a professional staff led by a full-time staff director. On the 9/11 commission, that title was executive director. All ten members of the commission had separate jobs and were volunteering their time to the investigation. Four of them, including Kean, lived far from Washington. Although Kean expected to keep a close watch on the commission, it would be mostly from a distance; he intended to continue to spend most of his time at home in New Jersey. It would be left to the executive director to manage the staff and set a direction for the investigation.

Many members of the commission's staff would later assume that the man selected as the commission's executive director—Philip D. Zelikow, a forty-eight-year-old historian and political scientist at the

University of Virginia—had been on that White House list of candidates. That was not true.

Over time, Zelikow would be seen by many of the commission's investigators, as well as by many of the 9/11 families, as a White House mole. They believed he had been put there to make sure that George Bush and especially Zelikow's close friend Condoleezza Rice were protected from too much scrutiny, particularly over the seeming failure of the White House to act on dire terrorist threats in the months before September 11. But if that was Zelikow's role on the commission, it was not because the White House had gotten him the job and asked in advance for his help. It appeared instead to be a role that the aloof academic had assigned himself.

— 7 —

CHARLOTTESVILLE, VA.

DECEMBER 2002

A t the University of Virginia campus in Charlottesville, Philip Zelikow was sulking, or so many of his colleagues thought in late 2002. Two years earlier, they would have guessed that he was a short-timer at Virginia. Zelikow seemed bound for Washington and great things in George W. Bush's White House. During the 2000 campaign, Zelikow made sure that others at Virginia knew of his close friendship with "Condi" Rice, who had emerged during the campaign as Bush's closest adviser on foreign policy. She was the president's tutor, really, since Bush had no experience in international affairs. Zelikow let people know he was on a first-name basis with many others who would take top jobs in the White House, including "Andy" Card.

Zelikow and Rice had known each other since the 1980s, when they were colleagues on the National Security Council in the presidency of Bush's father. Then, as always, the NSC was a heady place to work, a sort of rival State Department, Pentagon, and CIA all in one, in which even a junior White House staffer had the chance to shape national security policy. Zelikow left the NSC in 1991 to teach at Harvard, where he was a professor at the Kennedy School of Government, and then moved seven years later to Virginia to run the university's Miller Center of Public Affairs. The center is best known in academic circles for its authorized White House oral histories—collections of taped interviews from former presidents and their top aides, conducted shortly after leaving office.

After the White House, Rice returned to Stanford, where she had taught before the NSC. But she and Zelikow stayed in touch and published a book together in 1995 about Germany's reunification. Rice readily acknowledged that Zelikow had written the bulk of the book, and he was pleased to share credit with such an obvious up-and-comer as Rice. Zelikow was an elegant writer. His talent was evident on almost every page.

After the younger George Bush was declared president in the 2000 election, Rice was named national security adviser, and she in turn placed Zelikow on her transition team for the NSC. His work on the transition was not widely known outside the White House. That was no surprise. At a time when Washington was awaiting the arrival of a new president, few people paid attention to the names of middle-ranking members of the White House transition team, especially not in 2001, when the transition was brutally cut short because of the Florida recount debacle.

Zelikow was a Texan, raised in Houston, which was a useful thing in Bush's Washington, although it seemed hard for many people to believe that the tweedy historian hailed from the flatlands of central Texas. Zelikow could dress like an Oxford don; he seemed to have a closetful of tweed jackets. With his references to his "good years" in Cambridge, Massachusetts, he seemed to suggest that he had spent his undergraduate years along the pathways of Harvard Yard.

In fact, Zelikow had gotten his undergraduate degree at the University of Redlands, a small college not far from Los Angeles, where he had transferred in his senior year from the University of Houston. He had gone to both schools because of their nationally ranked debate teams. Zelikow was one of the country's best college debaters. His debate partner from Redlands, Mark Fabiani, went on to become a central political strategist—and scandal manager—for Bill Clinton's White House. The Zelikow-Fabiani team placed 16th at the national collegiate debate finals in 1976; among individual debaters, Zelikow came in 10th. The skills of a first-rate debater—the ability to argue any point of view on short notice and to crush an opponent's argument, no matter how valid it might be—served both men well in their careers in Washington.

Zelikow knew how to flatter people who might get him somewhere; that seemed to NSC colleagues to explain his close friendship with Rice. But he made many more adversaries with his outsize ego and fierce temper; his anger was a thing to behold, his face growing bright red, his well-chosen insults flying in every direction.

For someone who specialized in diplomatic history, Zelikow could be remarkably undiplomatic, most disastrously in 1992, when he was teaching at Harvard and attended a United Nations disarmament conference in Hiroshima, Japan. He declared at the conference that the atomic bombs dropped on Japan at the end of World War II had, in a sense, done Japan a service by shortening the war and saving perhaps a million other Japanese lives. Zelikow seemed oblivious to the fact that any attempt to justify the destruction of Hiroshima and Nagasaki would draw a fierce protest in Japan, and his statement led about fifty pacifists, including scarred survivors of the atomic bombs, to stage a sit-in protest. The protests—and Zelikow's remarks—drew news coverage around the world.

He attracted new, unwelcome headlines in 2000 with the disclosure of large numbers of errors in the transcripts of White House recordings that he had prepared for use in his otherwise well-reviewed book *The Kennedy Tapes: Inside the White House During the Cuban Missile Crisis,* written with Harvard historian Ernest May. In an article in the *Atlantic Monthly,* a former historian at the John F. Kennedy Presidential Library in Boston, Sheldon Stern, identified mistakes and omissions throughout the transcripts prepared by Zelikow and May. There were dozens in just the first twenty pages of *The Kennedy Tapes,* he said. Many of the errors were significant, changing the meaning of what was said during the nuclear showdown. (Two small but telling examples: The book had Attorney General Robert Kennedy referring to plans for the "invasion" of Russian ships heading to Cuba, when in fact he actually spoke of a much less confrontational "examination"; the flawed transcription suggested just the sort of showdown the Kennedy White House was trying to prevent. Zelikow and May also had CIA director John McCone referring to the need to call on former president Dwight Eisenhower as a "facilitator" in the crisis, when in fact McCone said "soldier.") Zelikow and May made major revisions in the book in later editions but said in a letter to the *Atlantic* that complaints from Stern had left them "bemused" and that "none of these amendments are very important." Stern said that he found Zelikow's dismissive response "shocking" and added, "When the words are wrong, as they are repeatedly, the historical record is wrong."

After Bush's victory in 2000, Zelikow thought he was in line for the job of Rice's deputy at the NSC, or so he led friends to believe, but the offer did not come. The job of deputy national security adviser went instead to Stephen Hadley, a Washington lawyer who was close to the new deputy defense secretary, Paul Wolfowitz.

Zelikow might have thought he was on the short list of any number of other important foreign policy jobs in the new Bush administration, but he was not offered those posts, either. Many people in the new Bush administration admired Zelikow's intelligence—"brilliant" was one of the adjectives often used to describe him—but found him impossible to work with. Andy Card had dealt with Zelikow at the Miller Center and bristled at his treatment by the "bully" historian.

So after he finished his duties on the transition team, Zelikow headed back to Charlottesville and the Miller Center. He stayed in touch with people at the White House he considered friends, including Rice. White House officials said he lobbied Rove for a commitment to designate the Miller Center as the official repository of the new administration's oral history.

If Zelikow did not get the job he wanted in the Bush administration, he was still handed an extraordinary assignment by the White House in the months after the 9/11 attacks. At Rice's urging, Zelikow was the principal—if initially secret—author of a national security strategy paper that would turn American military doctrine on its head and justify a "preemptive war" against an enemy that posed no immediate threat to the United States. It was being written with Iraq in mind; the administration needed a scholarly document it could point to in justifying the imminent invasion. When the existence of the new strategy paper became known late in 2002, it produced an uproar, which might explain why Zelikow made little effort at the time to publicize the fact that he had written it. That would become widely known only later. (For his part, Zelikow has insisted he had no idea that his paper, which was mostly written by the spring of 2002, might be used at the White House in justifying the overthrow of Saddam Hussein. "The subject of Iraq did not arise in the development of this document," he said later.)

In many ways, Zelikow had what should have been the job of his dreams at Virginia. He had an appointment at one of the country's best public universities and plenty of contact with the powerful in Washington, only 120 miles away up the highway. Zelikow was careful to fill the Miller Center's board with celebrities from the capital, including the fabled Watergate reporter Bob Woodward of *The Washington Post*. Zelikow was liked and trusted by other Washington journalists who knew that he was often well plugged-in with government officials; Zelikow understood what reporters needed on deadline and could be depended on for a pithy quotation.

Still, colleagues could see that Charlottesville was a small pond for a man as ambitious and talented as Zelikow. He was a historian who wanted to be part of history. He seemed perplexed that his talents had not been recognized by the people who handed out the best jobs in the Bush administration.

Zelikow was in his office when he got the call from Lee Hamilton in December 2002. Zelikow did not know Hamilton, but he certainly knew of him and of his long career in Congress. He also knew Hamilton had just been named vice chairman on the 9/11 commission. "Professor Zelikow, I'm wondering if we might talk," Hamilton said, introducing himself. Zelikow listened closely.

— 8 —

J. EDGAR HOOVER FBI BUILDING
Washington, D.C.
JANUARY 2003

FBI director Robert Mueller was horrified, too. But he could never admit that publicly when he was asked about the bureau's incompetence before 9/11.

On the morning of the attacks, he had been on the job at FBI headquarters for exactly one week. Seven days. He barely had time to figure out how to navigate the labyrinth of the J. Edgar Hoover Building and his suite of offices on the seventh floor before he was forced to organize the FBI's response to a terrorist attack that had left more than three thousand people dead on American soil. He was supposed to have arrived at the FBI earlier in the summer, but he delayed his swearing-in after he underwent surgery in August for prostate cancer. The bureau had been without a permanent director since June, when Louis Freeh retired abruptly. Whatever his arrival date, no one could blame Mueller for what had gone so wrong at the FBI in the months and years before the attacks.

But that did not make it easier for Mueller to hear the terrible stories—the drip-drip-drip of stories, a new one every news cycle for months, it seemed—about how the bureau might have prevented the attacks. *Should* have prevented 9/11. The what-if questions were being asked everywhere, and Mueller had to ask them, too.

What if someone in headquarters in Washington had acted on the pleas of FBI agents in Minnesota in August 2001 for a court warrant to inspect Zacarias Moussaoui's laptop? (The French-born Muslim extremist had been arrested near a Minneapolis flight school on immigration charges after alarming instructors there with his bizarre request to learn how to take off and land a Boeing 747 jumbo jet, even though he had no basic knowledge of flying.) What if one of the arrogant counterterrorism supervisors in Washington had taken a few minutes to read a memo sent in July from FBI agent Kenneth Williams in Phoenix? (Williams had urged FBI headquarters to open a nationwide investigation of why so many young Arab men connected to radical Muslim groups were seeking commercial flight training.) What if someone in San Diego had bothered to ask a veteran FBI informant to probe into the backgrounds of two mysterious young Saudi men who had been boarders in his house in 2000? (The Saudis, Hawaf al-Hazmi and Khalid al-Mihdhar, were among the hijackers on the American Airlines jet that crashed into the Pentagon on September 11.)

For weeks after September 11, Mueller sat there in his suite of offices overlooking Pennsylvania Avenue, trying to prevent his long Brahmin jaw from dropping to his desk in astonishment as yet another person arrived to give him more bad news—another belated discovery of a clue that, had somebody in the bureau followed up, might have allowed the FBI to roll up the hijackers before the attacks. What made it worse for Mueller was the fact that he had to demand to hear the bad news. Fairly or unfairly, Freeh, his temperamental predecessor, had a reputation of wanting only good news, and that's what he got. At the FBI under Freeh, it was often said that "we kill the messengers."

Even if he could legitimately duck blame for the bureau's pre-9/11 blunders, it was still left to Mueller to try to explain them and to fix them, if that was possible. And with each new disclosure, it seemed it was going to be left to Mueller to justify the bureau's very existence, at least in its current structure. By late 2002, it had gotten that bad.

There was sentiment on Capitol Hill and among the commissioners of the newly created 9/11 commission to break up the FBI, with terrorism investigations turned over to some sort of new domestic spy agency, perhaps one modeled on Britain's MI-5. Its critics believed the FBI was simply incapable of being anything more than a federal police force. Certainly 9/11 had proved that, as an institution, the FBI had no ability to deal with a sinister, shadowy force like al-Qaeda; it had no ability to use tools beyond basic law enforcement; it knew how to measure success only by arrest statistics.

On his senior staff, Mueller had deputies who had moved with him to the FBI and felt no special loyalty to the bureau, and some of them wondered if a breakup was not such a bad idea. To them, the ghost of

J. Edgar Hoover still haunted the FBI. "We need to junk this whole place," one of Mueller's senior aides blurted out after learning how an FBI agent in Minneapolis had warned FBI headquarters in August 2001, just weeks before the attacks, that Moussaoui seemed like a terrorist in training who might "fly a plane into the World Trade Center." After the briefing, the aide went to the men's room and vomited.

But Robert Swan Mueller III was not about to give up on the FBI. Mueller was many things—patrician, Princeton man, class of 1966, lawyer and prosecutor, passionately devoted husband and father—but he was, above all, a marine. And this battle-tested jarhead had been given a mission by his commander in chief to save the FBI.

Mueller rarely talked about his three years in the U.S. Marines, certainly not about his experiences in Vietnam in the late 1960s, where he won a Bronze Star for his valor in rescuing a trapped rifle platoon. He was far too modest for that. But there was a paper trail of his heroism. "2nd Lieut. Mueller fearlessly moved from one position to another, directing the accurate counterfire of his men and shouting words of encouragement to them," his Bronze Star citation read.

Mueller's performance after 9/11 was uneven. He was painfully shy—his comments at the White House press conference to announce his nomination in July 2001 lasted all of forty-eight seconds—and mostly hid from the press corps and the public in his first months after the attacks. He was happy to cede the public stage to Attorney General John Ashcroft, his patron, and the camera-loving Ashcroft was just as happy to take it.

When Mueller did make public statements about the 9/11 investigation and about the disclosures of FBI blunders, he often misspoke, raising early, unnecessary questions about his credibility.

He said repeatedly in the weeks after the attacks that there had been no clue within the FBI about Arab extremists seeking flight training in the United States, an assertion that would be contradicted with the disclosure of the Phoenix memo and the arrest of Moussaoui. In October 2001 and again in December 2001, when Moussaoui was charged with conspiring in the September 11 attacks, Mueller insisted that there had been insufficient evidence to justify a search of Moussaoui's laptop before September 11; the hard drive was later found to contain evidence linking Moussaoui to the hijacking plot. Mueller's claim of insufficient evidence was later shown to be wrong—astonishingly so.

His statements about Moussaoui were challenged most directly by a whistle-blower in the Minneapolis FBI office, Special Agent Coleen Rowley. She said in a letter to Mueller and congressional investigators that his comments on the case reflected a decision "to circle the wagons at FBI HQ in an apparent effort to protect the FBI from embarrassment." Her letter was leaked to *Time* magazine, which went on to name Rowley as one of its "Persons of the Year." Rowley and other agents in Minneapolis were also outraged by the news that Mueller, far from demoting or firing FBI supervisors in Washington who had tried to derail the Moussaoui investigation before 9/11, promoted them instead.

The creation of the joint House-Senate committee on 9/11 intelligence failures in 2002 had seemed an early opportunity for Mueller to demonstrate his willingness to cooperate with outside investigators. But the Democratic chairman of the congressional panel, Senator Bob Graham of Florida, accused Mueller of a "cover-up" to protect the bureau. Graham found that Mueller's newly discovered loyalty to the FBI trumped any commitment to allowing an open inquiry into the bureau's failings on 9/11. In its final report, the congressional committee urged the government to consider a breakup of the FBI.

The bureau's future appeared to be under a more serious threat with the creation of the 9/11 commission. It was one thing for the White House to ignore the findings of a congressional investigation, especially when it was led by a Democrat. It would be more difficult for the White House to ignore the findings of an independent commission led by a Republican and established by legislation that had been signed, albeit reluctantly, by Bush.

So Mueller was left with a decision: Would he follow the strategy that the bureau had used in dealing with congressional investigators—limit cooperation and hope that the investigators' fury would blow over? Or would he cooperate fully with the 9/11 commission in hopes that the commission would show leniency and give Mueller the time he needed to fix the FBI?

In New York, Mueller's immediate predecessor at the FBI, Thomas Pickard, a veteran agent who had been the bureau's acting director in the months before 9/11, had a similar decision to make. Should he tell the full, awful story? The story that might destroy John Ashcroft? Or something less?

Pickard was free of the bureau now. He was retired and living happily in New York, his hometown. He was no whistle-blower. Did he really want to tell the commission all that had happened at the FBI and the Justice Department in the spring and summer of 2001—how Ashcroft had ignored the flood of intelligence warnings of an imminent, cata-strophic attack? Pickard believed that the attorney general's indifference to terrorist warnings helped explain why the nation's law enforcement agencies were unprepared for what came on 9/11.

— 9 —

OFFICES OF THE SELECT
COMMITTEE ON INTELLIGENCE
The Senate

JANUARY 2003

Senator Bob Graham took a seat at a conference table in the offices of the Senate Intelligence Committee. Graham picked up and began paging through a document that he knew could—and almost certainly should—undermine Washington's relations with Saudi Arabia, supposedly one of America's closest allies in the Middle East. If the report ever saw the light of day, that was.

It was January 2003. Senator Graham, a Florida Democrat who had a reputation as a cautious, politically moderate lawmaker, had spent much of the past year consumed with his duties as chairman of a special House-Senate committee to investigate intelligence failures before 9/11.

The panel's final report was finished, but it could not be made public until the Bush administration completed a review of the voluminous secret material that it contained; it was left to the CIA and other spy agencies that answered to the White House to decide if the congressional report could be declassified. Graham suspected the Bush administration was in no hurry to complete the process.

That meant that, for now, Graham was required to read the report in the intelligence committee's thick-walled offices on Capitol Hill. The offices had round-the-clock guards and were swept regularly for eavesdropping equipment; cell phones had to be left outside. The walls were decorated with vintage World War II military posters—LOOSE LIPS SINK SHIPS—that reminded lawmakers of the need for secrecy in their committee work.

Graham felt the report made it clear that Saudi government officials had a role in 9/11—simple and shocking as that was. There was a "direct line between the terrorists and the government of Saudi Arabia," he believed. The draft contained a twenty-eight-page passage that detailed evidence that Saudis in the United States—Saudi government "spies,"

Graham called them—had provided financial and logistical support to at least two of the 9/11 hijackers while they lived in Southern California.

There was no allegation that senior members of the Saudi royal family were involved in the attacks or had advance knowledge of them. But Osama bin Laden and his call for jihad against America and the West had enthusiastic support among many Saudis, including government officials, before and after 9/11; bin Laden remained a hero to many of his former countrymen. And Graham and his investigators had become convinced that a number of sympathetic Saudi officials, possibly within the sprawling Islamic Affairs Ministry, had known that al-Qaeda terrorists were entering the United States beginning in 2000 in preparation for some sort of an attack. Graham believed the Saudi officials had directed spies operating in the United States to assist them.

It was an astonishing allegation, but Graham felt the facts were indisputable. The remaining question was whether any of the evidence could be made public and whether Graham could survive the efforts by the White House and congressional Republicans to portray him as a partisan conspiracy theorist—a headline-grabbing kook.

The early indications from the White House were that while most of the committee's report could be made public eventually, the twenty-eight pages about the Saudis would remain secret on national security grounds. Graham suspected the material would remain secret for far less noble reasons involving the Bush administration's determination to keep Saudi oil flowing to the United States.

He believed the Bush White House was determined to cover up Saudi involvement in 9/11—and that the administration had found an eager accomplice in the FBI; Graham knew the bureau was humiliated that it had missed so many clues before 9/11 that might have allowed it to prevent the attacks. Graham had come to believe that the new FBI director, Robert Mueller, had become a "facilitator of the ineptitude of the bureau" and was directly involved in the effort to hide the truth.

The evidence about the Saudi links to the hijackers was dug up because of the tenaciousness of the joint committee's staff director, Eleanor Hill, a veteran congressional investigator who had worked for both Democrats and Republicans, and Michael Jacobson, a former FBI lawyer and counterterrorism analyst who had joined the staff and was one of its most dogged investigators.

Jacobson had found the most important evidence about the Saudi connection to the hijackers buried in the files of the FBI's field office in San Diego and at FBI headquarters in Washington. Two of the Saudi-born 9/11 hijackers, Nawaf al-Hazmi and Khalid al-Mihdhar, had lived in San Diego for more than a year before the attacks while seeking flight training. They had lived in the open—amazingly so. Hazmi's name, address, and home phone number were listed in the San Diego phone book. The fact that they were in the United States at all reflected the most basic sort of incompetence by the nation's spy and law enforcement agencies, since both Hazmi and Mihdhar had been identified as al-Qaeda terrorists before their arrival in the United States in January 2000. The CIA claimed that it had almost immediately alerted the FBI to the fact that at least one of them might be in the United States, although there was no record at the bureau to support that.

What Jacobson found in searching through the FBI's files was that Hazmi and Mihdhar had been befriended shortly after their arrival in California by a mysterious Saudi expatriate, Omar al-Bayoumi; Bayoumi seemed clearly to be working on behalf of some part of the Saudi government. Bayoumi was in his early forties at the time. He entered the United States as a business student and had lived in San Diego since 1996. He was on the payroll of an aviation contractor to the Saudi government, paid about $2,800 a month, but apparently did no work for the company. Bayoumi was described by another worker as one of several "ghost employees" on the payroll. He instead spent much of his day at a mosque in El Cajon, about fifteen miles outside San Diego.

To Graham and several of his investigators, it seemed obvious that the amiable Bayoumi was a low-ranking Saudi intelligence agent. He was no James Bond, no cloak-and-dagger spy. But he was someone who had been put on the ground in San Diego by his government to keep an eye on the activities of the relatively large Saudi community in Southern California and to carry out whatever other tasks he was given from Riyadh.

Interviewed by the FBI after September 11, Bayoumi told an improbable tale of how he had met the two hijackers. He claimed that he had driven the 125 miles to Los Angeles in February 2000 for a previously scheduled meeting at the Saudi consulate there; it was later determined he met that day with a diplomat, Fahad al-Thumairy, who worked in the consulate's Islamic affairs office and was also a prayer leader at the King

Fahd mosque in Los Angeles. Thumairy, who was in his late twenties, had a reputation as fanatically anti-American and was later barred from reentering the United States because of possible ties to terrorists.

After the meeting at the consulate, Bayoumi drove an additional seven miles to an Arab food restaurant near Los Angeles, where he claimed to have overheard Arabic spoken by two men at a nearby table and stopped to introduce himself. The men were Hazmi and Mihdhar, who had arrived in the United States only two weeks earlier. Bayoumi said it was only natural for him—as a Saudi and as a follower of the Koran, which compels hospitality to strangers—to offer help to two fellow countrymen who had no friends in Southern California and spoke little English.

Over the next year, Bayoumi would offer assistance of almost every sort to the two Saudis. He helped Hazmi and Mihdhar move to San Diego from Los Angeles, find them an apartment, open a bank account, and obtain driver's licenses and Social Security numbers. He lent them thousands of dollars. He organized a party in San Diego to welcome them to the city's Muslim community.

As Jacobson and the other congressional investigators kept digging, they found more evidence that Bayoumi appeared to be part of a larger network of Arab expatriates who had been tasked to help Hazmi and Mihdhar. Bayoumi's income had grown dramatically in the period in which he had assisted the two hijackers—almost $40,000 above his usual salary from his "ghost" job. Jacobson had found evidence that another Saudi in San Diego who appeared to work as a spy, Osama Bassan, had funneled thousands of dollars to Bayoumi.

The source of Bassan's money was an additional shock to the congressional investigators: Much of it had come in the form of cashier's checks directed to his family by Princess Haifa al-Faisal, wife of the Saudi ambassador to Washington. The princess had a charity fund that assisted Saudis in distress in the United States, and she had supposedly sent the money to help Bassan's wife pay for thyroid surgery; Bassan's wife had signed a number of the checks over to Bayoumi's wife.

There was one more alarming surprise in the FBI files: Hazmi and Mihdhar had been in close contact in San Diego with a longtime FBI informant, Abdussattar Shaikh; they had both lived in Shaikh's home for a time. The FBI blocked the congressional investigators from interviewing the informant after Jacobson learned his identity. There was no evidence to show that Shaikh knew the two Saudis were terrorists, but Graham was astounded to discover that "terrorists were living under the nose of an FBI informant." It was just more proof of the FBI's incompetence, he thought.

More than a year after 9/11, Graham found it hard to believe that the FBI was ignoring the implications of what was in its own files. The special committee's report would not say so explicitly, but Graham believed that the evidence gathered by his investigators showed that Saudi officials sympathetic to al-Qaeda had done the terrorist network's bidding.

He imagined how the al-Qaeda middleman might have to put it to his contacts in the Saudi government shortly before Hazmi and Mihdhar landed in California: "We are going to be insinuating some of our people into the United States, and it's very important to us that they be able to carry out the mission with the maximum amount of anonymity."

Graham knew that many of his colleagues on the congressional committee, Democrats and Republicans alike, shared his view that the material that had been gathered in San Diego was explosive; they, too, felt it should be made public. But in what seemed to many of them to be a breach of the Constitution's separation of powers, they had been muzzled into silence by the White House and the FBI.

In January 2003, Graham and the other members of the committee were still the focus of a criminal investigation by the FBI into whether someone on the panel had leaked classified information. A report on CNN on June 19, 2002, revealed the wording of messages sent among al-Qaeda sympathizers in the days and hours before 9/11. The messages ("Tomorrow is zero day," "The match is tomorrow") were intercepted by the National Security Agency but not translated from the original Arabic until after the attacks. The CNN report aired only hours after the messages were shared with Graham's committee.

The leaks resulted in a fierce White House protest. Vice President Cheney called Graham at home.

"What the hell is going on, Bob?" Cheney asked. "We have tried to be as cooperative as possible, but we cannot tolerate this leakage to the press. If this continues, we will terminate our assistance to the committee." Graham thought Cheney's warning "disingenuous and pompous," but he felt compelled to call in the FBI. Without some sort of leak investigation, Graham thought, the White House would follow through on Cheney's threat and shut down all cooperation.

The FBI had responded aggressively to the request to find the leak, interviewing dozens of members of Congress and their aides. The bureau suggested it wanted to use polygraphs on some of the lawmakers.

To Graham and other lawmakers, the situation was "surreal." Members of Congress were under investigation by the FBI at the behest of the White House because, Graham believed, the lawmakers had brought such uncomfortable scrutiny to the FBI and White House. Graham thought the leak investigation was an obvious effort by the administration to intimidate Congress. And if that was the intention, it worked. Members of the joint committee and their staffs were frightened into silence about the investigation.

Graham was left as one of the only people who would talk openly—if more cautiously—about what the congressional investigation had found.

The only bit of good news in early 2003 for Graham was that Congress had finally overcome the administration's objections and created an independent commission to investigate the terrorist attacks. He knew and respected many of the 9/11 commissioners. With more time and a fresh eye, the 9/11 commission could do what Congress had been unable to do so far—reveal the truth about the duplicity of the Saudis and the FBI and expose what had really happened in San Diego. What reason would the new commission have to protect the Saudis and the FBI?

ONE OF Graham's former Republican colleagues, retired senator Warren Rudman of New Hampshire, had heard the rumors, too. His friends in Congress assumed he was going to be joining the 9/11 commission. His name had been circulating for weeks as a likely GOP member. He had years of background on terrorism and intelligence issues, and his candidacy was being championed by many of the 9/11 family groups.

But Rudman also figured—correctly, as it turned out—that the White House would bring pressure on Senate leaders to try to keep him off the investigation. "I've never had great relations with the Bush administration," he said, smiling at the understatement. Rudman was one of John McCain's best friends, and he had been instrumental in the Arizonan's victory over Bush in the 2000 New Hampshire primary, nearly derailing Bush's presidential campaign before it began.

Rudman said McCain came to him in late 2002 and told him—"in ultimate frustration"—that Rudman would not be invited onto the 9/11 commission. McCain did not give him the details why, but Rudman figured there was "pushback from the people at the White House."

Rudman suspected it might have gone beyond politics. There was another, possibly more important reason why the White House would want to keep Rudman off the investigation. Rudman had firsthand knowledge of how little attention the Bush administration had paid to domestic terrorist threats before 9/11. He had tried to deliver some of those warnings himself to President Bush in early 2001 and, to Rudman's astonishment, was rebuffed.

Throughout the Clinton administration, Rudman had been one of the Republican members of the President's Foreign Intelligence Advisory Board, which meant he had been briefed in detail by the CIA about the al-Qaeda threat as late as 2001. More to the point, Rudman had been co-chairman with former senator Gary Hart of a Pentagon-chartered commission on terrorist threats that released a report in January 2001 that predicted a catastrophic terrorist strike on American soil. The so-called Hart-Rudman report warned that "in the face of this threat, our nation has no coherent or integrated governmental structures" to respond to it.

Rudman had wanted to share those findings with President Bush, then newly arrived at the White House. Whatever the bad feelings about his support for McCain in the 2000 race, Rudman assumed that he would be given the courtesy of at least a brief meeting in the Oval Office with Bush. It was a federal commission. He was a former GOP senator. Rudman had wanted to deliver a "very blunt and very direct" warning to Bush that he needed to deal early in his presidency with the question of domestic terror threats.

But he could not get past Condoleezza Rice, Bush's national security adviser. She met with Rudman at the White House, heard his presentation about the committee's findings, and agreed to pass on his request to see the president. After that, Rudman heard nothing. He contacted Rice's office again several more times to push for a meeting with Bush. But there was no invitation. The new president was described as being too busy with other, more pressing issues. He was focused on his huge tax cut proposal.

"Offended is not the right issue, but I was disappointed," Rudman said later. He could not understand why Rice would not press harder to have the president briefed on such a clear national security threat—the certainty of a domestic terrorist attack in coming years. Wouldn't Bush want to know? "There's no question in my mind that somebody at the White House dropped the ball on this," Rudman said.

DREW UNIVERSITY
Madison, N.J.
JANUARY 2003

P hilip Zelikow had been recommended to Tom Kean and Lee Hamilton by one of the other Republican commissioners, former senator Slade Gorton. Gorton could not have been more effusive about Zelikow. "I picked up the telephone and called both of them and said that you couldn't possibly find a better person to direct the staff," he said.

Kean and Hamilton learned early on to pay attention to Gorton's advice. He seemed to be nothing like the harsh partisan they had been told to expect. Before his election to the Senate, Gorton had been Washington State's attorney general, and his instincts seemed to be those of a get-to-the-facts prosecutor, even when the facts might embarrass Republicans.

Gorton knew Zelikow from another federal commission—a blue-ribbon panel on electoral reform created in response to the 2000 recount fiasco in Florida. The commission was led by former presidents Jimmy Carter and Gerald Ford; Zelikow was staff director. Gorton had been wowed by Zelikow's intelligence, his writing skills, and his all-important ability to meet a deadline. Zelikow was known to be indefatigable, able to go without sleep for days, surviving off whatever was available from the nearest vending machine.

Gorton was also impressed by Zelikow's ability to quietly move the commission toward recommendations that he, Zelikow, supported. "He did a marvelous job of deferring to everyone but leading the commission in the direction that he wanted," Gorton said.

After his initial meeting at the White House, Kean went on a long-scheduled winter vacation to the isolated Caribbean island of Barbuda, which had only sporadic telephone service; he figured it would be his last real holiday for more than a year, and he was right. So Hamilton took on much of the job of vetting Zelikow as a prospective executive director of the 9/11 commission. He called around Washington and liked what he heard, and not just from Republicans. Zelikow had admirers among prominent Democrats, including Carter, who praised Zelikow's diligence in managing the staff of the electoral reform commission. Carter said he saw no evidence of political bias in Zelikow's work.

If Hamilton had talked to the staff of the Carter-Ford electoral commission, he would have heard a very different opinion of Zelikow. Many on that commission's staff, especially those who identified themselves as Democrats, found him arrogant and secretive. His success, they decided, rested largely on his ability to serve the needs—and stroke the egos—of the two former presidents and the other commissioners.

Zelikow provided Kean and Hamilton with a copy of his résumé. They found even more to like about Zelikow: author or editor of fourteen books, dozens of scholarly articles, an expertise in every sort of national security issue, including terrorism. They were both impressed with a remarkably prescient 1998 article that Zelikow and two coauthors had published in *Foreign Affairs* magazine. It was titled "Catastrophic Terrorism" and warned that the United States needed to ready itself for a massive domestic terrorist attack, possibly with nuclear, chemical, or biological weapons.

The résumé listed Zelikow's book with Condoleezza Rice and his appointment by Bush to a special White House intelligence advisory board in 2001; Kean and Hamilton knew that both of those entries would raise obvious concerns about a conflict of interest if they hired Zelikow for the commission. But Kean and Hamilton, who had no reason to believe that the résumé Zelikow had provided was incomplete, decided the conflict was not insurmountable.

Kean and Hamilton agreed that in the circles in which Zelikow traveled—and in which they traveled, for that matter—it was often impossible to avoid the appearance of a conflict. They could sympathize with Zelikow. In joining the 9/11 commission, both Kean and Hamilton had themselves faced allegations of conflicts of interest—Kean because he had been a director of companies with large business interests in Arab nations; Hamilton because he sat on advisory boards that oversaw the CIA and other national security agencies. Another of the Democrats, former deputy attorney general Jamie Gorelick, had been deeply involved in developing policies in the Clinton administration's Justice Department to deal with terrorist threats. Should the appearance of a conflict be enough to prevent people as obviously talented as Zelikow and Gorelick from contributing to the 9/11 investigation?

Zelikow's 1995 book with Rice was a special concern, given that Rice was likely to be such a central figure in the commission's investigation. But Kean decided that since both Zelikow and Rice were out of government service at the time it was published, the conflict was not obvious. "I thought they were both academics, so what's wrong with that?" he said.

After returning from his holiday, Kean asked Zelikow to travel up to New Jersey so they could talk, and Zelikow made the trip to Drew. Zelikow presented Kean with a plan for the commission that Kean found exciting, even thrilling. Zelikow proposed that the panel's final report be written for the general public, not in the bureaucratese of most government documents, and made available to the public on the same day it was presented to the White House and Congress. The commission should find a private publisher who would stock the report in bookstores around the country within hours of its release in Washington, Zelikow proposed. The idea had obvious appeal to Kean, who liked to consider himself "a historian who went into politics." Away from his duties as president, Kean also taught history at Drew, and he was proud of his master's degree in the teaching of history from Teachers College at Columbia University. This would not be another government report that would be ignored and gather dust on a bookshelf, thought Kean.

As far as Kean was concerned, Zelikow was the only choice for executive director of the 9/11 commission. After reviewing the résumés of about twenty candidates, including those proposed by the White House, "there wasn't anybody even close to Zelikow," he said. "Nobody else had the qualifications or anything even close to them. His experience, his brilliance, the fact that he was a historian."

Although Zelikow could not have been more polite in his initial phone contacts with them, Kean and Hamilton heard stories about his abrasiveness. Kean's staff at Drew experienced it directly. Just after Zelikow's visit to the university, Kean's office assistants at the university, veterans of several prickly phone calls with Zelikow, urged Kean not to hire him. "They just didn't like him," Kean recalled. He also talked with

Henry Kissinger, who knew Zelikow from projects at the Miller Center and Harvard.

"He's one of the most brilliant men I know," Kissinger told Kean. "But you will not like him. Nobody does."

Kean and Hamilton were hugely self-confident politicians who had spent their careers dealing with, and co-opting, people with big, abrasive egos. Kean was famous for it in New Jersey, making allies out of hard-nosed Democrats who spoke in the "dems and does" accent of the rougher parts of the state. So Kean and Hamilton were certain they knew how to rein in someone like Zelikow. "I figured he was going to break china, and I figured I'd have to clean it up," Kean said. Certainly, Kean thought, if there was any sign of partisanship in Zelikow's actions, the commission would put an end to it.

But could Kean and Hamilton rein in Zelikow if they did not know what he was up to? If they did not learn until much later what he had left off his résumé?

Zelikow has insisted that before he was hired, he made sure Kean and Hamilton knew about all of his connections to the Bush administration, including his work on the Bush transition team in 2001.

"In my very first conversations with Tom and Lee—on the phone— I discussed my past work and friendship with Rice and asked them whether they had considered that issue," Zelikow said later. "They said they were, of course, aware of that and had taken it into account." He said that none of the three of them realized how the issue might come back to haunt them later. "I don't think Tom or Lee or I anticipated the extent to which the commission's work would be used as a partisan battlefield."

But in interviews long after the commission had shut down, Kean and Hamilton seemed unsure of what Zelikow had told them. Kean acknowledged that he "wasn't sure" he knew anything about Zelikow's work on the Bush transition before hiring him. He said that when he did find out, he found it "worrisome" but consoled himself with the thought that Zelikow was brought into the transition because of his expertise as a historian, not because of his loyalty to Bush or the GOP. Hamilton said he thought he was aware that Zelikow had been on the transition team for Bush: "I think I did, but I don't think I'd swear to that." Whatever the case, Hamilton acknowledged that he did not know any of the details of what Zelikow had done during the transition.

Kean and Hamilton would learn all of those remarkable details, but not until much later—too late to think of removing him from the investigation.

On January 27, 2003, Kean and Hamilton issued a press release announcing Zelikow's hiring as the 9/11 commission's executive director. It identified Zelikow as director of the Miller Center and staff director of the Carter-Ford electoral commission. "Phil Zelikow is a man of high stature who has distinguished himself as an academician, lawyer, author, and public servant," Kean was quoted as saying.

The release was notable for what it did not say. It made no mention of the fact that Zelikow had worked on the NSC for the first President Bush. Nothing about the book with Rice. Nothing about Zelikow's role on the Bush transition team. Nothing about the fact that he had just written a policy paper for the White House that was going to be used within months to justify the American invasion of Iraq. Aides to Hamilton at the Wilson Center said they wrote the press release, based on the background information that Zelikow had provided to Hamilton. Zelikow reviewed it before it was handed out to reporters.

OFFICES OF THE NATIONAL
SECURITY COUNCIL
The White House
JANUARY 27, 2003

Z elikow? Philip Zelikow?
Richard A. Clarke could not believe what he was reading as he sat in his White House office. It was one of his last days on the job after almost a dozen years at the National Security Council, and this news was no retirement gift. On the afternoon of January 27, 2003, the Associated Press issued a short news report about Zelikow's appointment as executive director of the 9/11 commission.

"The fix is in," said Clarke. He knew and disliked Zelikow. Christ, how could anybody be so stupid? he wondered. Condi's friend?

Clarke understood that with Zelikow—Zelikow, of all people!—in charge, there was no hope that the commission would carry out an impartial investigation of the Bush administration's bungling of terrorist threats in the months before September 11. Could anyone have a more obvious conflict of interest than Zelikow?

It was not just that Zelikow was a close friend of Rice's from the first Bush presidency. That was the least of it. That was ancient history. Clarke wondered if the commission understood that it was Zelikow who, in his work on Bush's transition team in early 2001, had been the architect of the demotion of Clarke and his counterterrorism team within the NSC. Clarke's colleagues believed that Zelikow's "reorganization" had all but guaranteed that the White House would pay little attention to the flood of terrorist warnings in the months before 9/11.

Was it possible that Zelikow had not told Kean and Hamilton that he sat in on the briefings in the White House in January 2001 in which Rice was warned by her predecessor, Sandy Berger, that the biggest national security threat facing the country was al-Qaeda? Not the threats that she and President Bush had seemed so preoccupied with—Iraq, Iran, North

Korea. The threat was Osama bin Laden. "Zelikow was right there, sitting with her, listening with her," he said.

Clarke had worked at the NSC for three presidents, initially for Bush's father, and was given the counterterrorism portfolio under Clinton. Earlier, he had worked for years in the State Department and the Pentagon, where he earned a reputation as a gifted bureaucrat and briefer—no one gave a briefing like Dick Clarke, full of clever turns of phrase and almost theatrical urgency—and for razor-sharp elbows. At the NSC, he infuriated colleagues with "bold, red-type e-mail messages that ranged from the merely snide to the blatantly insulting," recalled Daniel Benjamin, a mostly admiring former colleague from the Clinton administration. He wrote later that within the White House, "few sentences were uttered with the same frequency as 'This time Dick has gone too far.'"

Clarke rarely discussed politics with his colleagues; many of them later said they had no idea if Clarke considered himself a Democrat or Republican. He seemed equally contemptuous of all politicians. Still, the last time he had been asked to declare his party loyalty publicly, in the 2000 primary for president in Virginia, where he lived, he had asked for a Republican ballot. He said later he voted for John McCain.

In his first years in the counterterrorism job at the White House, Clarke focused on Hezbollah and Hamas and the other well-established, well-understood terrorist groups in the Middle East. But by the mid-1990s, Clarke saw his job largely as the hunt for one man, Osama bin Laden, and the destruction of his al-Qaeda terrorist network; by then, Clarke was convinced that bin Laden's network surpassed all others as a threat to the United States. Clarke was among the first in the government to see the danger. He had long predicted that bin Laden would eventually attack on American soil, possibly with weapons of mass destruction. His passion was shared by his small, devoted staff on the NSC. One of his deputies, Lisa Gordon-Hagerty, would later startle investigators for the 9/11 commission by telling them that she had long expected to see terrorists strike in Washington with a nuclear device—"to drive to work one day and see a mushroom cloud rising over the White House."

In early 2003, Clarke's name was little known outside the government. But that anonymity would not last much longer. He had finally had enough. Clarke was planning to retire from the government in late January and finish his memoirs—a book that, his friends quietly suspected, could blow apart George Bush's hopes for a second term. Clarke had begun considering a title for the book. He was thinking about *Against All Enemies,* a phrase drawn from the military's enlistment oath; new soldiers swear to defend the Constitution "against all enemies." Clarke liked the title. Clarke knew that enemies could come from within.

He had not always been pessimistic about the 9/11 commission. When Congress finally overcame Bush's objections to an independent investigation and established the panel in late 2002, Clarke told colleagues that with the right commissioners and an aggressive staff, there was some hope that they would find out the truth of how Bush and Rice—Rice in particular—had repeatedly ignored the intelligence in 2001.

But the appointment of Zelikow suggested to Clarke that the commission had been turned into just another instrument for the Bush administration in trying to hide the truth. Zelikow, he figured, would serve as the administration's plant on the investigation, feeding information back to Rice and others that would allow them to deflect the commission's questions. Surely Zelikow would have no interest in a detailed public explanation of what had happened during the 2001 transition, since he had been such a central part of it. Zelikow had helped lay the groundwork for much of what went wrong at the White House in the weeks and months before September 11. Would he want people to know that?

THERE WAS someone else at the White House who found it difficult to believe that Zelikow had been hired by the 9/11 commission: Andy Card.

Just before announcing Zelikow's appointment, Tom Kean talked with Card at the White House. He wanted to give Card advance warning that the commission would not be hiring one of the White House candidates as executive director. Kean said he thought the panel had found the perfect candidate from outside the government.

"Do you know Philip Zelikow?" he asked.

Card hesitated before speaking. He knew Zelikow well, and he was surprised to hear the name. He wondered if Kean was aware of Zelikow's close relationship with Rice and others in the White House. He wondered if Kean was aware of Zelikow's difficult personality, his self-importance. Card had dealt with Zelikow during the 2001 transition and repeatedly during preparation of the Miller Center's oral history of the first Bush administration. He found Zelikow remarkably abrasive.

Almost as worrying, Card thought, was Zelikow's tendency as a historian to see his work as itself historic; Card had seen that in action in Zelikow's work on the transition team and at the NSC under the first Bush administration. "I think he is a historian who wants to live it," Card said, wondering how much of this he should tell Kean. "So sometimes he may overplay the historic work he is doing, believing that is historic rather than allowing it to be deemed historic by future generations."

Card did not think it was his place to tell Kean not to hire Zelikow, but he urged Kean to be careful before making a final decision. He put it to Kean diplomatically.

"I've had quite a bit of dealing with him before, and sometimes it was frustrating," Card said of Zelikow. "He has strong views. He's very intelligent, and he knows it." Zelikow has a mind "like a steel trap," but his secretiveness "sometimes invites conspiracy theories—he recognizes that knowledge is power, and he doesn't want to share the knowledge," Card said.

Card was not surprised that Zelikow had found his way onto the list of people being considered to run the commission. Among the nation's historians, Zelikow was about as well-known to prominent politicians as any in the country, thanks to his work at Harvard and the Miller Center. But the conflicts of interest—or at least the appearance of them—seemed so obvious to Card.

Card considered it part of his job to worry about "unintended consequences," and he saw the potential for endless trouble if reporters and congressional Democrats figured out all of Zelikow's connections to senior officials in the administration. Card did not want to have to spend the next year and a half trying to explain away all of Zelikow's conflicts of interest.

Since Kean said that there had been no final decision on Zelikow, Card hoped he had a little time. He decided to start asking around at the White House if others saw Zelikow's appointment to the 9/11 commission as a problem. He wanted it to be known that he had done his due diligence. Among the first people he went to see was Rice, Zelikow's friend and an obvious target of the commission's investigation.

"I raised this with Condi," he said. "She didn't have a problem with it."

In later interviews, Kean did not recall getting a warning from Card that he should not hire Zelikow. He did remember that Card had no special enthusiasm for the choice.

"Zelikow?" he remembers Card saying. "I guess we can live with that."

— 12 —

WOODROW WILSON INTERNATIONAL CENTER FOR SCHOLARS

Washington, D.C.

DECEMBER 2002

Tom Kean and Lee Hamilton bonded instantly. They met for the first time in December over a lunch of soup and turkey sandwiches in Hamilton's offices at the Wilson Center, a Washington think tank that he joined as president after retiring from Congress. Hamilton had a spacious suite of book-lined offices between Pennsylvania and Constitution avenues, a few blocks from the White House.

Kean decided before the meeting with Hamilton that he wanted to make an early, dramatic gesture of bipartisan unity. So between mouthfuls of his sandwich, he made what was, by Washington standards, a remarkable offer: He wanted to share power—cede power, even. Forget what the law said, he told Hamilton. As far as Kean was concerned, there should be no chairman, no vice chairman. He proposed that they would effectively be co-chairmen of the commission, with equal say on hiring and the structure of the investigation.

"I walked in with the idea that either he and I get along or this wouldn't work," Kean said. "I wanted him to understand that I wouldn't use the powers I had without his consent." He proposed to Hamilton, and Hamilton immediately agreed, that the two of them should be "joined at the hip"—always appearing together in public, certainly any time a television camera or microphone was nearby.

Hamilton thought the arrangement was especially important since he worried that he and Kean did not, individually, have the stature of the men they replaced. "Tom and I were both substitute hitters, and I wondered whether that would harm the prestige of the commission," he said. "Mitchell and Kissinger both have very prestigious reputations. Tom and I were not in their category."

Because the Christmas holidays were approaching, the full commission did not meet for another month. They all gathered for the first time on Sunday, January 26, 2003, for a dinner hosted by Kean and Hamilton at the Wilson Center. It was the night of the Super Bowl, and Kean hoped there were no fans of the Tampa Bay Buccaneers or Oakland Raiders among the commissioners. Just in case, there was a television nearby if anyone wanted to sneak out of the meal to watch Tampa Bay rout Oakland, 48–21.

Kean thought a relaxed supper would allow the commissioners to put aside their party affiliations for the evening and see one another, from the start, as friends. Or at least not as adversaries. But there was an edge to the meal, especially among the Democrats; they had gotten word of the selection of Philip Zelikow as executive director. The decision to hire Zelikow was made unilaterally by Kean and Hamilton. To the Democrats, it seemed to establish the wrong tone from the start. "It was presented as a fait accompli," recalled Richard Ben-Veniste, who was alarmed to learn some of the details about Zelikow's past relationship with Condoleezza Rice and others in the White House. Nor had the other commissioners been consulted in detail about Kean and Hamilton's plan to have a single, nonpartisan staff led by Zelikow.

Among the commissioners, Ben-Veniste and Max Cleland were especially upset by the way the investigation was being structured by Kean and Hamilton. In joining the commission, they assumed they could have a staff member of their own, typical on these sorts of independent commissions. Cleland had hoped he would have an office, possibly a secretary and driver; transportation around Washington was always a problem for the wheelchair-bound Cleland.

Other proposals from the Democrats were shot down. Ben-Veniste proposed that issues under investigation be divided up, with each of the commissioners developing an expertise in one of two areas. Over time Ben-Veniste would develop a special interest in the Federal Aviation Administration (FAA) and the Defense Department and why it had taken so long for the nation's air defense system to respond to the reports of the hijackings on September. 11. But Kean and Hamilton—and Zelikow—did not want a formal division of responsibilities among the commissioners. Kean and Hamilton made it clear that while the commissioners were invited to visit the panel's offices whenever they wished, they would not have a permanent presence there. Kean and Hamilton would not have separate offices at the commission, either. Everything would be run through Zelikow.

To Ben-Veniste, the way the staff was being organized guaranteed that the commissioners' involvement in the details of the investigation would be limited. It centralized control in Zelikow's hands.

The commission's first formal meeting was held the next morning—Monday, January 27, 2003—behind closed doors at the Wilson Center. Kean and Hamilton opened the session with a statement of purpose and with a warning. "There are two things that can destroy us," Kean said. "One is a leak of classified information. That would give the White House all the excuse it needs to deny us material. The second is politics." Kean reminded the other commissioners that he was an outsider in Washington but that it was clear to him that the city's vicious partisanship prevented the government from getting anything done. He did not want to see that repeated on the commission that was charged with getting at the truth about "a national tragedy."

"If we become like everybody else in Washington, if the Republicans on the commission start fighting Democrats, then we'll destroy our credibility," he said.

Zelikow was there to introduce himself to the commissioners, and he was invited by Kean and Hamilton to explain his vision for the investigation and the final report. His presentation was impressive. The Democrats were wary of Zelikow, but they could not deny that he was a graceful speaker and a true expert in the national security issues before the commission.

The conversation turned to the question of how the commission would gather information and how it would make use of its subpoena powers. To Jamie Gorelick, it was obvious: Every request made to the Bush administration for documents or other information should include a subpoena. Subpoenas did not have to be seen as threatening if they were issued routinely, she argued; a subpoena was simply evidence of the commission's determination to get what it needed. She explained there was a "nice" way of doing it. "You simply say, 'We're very serious and, therefore, here's a subpoena,'" she said. If the commission held off on subpoenas until late in the investigation, she warned, there would be no time to go to court to enforce them. The other Democrats, apart from Hamilton, agreed.

But Kean and Hamilton had already made up their minds on this issue, too. There would be no routine subpoenas, they decreed; subpoenas would be seen as too confrontational, perhaps choking off cooperation from the Bush administration from the very start of the investigation. Kean and Hamilton had the power to enforce the decision. The law creating the commission offered only two methods for issuing a subpoena: It required either an agreement between Kean and Hamilton or a vote of six of the ten commissioners. Given Hamilton's opposition to any early subpoenas, the other Democrats had little hope of mustering the Republican support they would need to issue one.

Kean played the role of stern headmaster at another early meeting of the commission. He arrived to see Democrats seated with the Democrats at one end of the room, Republicans gathered with Republicans at the other.

"I don't want to see this again," he declared in a surprisingly angry tone. Kean knew that the other commissioners probably saw him as a "stupid schoolteacher" at that moment. "They probably thought I was treating this like a kindergarten," he said. But he asked them—ordered them—to seat themselves Democrat, Republican, Democrat, Republican. He had already told the Republican commissioners that he did not want them to meet separately as a "caucus." He certainly would not participate.

MAX CLELAND sat glumly in his wheelchair. He did not like what he was hearing from Kean or Hamilton at the first meeting. Ultimately, he would never like what he heard.

It was obvious to him that "Bush and Rove and the other nutsos in the White House" would do whatever they needed to do to block the commission's access to evidence about intelligence blunders. Yes, Cleland was deeply depressed and angry after his election defeat; he admitted it probably made him more eager to be confrontational with the White House. But no subpoenas? A nonpartisan staff? An executive director who was close to Condi Rice? To Cleland, Kean and Hamilton were giving up the fight before it had begun.

Cleland had been named to the commission in December, a few days after Henry Kissinger, and unlike so many other Democrats, he was genuinely disappointed by Kissinger's resignation.

"With Kissinger, I thought we were going to get somewhere," Cleland said. "This is Henry Kissinger. He's the big dog."

Whatever his loyalties to the president and the Republican Party, Kissinger was not going to sacrifice his own legacy to George Bush's by covering up for the White House on 9/11, Cleland thought. In the Senate, Cleland had come to know Kissinger slightly over the years, "and he's too strong a personality to do anybody's business." He felt certain that Kissinger would not have tolerated any attempt by the White House to limit the commission's access to documents or to interviews with the president and his top aides. "We're talking about Henry Kissinger here," Cleland said. He was similarly impressed by the Democrats' choice of George Mitchell—"a man with a real power and gravitas all his own."

The departure of both Kissinger and Mitchell alarmed Cleland. He knew their replacements did not have similar stature in Washington. Kean had never worked in the capital—he seemed to take pride in it, in fact—and had no experience at all in foreign policy and intelligence. "You darn well know that an ex-governor who has no basic background in these issues is not going to be the world's greatest tiger in asking a difficult question," Cleland said. He certainly respected Hamilton, but he knew that Hamilton had a well-deserved reputation for cooperating with Republicans, not confronting them.

"It just didn't seem to me that Kean and Hamilton had the bite and the authority to tell the White House to go fly a kite," Cleland said.

He decided from the start that he would have to fight the battles himself—or at least constantly goad Kean and Hamilton to do battle. "You don't want to be the dog in the manger," Cleland would later say. "Nobody wanted to be that. I didn't want to be that." But if nobody else was going to make trouble for the Bush White House, Cleland would.

OFFICE OF THE COUNSEL TO THE PRESIDENT
The White House
JANUARY 2003

Philip Zelikow could not help himself. Whatever his instincts as a Republican partisan and friend of the Bush White House, his instincts as a historian overwhelmed everything else as he walked up the stairs to the second floor of the West Wing and entered the office of Alberto Gonzales. Zelikow did not consider this a negotiation. He was there to present Gonzales, Bush's White House counsel, with a list of highly classified documents and other material that the commission needed to see to do its job. To Zelikow, the access seemed nonnegotiable; he was there mostly to work out the logistics.

At the top of Zelikow's list were copies of the "crown jewels" of American intelligence—the president's daily brief, the intelligence summary delivered by the CIA to the Oval Office every morning. The PDB was a sort of supersecret newspaper, the information usually organized into short items, divided by bullet points, that summarized the latest, most important, or most sensational news gathered by the CIA and other spy agencies overnight. The readership was tiny. Copies were presented to Bush, Cheney, and a handful of their aides and to Secretary of State Powell and Defense Secretary Rumsfeld. Bush had cut back distribution of the PDB after he took office. While Clinton's attorney general, Janet Reno, had received the PDB, her successor, John Ashcroft, did not.

Zelikow believed the commission needed to see the PDBs given to Bush and Clinton in the years before 9/11 to determine what warnings they received about the al-Qaeda threat. Zelikow was well aware what an extraordinary concession that required from the White House. Although a handful of PDBs from the Nixon and Johnson administrations had been declassified over the years, the intelligence memos were, as a rule, never shared outside the executive branch. The PDBs had been denied to congressional investigators even after 9/11. But in an investigation by an independent commission of the worst surprise attack on the United States since Pearl Harbor, the rules were different, Zelikow believed. Surely the White House understood that.

There were a few pleasantries as Zelikow took a seat in Gonzales's office, which was decorated with mementos of his years in the service of George W. Bush, first in the Texas governor's office, then in Washington. Gonzales had left his treasured seat on the Texas Supreme Court to join his patron at the White House in 2001. The new president had an unfortunate habit of referring to Gonzales as *mi amigo* or *mi abogado*— "my lawyer," in Spanish—in gatherings in the White House. They were references to Gonzales's Mexican ancestry that drew cringes from others in the West Wing who thought them patronizing. But Gonzales was never heard to complain; he was absolute in his loyalty to Bush, describing the president in heroic terms. To Gonzales, Bush was a "great man."

Zelikow had thought the meeting might go well. He and Gonzales shared friends from the administration, so Gonzales might have had reason to see Zelikow as a potential ally. Gonzales was known to be unfailingly polite. He had a reputation as being one of the most mildmannered and self-effacing people in Bush's inner circle; when he was introduced at GOP gatherings, it was often noted that Gonzales was raised in the small town of Humble, Texas, near Houston. (Humble served as a metaphor in other ways: The town was in the noisy flight path of Houston's George Bush Intercontinental Airport, named for the first President Bush.)

But the meeting started going badly from the start. From his earlier conversations with Andy Card, as well as the assurances given to Tom Kean and Lee Hamilton, Zelikow believed that the commission already had an agreement from the White House for full cooperation. To Zelikow, that meant the commission would have access to virtually everything it wanted, including the PDBs and the files of the NSC.

"Given my belief about the president's commitment to cooperate fully with the commission, I came into the meeting pushing hard," Zelikow recalled. "I felt it important for folks to understand from the very start what full cooperation would entail."

He turned to Gonzales.

"The White House should be prepared to provide full access to documents and people," Zelikow began. He explained that Kean and Hamilton had to be able to assure the public at the end of its investigation that nothing was held back from the investigation. The commission's members "had to be in the position of saying publicly and truthfully, at the end of the day, that they had seen every document they wished to see," he said.

But Gonzales made it clear there would be no such cooperation. The commission, he said, "would receive the kind of access the White House has given to the joint inquiry" on Capitol Hill, nothing more. Anything more would be a clear violation of executive privilege, Gonzales said.

Zelikow hadn't expected this. He thought this had all been agreed to. "When I took the job, I thought that the White House had reconciled itself to the necessity of fully supporting such a commission, with all that implied," he remembered later. He was surprised by how dogmatic Gonzales seemed.

He tried to reason with Gonzales, reminding him that the legacy of other blue-ribbon federal commissions formed following a national crisis—the Warren Commission, the panels that investigated the Pearl Harbor attacks—had been tarnished after the discovery that they had been denied access to secret files. It proved to be a breeding ground for the sort of conspiracy theorists who were already beginning to swarm around 9/11.

He tried a brief history lesson, reminding Gonzales of the uproar that followed the discovery that the Warren Commission had never seen files from the CIA's "Operation Mongoose" to assassinate Fidel Castro during the Kennedy administration. The news gave birth to theories, long after the commission had gone out of business, that Castro had ordered Kennedy's murder in retaliation. Surely Gonzales understood that the 9/11 commission faced a "unique challenge" and would need much more material than the White House had provided Congress.

Gonzales was unmoved. He thought he was being lectured to by the arrogant historian.

Zelikow decided to up the stakes. If the White House would give the commission nothing more than it had given Congress, he would consider resigning from the 9/11 commission. It was not hard to imagine the damning headlines for the White House if the 9/11 commission's executive director resigned over White House stonewalling in the very first days of the investigation.

The White House offer was "unacceptable," Zelikow told Gonzales. "I would not want to serve with the commission if it ended up only receiving that kind of access."

Gonzales had nothing more to say. The meeting ended with Zelikow quietly seething and with Gonzales offended by Zelikow's tone and his threats. A day or so later, Tom Kean got a phone call from Gonzales about Zelikow, and the message was remarkably blunt and undiplomatic for a man as polite as Gonzales.

"I don't want to see him again," Gonzales declared to Kean. "I don't want to see Philip Zelikow again."

In the future, Gonzales would meet only with Kean and Hamilton themselves. There would be no intermediary.

CIA HEADQUARTERS
LANGLEY, VA.

Within days of his appointment to the commission, Zelikow also made arrangements to visit the CIA's headquarters in Virginia. He already knew many people at the agency, and this would be more than a friendly reintroduction. Zelikow wanted to make clear what he expected of the agency. Much as he had made an early enemy of the White House counsel, Zelikow was about to do the same with the CIA.

The agency's headquarters in McLean, Virginia, are about eight miles down the Potomac from the center of Washington, a ten-minute drive from the White House in good traffic. In the self-important bureaucratic shorthand of Washington, the 258-acre compound is known as "Langley" (as in "I was just out at Langley" or "Langley is calling"), which is actually the name of the McLean neighborhood where the CIA is found.

In 1999, the compound was renamed the George Bush Center for Intelligence. Cynical CIA colleagues saw the new name as a ploy by the agency's crafty, politically astute director, George Tenet, to curry favor with any Republican who might replace Bill Clinton in the elections the following year. Tenet loved the CIA job and would want to hold on to it. Was there anything better? Tenet wondered to himself. In his wildest dreams, could this former congressional staffer have imagined himself here? Tenet's aides said he had little to do with the renaming of the CIA headquarters, in fact. It was proposed by House Republicans and agreed to by Clinton in a generous moment. George Herbert Walker Bush had served as the director of central intelligence for less than a year in the mid-1970s. When his son was sworn in as president in 2001, the elder Bush urged that Tenet be kept on.

Zelikow drove past the agency's heavily guarded main gate, past the barbed-wire barricades and the nine-foot granite wall that served as a memorial to two CIA employees who were gunned down in January 1993 as they waited in their cars to clear the gate and go to work. The gunman, a twenty-eight-year-old Pakistani, Aimal Kasi, later confessed to the killings with an AK-47 rifle, saying he had wanted to punish the CIA for its meddling in Muslim nations.

Zelikow pulled up in front of the OHB, the Original Headquarters Building, where Tenet and the rest of the agency's senior leaders had their offices. He could see the evidence of how well Allen Dulles, Eisenhower's spy chief, had succeeded in his dream of creating a university-like setting for the CIA. For an agency that represented the darkest sort of malice to people in much of the world, the CIA had some of the most civilized offices in the federal government. The compound could pass for a college campus, with long stretches of well-tended, tree-shaded lawns. The OHB, designed in the mid-1950s by the same New York architects who designed the United Nations headquarters in Manhattan, had an airy, open feeling.

Zelikow headed to the seventh floor, where Tenet's suite was located, and went to see two of the director's most trusted lieutenants, Mark Lowenthal and Winston Wiley.

Lowenthal, a friend of Tenet's since they were staffers on Capitol Hill, had been hired by Tenet shortly after 9/11 to help him prepare for the congressional investigation of the attacks. With the creation of the 9/11 commission in November 2002, Tenet asked Lowenthal to deal with the commission as well. Lowenthal was quick-witted and had a detailed, scholarly knowledge of the intelligence community. (Lowenthal had a scholar's knowledge of many things; he had been a grand champion on the television show *Jeopardy!* in the 1980s, winning $154,000.) Wiley was the CIA's assistant director for homeland security, a job created after 9/11. Both men had met Zelikow before.

Wiley felt more strongly about the Virginia historian. "He reeks of arrogance," Wiley said of Zelikow, whose appointment to the 9/11 commission was no surprise to him. "Here's a guy who spent his career trying to insinuate himself into power so when something like this came his way, he could grab it."

There was a little chitchat before Zelikow took a seat in Wiley's conference room and slapped his palm on the table. "If you guys had a national intelligence director, none of this would have ever happened," he declared, according to Lowenthal's account.

Wiley remembers Zelikow saying that 9/11 represented a "massive failure" of the CIA and that the attacks had happened because "you guys weren't connected to the rest of the community."

Zelikow said later that he had no memory of the meeting or of the remarks attributed to him by Lowenthal and Wiley; he insisted later that he had taken no stand in 2003 on the idea of a national intelligence director. But the two CIA veterans recalled Zelikow's comments clearly and remembered being dumbfounded by his tone. They thought this was going to be a simple courtesy call. But Zelikow was apparently at the CIA to issue a verdict about the cause of 9/11—and pronounce sentence. The blame didn't rest with the FBI. Or with the Pentagon. And certainly not with Zelikow's friend Condoleezza Rice and the NSC.

To Lowenthal's mind, Zelikow had decided to scapegoat the CIA and Tenet; they were going to be blamed for 9/11. He could see where Zelikow was going: He was going to call for the elimination of Tenet's job—director of central intelligence, which gave him direct control over the CIA and at least nominal authority over other spy agencies. Zelikow was suggesting that the fix for 9/11 was to replace Tenet with a director of national intelligence, a sort of spy czar who would be above the CIA director.

"My God, he thinks he already has the answer," Lowenthal recalled thinking at the time. "He's going to make this all about the CIA."

Lowenthal figured it was a bad idea to confront Zelikow about the remark. He could only hope that this was Zelikow's bluster. "I purposely decided not to react," he said. "I was afraid I was going to provoke him some more." Wiley thought it was so typical of Zelikow to "come in with answers rather than questions." Wiley hoped that, unlike their staff director, the ten members of the 9/11 commission would not be so quick to reach judgment about the CIA.

But if he wasn't going to confront Zelikow, Lowenthal would certainly go see Tenet and warn him about what Zelikow had said. He went to Tenet's office that afternoon.

"George, Phil Zelikow has all the answers," Lowenthal said ominously. "He's going to create a national intelligence director. You mark my words, he's going to drive the idea through the commission with a truck."

Tenet shrugged. He was exhausted, and he did not have the time or energy to worry about Zelikow. At least not now. There would be time later to sort this out, he thought. The 9/11 commission had just opened for business; its final report was at least eighteen months away, and God knew what the world would look like then or where he would be. Maybe Lowenthal had misheard Zelikow, Tenet figured.

Single out the CIA for blame? It seemed crazy to Tenet that any legitimate review of what had gone wrong on 9/11 would end up with a conclusion that the CIA bore more responsibility than any other agency for the attacks. It was even nuttier, he told colleagues, to think that the answer was the creation of a new superspy to oversee the intelligence agencies. That would just add one more layer of bureaucracy to the layer cake of spy agencies that existed before the attacks.

He knew Zelikow a little—during his years at Harvard, Zelikow had helped prepare case studies for the CIA on intelligence issues—and Tenet was willing to be more charitable than others toward him. It was really true about Tenet: He was charitable about everybody. George Tenet wanted to be thought of as a very nice man. He wanted to be liked. He considered it a strength, his refusal to engage in backstabbing. He didn't criticize Condi Rice, and certainly not George Bush, for all of the bungling in the spring and summer of 2001, when the White House had apparently done so little in response to Tenet's repeated warnings of an al-Qaeda attack. He did not criticize Clinton, either, although hindsight showed that Clinton should have taken much bigger risks in the 1990s to destroy bin Laden's network.

Tenet did not criticize the FBI, at least not by name, even though it was common wisdom at Langley that if any one agency was responsible for 9/11, it was the bureau. The incompetent, arrogant FBI. How could anyone compare the pre-9/11 record of the CIA with the FBI's and decide that it was the CIA that needed to be shaken up?

The perfect anecdote? Zacarias Moussaoui, "the twentieth hijacker." Tenet was notified about Moussaoui's arrest a few days after he was picked up in Minnesota in August 2001. But no one had bothered to report it up the line in FBI headquarters in Washington until after 9/11. The FBI arrests a suspected Muslim terrorist in the "summer of threat" and nobody bothers to tell the FBI director? "Hell, it was the FBI's case, their arrest," Tenet would say later in exasperation. "I had no idea that the bureau wasn't aware of what its own people were doing."

Forget Zelikow. There was so much else on Tenet's mind at the start of 2003. He suspected Bush was only weeks away from ordering an invasion of Iraq, justified by CIA reports that concluded Saddam Hussein had hidden stockpiles of chemical and biological weapons. Tenet was "working my ass off." Zelikow? Zelikow was a "staffer," the dismissive title that Tenet had next to his own name earlier in his career in government. There would be plenty of time later to make sure the 9/11 commission got the story straight. Tenet was friendly with several of the 9/11 commissioners; he could talk to them if Zelikow got out of hand.

For his part, Zelikow and others on the commission's staff insisted that in the early stages of the investigation, they did not see Tenet as dishonest. They did not think that he would fudge the truth or lie outright—and under oath—to protect himself and the CIA. That realization would come only later, they said.

— 14 —

U.S. NAVY COMMAND CENTER
The Pentagon

His right hand flew up to his scalp to find the source of the terrible pain. Navy lieutenant Kevin Shaeffer could not feel his hair, he could feel only the heat from the flame; it was rushing over his head and neck. He threw himself to the ground, frantically rolling back and forth to smother the fire before it engulfed his face. The pain was secondary to Shaeffer's very conscious thought that he did not want this to be the day that he died.

Shaeffer was at work on the morning of September 11 in what he considered "the safest place the world," the navy's global command center in the heart of the Pentagon. He was on the staff of the chief of naval operations. It was a prestigious assignment for a young sailor. The command center, located on the first floor of the Pentagon's "C Ring" of offices, tracked the movement of the navy's ships and their crews around the world. The entire floor was blown apart when American Airlines Flight 77 crashed into the southeastern wedge of the Pentagon in a bright orange fireball at 9:37 a.m. Shaeffer was the only one of thirty people working nearby to survive.

The twenty-nine-year-old was burned over 40 percent of his body, losing most of the skin on his arms and back, and he survived by clawing his way toward daylight through mounds of red-hot rubble and shattered glass. Rescue workers used a pen knife to pry a metal ceiling beam from his back. His lungs were seared from inhaling the smoke from burning jet fuel.

Shaeffer arrived early for his job interview with the 9/11 commission, which had no permanent offices in the first weeks of 2003 and used a lounge in Philip Zelikow's downtown Washington apartment building to interview applicants. Shaeffer wanted desperately for the interview to go well. He had been seeking a job on the commission since mid-December, when he sent e-mails to Tom Kean and Lee Hamilton, recounting the story of his survival at the Pentagon and attaching copies of news articles about his recovery. He closed all of his e-mails with the words *Never Forget*. Hamilton met with Shaeffer, was impressed, and forwarded his name to Zelikow.

As Shaeffer took a seat for the interview, Zelikow and others in the room could not help but notice Shaeffer's injuries. He was missing part of his right ear. His hands and arms were covered in red, mottled skin from more than a dozen skin grafts. He sucked in air through a hole in his neck from a tracheotomy.

But Zelikow told himself he was damned if he was going to make a "pity choice" and hire a "token victim" for the commission.

"Why should I hire you?" he asked coldly, as if it were the most obvious, appropriate question in the world to ask of Shaeffer. "The commission does not really have a role for you."

Zelikow's dismissiveness shocked the others in the room.

Shaeffer seemed startled, too, by the callousness of the question. But he tried to keep himself calm. He explained to Zelikow that he thought his military background would be valuable to the investigation; he had glowing references from his former navy commanders and from his alma mater, the U.S. Naval Academy in Annapolis.

He did not want pity, he said. But he believed it would also be useful for the commission to have a staff member with the perspective of a victim of the 9/11 attacks. The commission offered him a way to understand—and in his own small way, even help bring to justice—the people who had done this to him. "No one has suffered the way I've suffered at the hands of terrorists," he said later.

Zelikow eventually offered Shaeffer a job on the commission—appropriately enough, on the team of staff members who investigated the emergency response at the Pentagon and the World Trade Center.

Zelikow later said that he had not intended to be rude to Shaeffer at the interview, but he'd wanted to make a point. He'd wanted Shaeffer to understand that "he needed to pass muster for his ability, not just his 9/11 experience. He had to be a real hire, able to do real work as a full colleague of his fellow investigators." He later praised Shaeffer's performance on the commission as "outstanding by any standard."

The story about Shaeffer's brutal job interview spread quickly among the commission's earlier hires. It was one more bit of lore about the personality of their new boss. Zelikow wanted to make it clear to everyone that he was in charge; the people being hired for the commission worked for him. Even a job applicant who had the support of Kean and Hamilton, even one with circumstances as extraordinary as Shaeffer's, had to have Zelikow's approval, too.

Before taking the job, Zelikow had insisted to Kean and Hamilton that he have responsibility for recruiting the staff, and they had readily agreed. Kean and Hamilton could veto Zelikow's staff selections, of course; they could insist that certain candidates be hired. But in the end, it was left mostly to Zelikow to choose who would conduct the investigation and how their responsibilities would be divided.

Zelikow had insisted that there be a single, nonpartisan staff because it would create a "collective identity" for the commission. Just as important, it would prevent any of the commissioners from striking out on their own in the investigation.

"If commissioners have their own personal staff, this empowers commissioners to pursue their own agenda," Zelikow said later to a Harvard researcher. "It doesn't mean that the commissioners are powerless. It means that they are powerless individually and powerful together."

It also meant that, ultimately, the staff answered to Zelikow. Every one of them. If information gathered by the staff was to be passed to the commissioners, it would have to go through Zelikow.

He put that in writing. As the first members of the staff began to arrive at the commission's newly opened offices on K Street in March, they were handed a five-page memo from Zelikow entitled "What Do I Do Now?" Much of the memo had a collegial, uncharacteristically friendly tone.

"Welcome," Zelikow wrote. "Thank you, once again, for joining up for an intense, challenging and rewarding period of public service. You are now part of a history-writing and history-making enterprise."

Some of the guidance in the memo was commonsensical, including Zelikow's request that—unless absolutely necessary—the staff not reveal the commission's exact address on K Street, a large thoroughfare that cut through the heart of Washington and was lined with the offices of lobbying firms.

The FBI and local police had warned that because of the commission's presence in the building, it could be a terrorist target, so Zelikow's warning was appropriate. He said in the memo that "our location is secure, but its security rests partly on its anonymity."

The offices were in a seemingly undistinguished nine-floor federal building between the White House and Georgetown. The building was secretly owned and operated by the CIA, used as downtown office space by the agency. It was ideal for the commission because it qualified as a so-called SCIF, the acronym for secure compartmentalized information facility, which meant that it had security measures that allowed for the storage of highly classified documents. Apart from witnesses called to private interviews with the commission, only people with security clearances would be allowed to enter the commission's offices; all cell phones and other electronic devices had to be left at the door. Each of the staff members at K Street was provided with two computer hard drives—one for classified information, one for unclassified information.

By page four of Zelikow's memo to his new staff, the tone was formal—and threatening. Here, he outlined the rules that, if broken, would get an investigator fired:

"You should not discuss the commission or its work with the press. Period. This is a bright line rule. Do not talk to the press at all. If you are contacted by a reporter, do not return the call." To Zelikow's mind, "there are no innocent conversations with reporters."

All reporters' calls had to be forwarded to Zelikow or Chris Kojm, a longtime congressional aide to Lee Hamilton who had been named the commission's deputy executive director. The mild-mannered, professorial Kojm was never seen by the staff as any sort of Democratic counterbalance to Zelikow. He often seemed cowed by Zelikow, in fact.

A ban on talking to reporters was not a surprise; most federal agencies bar workers from talking directly to reporters about government business.

But another rule on Zelikow's list was unusual—and worrying to the staff. It was one thing to tell the commission's investigators not to return a reporter's call. But Zelikow's memo also instructed them not to return calls from the ten commissioners, at least not without his permission. "If you are contacted by a commissioner, please contact Chris or me," Zelikow wrote. "We will be sure that the appropriate members of the commission's staff are responsive."

It occurred to several of the staff members, especially those with experience on other federal commissions, that Zelikow was trying to cut off their contact with the people they really worked for—the commissioners.

Democratic commissioner Jamie Gorelick saw a copy of Zelikow's memo and was furious. Through an arrangement with her law firm, she intended to spend nearly half of her work week on commission business, and she was not going to have Zelikow telling the staff that they could not speak freely with her—that they had to wait to get his permission to return her phone calls. She called Kean and Hamilton.

"This is totally unacceptable," she told them. "I'm going to have free access to the staff."

Max Cleland said he worried from the start that Zelikow was trying to "stovepipe" the investigation. It was ironic, said Cleland; it seemed Zelikow was going to duplicate just the sort of information bottlenecks that had plagued the FBI and the CIA and made them unable to "connect the dots" before September 11.

"It violates the whole spirit of an open look at what the hell happened on 9/11," he said.

Zelikow was forced to rescind that portion of the memo; the commission's staff would be permitted to talk to the commissioners.

But another Zelikow rule stayed in place. Some staff members did not have salaries large enough to require them to file government financial disclosure forms. But Zelikow still instructed them to "prepare a confidential memo to me that describes any potential conflicts of interest that may arise with your work on the commission." He added, "In making these judgments, consider outside perception—ask yourself how it would look if this information was made public and you had not disclosed it." Staff members who knew some of Zelikow's own conflicts of interest found it amusing that he was so worried about theirs.

Kean and Hamilton were the public face of the commission. But the staff could see that with every passing day, Zelikow was centralizing control of the day-to-day investigation in his own hands. He was becoming the eleventh commissioner and, in many ways, more powerful than the others. Kean and Hamilton stayed in close touch by telephone with the commission, and Hamilton could depend on Kojm to keep him informed about problems as they arose on the staff. But in the early months of the investigation, most of the commissioners rarely visited K Street. Zelikow was in charge.

THE COMMISSION's early hires for the staff were impressive. Even the Democratic commissioners who were most suspicious of Zelikow conceded that he had hired smart, experienced investigators. Few had any sort of political agenda that was detectable; Kean and Hamilton had not wanted staff members with close ties to the Republican or Democratic party organizations.

Zelikow had divided the investigation into nine teams:

- al-Qaeda and its history
- intelligence collection
- counterterrorism policy
- terrorist financing
- border security and immigration
- the FBI and other domestic law enforcement agencies
- aviation and transportation security
- emergency response in New York and around the Pentagon on 9/11
- the federal government's emergency response

Over time, "Team 1," the al-Qaeda team, would be divided into two—one focused on the terrorist network and its history, another on the 9/11 plot. The plot team was known as "Team 1A."

The counterterrorism team, "Team 3," would have responsibility for the most politically sensitive part of the investigation. It would review the performance of the Bush and Clinton administrations in dealing with al-Qaeda threats before 9/11.

Its investigators would be permitted into the files of the NSC and CIA to determine what happened in the spring and summer of 2001 and why the government had been unable to stop the attacks. It was the team that would draw judgments about whether Clinton had done enough to destroy al-Qaeda in eight years in office and why the Bush administration had seemed to do so little in response to the flood of terrorism warnings in the months before 9/11.

Zelikow chose the members of the team with special care. He knew it was a dream assignment for a historian or political scientist with a bent for national security issues, and he had reason to think that the team's members would be grateful to him for the assignment. Among the hires for the team were Warren Bass, a young Columbia PhD who was a terrorism researcher at the Council on Foreign Relations in New York, and Alexis Albion, a doctoral candidate in intelligence studies at Harvard. Bass would focus on the NSC. Albion would be the central researcher on the CIA.

Zelikow found someone with hands-on intelligence experience to lead the team: Michael Hurley, a taciturn Minnesotan who was the real thing—a battle-hardened spy on loan to the commission from the CIA. He had given up his "cover" at the agency a few years earlier, so he could tell people that he worked for the CIA. Still, what he had done immediately after 9/11, including his work on the ground in ousting the Taliban from Afghanistan, remained highly classified.

Zelikow made it clear from his earliest days on the commission that Team 3 was his priority. He gave special care to reviewing the lists of documents and interviews that were being requested from the Bush administration. He announced that he wanted to be present for all of its major interviews. At first, members of the team found it flattering that Zelikow wanted to spend so much of his own time and energy on the work of Team 3. Their suspicion of his motives grew later.

The commissioners presented Zelikow with strong candidates for other jobs. At the urging of Gorelick, Zelikow reviewed the résumé of Colonel Lorry Fenner, an air force intelligence officer who had worked closely with the National Security Agency, the government's eavesdropping agency, during portions of her career.

Fenner was hired and assigned to Team 2, which was reviewing the overall structure of the intelligence community. But she believed her knowledge of the workings of the NSA might be helpful to the teams that would be investigating the September 11 plot, especially when it came time for the commission to begin reviewing the NSA's vast archives of raw intelligence on al-Qaeda.

The CIA might be the agency that had the most direct contact with the White House in warning of al-Qaeda threats before 9/11. But much of the CIA's analysis of Osama bin Laden and the intentions of his terrorist network over the years had been built on the intelligence gathered by the NSA and its spy satellites circling the globe. Fenner knew the NSA archives would be a treasure trove—assuming somebody went to the NSA's headquarters in suburban Maryland to review them. Surely, she thought, somebody would.

DEALING WITH the 9/11 families was left mostly to two members of the commission's staff, Ellie Hartz and Emily Walker, who found the duty wrenching. They were the commission's "family liaison" team. For Hartz, the torment of the families was familiar. Her husband, John, had died in the South Tower of the World Trade Center; he had been a senior vice president of Fiduciary Trust. "John was just a pure and utter gentleman," she later told an interviewer. "I think that would be the word that most people would use to describe him. He was a very kind gentleman."

But Walker, who joined the commission from the executive ranks of Citibank, had known nothing like this. She had been at work in lower Manhattan on September 11, but she lost no close friends or relatives in the attacks. Now she found herself dealing with the concerns of men and women and children who felt they had lost everything that day—and wanted to know why. She got the job after innocently asking Zelikow, "Who is going to work with the families?" He had an answer a few weeks later: She would. "I was a banker," she said. "Emotionally, I worried I couldn't do it." She had no training at all as a grief counselor. She sought advice at the Justice Department from a woman who had worked as the department's go-between for families of the victims of the bombing of Pan Am 103 over Scotland in 1988. She told Walker that the 9/11 families would be traumatized—and angry—and that she would sometimes be the target of their fury. "Don't take it personally," Walker said she was told. "The process they are going through is normal."

Walker said her worst day on the investigation—and also maybe her best, in an odd way—was January 27, 2004. It was the day of a public hearing in Washington at which the commission heard a tape recording of the last known words of Betty Ong, a flight attendant for American Airlines Flight 11, the plane that crashed into the North Tower of the World Trade Center. Ong had used an on-board phone to call airline supervisors to alert them to the hijacking. In a remarkably calm, steady voice, she described the terror aboard the plane. "The cockpit's not answering, and somebody's stabbed in business class," she explained. "I think there's mace, that we can't breathe. I don't know. I think we're getting hijacked."

Shortly before the hearing, Walker and Hartz were given the job of escorting Ong's family to a special soundproof booth in the Senate hearing room so they could hear the tapes before they were played for the world. As they all listened together, Walker was struck by the family's composure. "Ellie and I were a wreck," said Walker, who remembered asking someone outside the booth to find paper towels for the two women to weep into. "But the family was so calm. Stoic. No tears. They had obviously prepared for this day."

— 15 —

K STREET OFFICES OF THE
9/11 COMMISSION
Washington, D.C.

P hilip Zelikow could not have been more deferential to Tom Kean and Lee Hamilton, returning their telephone calls instantly and praising them to the commission's staff at every opportunity. He was not about to offend them. But Kean could tell that Zelikow was not going to be so diplomatic with the staff; he heard early reports about Zelikow's harsh treatment of some of the commission's newly hired investigators. Zelikow was clearly off to a terrible start with two of the Democratic commissioners, Richard Ben-Veniste and Tim Roemer, who were most openly suspicious of his ties to the Bush White House.

Roemer was furious with Zelikow when he went to Capitol Hill in April to read classified interview transcripts and other documents from the joint congressional committee on 9/11—and was turned away. Zelikow had neglected to tell Roemer, who was a member of the joint committee in his final year in Congress, that he had reached a private agreement with the Justice Department to block access to the files of the congressional inquiry until the White House had a chance to review them first.

"Why is our executive director making secret deals with the Justice Department and the White House?" Roemer asked. "He is supposed to be working for us." Roemer believed, correctly, that it was a sign of much larger struggles to come with Zelikow.

Still, Kean and Hamilton were grateful for Zelikow's energy and obvious enthusiasm for the investigation. The commission had otherwise gotten off to a disastrously slow start. The withdrawal of Henry Kissinger and George Mitchell had eaten up almost a month of the commission's time, and the investigation's early logistical problems seemed endless.

Kean and most of the other commissioners did not have security clearances, nor did most of the new staff. That meant that even if the White House cooperated and began turning over classified files to the commission, there would be almost nobody to read them until the FBI completed the background checks needed for security clearances. That process could take several months, even if the FBI hurried.

The law creating the commission called for its work to be finished by May 2004, only sixteen months after the commissioners had met one another for the first time. The White House and the Republicans who controlled both the House and Senate made it clear from the start that they were opposed to any extension of the deadline; Bush and much of Congress would be up for reelection in November 2004, and GOP campaign strategists were worried enough about the impact of the commission's final report on a campaign that would be centered almost entirely on terrorism. The idea of a report issued on the eve of the November election was unimaginable.

The 9/11 commission faced overt hostility from House Republican leaders, who had been far more aggressive than their Senate counterparts in trying to block the panel's creation in the first place.

House Speaker Dennis Hastert of Illinois seemed almost irrationally antagonistic toward the investigation. It was a sign, in part, of just how much more poisonous the partisan divide had always been in the House. But with Hastert, it seemed to be more than that. Aides said Hastert saw the commission as a tool of congressional Democrats acting through— and manipulating—the families of the 9/11 dead. Kean would later describe his failure to open an early line of communication to Hastert and his formidable deputy in the Republican hierarchy, Majority Leader Tom DeLay of Texas, as his most serious mistake on the commission. It had long been assumed by Democrats on Capitol Hill that Hastert functioned as DeLay's puppet in the House; Hastert had gotten the Speaker's job in 1999 only when it became clear to DeLay, then in line for the job, that he would be too polarizing a figure as Speaker.

But when it came to his hostility to the 9/11 commission, Hastert seemed to be taking direction from no one.

Relations with Senate Republicans were easier since one of their own, former senator Slade Gorton, was on the panel. During the life of the commission, Gorton made a point of visiting Capitol Hill whenever he was in town from Seattle; he was a regular at the Senate Republicans' weekly strategy lunch.

The job of soothing Hastert was supposed to have been left to another of the Republican commissioners, former Illinois governor Jim Thompson. Hastert had personally selected Thompson for the commission; they were close friends. But to Kean's dismay, Thompson all but disappeared from the commission during the first year of the investigation.

Thompson was too busy trying to dig himself out of involvement in the scandals centered on media baron Conrad Black, former owner of the *Chicago Sun-Times* and the *Daily Telegraph* in London. Black had been accused by shareholders—and later by the Justice Department—of bilking his publishing company of tens of millions of dollars, some of it diverted to lavish parties, private jets, and upkeep of his palatial homes around the world. Thompson, a member of the board of directors of the company, Hollinger International, had been chairman of Black's auditing committee. That put Thompson at the center of many of the transactions that were the focus of the criminal prosecutors.

The commission's early logistical problems were more than a little humiliating to men like Kean and Hamilton, who had commanded vast staffs and virtually unlimited office space during their years in power in government. Now they were at the mercy of others if they wanted secondhand office furniture for the commission's cramped offices in Washington. It had taken several weeks to find the office space on K Street. Before that, the commission and the staff had no phones. No fax machine. No stationery. One of Zelikow's earliest hires was Stephanie Kaplan, a twenty-four-year-old political scientist who, Zelikow knew, was tough and seasoned beyond her years. Her cell phone functioned as the commission's initial operations center.

Kean's early worries went beyond office space. He was alarmed, too, to see signs of the partisanship that he had tried so hard to avoid on the commission in the first weeks of the investigation.

The Democrats were insistent that if Zelikow was going to remain as staff director, his Republican ties had to be balanced out by a Democratic general counsel, the title that would be given to the commission's chief lawyer. The Democrats wanted a counsel who had a prosecutorial bent and had overseen large, complicated investigations. Some of the

Republican commissioners bristled at the Democratic demands and quietly warned the White House what the Democrats were up to.

Kean heard within days from Andy Card and others at the White House. They were worried that the commission was going out of its way to find a partisan Democrat as counsel, someone who would be itching for a legal fight with the White House. "They were very, very alarmed when they heard some of the names being considered" for the counsel, Kean said.

Kean agreed in principle with the Democrats that the general counsel would be a Democrat. But he and Hamilton were determined not to choose someone with a clearly partisan background; they also did not want a candidate who seemed eager to confront the Bush administration. The Democrats offered up several candidates, including James Hamilton, who had been a lawyer on the Senate Watergate committee (he was no relation to Lee Hamilton).

Kean went to a computer to do his own Google search and discovered that Hamilton had participated in the Al Gore campaign's legal team in the 2000 Florida recount; to Kean, that made Hamilton too partisan to be considered for such an important job on the commission.

Weeks later, Jamie Gorelick thought she had the perfect candidate for the job: Carol Elder Bruce, a respected Washington lawyer who had worked for years in the Justice Department as a career prosecutor. Bruce was a veteran investigator. She was familiar with national security and intelligence issues; in the 1980s she led the high-profile prosecution of Edwin Wilson, a former CIA officer convicted of selling weapons to Libya; Wilson was later taped in prison trying to arrange Bruce's murder. She had been a special federal prosecutor in both the Reagan and Clinton administrations. She was a registered Democrat but was not active in party politics.

She was invited in for an interview with Kean and Hamilton in Hamilton's offices at the Wilson Center. She was surprised to see Zelikow in the room, if only because she knew that the commission was looking for a tough-minded general counsel to "balance out" Zelikow.

Kean asked what her priorities would be if she was chosen as general counsel. She was direct: She said that the commission would be making a terrible mistake if it did not quickly issue subpoenas to the Bush administration, including to the White House, for documents and interviews.

"I've been in this town for a long time, and there is nothing extraordinary about issuing subpoenas," she explained. "That's the way it's done in Washington. There would be no offense taken. It would not be considered too aggressive. It would be expected."

Bruce explained that for a veteran criminal investigator, this was a "no-brainer." In an investigation of this significance, she said, the subpoena would establish the commission's seriousness about its mission—and avoid court delays later on if the White House or federal agencies refused to cooperate.

Bruce could sense that she was going over with Kean, Hamilton, and Zelikow—especially Zelikow—like a particularly odiferous skunk at their garden party. Her instincts were right.

As far as Kean as concerned, the interview was over at her first mention of subpoenas. "She was a very able woman, but it was the dead opposite of what Lee and I wanted to do," he said. Bruce was just repeating what Gorelick and the other Democrats had suggested—and Kean and Hamilton had rejected—at the commission's first meetings. Kean and Hamilton were sticking by their decision to use subpoenas only when all other options had failed. They did not want unnecessary battles with the White House.

The search for a general counsel went on for weeks, and Kean found himself dispirited that it had become a subject of such partisan rancor.

Gorelick found another candidate: Daniel Marcus, a partner in her law firm and a Democrat. He had worked in the White House Counsel's Office and at the Justice Department during the Clinton administration, but he had no ties to Democratic political operations. He had not worked as a criminal prosecutor; his specialties were constitutional and regulatory law. He was known by colleagues in the Clinton administration for his intelligence, level head, and good humor. Kean called around to Republican friends in Washington legal circles.

"He's obviously a Democrat, served in the Clinton administration, but everyone said this is a very fine lawyer," Kean said. "This is a very fine man."

The Democrats would still have preferred a prosecutor, certainly someone with more experience in the corridors and back rooms of the CIA and the Pentagon. But after weeks of battling it out with the Republicans, they agreed on Marcus. It was time to move on.

"Dan was just the sort of general counsel they wanted," Gorelick said of Kean and Hamilton. "They wanted to assure themselves they got all the information, but they did not want to engage in fisticuffs." Marcus, she said, "was a general counsel in the Kean-Hamilton mold"—willing to fight for information if that was what it came to, but willing to wait to strike the first punch.

— 16 —

CITY HALL
New York, N.Y.
MARCH 2003

I t was never clear if Michael Bloomberg was genuinely furious or if his anger was a well-choreographed show by the billionaire mayor to intimidate the 9/11 commission. But Bloomberg's staff made it instantly clear that the commission was not welcome in the city.

"What the *fuck* are you doing here?" one of Bloomberg's senior aides barked to Philip Zelikow in City Hall.

Zelikow was startled. He and a group of the commission's staff had traveled to New York in preparation for the commission's first public hearing; it was scheduled for late March at the Customs House in lower Manhattan, only a few blocks from ground zero. The rest of Bloomberg's staff was just as rude to Zelikow's delegation on that first day of meetings in City Hall, just without the profanity. They wanted Zelikow and these other out-of-towners to turn around and go back to Washington or wherever else they had come from; the commission had no business in New York.

"Their position was this: New York City didn't cause the 9/11 attack," Zelikow said of Bloomberg's aides. They believed "the 9/11 commission had nothing to do with them and we should leave them alone."

That was not going to happen. The mayor's staff did not understand what they were up against in Zelikow. He coolly explained to Bloomberg's aides that they were wrong about the commission's mandate and that the mayor had better get used to the scrutiny. The commission was not going away. The law establishing the panel gave it the authority to investigate what had happened in New York on September 11, especially the city's emergency response at the World Trade Center. The commission expected the city's cooperation in the investigation. If Bloomberg did not cooperate, the commission always had the option of a politically damaging subpoena.

Tom Kean, in particular, had felt strongly that the commission needed an early public hearing, if only to prove to the increasingly anxious 9/11 families that the investigation really was up and running. And he felt that the first hearing should be in New York City, where most of the lives had been lost.

Kean probably should have known better. He had lived much of his life less than an hour's drive from Manhattan and the theaters of Broadway. As much as anyone on the commission, he should have understood that it was better to open a production out of town than to debut in New York. The logistics are difficult. New York audiences are as tough as they come when the curtain goes up. The commission's first public hearing came close to being a disaster.

UNTIL HE arrived in New York for the hearing, Lee Hamilton had not seen ground zero for himself. The commissioners were staying at the Millenium Hilton Hotel in lower Manhattan, directly across Church Street from where the Twin Towers had stood. The fifty-five-story hotel had been badly damaged during the 9/11 attacks and had undergone a complete structural renovation, essentially stripped to its Sheetrock frame, before reopening a year later. Hamilton arrived in his hotel room, pulled back the curtains, and looked out the window to see the vast gray emptiness—sixteen acres—that was now called ground zero. He wrote later that he had to sit down to collect himself.

The commissioners had decided to hold off on testimony from former mayor Rudolph Giuliani until later in the investigation, when they would have a better sense if Giuliani's hero status from his performance as mayor on 9/11 was as well deserved as his growing army of political consultants wanted the public to believe. By early 2003, Giuliani was already laying the groundwork to succeed George Bush in the White House.

The commission did schedule testimony at the first hearing from other New York politicians: Bloomberg, Governor George Pataki, and the state's two senators, Hillary Clinton and Charles Schumer. But the witness list was thrown into chaos four days before the hearing, when former senator Patrick Moynihan of New York, arguably the state's most beloved politician, died suddenly. His burial service at Arlington

National Cemetery, across the Potomac from Washington, was scheduled for the same day as the hearing. So Clinton and Schumer canceled. It was not immediately clear that Pataki or Bloomberg would show up for the hearing, either.

Kean had hoped the hearing would offer the commission the chance to show the public and the families that the investigation was making progress, that the commission was really moving forward. But the truth was that the investigation was barely under way; the commission was only just settling into its offices in Washington; it was still searching for space for a satellite office in New York. Almost four months after the commission's creation, many staff members did not have security clearances to begin the hard work of digging in classified government files. Negotiations with the White House over access to the most important and most secret intelligence documents were still weeks, if not months, away.

For many of the younger staffers who traveled up to Manhattan to prepare for the hearings, New York was unknown, unfriendly territory, and it showed in the amateurish preparations for the hearing.

Kean arrived at the Customs House to discover that no one had thought to bring a gavel for him to use to open the hearing. One of the staffers ran to a nearby courthouse and asked to borrow a gavel for the day. The Customs House, the stately Beaux Arts federal building that had once served as the New York offices of the U.S. Customs Service, had no spare water pitchers to share with the commission, so they had to be hurriedly rented.

The commission had expected a huge turnout for the hearing on March 31 and warned the 9/11 victims' families to show up early or they might not find a seat. But as Kean arrived in the Customs House auditorium that morning, almost two-thirds of the 350 seats in the auditorium were empty. The audience was made up mostly of the 9/11 family members, many clutching poster-size photographs of their dead loved ones, and they were furious. They could see that the commission had so botched publicity for the hearing that few people—other than a group of reporters and cameramen and them—had shown up.

Kean was about to make many of the families even angrier with his opening statement. He was going to tell them exactly what they did not want to hear.

"I am honored and humbled to convene this first public hearing," he began. "The American people want the answers to so many questions around 9/11. They want to know who were these people and how could they have done this terrible thing to so many innocent people. What kind of fanaticism drove them to do this? They also want to know how such a dastardly attack could occur and succeed in a nation as strong as ours." He vowed to get the answers to those questions.

But there was a rumble in the audience, even a few groans, as Kean revealed what the commission would not do: It did not intend to make a priority of blaming individual government officials for 9/11.

"We will be following paths, and we will follow those individual paths wherever they lead," he said. "We may end up holding individual agencies, people, and procedures to account. But our fundamental purpose will not be to point fingers."

A few of the family advocates cocked their ears, wondering if they had heard Kean properly. They had pushed so hard to create the commission because they *wanted* fingers pointed at the government. And Kean knew it; the families had told him that over and over again in their early meetings. For many families, this investigation was supposed to be all about finger-pointing. They wanted strict accountability, especially at the White House, the CIA, the FBI, the Pentagon, and other agencies that had missed the clues that might have prevented 9/11. The families wanted subpoenas—and indictments and jail sentences, if that was where the facts led.

As Kean finished his statement, many of the family advocates were all but sneering at him. George Bush? Bill Clinton? Condoleezza Rice? Sandy Berger? George Tenet? Louis Freeh? Were they all suddenly in the clear?

"Kean is following orders," Lorie Van Auken, one of the widows known as the Jersey Girls, mumbled to herself. "He's taking orders from the White House." Kean certainly did not think he was taking orders from anyone. But he could sense the families' anger.

With Kean running the hearing, Hamilton was left to rush back and forth to the room where witnesses waited to testify. Hamilton was getting a quick education in how different things were in New York. He was a creature of Washington and of Capitol Hill, where a veteran congressional committee chairman had near dictatorial power at a public hearing; congressional witnesses sat and waited patiently until they were called. They did not dictate the schedule of their testimony.

But this was New York, and Hamilton could see that it was the witnesses who were trying to call the shots.

Pataki had arrived early for the hearing, and his staff warned Hamilton that the governor could not wait around to testify. If the commission wanted to hear from the governor, it would have to be now, this minute. That was awkward; Kean had turned over the hearing to the other commissioners to give opening statements. It was an important moment for them. Several had been at work for weeks to craft a statement that conveyed the importance of the commission's work and their pride in serving on the investigation; this was their first moment in the spotlight, in front of the television cameras. Now, it seemed, Pataki's hotheaded staff was about to push them aside.

Kean and Hamilton agreed that they could not offend Pataki; he would have to be accommodated. Tim Roemer was about to make his opening statement when Kean went to the microphone: "We are going to interrupt the statements from the commissioners because Governor Pataki has arrived."

Pataki took his seat at the witness table and read out a brief, unmemorable statement in which he pledged the state's cooperation with the investigation. He left without taking questions.

Things were even trickier with Mayor Bloomberg. When he was initially offered an invitation to appear at the hearing, he declined, saying he would instead issue a written statement to the commission and would not be present to read it. Then he informed Kean and Hamilton that he would testify but not answer questions. Then he agreed to answer questions but insisted that his police and fire commissioners would not appear for the hearing.

When Bloomberg finally arrived at the Customs House the morning of the hearing, he was in the company of Police Commissioner Ray Kelly and Fire Commissioner Nicholas Scoppetta; and he announced that they were all ready to testify.

It was clear to the commissioners and the staff that the mayor was trying to blindside them; the commission had not prepared itself to question the police and fire commissioners, who would be vital witnesses in discussing the emergency response on 9/11.

Bloomberg also made it clear that he, like Pataki, did not want to wait to testify. The commission's staff pleaded for a little patience.

When Bloomberg was invited into the auditorium several minutes later, he appeared to be seething. In a gesture that seemed designed to make his disdain even clearer, he casually tossed his prepared testimony onto the witness table before taking his seat, as if this were a routine meeting of the zoning board.

Bloomberg's testimony offered an unapologetic defense of the city government's performance on September 11: "We have examined the city's response to 9/11 thoroughly, and I can tell you that it was swift, massive, heroic, and extraordinarily effective."

His testimony included an angry—and, the commissioners agreed, justified—attack on the way Washington had divided up the federal antiterrorism budget after 9/11. Bloomberg noted that even though New York City had been targeted repeatedly by terrorists over the years, including on September 11, it received only a small percentage of the billions of dollars that the government had allocated for counterterrorism preparations in 2002 and 2003. Per capita antiterrorism spending was far higher in Casper, Wyoming, and Biloxi, Mississippi, than in the city that almost certainly remained the world's number one terrorist target.

"To argue that most other cities have comparable threats is just ridiculous," Bloomberg said. "If we distributed moneys for the military this way, our troops in Iraq would have bows and arrows to fight with."

A few minutes into his testimony, Bloomberg looked up toward the dais and scowled. He could see that Kean and Zelikow were deep in conversation about something, whispering to each other and apparently ignoring what he had to say. (Bloomberg had no way of knowing it, but Kean and Zelikow were discussing how the commission should deal with the unexpected arrival of the police and fire commissioners.)

"Would you like me to wait while you finish?" Bloomberg asked Kean, the mayor's face a mix of annoyance and contempt. "I'd be happy to wait while you finish up. It's quite all right. I have plenty of time." Bloomberg rested his chin on his hand.

Kean tried his best to smile apologetically, but it was a strain. After all those years as governor in neighboring New Jersey, he had dealt with more than his share of difficult New Yorkers, including more than a few nastily combative New York City mayors. It was one more reason he would be happy to head back across the Hudson River to New Jersey when the hearing was over.

A PANEL of 9/11 survivors was scheduled to testify next, and they were a reminder to the commissioners that, whatever the political theatrics of the morning, this investigation would likely be the most important public service of their lives.

Harry Waizer, a bond trader who had worked in the North Tower of the World Trade Center, told of being in an elevator on its way to his offices on the 104th floor when it suddenly began to rumble; fire shot into the elevator from the seams in the door. The elevator stopped on the 78th floor, where Waizer jumped out and tried to join the exodus down the stairwell to the lobby. Others in the stairway looked in horror at the terrible burns across his face and his body; it was as if his flesh were melting off.

"I noticed a large flap of skin hanging on my arm," said Waizer, whose face still bore large, purplish scars. As he continued down the stairwell, he remembered, he forced himself not to look at what remained of the skin on his other arm and the rest of his body. "I did not look any further."

Another of the survivors, New York City fireman Lee Ielpi, told of being dispatched to the World Trade Center on September 11 and discovering that his twenty-nine-year-old firefighter son, Jonathan, was missing in the South Tower. Ielpi said he considered himself lucky because when he finally recovered his son's body, it was intact—two arms, two legs. Of the 2,750 people who died at the World Trade Center, only 292 whole bodies were ever found. Ielpi said that before he buried his son, he took the corpse back home to Great Neck, Long Island, and "put him to bed at home, where he belonged."

It had been difficult for the commission's staff to organize the day's next panel of witnesses—the families of the victims—because so many of the family advocates wanted to testify. The commission compromised by allowing one witness to testify from each of four of the major family groups.

Many of them wanted to voice their anger with the commission—the slowness of its investigation, the lack of subpoenas, the fact that Kean and others were now publicly dismissing the idea that individuals should be held accountable for their actions on September 11.

"I think the commission *should* point fingers," testified Stephen Push of Arlington, Virginia, whose lobbyist wife died aboard American Airlines Flight 77, the plane that struck the Pentagon.

"I'm not suggesting you find scapegoats—someone to hang out to dry. But there are people, people in responsible positions, who failed us on 9/11. They didn't just fail us once; 9/11 occurred because they were failing us over a long period of time. Some of these people are still in responsible positions in government. Perhaps they shouldn't be."

One of the Jersey Girls, Mindy Kleinberg of East Brunswick, New Jersey, was next to testify. She, too, wanted the commission to hold someone accountable for September 11—for the death of her husband, Alan, who was trapped on the 104th floor of the North Tower.

She was tired of hearing the constant refrain—the constant excuse, really—from the Bush administration about how difficult it was to stop terrorist attacks. How often had she heard Condoleezza Rice and others at the White House say it? "The terrorists only have to be lucky once, while the government needs to be right 100 percent of the time." It seemed to Mindy that there was plenty of evidence that the 9/11 terrorists were lucky only because bungling at the White House, the FBI, the CIA, the FAA, and the Pentagon had made their luck possible. She asked: "If at some point we don't look to hold the individuals accountable for not doing their jobs properly, then how can we ever expect for terrorists to not get lucky again?"

THERE WAS one more panel of witnesses that day—a group of foreign policy and terrorism specialists from around the country. Zelikow had drawn up the witness list, and the lead-off witness—the first outside expert of any sort to testify before the 9/11 commission—was Abraham Sofaer, a fellow at the Hoover Institution, the conservative think tank at Stanford. Sofaer was the State Department's legal adviser in the Reagan administration and a widely admired federal judge before that. It was certainly worth the commission's time to hear from Sofaer, whose expertise in the intersection of foreign policy and the law was of obvious value.

But it seemed odd that he was the commission's very first expert witness. Sofaer had no special expertise on the events of September 11. He appeared there, mostly, as an advocate for the American invasion of Iraq—the invasion had been launched a week earlier—and a champion of the concept of "preemptive defense" or "preemptive war."

The doctrine of preemptive defense, which held that an adversary like Iraq that posed no imminent military threat could still be attacked, had been formally adopted a year earlier by the Bush administration. The decision was hailed by Sofaer. The administration argued that Iraq had worked closely for years with al-Qaeda.

"The president's principles are strategically necessary, morally sound, and legally defensible," Sofaer said in praising Bush. He criticized the Clinton administration for relying on law enforcement instead of military force in dealing with terrorist threats. "The notion that criminal prosecution could bring a terrorist group like al-Qaeda to justice is absurd," he said. Under Clinton and his predecessors, counterterrorism was treated as "a game" in which "the FBI, prosecutors, and intelligence personnel attempted to learn where and when attacks were to occur before they actually happened so they could do their best to prevent it," he continued. "This commission should, I think, make it clear that presidents don't have the option of sitting back and playing that game." In the future, he said, when an enemy "rises up to kill you," the United States should "rise up and kill him first." He called on the commission to endorse Bush's new policy—in effect, to endorse the president's decision to invade Iraq and overthrow Saddam Hussein.

Members of the commission's staff would look back on Sofaer's testimony as the first evidence that Zelikow might try to use the commission to promote the war with Iraq. Few people outside the Bush administration knew at the time that Zelikow was the author of the White House's "preemptive defense" doctrine—that it was his scholarly document that had been used to justify the invasion. Sofaer later recalled how pleased he had been to receive the invitation from Zelikow for the hearing. He knew what an honor it was to be the first expert called to testify before the 9/11 commission.

K STREET OFFICES OF THE
9/11 COMMISSION
Washington, D.C.
APRIL 2003

Karen Heitkotter was one of those dedicated women who, for generations, had made the State Department work. Her job title used to be "secretary." Then in the 1980s and 1990s the single-word title mostly disappeared, seen as sexist, and Heitkotter became an "executive secretary" or "executive assistant" to several ambitious American diplomats. She lived—and thrived—in American embassies in Europe, where she worked for the ambassadors to Italy and Norway. It was impossible to guess her age. She was timelessly pretty, poised, cheerful, full of the common sense that came from her family's roots in Nebraska; she was just as smart as many of the diplomats she worked for, although she never felt the need to make that obvious.

Friends passed her name to Philip Zelikow and the 9/11 commission; Zelikow and the "front office" needed someone in a hurry to deal with secretarial duties—answering the phone, arranging travel, filling out paperwork. Heitkotter was a natural candidate for the job. Her résumé was especially appealing to the commission because she had been given every sort of security clearance in her years in government. She had worked with top-secret documents for most of her career. Unlike so many other new staff members on the commission, she could go to work without a long FBI background check.

She arrived at the commission's offices on K Street to find chaos. "We didn't have phones, we didn't have computers, we didn't have fax machines," she recalled. She was given a desk near the lobby door that offered no privacy at all, which was painful for a woman who valued her privacy so highly. The consolation, she figured, was the chance to say that she had a ringside seat to the most important government investigation of her lifetime. She could see almost everything that went on.

Heitkotter had worked for difficult, dismissive bosses throughout her career, but it was clear to her and her colleagues on the commission that Zelikow was going to be in a category all his own. He was undeniably smart, but he was nasty, insecure, and prone to red-in-the-face outbursts. She was rarely the victim of his outbursts—maybe Zelikow couldn't be bothered to waste his anger on someone at her level—but Heitkotter cringed when she saw him savage others.

Although it was unpleasant to deal with Zelikow, Heitkotter quickly made friends on the commission's staff, and she found much to admire among the ten commissioners, especially Tom Kean. It was obvious that Kean was "wellborn," the sort of aristocrat who had been taught at an early age to be polite to everyone, regardless of station. "A lot of people don't treat administrative staff well, but Kean always did," she said. It was the same sort of confidence and patrician good manners she saw in John Lehman; his family was prominent on Philadelphia's Main Line. Grace Kelly, the actress-turned-princess, was Lehman's cousin.

Part of Heitkotter's job was taking Zelikow's phone calls and setting up his appointments. Since the commission did not even have office supplies at the start, she brought a small spiral notebook to work that would serve as her telephone log. She began recording the phone calls that Zelikow received at the office. (She knew only who called in; Zelikow lived on his cell phone and preferred to use it to return most of his calls.)

When a phone call came into the office for Zelikow, she would log it with a date and time. In the first months of the investigation, most of Zelikow's callers were those Heitkotter would have expected: Tom Kean and Lee Hamilton and the other commissioners; middle-ranking government officials who were serving as their agencies' liaison to the investigation; and reporters. Although Zelikow had hired a press spokesman, he often preferred to return calls from reporters from large news organizations.

But then on Monday, June 23, 2003, at 4:40 p.m., Heitkotter picked up the phone and was startled to hear the voice of one of the most powerful men in Washington.

"This is Karl Rove," he said. "I'm looking for Philip."

Heitkotter wondered why Bush's political adviser would want to talk to Zelikow. She knew that Zelikow had promised the commissioners he would cut off all unnecessary contact with senior Bush administration officials to avoid any appearance of a conflict of interest, given his close ties to Condoleezza Rice and others at the White House. So why would he be talking to Rove? It was not a mystery she could answer; it was not her place to ask why someone like Rove would be calling. She explained to Rove that Zelikow was out of the office and gave him Zelikow's cell phone number. She logged the call in the spiral notebook: "Karl Rove— gave PZ cell #."

At 11:35 the next morning, the phone rang and it was Rove again, eager to find Zelikow. She took a message for Zelikow.

How odd, she thought, that Rove would be so insistent on tracking down Zelikow personally.

It was not the last time Zelikow would hear from Rove and others at the White House. Rove called again on September 4 and again on September 15. And Rove was not the only senior administration official in contact with Zelikow.

While Zelikow was telling people how upset he was to cut off contact with his good friend Rice, Heitkotter knew that he hadn't. More than once, she had been asked to arrange a gate pass so Zelikow could enter the White House to visit the national security adviser in her offices in the West Wing. In September, he had gone over to the White House to have lunch with her and her staff.

Zelikow would later claim that he had no idea Heitkotter was keeping a log of his phone calls. But the existence of the log—and Zelikow's contacts with Rove and Rice—did become widely known within the commission that fall.

A staffer passing Heitkotter's desk late one evening noticed the phone log, which was open to a page that made reference to a call from "Rove." Alarmed to see the name of Bush's top political adviser in the commission's phone logs, the staffer picked up the notebook and paged through the rest of it, finding references to the additional contacts with Rove—and with Rice.

The next day, word of Zelikow's contacts at the White House began to spread wildly through the commission. For many of the staff, it was just what they had suspected: Zelikow was some kind of White House mole, feeding information back to the administration about the commission's findings. Now, they thought, they had proof of it.

PERHAPS ZELIKOW never understood how badly he came off to the staff. Some of his detractors on the commission worried that they assumed the worst about Zelikow because they simply did not like him. Or they feared him. "I'm very conscious of my many weaknesses," Zelikow said later when told of the harsh appraisals of his management style. But as a historian, he said, he had often seen words like "obnoxious" and "nasty" and "bully" applied to people who would later be remembered and admired as "change agents" in government—leaders "who have to drive an institution or set of issues very hard." The commission "needed high-intensity, high-energy staff leadership," he said.

Yes, he was a friend of Condi Rice's; that was well known on the staff from early in the investigation. And yes, he knew and respected Rove, a fact that became clear to the staff only later. But there were others on the staff who faced their own conflicts of interest, or at least the appearance of a conflict, involving their ties to the Democratic Party. Zelikow had hired investigators for the 9/11 commission who had worked in the White House for Democrats or for Democratic leaders in Congress. Dan Marcus, for instance, had worked in Bill Clinton's White House and was the number-three official at the Justice Department under Janet Reno. On the commission, Marcus was involved in the investigation of the performance of the Clinton Justice Department on terrorism. So were there similar complaints that Marcus was a Democratic partisan who might protect Clinton or Reno from scrutiny? No, Zelikow knew. Zelikow felt he was being singled out.

Whatever others thought of him, Zelikow never considered himself a partisan Republican. Certainly he would never admit that to himself. Until 1991, he said, he had always registered to vote as a Democrat or an independent; he had worked for Jimmy Carter's first presidential campaign, in 1976. In his earlier career practicing law in Texas, his work often allied him with civil rights and civil liberties groups that were hardly under the sway of the GOP. In the early 1980s, he had worked with the Southern Poverty Law Center to seek court protection for Vietnamese-American shrimpers who were being harassed by the Ku Klux Klan and other racist groups. In 1980, he had sued the University of Houston for giving way to perceived pressure from the Saudi government in blocking the school's PBS station from showing a controversial British docudrama, "Death of a Princess," apparently based on the true story of a Saudi princess who was executed for adultery. He became a Republican only after entering the foreign service in 1985 and finding himself at the White House, working for the first President Bush on the National Security Council. Zelikow was impressed by what he saw of Republican leadership, especially during the 1991 Gulf War, and he worked actively in Bush's reelection bid in 1992, when he lost to Bill Clinton.

DANA LESEMANN was Zelikow's nightmare. At the suggestion of former congressman Tim Roemer, she and another investigator—Mike Jacobson—had been hired from the joint congressional committee on pre-9/11 intelligence failures. Roemer had gotten to know them both during the House-Senate inquiry, which was shutting down just as the 9/11 commission was opening its doors. On the commission, Lesemann and Jacobson were assigned to the team that was responsible for trying to unravel the September 11 plot. That meant they could continue the digging they had begun on Capitol Hill.

Lesemann was that rare thing on the commission: She was not afraid of Zelikow; she would not be intimidated by him. In fact, from the moment she arrived at the commission's offices on K Street, she seemed almost to relish the daily combat with Zelikow, even if she wondered aloud to her colleagues why there had to be any combat at all.

Lesemann and Jacobson had become friends on the congressional investigation. Both were lawyers in their mid-thirties and had backgrounds in federal law enforcement. She was on leave from the Justice Department, where she had overseen the preparation of wiretap warrants in terrorism cases; he was a former FBI intelligence analyst. They shared a mutual skepticism, if not contempt, for the FBI, made all the stronger after their work on the congressional investigation of 9/11.

That was where the similarities between the two of them ended. Lesemann could be blunt-spoken to the point of rudeness—a self-described "pain in the ass"—and did not seem aware that she often left bruised feelings in her wake. Jacobson was slow to anger and could be shy, as eager to avoid confrontation as Lesemann was to embrace it. Instead, he tended to intimidate people with his physical presence: At six feet three and 210 pounds, he had the height of a basketball player and the bulk of a wide receiver. For relaxation, Lesemann went scuba-diving in New Zealand; Jacobson played the flute.

Both welcomed the chance to continue the lines of inquiry they had opened in the congressional investigation. In their work on Capitol Hill, they had come to the conclusion that FBI officials had tried to hide the truth of what had happened in San Diego with Nawaf al-Hazmi and Khalid al-Mihdhar, the two 9/11 hijackers who had lived in the open in Southern California for nearly a year. It was Jacobson who, digging through FBI files, discovered that Hazmi and Mihdhar had lived in the home of an FBI informant in San Diego, an astonishing fact that no one had shared for weeks after 9/11 with the bureau's headquarters in Washington.

Jacobson was convinced that a network of Saudis and other Arab expatriates living in California had assisted the two terrorists. It was Jacobson's work that had led Senator Bob Graham and others in Congress to accuse the White House of covering up a Saudi role in the attacks. Jacobson was the primary author of the twenty-eight pages in the final congressional report that the White House refused to declassify because it contained evidence suggesting that Saudi government officials, including Fahad al-Thumairy, the Saudi diplomat in Los Angeles, were part of the support network.

Both Lesemann and Jacobson came to the commission from Congress with security clearances, which meant that they, unlike so many of the other staff members, could go straight to work. And because they knew the issues so well and the questions that were left unanswered by the congressional inquiry, they knew exactly what documents and interviews the commission needed to request from the Bush administration.

Shortly after she was given a desk at the offices on K Street, Lesemann presented Zelikow with a list of about twenty people that she and Jacobson wanted to interview, including senior FBI officials. She also asked Zelikow for a copy of Jacobson's still classified twenty-eight pages; the law creating the commission had required that it build upon the record of the congressional investigation, and the twenty-eight pages included the most explosive allegations that she and Jacobson needed to pursue. Jacobson did not have a copy, either, and he could not remember every detail of what he had written. Although the twenty-eight pages were not available to the public, they were certainly supposed to be available to the commission.

Lesemann was startled when, after several days, Zelikow's office came back with an answer to her request for the interviews. She could not ask for twenty interviews, he told her. She could ask for half of that.

"What?" she asked. "Why?"

Zelikow did not like to explain himself to the staff; he wanted his orders followed without question. But in this case, he made an exception. He explained to Lesemann that the commission did not want to overwhelm federal agencies with documents and interview requests at such an early stage in the investigation.

That seemed preposterous to Lesemann—and to many of the other staff members on the commission. It was a tradition at the Justice Department, and a good one, to demand the widest range of documents and interviews early on from the target of an investigation and then, if necessary, cut back the requests through negotiation. A good investigation didn't limit itself from the start, especially since the staff had been told that subpoenas were going to be a last resort.

"This seems very arbitrary," she said. "This seems crazy."

Zelikow was done explaining. He was not in the business of negotiating with staff who worked for him.

"Philip, this is ridiculous," she said, almost pounding him in the chest with her outstretched index finger. "We need the interviews. We need these documents. Why are you trying to limit our investigation?"

It was the first of several similar confrontations between the two, and they became the talk of the K Street offices, with some of the investigators quietly cheering on Lesemann. She could be obnoxious, sure, but she was fearless. Jacobson and others on the staff worried that Lesemann would push Zelikow too far.

Their battles also involved the twenty-eight pages from the congressional report. Weeks after she had requested a copy, Zelikow had still not obtained it for the commission. Finally, Lesemann stopped him in the hallway.

"Philip, how are we supposed to do our work if you won't provide us with basic research material?" she said. Her colleagues said that Zelikow stormed away.

Lesemann made a decision: If Zelikow wasn't going to get her a copy, she would get one herself. She apparently did not understand that she was about to give Zelikow the ammunition he would need to fire her.

———

ZELIKOW LEARNED that spring that Lesemann had broken the commission's rules and obtained a copy of classified portions of the congressional report on 9/11, including the twenty-eight pages. News that she had the material came to Zelikow from another staff member on a different team who had tangled with Lesemann and wanted to see her removed from the investigation. It took only hours for Zelikow to fire her.

To some of her colleagues, what Lesemann had done seemed a minor infraction of the rules. It was a mystery to them how she had gotten the documents. But she certainly had the security clearances needed to read them, even if she did not have the authorization to keep them in her possession. There was no allegation that any classified documents had left the K Street offices. She had locked them away at night. There was no doubt that she needed them to do her job.

But Zelikow had what he needed to argue to Kean and Hamilton that Lesemann had, technically, broken the law by mishandling a classified document. He believed she needed to be dismissed—instantly. "Lesemann committed a set of very serious violations in the handling of the most highly classified information," Zelikow said later. She had violated the commission's "zero-tolerance policy on the handling of classified information."

Dan Marcus agreed with Zelikow that Lesemann had to go. To their minds, it was an infraction that put the entire investigation in jeopardy. If the White House learned that the commission had mishandled secret material, it would be all the excuse the administration needed to cut off cooperation with the commission. "The administration would have seized upon any negligence on our part," Zelikow said.

Lesemann was called into Zelikow's office and emerged a few minutes later, ashen-faced. She walked out of the commission offices without emptying her desk. Zelikow had fired her on the spot. He would not hear her appeals. There was no announcement of what had happened.

Raj De, a newly minted graduate of Harvard Law School who was on the "plot" team, was told to empty out Lesemann's desk; he was not told why she had gone. Only later did word begin to spread about the reasons for Lesemann's abrupt departure. It was Lesemann's good fortune, and the commission's, that word of her firing did not reach the press or the investigation's Republican critics on Capitol Hill. The fact that the news did not leak was proof of how tightly Zelikow was able to control the flow of information on the commission.

To Lesemann's friends, it seemed that Zelikow had accomplished all of his goals with her departure. He had gotten rid of the one staff member who had emerged early on as his nemesis; he had managed to eject her without attracting the attention of the press corps or the White House. And he had found a way to send a message to the staff: *Do not cross me.*

K STREET OFFICES OF THE
9/11 COMMISSION
Washington, D.C.
APRIL 2003

S lade Gorton had to catch his breath as the nearly four-inch blade was passed around for the commissioners to inspect. It was shocking to see the sort of weapon that was used to butcher some of the pilots and passengers aboard the four planes on 9/11. The staff investigators wanted the ten commissioners to see for themselves exactly what the hijackers had been allowed to carry onto the planes. So they went out and purchased a plierslike utility tool common among building contractors and known as a Leatherman. It had an exceptionally sharp, forged-steel blade that folded out and locked into place. Obviously it could maim. How could anyone have doubted that it could kill with a well-directed plunge into a victim's neck or chest?

Yet on the morning of September 11, 2001, the rules of the Federal Aviation Administration allowed a metal blade up to four inches long to be taken aboard a passenger plane. If it was detected by a magnetometer at an airport security checkpoint, the FAA's rules called for the knife to be inspected and then returned to the passenger. The FBI believed that at least two Leatherman-like tools were among the weapons used by the 9/11 hijackers to take control of the planes.

The blade was just one more bit of proof to Gorton that if one agency of the government above all others bore responsibility for 9/11, it was the FAA, which was supposed to maintain safety in the skies and at the nation's airports. It was not a view shared by most of his colleagues on the commission, who were much more likely from the start to single out the FBI and CIA for blame. But Gorton thought he could make a strong argument that the FAA deserved the shameful distinction of being the most culpable for the attacks.

It went far beyond the lunacy of FAA rules that allowed an obviously lethal weapon like a nearly four-inch steel blade to be carried onto a passenger plane. To Gorton, it was a question of the basic competence of senior FAA officials who were aware in the summer of 2001 that there was a grave terrorist threat that could involve the hijacking of civilian airliners yet did almost nothing to respond to it. It was a view shared by the commission's staff. In their early interviews at the FAA, the panel's investigators were often impressed by agency officials who worked outside Washington, especially the air traffic controllers around the country who responded to the hijackings on 9/11. But almost uniformly, the commission's staff held FAA leaders at headquarters in contempt. Many of them seemed the definition of careerist bureaucrats.

For Gorton, the FAA's incompetence was embodied in the fact that its official no-fly watch list of potential terrorists had fewer than twenty names on September 11. The State Department had its own watch list, known as TIPOFF, which included sixty-one thousand names of possible terrorists. Among the names on the TIPOFF list on September 11 were those of Nawaf al-Hazmi and Khalid al-Mihdhar, the two hijackers who had lived in San Diego for much of the year before the attacks. TIPOFF was considered the government's most authoritative terrorist watch list, and it was readily available to the FAA and the airlines; the State Department was eager to share it.

But the FAA's chief of civil aviation security in 2001, Cathal L. Flynn, had admitted sheepishly to the commission's staff early in the investigation that he had been unaware before September 11 that the State Department's watch list even existed. "I regret to say that I was unaware of the TIPOFF list," said Flynn. Gorton thought that Flynn's humiliating acknowledgment was among the most telling moments in the commission's investigation—"stunning, just unbelievable," and an "example of the absolute incompetence" of the FAA and other government agencies in sharing information.

Others at the FAA said that while they were aware of TIPOFF and made use of it on occasion, they and the airlines found it difficult to take advantage of a list that included tens of thousands of names, many of them foreigners. Gorton thought that ridiculous; during his Senate career, he had flown home to Seattle almost weekly, and the airlines had little difficulty cross-indexing his name and ticket with his frequent flier account and properly crediting his mileage, just as they did for millions of other passengers who had names far more exotic than his.

The performance of the FAA's parent organization, the Department of Transportation, was not much more reassuring. One of the commission's earliest witnesses at its public hearings in 2003 was Transportation Secretary Norman Mineta, a genial former Democratic congressman from California who was considered the token Democrat in George W. Bush's cabinet.

If the commission was looking for early proof of how little the Bush White House had done to prepare domestic agencies for a terrorist attack that summer, Mineta offered it up, perhaps unintentionally.

As head of the Department of Transportation, he oversaw the FAA, the Coast Guard, and other agencies that should have played some role in preparing for a domestic terrorist attack in 2001. But Mineta revealed that the White House had made no special effort to warn the Transportation Department to be ready for an al-Qaeda strike that spring and summer. He could not remember any special interagency meetings at the White House about the threats, when the CIA was warning President Bush almost daily of an imminent attack.

Mineta seemed wary of saying it directly—and proving how far out of the intelligence loop he had been in the Bush administration—but it was clear from his answers that he and the Transportation Department had no sense at all of how dire the terrorist warnings were in 2001. Nobody had told him.

John Lehman, the former navy secretary, reviewed the long timeline of terrorist warnings that summer and then asked Mineta: "Wouldn't you view it as a failure of our intelligence community not to tell the secretary of transportation that there was such a conceivable threat?"

"We had no information of that nature at all," Mineta replied.

ON SEPTEMBER 11, two federal agencies had the duty of making sure the skies above the United States were free of threats: the Federal Aviation Administration and the Department of Defense. In the event of hijackings, they were supposed to work together. The FAA was supposed to alert the Pentagon—specifically the North American Aerospace Defense Command, or NORAD—at the first sign that a passenger plane had been commandeered.

Understanding what happened in the skies on September 11 was the job given to a team of investigators on the commission led by John Farmer, a former attorney general of New Jersey. He had been recruited by Tom Kean, who would later say that Farmer was one of the commission's best hires.

Farmer was known as a dogged investigator, and he had been at the center of the New Jersey government's response on 9/11. His loyal staff at the attorney general's office had organized the search that turned up key evidence discarded before the attacks by the United Flight 93 hijackers. The evidence was found in garbage bins at Newark International Airport, where the Boeing 757 had begun its last flight, and at nearby hotels. It included a large poster of the computerized flight controls of a 757; the terrorists had used the poster as part of their training. Farmer has also overseen the state's end of the investigation of five deaths caused by anthrax-laden letters mailed in the days after September 11 from a post office in Hamilton Township, New Jersey.

Farmer would also prove invaluable to the commission because he knew how to write. His father had been a popular columnist at the Newark *Star Ledger,* and Farmer had considered following his father into a writing career. While in college, Farmer had won a summer fellowship to the University of Iowa's famed writing school. Ultimately, though, he opted for a law degree at Georgetown and went to work as a prosecutor. Friends thought he still harbored dreams of a second career as a novelist or poet.

On the commission, Farmer was named to lead the team that would investigate what happened in the skies on September 11 and detail—hour by hour, minute by minute—what had happened aboard the four planes and how the government had responded to the attacks. Farmer knew that it would be the best, if most difficult, writing assignment on the commission.

When he joined the commission in early 2003, Farmer was eager to get back into the middle of the investigation of September 11. Only four months after the attacks, his term as the state's attorney general expired, and he had returned to private legal practice. When Kean offered him a job on the commission, Farmer quickly accepted, as long as he could work out of the panel's New York office. He did not want to move to Washington. Kean, who was just as eager not to relocate to Washington, agreed.

Farmer began to educate himself about the workings of the FAA, responsible mostly for the safety of commercial and private aircraft, and NORAD. And it did not take long for him to realize that he had taken on the role of the commission's chief debunker of conspiracy theories. Because the FAA and NORAD had found it difficult, if not impossible, to offer a coordinated story about their actions on September 11, they had given the conspiracy theorists plenty to work with.

THE CONSPIRACY theories about 9/11 began to circulate long before the ashes had stopped smoldering at ground zero. That was no surprise. After an event as horrifying and—to the public—unexpected as 9/11, the darkest theories about its cause did not seem beyond belief.

But by the time the 9/11 commission opened its doors in 2003, many of the most outrageous, if well circulated, of the theories—that the attacks were an inside job by the Bush administration, that the Twin Towers were brought down by preplaced explosives, that the Pentagon was hit by a missile and not a plane—had been well debunked.

The evidence was incontrovertible that al-Qaeda was behind the September 11 attacks; Osama bin Laden had been videotaped bragging to his colleagues about his role in the preparations. There was clear-cut documentation to show that bin Laden had dispatched nineteen young Arab men to the United States to carry out the hijackings—he had chosen them personally for the mission—and that those same men were aboard the four planes. There was a well-documented money trail for the plot. Independent scientists and engineers had plausible explanations for the physical collapse of the Twin Towers and other buildings nearby.

But there was one important set of conspiracy theories that would not be dismissed so easily, and they involved how government agencies—specifically the FAA and NORAD—had reacted to first reports of the hijackings. Officials at the FAA and the Pentagon had no one to blame but themselves for the confusion. Over the course of two years, they released a series of timelines that fueled the skeptics by suggesting that the government should have had time to shoot down at least one of the planes before they hit their targets.

The first of the planes was reported hijacked to the FAA at 8:24 a.m.; the last of them would not crash until 10:03, which meant that the supersonic military jet fighters stationed up and down the East Coast to defend American borders had at least one hour and thirty-six minutes to try to reach some of the planes. That should have been plenty of time to apprehend and shoot down at least one or two of the hijacked airliners.

Even from his earliest review of the evidence, Farmer could see that the FAA and NORAD had never presented the public—or the White House, for that matter—with a consistent timeline for the events of the morning of September 11. And they seemed bizarrely uninterested in trying to correct the record.

It was remarkable, he thought, how often the inaccurate statements were made by senior government officials in public testimony—and under oath.

On September 13, 2001, two days after the attacks, U.S. Air Force general Richard Myers appeared before the Senate Armed Services Committee for his confirmation hearing as chairman of the Joint Chiefs of Staff. Myers, then the number two officer on the Joint Chiefs, was a veteran air force fighter pilot. He had flown more than six hundred hours of combat in the Vietnam War and was twice awarded the Distinguished Flying Cross.

It seemed obvious that Myers, of all people at the Pentagon, would want to know—would demand to know—how jet fighters under NORAD's control had responded on the morning of September 11 to the threat in the skies.

But in his testimony, Myers offered the first of what would be several contradictory—and flatly inaccurate—statements from the Pentagon about the military response on September 11. He asserted that military fighters were not scrambled to respond to the hijackings until after the Pentagon had been hit at 9:37 a.m. That was wrong; it would later be demonstrated that the first fighters had been scrambled almost an hour earlier than Myers suggested.

Farmer could not understand why it was so difficult to establish an accurate timeline—surely the military and FAA had logs and computer records that documented what had gone on. It seemed all the more remarkable to him that the Pentagon could not establish a clear chronology of how it responded to an attack on the Pentagon building itself. Wouldn't the generals and admirals want to know why their own offices—their own lives—had been put at risk that morning?

He was pleased that the commission scheduled its second set of hearings, in May 2003, to take testimony from NORAD commanders. Surely by then, a year and eight months after the attacks, the Pentagon would have figured out what happened on September 11.

The key witness was retired air force major general Larry K. Arnold, who had overseen NORAD's efforts on September 11 to respond to the attacks. Given his retirement, Arnold testified before the hearing in civilian coat and tie. But the fact that he was no longer in uniform did not mean that Arnold's information was out of date. He had been briefed in detail by his former air force colleagues before the hearing about the questions to expect.

As Farmer later reflected on Arnold's testimony, he was startled to realize that NORAD still had its facts wrong in the spring of 2003—and either it did not care or was misstating the record intentionally.

Arnold was questioned by Richard Ben-Veniste about the timeline on the morning of September 11, specifically about when the FAA notified NORAD of each of the hijackings and how long it had taken to scramble jet fighters to respond.

Ben-Veniste was especially interested in what had happened with American Airlines Flight 77, the plane that crashed into the Pentagon, and United Airlines 93, which plunged into the field in Pennsylvania. They took off and crashed later than the pair of planes that hit the World Trade Center. Presumably there was more time for fighter jets to intercept them.

Ben-Veniste asked Arnold when NORAD had been notified that American 77 might have been hijacked.

"I believe that to be a fact: that 9:24 was the first time that we had been advised of American 77 as a possible hijacked airplane," Arnold replied. He said that if NORAD was distracted in responding to Flight 77, which crashed into the Pentagon at 9:37, it was because "our focus—you have got to remember that there's a lot of other things going on simultaneously here—was on United 93."

Arnold testified that the FAA had urged NORAD to pay special attention to tracking down United 93, which he believed might be headed toward Washington. "It was our intent to intercept United Flight 93. And in fact, my own staff, we were orbiting now over Washington, D.C., by this time, and I was personally anxious to see what 93 was going to do, and our intent was to intercept it."

The retired two-star general was suggesting that there had been time to shoot down United 93 and that the shoot-down was made unnecessary because of the sacrifice of passengers who had stormed the cockpit and provoked the hijackers to crash the plane. "The brave men and women who took over that aircraft prevented us from making the awful decision," Arnold testified somberly.

When Farmer and his team of investigators looked back at Arnold's testimony later, they were astonished; Farmer believed the testimony from Arnold and other NORAD generals should have been referred to the Justice Department for possible prosecution. It would later be determined that almost every one of those assertions by General Arnold in May 2003 was flat wrong, most startlingly his claim that the military had close-tracked United 93 and was prepared to intercept it. In fact, it was later shown, NORAD knew nothing about the hijacking of the United plane until after it had crashed into that lonely rural field in western Pennsylvania. Luckily for Arnold, the commission had not put him under oath on the first day he testified. Farmer would make sure that did not happen again.

OFFICE OF THE COUNSEL
TO THE PRESIDENT

The White House

JUNE 2003

With each meeting, Tom Kean grew more exasperated with Alberto Gonzales.

"This is not a viable position for the White House, Judge," Kean told Gonzales, trying not to raise his voice, not to show anger. "You've got to move off this."

Kean and Lee Hamilton sat in Gonzales's second-floor corner office in the West Wing hour after hour, meeting after meeting, in 2003, haggling over the White House's refusal—Gonzales's refusal—to turn over classified documents to the investigation and to help the commission arrange interviews.

Kean kept asking himself the same questions: Did Gonzales understand the political damage he was doing to President Bush? Did the president understand what was being done by Gonzales in his name?

Kean found Gonzales, an original member of the "Texas mafia" who had moved to Washington with Bush, to be polite and formal to the point of theatricality: "He was one of the politest men I've ever worked with, always very even in tone, always very polite. 'Governor this,' 'Governor that.'"

Kean could not help but be impressed by Gonzales's life story. In a sense, the fact that a man like Gonzales had found his way into the Republican Party was the fulfillment of one of Kean's lifelong political goals: to broaden the GOP beyond its staunchly Caucasian, Protestant, moneyed roots. Gonzales was one of eight children of a Mexican-American couple who had met as migrant workers, picking cotton in the fields of South Texas in the early 1950s. His father, who never finished grade school, built the two-room, wood-sided house near Houston in which Alberto and his brothers and sisters were raised; the home had no running water or telephone. From this, Alberto Gonzales made his way to the air force and then to Harvard Law School, the governor's office in Austin, and finally the White House. Despite all of his accomplishments, Gonzales did not display an ounce of arrogance or self-importance.

But Gonzales's good manners did not mask the fact to Kean that the White House counsel was stonewalling the 9/11 commission.

The White House, through Gonzales, was refusing to provide the commission with essential documents, including the president's daily briefs that went to Bush in the months before 9/11.

Gonzales also made clear that "my client"—the way he always referred to President Bush—would also not be made available for a formal interview with the full commission. Nor would Vice President Dick Cheney. Nor would National Security Adviser Condoleezza Rice be allowed to testify in public to the commission or under oath. "No, no, no," Kean kept hearing.

Gonzales's argument never varied. It was an absolutist view of executive privilege—the concept that advice given to a president by his staff needed to remain secret if it was to have value.

"My client believes that the material and interviews being sought by the commission are protected by executive privilege," Gonzales told Kean and Hamilton more than once. If the White House made compromises with the commission, he said, it would soon be forced to compromise with hostile lawmakers in Congress.

Kean took pride in his lack of a law degree. "Don't like lawyers," he would often taunt the many lawyers on the commission's staff, almost always with a wink and a playful smile. But although he did not claim to know the law, he knew politics. He really knew politics. And he knew from his first dealings with Gonzales that the White House was going to have to compromise.

Kean could not tell if Gonzales was speaking for the president—if the president really knew and believed in what Gonzales was saying— or if Gonzales was being directed by someone else. "We never knew," Kean said. Either way, he thought, George Bush's lawyer was doing his "client" no favors.

It was often thought among the commissioners that Gonzales was taking his direction not from the president but from Vice President Cheney and his powerful counsel, David S. Addington. Gonzales had no experience at all in national security law or issues of executive privilege before arriving at the White House in 2001. Cheney and Addington knew those subjects as well as anyone in Washington, even if their views were considered extreme. No one was more of an executive privilege absolutist than Addington. Other White House lawyers believed him to have ghostwritten a January 2002 document signed by Gonzales that became known as the Bush administration's original "torture memo." It argued that Bush had authority under the Constitution to ignore the Geneva Conventions when it came to the detention of al-Qaeda followers and other prisoners captured in a "war on terror." The opinion opened the door to harsh interrogation techniques that the United States had previously outlawed as torture, including waterboarding. In waterboarding, American interrogators pour water over the face of a prisoner whose head is covered with cloth or cellophane, simulating drowning. It was widely reported that the CIA "waterboarded" at least three senior al-Qaeda leaders apprehended after September 11.

Kean knew that if all else failed, he could issue subpoenas to the White House, potentially setting off a constitutional fight that would do even more damage to Bush. He never used the word *subpoena* in his conversations with Gonzales. He thought Gonzales was well aware that the threat of a subpoena was always on the table.

The script for these meetings was almost always the same. Gonzales would greet Kean and Hamilton cordially and invite them into his West Wing office. Coffee, tea, a glass of spring water? He was usually in shirtsleeves and invited his visitors to take a seat around his coffee table. Then he would spend thirty minutes saying no to all of Kean and Hamilton's requests. And Kean and Hamilton—Kean, mostly—would insist that Gonzales reconsider for the sake of his "client."

Gonzales would often fall back on the argument that because the commission was created under a law approved by Congress, the investigation fell under the purview of the legislative branch. A decision to hand over the PDBs would therefore set an unacceptable precedent requiring future presidents to provide them to congressional investigations. He said Rice could not testify in public, or under oath, to the commission because of the long, well-established tradition that White House national security advisers do not appear before Congress.

Gonzales argued, and Kean knew it was true, that presidents and vice presidents traditionally did not give testimony—or even private interviews—to outside investigations. Lyndon Johnson had refused to be interviewed by the Warren Commission, even though the subject was his predecessor's assassination.

"But we believe there are no precedents for our investigation," Kean argued back. He reminded Gonzales, over and over again, that 9/11 was unlike anything in modern American history—an attack within American borders in which thousands of civilians were murdered, the deadliest attack on the continental United States by a foreign aggressor since the War of 1812.

"We've never had an attack like this in American history. You can't say we're setting a precedent by letting us see the PDBs or talk to Condoleezza Rice or anything else," he told Gonzales.

Gonzales would reply with almost the same words each time, always in the same quiet, infuriatingly calm voice. "I don't think we can do that," he said. "My client can't do that."

DAN MARCUS, the new general counsel, was left to conduct legal negotiations with the White House by an odd triangulation. Gonzales refused to see Marcus. After announcing in the first weeks of the investigation that he would not meet with Zelikow again, Gonzales insisted on dealing only with Kean and Hamilton.

When Kean and Hamilton returned from meeting with Gonzales at the White House, Marcus would try to sit them down and debrief them. And then Marcus, based on what he thought had gone on at the White House, would need to plot counterproposals for Kean and Hamilton to take back to Gonzales. "It was very messy," Marcus recalled.

It was a crazy way to do business, he knew, but there was so much that was crazy about the way the White House and its lawyers were dealing with the commission. Like virtually every other lawyer on the commission and its staff, Marcus questioned whether Gonzales understood what he was doing and how badly—as a lawyer—he was serving the president.

"Gonzales didn't have good political judgment and staked out positions that got the White House in trouble—these kinds of wooden separation-of-power arguments," Marcus remembered.

Some of the commissioners framed the questions about Gonzales more directly: Was the president's counsel competent?

If anyone on the commission understood the issues before Gonzales, it was Fred Fielding, the Republican commissioner who had been Ronald Reagan's White House counsel; Fielding had also been deputy White House counsel during the worst of the Watergate scandal in the Nixon administration, when questions of executive privilege were tested almost daily in the federal courts.

Fielding could see how this was going to turn out: The Bush White House would have to back away from its absolutist arguments—its refusal to turn over the PDBs and other documents, its refusal to make Rice and others available—if only because the political pressures would simply be too great.

A good White House counsel would have understood that—the counsel's ultimate responsibility was to defend the president in every way, including protecting the president's hopes for a smooth route to reelection.

To Fielding, it was only a question of when the White House would compromise; the longer Gonzales and others waited, the more damage would be done to the president from the barrage of headlines about White House "obstruction" and "stonewalling."

If Fielding was back at the White House, this would have been a reasonably simple, if time-consuming, give-and-take with the commission. Fielding would have started by offering the commission 25 percent of what it wanted and then, as a "generous" compromise, would have eventually agreed to turn over 50 percent. Maybe some of the less damning PDBs. Maybe a limited chat for several of the commissioners with Bush and Cheney. The grateful commissioners could argue that they were "victorious" because they had pressured the White House to meet them halfway.

Fielding could see that Gonzales, by offering the commission nothing and antagonizing its members, including the Republicans, might eventually be forced to turn over everything, compromising the prerogatives of the White House in ways that might damage the presidency for generations.

K STREET OFFICES OF THE
9/11 COMMISSION
Washington, D.C.
MAY 2003

T o the alarm of some of the more publicity-hungry commissioners, the investigation fell out of the headlines for several months in the spring and summer of 2003. It was mostly ignored by the Washington press corps, which had a much bigger story to cover at the time. In March, only four months after the creation of the commission, President Bush ordered the invasion of Iraq. The overthrow of Saddam Hussein was described by the White House as the next logical chapter in the "war on terror" that began on September 11.

The White House had originally justified the invasion as necessary because of intelligence that Baghdad was hiding stockpiles of chemical and biological weapons—maybe even nuclear material—from United Nations inspectors.

After the invasion, when it became clear that the intelligence was disastrously wrong and there were no such deadly weapons, the administration shifted its argument. Now it justified the war by focusing almost exclusively on the purported collaboration between Iraq and al-Qaeda. The White House played endless semantic games on the issue. When pressed, Bush was careful not to allege that Iraq had any role in the 9/11 attacks, at least no direct role. But he insisted that if Saddam Hussein had remained in power, he would have continued his hunt for weapons of mass destruction and would have been tempted to hand them over to his supposed ally Osama bin Laden.

Vice President Cheney went further, subtly contradicting the president and suggesting repeatedly, almost obsessively, that Iraq may in fact have been involved in the September 11 plot.

In speeches and interviews throughout 2002 and 2003, Cheney kept citing a Czech intelligence report that Mohammed Atta, the Egyptian-born ringleader of the 9/11 hijackers, met in April 2001 with a senior Iraqi spy in Prague, the Czech capital. Cheney kept promoting the report as credible even though his White House staff knew it had been knocked down by both the CIA and the FBI; the bureau had found cell phone and banking records to show that Atta had been in Florida in April. The Iraqi spy who supposedly met with Atta in Prague was captured after the Iraq invasion and denied there had been any such meeting.

MOST OF the commissioners and the staff did not know it until much later, but Philip Zelikow had an important role at the White House in developing the scholarly underpinnings for the Iraq war.

His thirty-one-page "preemptive war" doctrine, written anonymously and at Condoleezza Rice's request, was released by the White House in September 2002 under George W. Bush's signature. It had the simple, magisterial title "The National Security Strategy of the United States."

"In an age where the enemies of civilization openly and actively seek the world's most destructive technologies, the United States cannot remain idle," it declared. "The United States will, if necessary, act pre-emptively." It was a remarkable document, a reversal of generations of American military doctrine, which had previously held that the United States would launch a military strike against an enemy only after it had been struck or if American lives were in immediate jeopardy.

When commission staffers learned that Zelikow was the principal author, many were astounded. It was arguably his most serious conflict of interest in running the investigation. It was in his interest, they could see, to use the commission to try to bolster the administration's arguments for war—a war that he had helped make possible.

Zelikow's participation in preparing the White House strategy paper was mentioned in passing in a few news accounts in 2003. But the extent of his involvement was not revealed until publication of a book in March 2004 about Bush's war cabinet by journalist Jim Mann. Zelikow's support for the concept of preemptive war had not been a secret in the run-up to the Iraq war, however. In June 2002, nine months before the invasion, Zelikow was quoted by the Associated Press as saying that "we're now beginning to understand that we can't wait for these folks to deliver the weapons of mass destruction and see what they do with them before we act." He referred specifically to Iraq: "We're beginning to understand that we might not want to give people like Saddam Hussein advance warning that we're going to strike."

In the commission's early private meetings, Max Cleland felt passionately that the commission needed to investigate the Bush administration's reasons for going to war in Iraq—specifically, whether the president had used the 9/11 attack as an excuse to launch an invasion that he had planned to carry out from his earliest days in the White House.

Cleland felt that the White House's early "obsession" with Iraq resulted from Bush's belief that his father had made a mistake by not finishing off Saddam Hussein in the 1991 Gulf War. Iraq was part of the reason the White House had paid so little attention to al-Qaeda terrorist threats in the spring and summer 2001, Cleland believed. Bush was targeting a different enemy, the one in Baghdad that his father had failed to overthrow. "They were focused on Iraq, they were planning a war on Iraq, they were not paying attention to the business at hand," he told the other commissioners.

But he could see that Kean, Hamilton, and Zelikow had no interest in pursuing any line of inquiry involving the Iraq war. The war had overwhelming public support at the time, largely because most Americans saw it as a response to 9/11.

Cleland found the opinion polls on the subject of Iraq astounding—the public had "drunk Cheney's Kool-Aid" and believed, despite all evidence to the contrary, that Iraq was somehow involved in September 11. He was astonished by a *Washington Post* poll that summer showing that seven in ten people believed Saddam Hussein had helped direct the attacks on the World Trade Center and the Pentagon. A Time/CNN poll found that 80 percent of Americans suspected Iraq's involvement in 9/11.

Cleland could tell that his harping on Iraq and the war was making him even more unpopular among the other commissioners, especially the Republicans. Several of the GOP members had already made it clear they were offended by his insulting comments behind closed doors about Bush, Karl Rove, and the other "nutsos" in the White House. Even some of the Democrats were distancing themselves from him. Cleland knew he was quickly becoming a pariah.

"It was painfully obvious to me that there was this blanket over the commission," he said. "Anybody who spoke out or dissented, whether against George Bush, the White House, or the war against Iraq, was going to be marginalized." The investigation was only a few months old, but Cleland was already wondering if he had to find a way off the 9/11 commission.

THE COMMISSION scheduled a third set of public hearings in July 2003. The subject this time was al-Qaeda, its history and its relationship with other terrorist groups and governments. And to the surprise of some of the commission's staff who knew something about Laurie Mylroie of the American Enterprise Institute, Zelikow made sure that she had a prominent place at the witness table.

Mylroie was considered the intellectual godmother of the Iraq invasion. She and her theories about Iraq and al-Qaeda had been embraced by the Bush administration. Mylroie argued that Iraq had played a role in every major terrorist attack against the United States since the early 1990s, including September 11 and the 1993 bombing of the World Trade Center. She even saw a link between Iraq and the 1995 Oklahoma City bombing. She was certain, she believed, that Baghdad was working with al-Qaeda to plan new terrorist strikes on the United States.

What more could the White House want? A politial scientist at a respected conservative think tank who had all the right credentials, including a Harvard PhD, and who was eager to promote the idea that Iraq and al-Qaeda were effectively one and the same. If Mylroie was right, it almost did not matter that no weapons of mass destruction were found in Iraq; Saddam Hussein deserved to be brought down, she argued, because of his role in 9/11.

Zelikow would later say that he had never met Mylroie prior to her testimony and was skeptical of her views. But he said that at least one of the commissioners "felt those views should be heard," and he agreed. Zelikow surely knew that many in the Bush administration wanted her theories promoted as widely as possible; he knew that she had extraordinary access to the White House and the Pentagon.

Her biggest booster in the government was Deputy Defense Secretary Paul Wolfowitz, a key architect of the Iraqi invasion. In November 2001, Wolfowitz's Pentagon office issued an unusual statement of praise for

Mylroie's newly published book, *Study of Revenge: The First World Trade Center Attack and Saddam Hussein's War Against America,* describing the book as "provocative and disturbing" and saying Mylroie "argues powerfully that the shadowy mastermind of the 1993 World Trade Center bombing was in fact an agent of Iraqi intelligence." Mylroie thanked Wolfowitz in the prologue and said his wife, Clare, had "fundamentally shaped this book." She also thanked Vice President Cheney's chief of staff, Lewis "Scooter" Libby, for his "timely and generous assistance."

At the time, few members of the commission's staff understood the full significance of Zelikow's invitation to Mylroie to testify before the commission; the investigation was barely under way, and they had little say in the makeup of the witness lists. Zelikow made those decisions.

But they would later realize how troubling it was that the 9/11 commission had suggested—early in its investigation, at one of its first substantive public hearings—that the most credible academic in the United States on possible ties between Iraq and al-Qaeda was one who believed firmly that there *were* such ties.

By giving Mylroie such a prominent public platform before the 9/11 commission, Zelikow may not have gotten what he bargained for, however. Several of the commissioners thought that Mylroie came off as batty, if not actually disconnected from reality.

JUDITH YAPHE of the National Defense University took one look at the witness list for the July 2003 hearing, and she could see this was a "setup" by the staff of the 9/11 commission.

She had spent twenty years at the CIA and was considered one of its most experienced analysts on Iraq. She retired in the 1990s and joined the National Defense University, the Pentagon's prestigious military studies college in Washington. Given her credentials, it was no surprise that she was called as a witness before the 9/11 commission to discuss Iraq. Yaphe was widely admired in and out of the intelligence community for her sober analysis of events in the Persian Gulf.

Like most researchers on the subject, she was convinced there had never been a close relationship between Saddam Hussein and Osama bin Laden, certainly nothing like the relationship the Bush administration kept suggesting had existed.

Yes, she agreed, there had been plenty of contact between Iraq and al-Qaeda over the years. In the 1990s, Iraq had probably given weapons training to some of bin Laden's followers in Sudan. But Saddam Hussein would have known he was writing his death warrant if he coordinated terrorist attacks with bin Laden, whose ultimate goal was a bloody end to secular Arab governments—just like his. "Saddam Hussein knew he would be next on their hit list," she said.

So Yaphe was taken aback when she saw the rest of the witness list for the commission's hearing and realized who else would be at the witness table. Seated right next to her, in fact. Laurie Mylroie.

To Yaphe's thinking, Mylroie's crazed theories about Iraq and al-Qaeda had been discredited by other intelligence analysts and scholars years earlier. Had the commission not done enough research to understand that? Did they really want to give an audience to someone who wanted to blame Saddam Hussein for 9/11?

Yaphe decided to go ahead with her testimony despite Mylroie's presence; at least the commissioners could hear for themselves just how bizarre Mylroie sounded when someone tried to pin her down on the details of her eccentric conspiracy theories about Iraq and al-Qaeda. "I thought this might be interesting," Yaphe recalled thinking. Still, she wondered why the 9/11 commission would want to risk its credibility by giving this sort of publicity to Mylroie.

MYLROIE'S TESTIMONY before the 9/11 commission was a bizarre bit of political theater. Here was the woman who was, arguably, one of the most influential academics of her generation, whose research was cited by the United States government to justify a war. And she was spouting what would later be shown to be—and what many other experts in the field already knew to be—nonsense.

"A major policy and intelligence failure occurred in the 1990s, namely the emergence of a serious misunderstanding about the nature of major terrorist attacks on the United States," Mylroie began.

"Prior to the 1993 bombing of the World Trade Center, it was assumed that all major attacks against the United States were state sponsored. The Trade Center bombing is said to mark the start of a new kind of terrorism that does not involve states, and that is simply not true."

According to Mylroie, both the 1993 bombing and September 11 were the work of Iraqi intelligence agents. She insisted the men known as Ramzi Youssef, the 1993 World Trade Center bomber, and Khalid Sheikh Mohammed, the mastermind of the 9/11 plot and supposedly Youssef's uncle, were Iraqi spies. Her byzantine theories centered on her belief that Iraq had planted phony identification papers—"legends," she called them—in Kuwaiti government offices for the two men during the Iraqi occupation of Kuwait in 1990.

"The odds are high that these people are not whom they claim to be, and demonstrating that would constitute a clear link between Iraq and the 9/11 attack, as reasonably only Iraq could have created these legends while it occupied Kuwait," she said.

"Al-Qaeda was a front for Iraqi intelligence in much the same way that Hezbollah is a front for the Iranians and the Syrians," she testified. "We went to war because senior administration officials believe Iraq was involved in 9/11."

Yaphe looked appalled by what she was hearing.

"Dr. Mylroie's answer leaves me kind of breathless," she said in her testimony. "I think she's doing exactly what troubles me the most about leaping to great conclusions that al-Qaeda was a front for Iraqi intelligence. I'm sorry. I need evidence."

Richard Ben-Veniste knew something about Mylroie's background, and he could see how the Bush administration had cynically tried to seize on her theories to justify the Iraq war. He could not understand why the commission's staff had called her to testify. What is she doing here? he asked himself.

Like the talented prosecutor he had been, Ben-Veniste bored in on Mylroie, getting her to acknowledge that "95 percent" of Middle Eastern scholars did not accept her theories about a link between Iraq and al-Qaeda.

Yaphe felt vindicated by the hearing; it seemed to her that Mylroie had been shown for what she was.

Yet if Zelikow was trying to give credibility to Mylroie's views, it may have worked, at least as measured by the respectful news coverage of the hearing, and specifically of Mylroie's testimony. At that moment, there was little of the cynicism that later became almost universal, both in the public and in the press corps, about the Bush administration's justification for the war. The public clearly wanted to believe there was a relationship between Iraq and al-Qaeda. So did many reporters. Otherwise, why had the United States gone to war to overthrow Saddam Hussein?

But if most of the reporters in the hearing room knew nothing about Mylroie, the Jersey Girls knew plenty. From her months of research on the history of al-Qaeda, Lorie Van Auken, who was at the hearing, knew about Mylroie and her "loony" claims of a close alliance between Iraq and bin Laden. Lorie thought the invasion of Iraq was a farce. She thought the White House was ignoring the real enemy, al-Qaeda, to focus on Saddam Hussein. She confronted Zelikow at a meeting between the families and the commission's staff shortly after the hearing.

"That took a lot of nerve putting someone like that on the panel," she told him. "Laurie Mylroie? This is supposed to be an investigation of September 11. This is not supposed to be a sales pitch for the Iraq war."

She remembered that a sly smile crossed Zelikow's face. He said nothing to her. "He knew exactly what he was doing," Lorie recalled. "He was selling the war."

Zelikow was certainly not done with this issue. After the hearing with Mylroie, he made it clear to the commission's staff that he wanted the issue of al-Qaeda–Iraq links pursued aggressively. To some members of the staff, Zelikow seemed determined to demonstrate that whatever the evidence to the contrary, Iraq and al-Qaeda had a close relationship that justified the toppling of Saddam Hussein.

DEPARTMENT OF HISTORY
Harvard University
Cambridge, Mass.
MARCH 2003

In Harvard's History Department, the other doctoral candidates were jealous of Alexis Albion. She was actually having fun. She was at Harvard to earn her PhD, in part, by reading spy novels.

It was a childhood fascination for Albion, the world of espionage—"assignments in exotic lands, slinky black catsuits," as she imagined it. But rather than living out her "spy girl" fantasies by joining the CIA after earning her bachelor's degree from Princeton, Albion had opted to become an intelligence historian. She knew enough about the CIA to understand that the reality of being a spy—long assignments in dreary, lonely places—could be "less Pussy Galore than Bridget Jones."

So Albion decided instead on a career in which she researched and wrote about the history of spies, real and fictional. She had a special interest in James Bond and wrote an unlikely scholarly paper, at least by the standards of Harvard's History Department, on the subject of 007 and "the global historical moment of Bond in the mid-1960s." Her dissertation was titled "The Spy in All of Us: The Public Image of Intelligence."

With her background in history and her appreciation of popular literature, her professors felt she was a natural choice to join the staff of the 9/11 commission. If Philip Zelikow was serious about turning the commission's final report into a work of popular history that the public would want to read and understand, there were few young historians better qualified than Albion to help. Thanks to Ian Fleming and John le Carré, she knew what a page-turner was.

Zelikow recruited her for the commission and she was placed on Team 3, the counterterrorism policy team. It was a dream assignment; it might well be the best research opportunity of her career. She would be the commission's chief investigator on the CIA and its archives. It would be her responsibility to spend days at CIA headquarters at Langley, searching through the agency's files for anything that involved al-Qaeda and the CIA's response to terrorist threats.

She was all of thirty-three when she joined the commission in April and looked several years younger. Elsewhere on the staff, Albion was perceived—incorrectly, it later turned out—as another young intellectual pawn of Zelikow's. Like Warren Bass, who was her counterpart in dealing with the National Security Council archives, Albion would end up having to fight Zelikow to make sure the truth about 9/11 was fully told.

While she waited in 2003 for her security clearance, Albion read through book after book about al-Qaeda and its history, as well as the modern history of the CIA. She read through the full library of Bob Woodward's best-selling fly-on-the-wall books about the workings of the CIA, the Pentagon, and the White House.

It was her first security clearance, and it meant that her family and friends were interviewed about every detail of her life. She got calls from friends who had always suspected she was a spy, and now—they thought—they had proof of it.

When the security clearance finally came through that summer, Albion began her real work: driving to Langley in the morning to sit down and read through years' worth of case files on the CIA and its history of dealing with terrorist threats. Whatever the commission's later disagreements with George Tenet and his deputies, the staff found the CIA to be surprisingly accommodating on opening up its files to Albion and her colleagues.

She was provided with a secure reading room of her own at the agency. She was given the electronic codes needed to enter the suite of offices where the room was located. She had remarkably free rein in the building; when she needed a break, she headed off to the CIA cafeteria for a cup of tea.

She took notes on a laptop. Because her notes were as classified as the documents she was reading, they needed to be reviewed by a CIA lawyer before they left the agency as a printout. The lawyer who worked with Albion was concerned above all else with trying to protect information that would reveal "sources and methods"—the source of the information in the documents and how it was gathered. Albion and the lawyer got along well. Once her notes were released to the commission, Albion would transport them back to downtown Washington in a special lock bag.

Rudy rousseau did not volunteer for the job he was given by George Tenet. But after 9/11, Tenet needed someone he trusted to help organize the agency's vast archives on its counterterrorism programs over the years. The agency wanted to know what it had done—and more important, what it had not done—in response to the rise of Osama bin Laden beginning in the early 1990s. After Rousseau and his team had gathered the material, the CIA would have to decide which of the information could be released to congressional investigators and, eventually, to the 9/11 commission.

Rousseau understood immediately what a terrible assignment it would be, given how many divisions of the CIA had some responsibility for terrorism—and, therefore, how far he would have to dig to make sure that Tenet saw everything he wanted to see.

"You'd have to have your head examined to want the job," Rousseau said.

But he also knew that he was an obvious candidate for the assignment, given his past work in the CIA's Inspector General's office, where digging through classified archives was routine, and at the agency's counterterrorism center. He had also been a Senate staffer for a decade before joining the agency in the 1980s, so he had a good idea what congressional staffers investigating 9/11 would want from the agency.

In Albion's first few days reviewing documents in August 2003, Rousseau had something special to show her. He had arranged for her to look over "the Scroll," a massive chronology prepared after 9/11 to document every element of the CIA's antiterrorist effort before the September 11 attacks.

Albion's eyes widened as they rolled it out for her for the first time on the table in the reading room. It was a remarkable document, produced on a special agency printer that allowed vast amounts of data to be displayed on long rolls of thick white butcher paper. No one had ever measured it, but Rousseau thought the Scroll must have measured about 150 feet across—a day-by-day, hour-by-hour, almost minute-by-minute chronology of the agency's battles against al-Qaeda.

The information was broken down by activity. On one line was a timeline of the CIA's covert operations, set against another line that offered a chronology of the work of the agency's analysts; another line showed the agency's counterterrorism budget over time. The entries on the scroll were carefully footnoted to refer to the underlying documents, so Albion could go back and read the raw material for herself, if she wanted.

When she finished the Scroll, she moved on to the first of thousands of other documents that Rousseau had gathered for her. She would arrive in the reading room to find huge stacks of documents wrapped with rubber bands, many of them from the files of "Alec Station," the special office the CIA had set up in 1996 to do nothing but track al-Qaeda. (It was also known as the "UBL unit," for "Usama Bin Ladin"—the CIA's in-house spelling of his name.)

Albion was impressed. Over time, she came to see there was truth in what many at the agency had told her from the start: There were true heroes at the CIA in the war against bin Laden.

In the aftermath of 9/11, the CIA had been subjected to relentless and often justifiable criticism about its failures before the attacks. But Albion could also see that there were men and women—and a remarkably large number of them were women—who had given up the rest of their lives to the mission of tracking down Osama bin Laden. She could see that the UBL unit and its first director, Michael Scheuer, had crafted detailed plans to capture or kill bin Laden from his sanctuary in Afghanistan in the late 1990s; why the operations were called off was a mystery that Albion would spend months trying to understand. She wanted to be certain that whatever the conclusions of the commission's final report, it saluted the people who had done their jobs well.

She could also see that within the CIA, information did travel up and down the agency quickly and with reasonable ease, certainly better than at the FBI. There was no better evidence of the differences at the two agencies than what Albion discovered about the Moussaoui case.

Working with the FBI, federal immigration officers in Minneapolis arrested Zacarias Moussaoui on August 16, 2001. Based on his bizarre behavior at a local flight school, FBI agents were convinced Moussaoui, who held a French passport, was a Muslim extremist interested in hijacking a commercial jet. In searching through PowerPoint slides that had been prepared for briefings for George Tenet that month, Albion found an amazing sequence of slides dated August 23. One was labeled "Islamic Extremist Learns to Fly." It was about Moussaoui. The acting director of the FBI, whose agents had taken Moussaoui into custody and believed him to be a terrorist, would not learn about the arrest for another three weeks, not until the afternoon of September 11. Tenet, whose agency was watching the Moussaoui case only from a distance, knew about the arrest a week after it occurred.

WITHIN GEORGE Tenet's inner circle, a dangerous decision had been made in 2003 about the CIA's dealings with the 9/11 commission and other outside investigations. Tenet and his aides were going to try to make the argument that whatever had gone wrong in the months and years before 9/11, the CIA had actually done its job remarkably well on al-Qaeda. There would be none of the bowing and scraping that, they later learned, the FBI had done to try to placate the commission.

As Albion was discovering, the CIA had warned—consistently, for years—that al-Qaeda was a grave threat to the United States. There were many people in the agency, Tenet among them, who saw al-Qaeda and other terrorist groups as the most serious threat of the new century. A review of Tenet's congressional testimony and his speeches showed that he had warned, time after time before September 11, about bin Laden's intentions, including the possibility that he would acquire weapons of mass destruction.

In 1995, the CIA provided the White House with a national intelligence estimate, the term used for the agency's most authoritative, all-sources analysis of a particular national security threat, that was entitled "The Foreign Terrorist Threat in the United States." As Tenet reminded investigators later, the preposition in the NIE's title was not "against" or "to." The preposition was "in." It warned specifically that the sort of stateless Islamic terrorists who had bombed the World Trade Center in 1993 intended to continue to "operate in the United States." Their future targets would likely include "national symbols such as the White House and the Capitol and symbols of U.S. capitalism such as Wall Street."

In 1998, in the wake of the bombing of two American embassies in East Africa, Tenet issued a memo to employees at the CIA, the NSA, and other spy agencies about the threat of new al-Qaeda attacks. It was titled

"We Are at War." The question for Albion and her colleagues on the 9/11 commission was why so little seemed to have been done to respond to Tenet's government-wide battle cry.

From his initial sweep of the documents, Rudy Rousseau could see that the CIA had also repeatedly warned against just the sort of terrorist attack that had taken place on 9/11—airplanes as weapons. Rousseau had found several agency documents that reported on the possibility that al-Qaeda and other terrorists would use planes as missiles. He knew that this had been a specific concern just two months before 9/11, when Bush traveled to Genoa, Italy, for a meeting of the leaders of the so-called Group of Eight (G-8) of industrialized nations.

Rousseau also thought that the CIA's archives showed that the common wisdom in Washington about the CIA and the FBI—that they were locked in a tortured rivalry that prevented the sharing of information—was in many ways untrue. FBI agents and analysts were assigned to the CIA's bin Laden unit, just as CIA analysts worked at FBI headquarters.

For many weeks after 9/11, John Moseman, Tenet's world-weary chief of staff, was feeling surprisingly, if still warily, optimistic. He thought that when the full story of the agency's performance was told, the agency would weather the many outside investigations.

His confidence was shaken when he attended one of the weekly meetings on Fridays at which Rousseau's group updated Tenet and his aides on the seventh floor about the status of their work. They had terrible news. The team had gathered the files about Nawaf al-Hazmi and Khalid al-Mihdhar, the two hijackers who had lived in San Diego before 9/11, and determined that the CIA might have failed for more than a year to notify the FBI of the pair's presence in the United States. Even though the CIA had strong reason to believe in 2000 that Hazmi and Mihdhar were both at large somewhere within American borders, the agency had waited until just days before 9/11 to ask that they be added to the government's terrorist watch lists.

Moseman understood instantly what this meant. This would be the "smoking gun" anecdote that the investigators would seize on to blame the CIA for 9/11.

All of the good news about the agency's performance for the years before that would not matter. Tenet agreed. Rousseau tried to convince Tenet that there was a lot of "good news" about the agency's ingenuity in tracking Hazmi and Mihdhar until the moment they arrived in the United States.

"No," Tenet corrected him. "This is bad news."

BEFORE THAT, the agency felt, there was a remarkable, almost heroic story to be told about what had happened at the agency in late 1999 and early 2000 in the struggles against al-Qaeda. The CIA had managed to conduct surveillance of what amounted to an al-Qaeda summit meeting in Kuala Lumpur, the steamy capital of Malaysia, on January 5, 2000. Malaysia, a predominantly Muslim nation, was known to be home to a small but growing group of extremists loyal to al-Qaeda.

The impressive detective work had begun in late 1999, when the National Security Agency, through its electronic eavesdropping of a telephone number in Yemen used by al-Qaeda to relay messages, learned that several members of an "operational cadre" planned to travel to Malaysia in January. One of the men had the first name "Khalid," and the CIA was able to determine quickly that he was Khalid al-Mihdhar, a known al-Qaeda operative from Saudi Arabia. Another of the terrorists had the first name "Nawaf"; the agency would learn later that his full name was Nawaf al-Hazmi.

While Mihdhar was en route to Malaysia for the meeting, the CIA performed a bit of espionage wizardry. Through contacts at Persian Gulf airports on his route to Southeast Asia, the agency managed to get hold of Mihdhar's passport for a few minutes and photocopy several pages. The passport contained a multiple-entry American visa, an alarming bit of news. The surveillance information about the Kuala Lumpur meeting was widely shared within the American government in close to real time. Both National Security Adviser Sandy Berger and FBI director Louis Freeh were briefed on what was happening in Malaysia.

But the good work of the CIA ended there. The CIA learned that Mihdhar and two of the other Arabs had suddenly left Kuala Lumpur on January 8, headed to Bangkok, Thailand, where the local CIA station and its Thai counterparts lost track of them in that city's traffic-clogged streets.

In March 2000, the CIA's Bangkok station alerted CIA headquarters that "Nawaf" was Hazmi, now identified as one of the men who had met with Khalid, and that he had left Bangkok aboard a United Airlines flight to Los Angeles. Presumably, he was now on American soil.

Yet this critical piece of information—that a man closely identified with al-Qaeda terrorists, if not a terrorist himself, was in the United States in early 2000—apparently went no further for more than a year. The CIA would learn that Mihdhar had also reached the United States; he had traveled with Hazmi aboard the same United Airlines flight from Bangkok.

But none of that information was given to the State Department for its TIPOFF terrorist watch list. More important, it did not appear to have gone to the FBI. CIA files seemed to suggest that the agency's analysts intended to share the information with the bureau, but the FBI's files showed no indication that it was ever received.

Moseman came to believe there was a simple, innocent explanation for why the information about Hazmi and Mihdhar had not been watch-listed in early 2000: simple, total exhaustion.

The Kuala Lumpur meeting occurred at a time when the CIA and its analysts were recovering from weeks of some of the most frantic activity in the agency's history. The CIA had expected a series of massive terrorist attacks around the millennium—one, the bombing of Los Angeles International Airport, had been foiled—and its counterterrorism teams had been working round-the-clock for weeks. Many counterterrorism analysts had given up holiday celebrations with their families to be at their stations in case al-Qaeda attacked. By January 5, 2000, when the terrorist summit was underway in Malaysia, the agency's analysts were bone-tired; they were not much recovered by January 8, when the two hijackers left for Bangkok and disappeared.

But although that might be the explanation, Moseman also knew that fatigue would not be accepted by the 9/11 commission or anyone else as an excuse. He feared the CIA's failure to watch-list Hazmi and Mihdhar would be the "gotcha" anecdote that would threaten the CIA's very existence if investigators seized on it. "I kept wondering how it could have happened," he said of the day he learned of the blunder with Hazmi and Mihdhar. "I know that the rest of our record was so strong. Up to that moment, I thought we had tried our damnedest in every way to stop the attacks."

ROOM 5026
New Executive Office Building
Washington, D.C.
AUGUST 2003

There was a window in the reading room that had been set aside for Alexis Albion, the commission's chief researcher on the CIA, for her visits to Langley. When she needed a break, she could push aside the stacks of classified documents in front of her and admire the view out onto another part of the CIA's airy headquarters building. But Warren Bass, who had been assigned to review the archives at the National Security Council, had no view at all from room 5026 in the New Executive Office Building on 17th Street. The building was in the heart of downtown Washington, and the blinds had to be drawn at all times as a security measure, given how highly classified the documents were.

The room had been designated by the White House as the commission's reading room for documents from the National Security Council, and it was as dreary as the building itself. The New Executive Office Building, built in the 1960s to house the offices of lesser federal agencies, was a soulless bit of redbrick construction that had the only advantage of location. It was right behind Blair House, where the White House housed visiting heads of state, and only a block and a half from the West Wing. The commission's K Street offices were a ten-minute walk away.

Inside room 5026 was a thick-walled safe, where the secret files were stored between visits from Bass and others from the commission; a table where Bass could spread out documents; and a pair of computer terminals for note taking. The furniture in the room was standard government issue; in one of the chairs sat Bass's "minder," a lower-level White House official who had been assigned to keep watch on Bass as he worked.

As at the CIA, notes taken by the commission's staff needed to be reviewed by a White House lawyer and given a security classification before they could be moved to K Street. With few exceptions, the documents themselves could not be removed from room 5026. (In general, notes were classified at the same level as the documents they referred to, so Bass's notes about a "top secret" document would also have been stamped "top secret.")

It might have seemed a depressing place to contemplate spending weeks of his life in 2003. But Bass was exhilarated by his assignment. His doctorate from Columbia was in history, with a specialty in American diplomatic history, so the files stored in this reading room—the most secret documents maintained by the National Security Council under two presidents—would likely be the prize reading of his career.

Long before his first visit to the New Executive Office Building, Bass had an idea what he was searching for. He certainly knew he wanted to see the personal files of National Security Adviser Condoleezza Rice; her predecessor under Clinton, Sandy Berger; and Richard Clarke, the NSC's counterterrorism czar for both Clinton and the second President Bush.

Clarke's name was essentially unknown outside the government until 2004 and his startling public testimony before the 9/11 commission. But it was well known within the government, and there were rumors in 2003 at the State Department and the Pentagon that Clarke had left the Bush White House earlier that year in dismay over its performance on terrorism before and after 9/11. Clarke's small staff at the NSC knew the rumors were true, that Clarke was planning to go public, and that his NSC files would be a revelation for the 9/11 commission. Clarke's files, they knew, would help explain the mystery of why the Bush administration did so little in the spring and summer of 2001 to respond to the urgent warnings of an imminent al-Qaeda attack. They knew that much of what Clarke had written in the months before 9/11—his e-mails and memos and policy papers warning of catastrophe—had gone straight to his boss, Condoleezza Rice.

Bass was an urbane, quick-witted historian who had been recruited for the 9/11 commission from the Council on Foreign Relations in New York, where he ran a terrorism research program. Born in Boston and raised in Toronto, he was a citizen of both the United States and Canada.

His Canadian citizenship created complications when he sought a high-level security clearance to work for the commission. At an interview for his clearance, he was startled to be asked, apparently seriously, "If Canada and the U.S. went to war, which side would you be on?" He was asked if he would be upset if the United States bombed Toronto. After some delay, the security clearance came through. He was a fine writer, maybe the best on the commission. His first book, a well-reviewed history of the origins of the alliance between the United States and Israel, was published by Oxford University Press just as he was joining the commission. He signed on to the investigation knowing that Zelikow would be a difficult boss—in scholarly circles, Zelikow's ego and abrasiveness were no secret—but one still worth working for. Like Alexis Albion, Bass was only thirty-three, and for a young historian, Zelikow was a wonderful contact to have.

But the relationship quickly turned difficult. Bass and other members of Team 3, the commission's counterterrorism policy team, were startled to discover that Zelikow expected to be involved in the smallest details of their work. He virtually ignored the work of other teams of investigators; by mid-2003, many of the other teams had been pushed far across town to the commission's overflow space in an office building that housed employees of the General Services Administration, the agency that functioned as the government's real estate manager. The dark, claustrophobic GSA offices were known to investigators sent there as "the Cave."

The members of Team 3 were also alarmed by the revelations, week by week, month by month, of how close Zelikow was to Rice and others at the White House. They learned early on about Zelikow's work on the Bush transition team in 2000 and early 2001 and about how much antipathy there was between him and Richard Clarke. They heard the stories about Zelikow's role in developing the "preemptive war" strategy at the White House in 2002. Zelikow's friendships with Rice and others were a particular problem for Bass, since Rice and Clarke were at the heart of his part of the investigation.

It was clear to some members of Team 3 that they could not have an open discussion in front of Zelikow about Condoleezza Rice and her performance as national security adviser. They could not say openly, certainly not to Zelikow's face, what many on the staff came to believe: that Rice's performance in the spring and summer of 2001 amounted to incompetence, or something not far from it. David Kay, the veteran American weapons inspector who was dispatched to Iraq by the Bush administration in 2003 to search for weapons of mass destruction, passed word to the commission that he believed Rice was the "worst national security adviser" in the history of the job, a statement he would later repeat to Bob Woodward for one of his books.

For Team 3, there was a reverse problem with Clarke. It was easy to talk about Clarke in Zelikow's presence, as long as the conversation centered on Clarke's failings at the NSC and his purported dishonesty. Long before Bass had seen Clarke's files, Zelikow made it clear to Team 3's investigators that Clarke should not be believed, that his testimony would be suspect.

"I *know* Dick Clarke," he said; he argued that Clarke was a braggart who would try to rewrite history to justify his errors and slander his enemies, Rice in particular. The commission had decided that in its private interviews with current and former government officials, witnesses would be placed under oath when there was a substantial reason to doubt their truthfulness. Zelikow argued that Clarke easily fell into that category; Clarke, he decreed, would need to be sworn in.

WHEN HE finally got his security clearance and was allowed into room 5026, Bass discovered he could make quick work of Rice's e-mails and internal memos on the al-Qaeda threat in the spring and summer of 2001. That was because there was almost nothing to read, at least nothing that Rice had written herself. Either she committed nothing to paper or e-mail on the subject, which was possible since so much of her work was conducted face-to-face with Bush, or terrorist threats were simply not an issue that had interested her before 9/11. Her speeches and public appearances in the months before the attacks suggested the latter.

Tipped by an article in *The Washington Post*, the commission discovered the text of a speech that she had been scheduled to make on September 11, 2001—the speech was canceled in the chaos following the attacks—in which Rice planned to address "the threats of today and the day after, not the world of yesterday." The speech, which was intended to outline her broad vision on national security and to promote the Bush administration's plans for a missile defense system, included only a passing reference to terrorism and the threat of radical Islam. On the day that Osama bin Laden launched the most devastating attack on the United States since Pearl Harbor, bin Laden's terrorist network was seen by Rice as only a secondary threat, barely worth mentioning.

But if Rice had left almost no paper trail on terrorism in 2001, Clarke's files were everything that Bass could have hoped for. Clarke wrote down much of what he saw and heard at the White House, almost to the point of obsession when it came to al-Qaeda. Bass and his colleagues on Team 3 could see that Clarke had left behind a rich narrative of what had gone so wrong at the NSC in the months before 9/11, albeit filtered through the writings of the very opinionated Clarke.

Repeatedly in 2001, Clarke had gone to Rice and others in the White House and pressed them to move, urgently, to respond to a flood of warnings about an upcoming and catastrophic terrorist attack by Osama bin Laden. The threat, Clarke was arguing, was as dire as anything that he or the CIA had ever seen.

He pushed for an early meeting in 2001 with President Bush to brief him about bin Laden's network and the "nearly existential" threat it represented to the United States. But Rice rebuffed Clarke. She allowed him to give a briefing to Bush on the issue of cyberterrorism, but not on bin Laden; she told Clarke the al-Qaeda briefing could wait until after the White House had put the finishing touches that summer on a broader campaign against bin Laden. She moved Clarke and his issues off center stage—in part at the urging of Zelikow and the transition team.

Rice had admirably resisted calls to remove Clarke entirely from the White House staff, a fact that she would recall repeatedly after 9/11 in defending herself. But she had pushed Clarke so far away from the center of power that his warnings through 2001 about an imminent terrorist attack could be—and were—ignored.

By comparison, Clarke's files from the Clinton administration showed that he and the NSC's Counterterrorism Strategy Group, which he led, had enjoyed easy access to the Oval Office in the Clinton years. Bass could see from the paperwork that Sandy Berger, Rice's predecessor, had forwarded Clarke's e-mails and CSG memos directly to Clinton, often without changing a word. At Berger's recommendation, Clarke was made a de facto member of the White House Principals Committee when it discussed terrorist threats; that gave him regular face-to-face contact with the secretaries of state and defense, as well as with George Tenet at the CIA. Rice removed Clarke from the Principals Committee and forced him in 2001 to report up through the Deputies Committee, made up of the number two officials from the cabinet departments.

Bass told colleagues that he gasped when he found a memo written by Clarke to Rice on September 4, 2001, exactly a week before the attacks, in which Clarke seemed to predict what was just about to happen. It was a memo that seemed to spill out all of Clarke's frustration about how slowly the Bush White House had responded to the cascade of terrorist threats that summer. The note was terrifying in its prescience.

"Are we serious about dealing with the Al Qaeda threat?" he asked Rice. "Decision makers should imagine themselves on a future day when the CSG has not succeeded in stopping Al Qaeda attacks and hundreds of Americans lay dead in several countries, including the U.S. What would those decision makers wish that they had done earlier? That future day could happen at any time."

Bass's colleagues said he knew instantly that the September 4 e-mail was so sensitive—and potentially damaging, especially to Rice—that the White House would never voluntarily release a copy to the commission or allow him to take notes from the room if they came close to reproducing its language. Under a written agreement between the commission and the White House, notes could not "significantly reproduce" the wording of a classified document.

Bass decided he would have to try to memorize it in pieces, several sentences at a time, and then rush back to the commission to bat them out on a computer keyboard.

The day he discovered the document, Bass all but burst into the commission's offices on K Street and rushed over to Mike Hurley, the Team 3 leader. Bass had taken to calling Hurley "Chief" as a sign of humorous affection—he was Jimmy Olsen to Hurley's Perry White. Hurley, the veteran spy, was uniformly admired by his team members. Zelikow seemed a little intimidated to have a true spy on his staff. It was not so long ago, Zelikow and others knew, that Hurley was in Afghanistan, calling in air strikes that left the smoldering remains of Taliban and al-Qaeda fighters littered across the desert.

"Holy shit, Chief," Bass said excitedly. "You won't believe what I found."

He told Hurley that Clarke's September 4 memo was a "document that grabs you by the throat, a document that you write when you're at the end of your tether—or well past it," as Clarke clearly was in the weeks before September 11. Hurley instantly understood the significance of what he was being told by Bass. The question for both men was whether Zelikow would allow them to share any of it with the public.

Months later, Bass could not take it any longer. He was going to quit, or least threaten to quit, and he was going to make it clear that Zelikow's attempts at interference—his efforts to defend Condi Rice and demean Clarke—were part of the reason why. He marched into the office of Dan Marcus, the general counsel, to announce his threat to leave the investigation.

"I cannot do this," he declared to Marcus, who was already well aware of Bass's unhappiness. "Zelikow is making me crazy."

If he had ever felt any loyalty toward Zelikow from the early days of the investigation, it had evaporated. He was outraged by both Zelikow and the White House; Bass felt the White House was trying to sabotage his work by its efforts to limit his ability to see certain documents from the NSC files and take useful notes from them. Marcus urged him to calm down: "Let's talk this through."

The tensions between Bass and Zelikow had been building for months. Zelikow described his struggles with Bass as the result of an honest difference of opinion between two historians with a mutual admiration. Colleagues said Bass saw something much less innocent.

For a while, their struggles had seemed almost comical. Alexis Albion tacked up a poster from the Tom Cruise film *The Last Samurai,* with a photograph of Bass's head pasted over Cruise's. A photo of Zelikow's head was taped over that of Cruise's sword-wielding Samurai rival. Even Zelikow found that funny.

But as time had gone on, Bass had lost his sense of humor on the subject. He made it clear to colleagues that he believed Zelikow was interfering in his work for reasons that were overtly political—intended to shield the White House, and Rice in particular, from the commission's criticism. For every bit of evidence gathered by Bass and Team 3 to bolster Clarke's allegation that the White House had ignored terrorist threats in 2001, Zelikow would find some reason to disparage it.

Marcus and Hurley managed to talk Bass out of resigning, although the threat lingered until the final weeks of the investigation. Hurley thought that Bass's departure would have been a disaster for the commission; Bass was the team's institutional memory on the NSC, and his writing and editing skills seemed irreplaceable. Hurley could see that Bass's punishing workload was part of the problem; the whole team was overworked to the point of exhaustion. By the end of 2003, working past midnight and through the weekend had become routine on Team 3. Hurley asked Zelikow if he could hire a friend, Leonard Hawley, a retired West Point–educated solider who had worked in the State Department and the NSC, as a consultant. It would ease the workload on everyone. Hawley's calm and his sense of humor would be welcome on the staff, Hurley said.

Zelikow interviewed Hawley before agreeing to hire him. Zelikow seemed concerned by Hawley's work on the NSC in the Clinton administration, specifically about whether he had a friendship with Zelikow's nemesis Richard Clarke. Hawley did not deny that he admired Clarke. "But I think I'm a fairly independent guy," he told Zelikow. It was another hiring decision that Zelikow might quickly come to regret.

Washington, D.C.

SEPTEMBER 10, 2001

I n the summer of 2001, the nation's news organizations, especially
the television networks, were riveted by the story of one man. It
wasn't George Bush. And it certainly wasn't Osama bin Laden.

It was the sordid tale of an otherwise obscure Democratic congressman from Modesto, California, Gary Condit, who was implicated—
falsely, it later appeared—in the disappearance of a twenty-four-year-old
government intern later found murdered. That summer, the names of
the blow-dried congressman and the doe-eyed intern, Chandra Levy,
were much better known to the American public than bin Laden's.

Even reporters in Washington who covered intelligence issues
acknowledged they were largely ignorant that summer that the CIA and
other parts of the government were warning of an almost certain terrorist attack. Probably, but not necessarily, overseas.

The warnings were going straight to President Bush each morning in
his briefings by Tenet and in the PDBs. It would later be revealed by the
9/11 commission that more than forty PDBs presented to Bush from January 2001 through September 10, 2001, included references to bin Laden.
And nearly identical intelligence landed each morning on the desks of
about three hundred other senior national security officials and members
of Congress in the form of the senior executive intelligence brief, or SEIB,
a newsletter on intelligence issues also prepared by the CIA.

The SEIBs (pronounced "*seebs*") contained much of the same information that was in the PDBs but were edited to remove material considered too
sensitive for all but the president and his top aides to see. Often the differences between the two documents were minor, with only a sentence or two
changed between them. Apart from Philip Zelikow, the commission's staff
was never granted access to Bush's PDBs, except for the notorious August

2001 PDB that warned of the possibility of domestic al-Qaeda strikes involving hijackings. But they could read through the next best thing: the SEIBs.

It was startling to Mike Hurley and the other investigators on Team 3 just what had gone on in the spring and summer of 2001—just how often and how aggressively the White House had been warned that something terrible was about to happen. Since nobody outside the Oval Office could know exactly what Tenet had told Bush during his morning intelligence briefings, the PDBs and the SEIBs were Tenet's best defense to any claim that the CIA had not kept Bush and the rest of the government well-informed about the threats. They offered a strong defense.

Team 3's investigators began to match up the information in the SEIBs—and therefore, they knew, in the PDBs—with the discoveries being made by Warren Bass in the NSC files and by Alexis Albion at the CIA. And it showed that the chronology of warnings to the White House about "UBL" was long and troubling.

Team 3 pulled together a timeline of the headlines just from the SEIBs in the spring and summer:

"Bin Ladin Planning Multiple Operations" (APRIL 20)
"Bin Ladin Public Profile May Presage Attack" (MAY 3)
"Terrorist Groups Said Cooperating on US Hostage Plot"
    (MAY 23)
"Bin Ladin's Networks' Plans Advancing" (MAY 26)
"Bin Ladin Attacks May Be Imminent" (JUNE 23)
"Bin Ladin and Associates Making Near-Term Threats"
    (JUNE 25)
"Bin Ladin Planning High-Profile Attacks" (JUNE 30)
"Bin Ladin Threats Are Real" (JUNE 30)
"Planning for Bin Ladin Attacks Continues, Despite Delays"
    (JULY 2)

It was especially troubling for Team 3 to realize how many of the warnings were directed to the desk of one person: Condoleezza Rice.

Richard Clarke's e-mails showed that he had bombarded Rice with messages about terrorist threats. He was trying to get her to focus on the intelligence she should have been reading each morning in the PDBs and SEIBs.

From Bass's notes, Team 3 pulled together a chronology of the most alarming of Clarke's e-mails to Rice from the NSC archives, and they could see that a number of them involved the threat of a terrorist attack within American borders:

On March 23, Clarke warned Rice of the existence of Islamic terrorist cells in the United States and his fear that they might use a truck bomb on Pennsylvania Avenue, resulting in the destruction of the West Wing. Truck bombs were their "weapons of choice," he wrote.

In late March and early April, he relayed a number of reports to Rice from the CIA that Abu Zubaydah, al-Qaeda's planning chief, was making preparations for a major attack in a foreign country, possibly Israel.

On May 17, Clarke's Counterterrorism Strategy Group circulated an agenda for a meeting that would, as its first item of business, focus on "UBL: Operation Planned in U.S." It was a reference to an uncollaborated warning phoned into an American embassy the day before that bin Laden and his followers were planning a "high explosives" attack in the United States.

On May 29, Clarke suggested to Rice that she ask Tenet if there was more that could be done to preempt "a series of major terrorist attacks" organized by Zubaydah. "When these attacks occur, as they likely will, we will wonder what more we could have done to stop them," Clarke wrote; he would use similar wording in his "Americans lay dead" memo on September 4.

On June 25, he warned Rice that six separate intelligence reports showed that bin Laden's followers were warning of an imminent, calamitous attack.

On June 28, he told her the al-Qaeda threats had "reached a crescendo."

"A series of new reports continue to convince me and analysts at State, CIA, DIA and NSA that a major terrorist attack or series of attacks is likely in July," he wrote. He pointed out to her that an intercepted message between al-Qaeda followers warned of something coming that would be "very, very, very, very big."

Other parts of the government did respond aggressively and appropriately to the threats, including the Pentagon and the State Department. On June 21, the United States Central Command, which controls American military forces in the Persian Gulf, went to "delta" alert—its highest level—for American troops in six countries in the region. The

American embassy in Yemen was closed for part of the summer; other embassies in the Middle East closed for shorter periods.

But what had Rice done at the NSC? If the NSC files were complete, Bass and the others could see, she had asked Clarke to conduct inter-agency meetings at the White House with domestic agencies, including the FAA and the FBI, to keep them alert to the possibility of a domestic terrorist strike. She had not attended the meetings herself. She had asked that John Ashcroft receive a special briefing at the Justice Department about al-Qaeda threats. But she did not talk with Ashcroft herself in any sort of detail about the intelligence. Nor did she have any conversations of significance on the issue with FBI director Louis Freeh or with his temporary successor that summer, acting director Tom Pickard.

The records showed she had otherwise focused on al-Qaeda threats in detail only once that summer—and remarkably enough, it would involve the possibility of a suicide attack by al-Qaeda from the air. The threats centered on the G-8 summit in Genoa in July. Both the German and Russian intelligence agencies had warned of an al-Qaeda plot involving an aerial attack on the summit, and as a result, the Italians placed a battery of surface-to-air missiles near the seaport. The threats were taken so seriously that Bush's nighttime whereabouts were kept secret; he was reported to have slept aboard an American aircraft carrier that was stationed nearby.

There is no record to show that Rice made any special effort to discuss terrorist threats with Bush. The record suggested, instead, that it was not a matter of special interest to either of them that summer.

Bush seemed to acknowledge as much in an interview with Bob Woodward of *The Washington Post* that Bush almost certainly regretted later. In the interview in December 2001, only three months after the attacks, the president said that "there was a significant difference in my attitude after September 11" about al-Qaeda and the threat it posed to the United States.

Before the attacks, he said:

"I was not on point, but I knew he was a menace, and I knew he was a problem. I knew he was responsible, or we felt he was responsible, for the previous bombings that killed Americans. I was prepared to look at a plan that would be a thoughtful plan that would bring him to justice, and would have given the order to do that. I have no hesitancy about going after him. But I didn't feel that sense of urgency, and my blood was not nearly as boiling."

If anyone on the White House staff had responsibility for making Bush's blood "boil" that summer about Osama bin Laden, it was Condoleezza Rice.

LORRY FENNER was dumbfounded by what she was hearing. No one from the commission—no one—would drive the twenty-seven miles from downtown Washington north to the headquarters of the NSA, in Fort Meade, Maryland, to review its vast archives of material on al-Qaeda and terrorist threats.

There was no problem on the commission's staff finding people willing, eager, to spend their days at the CIA's headquarters in Virginia to review its files. Philip Zelikow had made it clear that he was fixated on George Tenet and the CIA's performance before 9/11, and his obsessions drove the workings of the rest of the staff.

But no one seemed worried about what the NSA knew, even though it was the NSA and its eavesdropping satellites circling the earth that allowed the CIA's analysts to do their jobs. In the case of al-Qaeda and other terrorists groups, the NSA's satellites and its ground-based wiretapping technology had managed at times to track the telephone conversations of Osama bin Laden and his sympathizers—and the terror networks' e-mail and faxes and every other form of communication that involved data transmitted by electronic pulse. Often, the CIA's analysts had little to go on beyond what the NSA's intercepts were telling them. Sometimes the NSA material was all that the CIA had.

So why wouldn't anyone drive up to Fort Meade? Assuming there was no traffic jam on the expressway between Washington and Baltimore—the NSA had its own exit from the road, marked with a sign that warned NSA EMPLOYEES ONLY—the drive to the NSA could actually be quicker than the drive to Langley. But for the commission's staff, Fort Meade might as well have been Kabul, it seemed so distant.

Fenner could see that some of the 9/11 commissioners and staff simply did not understand what the NSA was and what it did.

In terms of budget and people, the NSA was the nation's largest spy agency, much larger than the CIA. Their budgets were supposed to be secret, but the NSA was reported in 2003 to have a budget of about $6 billion, compared with $4 billion for the CIA. The NSA was an agency of superlatives; it was reported to be the world's largest owner of super-computers and the largest single employer of mathematicians. But for Zelikow and other staff on the commission, it was just more interest-ing—sexier—to concentrate on the CIA. To outsiders, the CIA was Hollywood; the NSA seemed like a geeky corner of Silicon Valley. Spies seemed more interesting than satellite hardware.

It was all the more frustrating to Fenner given the obvious willing-ness of the NSA, unlike so many other parts of the government, to coop-erate with the 9/11 commission. The NSA's director, General Michael Hayden, had thrown open its archives on al-Qaeda; Zelikow and others were impressed by his eagerness to help. But perversely, the more eager General Hayden was to cooperate, the less interested Zelikow and oth-ers at the commission seemed to be in what was buried in the NSA files.

Reviewing the NSA's terrorism archives was not part of Fenner's job. She had been assigned by Zelikow to a team of investigators that was supposed to be reviewing the overall structure of the intelligence com-munity and whether it needed revamping, not how the individual spy agencies had actually performed before 9/11.

But she knew the NSA and how valuable the archives would be, and she was determined to make sure somebody looked them over. She con-tacted the agency and organized a transfer of the archives—several file cabinets packed with documents—to a special reading room in the NSA's offices in downtown Washington. The NSA readily agreed. The files were moved to Washington at the end of 2003, which meant that the commis-sion would have several months to get into the archives before issuing its final report.

Weeks later, she was astonished to discover that no one from the commission's staff had walked the few blocks across town in Washing-ton to begin reading through the files. She thought about pressing the issue with the leader of her team, Kevin Scheid, a CIA budget officer on loan to the commission. But Scheid, like so many others on the com-mission, resisted any sort of confrontation with Zelikow; it was just too unpleasant.

She could go to Zelikow herself to urge him to assign someone to read through the NSA files. But to her later regret, Fenner decided she was too much of a military officer to violate the chain of command like that. She decided she would have to do this herself. Scheid would be annoyed at her absence, but she began to take trips to the NSA reading room to begin paging through the archives herself.

The reading room was only a short walk from the commission's offices on K Street. On the first visit, Fenner entered the reading room with trepidation, given the size of the task she had assigned herself. The file cabinets bulged with tens of thousands of pages of documents about the NSA's efforts to track bin Laden and al-Qaeda since the mid-1990s; she knew most of the documents would be densely written, with code names and abbreviations and acronyms and geographic locations that she would not understand. It would take several days of reading to get through even a small portion of it.

But it was soon clear that they were a gold mine of information about al-Qaeda and its connections—or lack of connections—to other terrorist groups and to other countries.

After several visits, Fenner came across a file that included references to Iran and the Iranian-backed Lebanese terrorist group Hezbollah and their possible ties to al-Qaeda. That was odd, even alarming, she thought. The United States had invaded Iraq that March; the Bush administration justified the war in part by arguing that Saddam Hussein was somehow connected to al-Qaeda. The government's concern was about Iraq, not Iran. Fenner kept reading, growing more worried about what she had found. Had the CIA just missed the Iranian connection to al-Qaeda in the Bush administration's single-minded focus on Iraq? Why wasn't anyone else interested in this? What else was in these files? The more she read, the more the knot in her stomach tightened.

— 24 —

K STREET OFFICES OF THE
9/11 COMMISSION
Washington, D.C.
JUNE 2003

Max Cleland said the "second grenade" hurt as much as the first, maybe more.

The first grenade was a real one, which went off at Cleland's feet as he stepped off a helicopter during the siege of the Vietnamese village of Khe Sanh in 1968. It blew off the twenty-five-year-old army captain's legs and his right arm.

What he called the "second grenade" was Cleland's defeat in his 2002 campaign for a second term in the United States Senate. As anyone who suffers from depression knows, there is physical pain attached to the mental anguish. And for Cleland, the pain after the 2002 defeat was searing—similar to what he remembered from all those years ago in Vietnam. "It was like that pain all over again," he told almost anyone who would listen after the election.

Cleland blamed the Senate defeat on two men: President George W. Bush, who had traveled to Georgia half a dozen times to campaign for Saxby Chambliss, Cleland's victorious Republican challenger; and Karl Rove, Bush's "hatchet man" in the White House.

They had turned the Senate campaign into a cynical referendum on Bush's performance in the fight against terrorism. The GOP was determined to take Cleland's seat, even if that meant suggesting to Georgia voters that a man who had left three limbs on the battlefield in Vietnam lacked patriotism. Cleland could not prove it, and Rove denied it, but Cleland believed Rove must have been behind the notorious television attack ads that fall that tried to link Cleland's image with that of Osama bin Laden and Saddam Hussein.

"Evil," he later said of the GOP's tactics in the race. "It's evil in its purest form, because George Bush and Karl Rove and Dick Cheney do not care who they go after, whose character they assassinate. If you stand in their way and disagree with them, they will try to kill you politically. They will trash you. They will bring up lies."

After the defeat, his friends from the Senate worried about Cleland's emotional state, even his stability. The ebullient, bearlike Cleland they knew from Congress was gone. He was replaced by a man consumed by the demons that he had first encountered thirty-four years earlier, when he woke up in a military hospital to discover what was left of his shattered body.

To his credit, Cleland did not deny what was happening to him as the depression worsened in early 2003. He was close to other Vietnam veterans from his years in the Senate, including John McCain, John Kerry of Massachusetts, and former senator Bob Kerrey of Nebraska, and they grew used to Cleland's late night telephone calls for consolation. Cleland would talk of how little the future seemed to hold away from the Senate, questioning whether he had a future at all. Some of his friends worried that Cleland was so despondent during those weeks that he might try to take his life.

He had thrown himself into politics in his native Georgia in the early 1970s, describing it as a type of "therapy." Two years after his return from Vietnam, at the age of twenty-eight, he was elected to the state senate in Georgia; he was the youngest senator in the state's history. In 1977, President Jimmy Carter brought him to Washington to run the Veterans Administration. In 1996, Cleland won the U.S. Senate seat. But his luck ran out in the 2002 election. If politics had been Cleland's "therapy," it now seemed that the therapist who helped him create this good, rewarding life had cruelly abandoned him.

He had lived off his Senate salary. The Senate had made his life comfortable in so many other ways; he had easy access to cars and drivers and a large staff on Capitol Hill and at home in Georgia. Now, it was all gone. His lowest moment in the weeks after the election came in December, when a restaurant valet in Washington, failing to understand the special driving controls in Cleland's 1994 Cadillac, plowed the car into a telephone pole. The car, which had allowed Cleland to travel around the city without help, offering him one treasured taste of freedom in his day, was totaled.

The bill creating the 9/11 commission was approved in Congress just days after the election, and it seemed a godsend to Cleland and to

Democratic leaders in the Senate. Majority Leader Tom Daschle was eager to create a soft landing for his old friend Cleland, a new job that would give him real purpose. The commission was ideal. It meant that Cleland could stay in the public spotlight on the national security issues that were his passion in the Senate.

Cleland was grateful to Daschle for the assignment, and friends could see a small glimmer of the old optimism as he prepared for his duties on the commission.

But the optimism evaporated as quickly as it had appeared.

By the spring of 2003, several of the other 9/11 commissioners had come to believe that the biggest threat to the investigation did not come from the intransigence of the Bush White House or the FBI or the CIA; it did not come from the refusal of the Pentagon and the FAA to hand over its full records from the morning of the attacks. The threat appeared to come from within the commission itself—from Cleland.

They felt that Cleland was so combative and harshly partisan in the commission's early private meetings—so angry at the mention of the names of Bush or Rove, so obsessed with what was happening in Iraq—that it threatened any hope of a unanimous final report.

Former senator Slade Gorton, who was considered second only to Tom Kean among the Republicans in his willingness to cooperate with the Democrats and to incur the wrath of the White House in the process, felt that if Cleland had remained on the investigation, it would have failed. "Max Cleland is an extremely embittered individual, and all he wanted to do was 'get' the president," Gorton said later.

It had come to the point where commissioners began to hope that Cleland would not show up for the commission's meetings. "He stirred things up every time he came," Gorton said. Lee Hamilton had not realized, and was startled by, "the depth of Max's bitterness about the Senate race—it hit him hard."

In the early closed-door meetings in 2003, Kean had struggled to convince the other commissioners that they needed to put aside their partisan differences for the good of the investigation. "We owe nothing to our political parties, and we owe everything to the people who died in New York and Washington," Kean would say.

Cleland's presence threatened to make it impossible. He demanded again and again that the commission investigate the Bush administration's reasoning for invading Iraq in March. He kept revisiting the question even after Kean and Hamilton made clear that they did not consider it part of the commission's mandate.

Kean had hoped that, with time, Cleland's outbursts would stop, or that at least he would tone them down. But the situation grew worse when Cleland decided to go public with his attacks on the president, the White House staff, and eventually the commission itself.

Cleland understood how alarmed others on the commission were becoming about the harshness of some of his rhetoric on the question of the Bush White House, but he felt he had no choice. He was just so mad. "I was about as hot as I could get," Cleland acknowledged later.

Quietly, Kean and the other commissioners began to look for a way to remove Cleland from the commission, fearing that if he remained on the panel, his outbursts would provide the White House with the political cover it needed to withhold any cooperation from the investigation.

Kean knew that Cleland's departure would have to be orchestrated with extraordinary delicacy. Cleland had become a hero to many of the 9/11 families early on with his eagerness—apparently not shared by the rest of the commission—to confront the White House.

Cleland's departure would mean the loss of the Bush administration's toughest critic on the investigation. Kean could imagine the headlines if word of Cleland's departure leaked prematurely or if it was depicted by the family groups as a move by the commission to placate the White House. Warily, Kean picked up the phone to call Tom Daschle and discuss the "concerns about Max."

CLELAND INSISTED it was his decision to leave the commission. He said he did not want to participate in anything that might be depicted in history as a whitewash of 9/11. "They didn't get rid of me," he said of the commission bitterly. "I got rid of them."

He was convinced, he said, that the Bush White House was orchestrating a "cover-up" of its intelligence blunders before 9/11 and that the commission was frightened of taking on a president who was then riding so high in opinion polls. "There was a desire not to uncover bad news, a desire to leave rocks unturned—both in the White House and, to a certain extent, on the leadership of the commission," he said.

Cleland said the final straw for him was Kean and Hamilton's refusal to draw an end to negotiations with the White House over the commission's access to classified documents, especially the presidential daily briefs. Cleland and other Democrats on the commission were convinced they should have been subpoenaed from the start.

"When I saw Mr. Hamilton and Governor Kean go hat in hand to the White House, I said, bullfeathers, we shouldn't be negotiating with anybody," he said. "When we were denied full access by every member of the commission to all of the presidential daily briefs, I knew this was ultimately going to be a sham."

At the urging of Kean and others on the commission, Tom Daschle arranged a new, soft landing for Cleland, this time on the board of directors of the Export-Import Bank, a federal agency that helps American businesses sell their products overseas. Two of the five seats on the bipartisan board were set aside for Democrats, and there was a vacancy in the summer of 2003. The appointments were much sought after, since they were full-time jobs that came with a salary of $136,000 a year, plus a full staff and spacious government offices on Lafayette Park, a block from the White House. Daschle submitted Cleland's name to the White House—the president has final say on the nominations—in July. The White House announced the nomination four months later.

It was an awkward decision for the White House. It pained administration officials to arrange a new, high-paying government job for someone who was such a venomous critic of the president and his top aides. At the same time, they were eager to see an end to Cleland's attacks on Bush and his "stonewalling" of the 9/11 commission; he would lose the platform that the commission had offered him.

At a news conference in Washington in December, Kean was asked about the reasons for Cleland's departure. A reporter noted that the circumstances of his White House nomination to the Export-Import Bank were "rather suspicious" given Cleland's public attacks on both the White House and the commission. Why would the White House agree to give the job to Cleland? Why was the commissioner who was most openly critical of President Bush leaving the 9/11 investigation?

"Anybody who knows Max Cleland would never question his integrity," Kean replied with what appeared to be anger, responding to an attack on Cleland's integrity that the reporter really had not made. "He would never take an appointment as a payoff, which you imply, at all. I just resent that on his behalf. Senator Cleland is an American hero, as far as I'm concerned."

Because it had taken several months to get Cleland nominated and confirmed to the Export-Import Bank, Daschle had much of the autumn to find a replacement. The commission's final report was due in May 2004, only several months away, and he needed to find a loyal Democrat who did not face a steep learning curve on national security issues.

He offered the job in December to one of his closest friends, Bob Kerrey, the former senator from Nebraska. Three years earlier, Kerrey had startled Senate colleagues with his announcement that he was retiring from Congress. He was leaving Capitol Hill for Manhattan, politics for academia. He had accepted the presidency of the New School, a university based in Greenwich Village that was best known for its respected, if eclectic, group of graduate schools, including the Parsons School of Design, the nation's best-known fashion school, and the Actors Studio, the famed drama academy.

Life in New York suited Kerrey. As often happens to politicians of a certain charisma and glamour, he seemed to outgrow Washington; the capital was too much of a gray, one-company town. By Washington standards, Kerrey had plenty of star power; he had famously dated the actress Debra Winger before marrying Sarah Paley, a screenwriter and former writer for *Saturday Night Live*. He had a heroic personal story before joining the Senate, which included combat duty in Vietnam as a navy SEAL; he lost half of his right leg to a land mine in Vietnam and was awarded the Medal of Honor.

His war record would be tarnished with news reports in early 2001, shortly after he left the Senate, that he led a raid on a Vietnamese village in 1969 in which as many as twenty-one unarmed civilians were massacred, including women and children. Kerrey did not dispute the essential details of the reports, acknowledging he was still haunted by the killings. "I thought dying for your country was the worst thing that could happen to you, and I don't think it is," he said. "I think killing for your country can be a lot worse."

Kerrey was tempted by Daschle's offer to replace Cleland. In the

Senate, Kerrey's expertise was in just the sorts of national security issues that were before the 9/11 commission; he had been the ranking Democrat on the Senate Intelligence Committee in the 1990s, when the al-Qaeda threat first emerged. But he did not accept Daschle's offer immediately; he asked for time to think it over. Kerrey had only recently married and had a two-year-old son—the boy, Henry, was born on September 10, 2001—and he told Daschle that he did not relish the prospect of being away from his new family in Washington for days or weeks at a time.

Finally, Daschle won him over. Daschle's aides knew that the commission offered Kerrey a chance to reintroduce himself to the public in a setting that would show Bob Kerrey at his best—smart, subversively funny, iconoclastic—and might dull the memory of the ugly stories about the 1969 massacre.

After accepting the job, Kerrey called his wife to tell her that he would need to cancel the couple's plans for a two-week Christmas vacation to Italy; he would spend it instead commuting to Washington to read up on the commission's work. He met Philip Zelikow in the offices on K Street, was given a desk, and got to work, grabbing the first of dozens of files of classified summaries of the commission's investigation to date.

On that first day, Kerrey came across a document that would almost end his work on the commission before it began. It was a written statement prepared by Zelikow for the commission's files about his ties to Condoleezza Rice and his work on the White House transition team in 2001 in reviewing Richard Clarke's counterterrorism operation.

Kerrey could not believe what he was reading—"just could not believe it." He had not known any of this. Zelikow's friendship with Condoleezza Rice was bad enough, but was it really possible that Zelikow had been an architect of Clarke's demotion only months before 9/11? Kerrey thought Zelikow's 2002 "preemptive war" strategy paper amounted to the "gene code" for Bush's Iraq policy. Kerrey wondered how Kean and Hamilton could have agreed to put someone with such an obvious conflict of interest in charge of the investigation.

He had a lunch scheduled the next day with Kean, and he confronted him about Zelikow.

"Look, Tom, either he goes or I go," Kerrey declared. "I don't know what you were thinking about putting him on the investigation. But you can't expect me to stay."

Kean tried to talk Kerrey out of any rash decisions. He explained that Zelikow's conflicts of interest had been a concern to the commission from the start and that Kean and Hamilton had kept a close eye on Zelikow for any action that hinted of partisanship. So far, he said, there was no evidence of it.

Kerrey was not convinced. He still held out the possibility that he would resign from the commission, but he agreed to continue the conversation with Kean. For Kean, it was hard to see which would be worse, the loss of Zelikow so late in the investigation or the angry resignation of a newly arrived commissioner because of Zelikow's conflicts of interest.

Kean agreed to meet up with Kerrey on an Amtrak train heading to Washington for the commission's next meeting, and the men talked for much of the trip. Kerrey learned what a generation of New Jersey politicians already knew—that Tom Kean was a grand master in the art of persuasion. Whatever his suspicions about Zelikow, Kerrey agreed to stay.

Kerrey's appointment to the commission was not considered good news throughout the Democratic Party, certainly not among officials of the former Clinton administration. Daschle had picked Kerrey over the opposition of other Democrats who knew that Kerrey's reputation in the Senate was that of a contrarian.

During Clinton's White House years, Kerrey had seemed to revel in attacking the administration. Certainly, Kerrey had never hidden his dislike of Bill Clinton. When both men were running for the 1992 presidential campaign, Kerrey had publicly described Clinton as an "unusually good liar," an insult that had lived on in virtually every political biography written about Clinton.

As he was about to prove on the 9/11 commission, Kerrey believed that Bill Clinton deserved just as much scrutiny as George Bush for the government's failures before 9/11 to deal with Osama bin Laden. Bush had eight months to worry about bin Laden before he attacked on American soil; Clinton had eight years. Democrats other than Daschle worried that they had just replaced the commission's fiercest critic of George Bush with a man who would prove equally critical of Bush's Democratic predecessor.

— 25 —

HOME OF LORIE VAN AUKEN
East Brunswick, N.J.
OCTOBER 3, 2003

The leaders of the Family Steering Committee could not put up with it—with him—anymore. By fall, the committee, which included the Jersey Girls and was the most aggressive of the 9/11 family groups, was convinced that Philip Zelikow had to go. It was not just his connections with Condoleezza Rice and his friendships with so many others in the Bush administration; the basic information about his conflicts of interest had been known for months. It was his arrogance in his meetings with the families. His haughtiness. His secretiveness.

The families had a justifiable sense of entitlement about the 9/11 commission. It was *their* commission, this was *their* investigation. The families knew for a fact, and no one disputed it, that the commission would never have been created without them. It was their daylong vigils on Capitol Hill and in front of the White House in 2002, their button-holing of lawmakers in the House and Senate parking lots, and those endless rounds of television and radio interviews that had shamed the White House and Congress into agreeing to an independent investigation of why their loved ones had been murdered.

So why was Zelikow, of all people, running this investigation? With each new disclosure about his relationships in the Bush White House, why did Tom Kean and Lee Hamilton choose to stand by him? To many of the families, it was clear that Zelikow was overseeing an investigation that would be—or at least should be—targeting people who were among his best friends and patrons. Rice in particular.

The Jersey Girls were fixated on Rice; they believed she was at the center of all that had gone wrong in the White House in the spring and summer of 2001 in its failure to respond to warnings that al-Qaeda was

about to strike. Among themselves, the Jersey Girls had taken to referring to Condoleezza Rice as "Kinda-Lies-a-Lot" Rice.

When challenged rudely by the families, Zelikow would be rude right
back, which only fed the families' anger. Kean and most of the other
commissioners were smarter than that. Kean was known for agreeing
to painfully long private meetings with the Jersey Girls and other 9/11
families and letting them vent their anger, sometimes for hours, about
the perceived failings of the investigation. He said he thought it was
their right to yell at him.

"I'd be yelling at somebody, too, if I had gone through what they had
gone through," he said. "I always had a feeling that, rational or irratio-
nal, they deserved to be heard."

A reporter from the Newark *Star-Ledger* was sitting outside Kean's
office at Drew University, waiting for an appointment, when he overheard the Jersey Girls laying into Kean from behind the closed door.
The reporter was so astounded by the attacks that he reported them on
the front page of the paper the next day. The story bore the headline
KEAN FEELS THE WRATH OF IRATE 9/11 FAMILIES. It reported that the meeting was "punctuated by shouts and table-pounding."

Zelikow was apparently able to put aside any sympathy he might have
had for the families. He would shout back. He stormed out of a meeting with the families held at a downtown Starbucks in Washington—the
families were not allowed into the commission's offices because they
did not have security clearances, which only added to their fury—after
Kristen Breitweiser, one of the Jersey Girls, challenged him again about
his conflicts of interest with Rice and others.

"That's right, Kristen," he said sarcastically, his face growing bright
red with anger as he stood up to march out the door of the coffee shop.
"Everything is connected. The hip bone is connected to the thigh bone
is connected to the knee bone is connected to the ankle bone. It is all
connected." He said later that many of the 9/11 family advocates had
gone beyond grief to "a further level of anger, which in some cases had
hardened into deep bitterness and mistrust."

By October, the committee felt it had cataloged enough evidence of
Zelikow's conflicts to go public and call for his ouster.

In a letter to Kean and Hamilton on October 3, 2003, they said the
commission had only two options—force Zelikow's resignation or

demand that he recuse himself from any part of the investigation involving the National Security Council; the second option would have effectively ended Zelikow's involvement in the parts of the investigation that
were most important to him.

Kean and Hamilton immediately rebuffed the committee's demands.
They wrote back to the families that Zelikow's ties to the Bush White
House were "not news to us" and that "Dr. Zelikow explained fully his
past association with government agencies and the breadth and depth of
his work experience before he was retained in his present position." They
said his "experience makes him an invaluable asset to the commission."

But were Kean and Hamilton right that Zelikow's conflicts were not
"news" to them? Had Zelikow really explained his background to the
commission in detail before he was hired?

Zelikow was clearly rattled by the call for his resignation. The families appeared to have sources on the commission's staff, and it seemed
only a matter of time before they figured out all of his ties to the Bush
White House, especially to Rice and Karl Rove. Would they learn about
the phone calls to Rove, all of the details about Zelikow's work on the
transition team? Better for Zelikow to tell the story himself than to leave
it to the families and the press to distort it and try to make a scandal of it.

Determined to remain on the investigation, Zelikow decided on a
preemptive strike. He wanted to turn himself into a subject of the investigation.

"I want to be interviewed," he told Kean and Hamilton. "I want to
be on the record about this." He wanted the commission's staff to conduct a sworn interview with him about his work on the Bush transition
team and his associations with senior officials in the Bush White House.
(Zelikow has said that he actually volunteered to be interviewed in the
summer of 2003 but that the staff was not "ready to conduct the interview until early October.")

The job fell to Dan Marcus, the general counsel, who readied himself
for the interview by gathering all the material that Zelikow had submit-
ted to Kean and Hamilton in the weeks before he was hired in January. He brought a copy of Zelikow's résumé to the interview, which was
held in the commission's conference room on K Street on October 8,
2003, only five days after the commission had received the families' letter demanding his removal.

Marcus thought it was silly to place Zelikow under oath, but Zelikow had insisted: It would be proof, he said, of his eagerness to tell the truth.

In personality, Marcus was Zelikow's opposite. Marcus was open, unpretentious, slow to anger. Where Zelikow saw information as something to hoard in accumulating power, to keep secrets to himself, Marcus was garrulous. He liked to talk—sometimes too much, he admitted. The principal criticism of Marcus from some of the Democratic commissioners and staff members was that he was too nice a guy, too unwilling to take on Zelikow.

From his first days at the commission that spring, Marcus had been concerned about Zelikow's conflicts of interest.

"Let me tell you something: I always worried about him, and so did a lot of other people," Marcus said later. He thought that perhaps Zelikow was just oblivious to the whole concept of a conflict of interest, that his ego was so large that he simply could not fathom the idea that he would be capable of something so pedestrian as protecting friends for some partisan reason.

Zelikow was "just blind to this stuff," Marcus said. "For a guy who is as smart and savvy as he is in some ways, he's just totally unaware, doesn't worry about these conflicts. I viewed it as one of my jobs to help protect him from himself."

Kean and Hamilton made it clear to Marcus that they wanted to keep Zelikow on, regardless of what Marcus found. It was too late to find a new executive director. Besides, Zelikow had made himself indispensable, if only because he had so tightly controlled the flow of the information within the commission that only he really knew all that was going on among the teams of investigators.

Kean and Hamilton believed that if Marcus determined Zelikow had major conflicts of interest, he could be recused from those areas of the investigation.

"I think Tom and Lee basically made the decision that they were going to stick with this guy, that it was too late in the game to make a change," Marcus said. "I don't remember whether I had a specific conversation with Tom or Lee about it. But it was pretty clear that my instructions were to do what we needed to do on the recusal front and to make it work. We were going to make it work." He said that Kean and Hamilton appeared to be motivated by a "combination of practical considerations and loyalty to Philip."

Zelikow was sworn in and took a seat at the commission's conference table. And over the next ninety minutes, he told a story that was especially shocking when heard in this much detail.

Yes, he had worked on Bush's White House transition team. Yes, he had, on Rice's behalf, reviewed the operations of Richard Clarke and the NSC's counterterrorism operation—the review that ended with what amounted to Clarke's demotion. Yes, he had written the national security strategy in 2002 that would later be used to justify a preemptive strike on Iraq. No, he did not see any of this as a major conflict of interest.

Marcus ran his eyes down Zelikow's résumé once again. There was nothing on it about his role on the Bush transition. Certainly nothing about his review of the performance of Clarke's operation. Nothing about the fact that he was the author of the "preemptive war" strategy paper.

Marcus shook his head. He was certain that Kean and Hamilton had not known these things; if they had, they never would have hired Zelikow. Certainly if some of the Democratic commissioners had known, they would have insisted back in the early weeks of the investigation that Zelikow be fired.

Marcus and others on the staff tried to imagine how Zelikow's conflicts could be any worse. They tried to imagine a comparable conflict on other important blue-ribbon commissions. It became a little parlor game in the office. Would the commission that investigated the *Challenger* disaster have hired a staff director who was a NASA lobbyist or an executive of one of the contractors that built the faulty shuttle? Would the Warren Commission have hired the chairman of the Dallas tourism board?

Marcus could not be certain, but he suspected that Zelikow might have kept the information from Kean and Hamilton intentionally, in the knowledge that he would never have been hired otherwise.

He could not say that definitively. "I have no idea whether they were deliberately blindsided or not," he said of Kean and Hamilton. But it was obvious that Kean and Hamilton had been blindsided. Zelikow, he said, "should never have been hired for this job."

Marcus took his findings back to Kean and Hamilton. If they were insistent that Zelikow remain on the investigation, his responsibilities would have to be curtailed sharply. At the very least, he needed to be recused from any part of the investigation dealing with the 2001 White House transition, and perhaps he should be excluded from anything involving the NSC, as the families had recommended.

Kean and Hamilton were surprisingly unconcerned at the discoveries about Zelikow. It reflected what Marcus saw as misplaced confidence by Kean and Hamilton and the other commissioners about their role in the investigation. Hamilton in particular seemed to believe that Zelikow and the staff were secondary to the investigation—that it mattered only what the ten commissioners thought and did.

"Lee had this view, which was somewhat unrealistic, that the staff was not important," he said. In Hamilton's view, Marcus thought, Zelikow might be the most important person on the staff, but he was still a "staffer" and was not capable of "sneaking something" by the commissioners.

The decision by Kean and Hamilton, at Marcus's recommendation, was that Zelikow recuse himself from all issues involving the transition from the Clinton to the Bush administrations and that he be barred from participating in any interviews of senior Bush aides, including Rice.

Zelikow was angry about the recusals, but he accepted them. He would have left the commission, he said, if he had been forced to accept the more sweeping recusals sought by the families. If the commission had tried to force him off all parts of the investigation involving the NSC, "it would have had the prompt and foreseeable effect of forcing my resignation."

MARCUS HEARD a knock on his door. Karen Heitkotter, the commission's executive assistant, entered. She was obviously nervous and upset.

"Dan, I need to talk to you about something," she said. "I'm not comfortable with an order that Philip has given me. He asked me to stop keeping records—phone logs—for his contacts with the White House."

She said that Zelikow had called her into his office, shut the door, and given her the order. He had not explained why he wanted no more records of the White House conversations; Heitkotter and Marcus both knew that it was not like Zelikow to explain anything he did. But Zelikow was insistent about it, Heitkotter said. She was worried that she was being asked to do something improper; one of her friends on the commission's staff, a lawyer, had urged her to tell someone in authority to protect herself if the information ever became public.

"I thought I should let you know," she told Marcus.

Marcus did not alert Kean or Hamilton to what had happened, nor did he confront Zelikow. He acknowledged that Zelikow's order on the phone logs "looks bad—it certainly doesn't look good."

But he figured that by late 2003 Zelikow's conflicts of interest were well-known to everyone on and off the commission; Marcus certainly did not want another fight with Zelikow, who was clearly growing paranoid about how closely he was being watched.

He thought there was a simple solution. He told Heitkotter just to ignore Zelikow's order. She should keep recording the calls.

"I told her to forget about it," he said. For his part, Zelikow later said that he issued no such order to Heitkotter, nor was he aware that any phone logs were being kept. "I don't think my office kept phone logs," he said. "I think this is recycled, garbled office gossip."

The existence of the logs and Zelikow's contacts with the White House were the talk of the commission's staff for weeks. Many staff members were furious about what appeared to be his surreptitious communications with Karl Rove and Condoleezza Rice. (Hamilton would later say he had authorized some limited contacts between Zelikow and Rice, especially over the logistics of a trip by the commission's investigators to Afghanistan and Saudi Arabia in 2003; but both Kean and Hamilton said they knew nothing about the calls between Zelikow and Rove.)

Several staff members debated whether to make a formal protest to Kean and Hamilton about Zelikow's continuing communications with his friends in the White House. They decided against it out of fear that it would throw the commission into scandal if it ever leaked out, jeopardizing so many months of their own hard work. It was a moment in which Zelikow's decision to hire so many young, ambitious people for the staff may have paid off. They were furious with what Zelikow had done and how his conflicts had threatened the integrity of the investigation. But they knew how valuable this work was and how valuable their affiliation with the 9/11 commission would be to their careers. They wanted its legacy to be untarnished.

Word about the phone logs also reached some of the 9/11 families, including the Jersey Girls, and they alerted the Washington bureau of *The New York Times* in November 2003.

It was a remarkable tip—why was the executive director of the 9/11 commission, already under suspicion because of his ties to the White House, swapping telephone calls with President Bush's top political adviser?

A reporter telephoned Zelikow, who seemed alarmed that the *Times* knew about his contacts with Rove and eager that this not become a story for the paper. It is not clear if it was the reporter's phone call that prompted Zelikow to order Karen Heitkotter to stop keeping logs of his White House calls, although that is a theory offered by some members of the commission's staff.

Zelikow said that there had been only one exchange of phone calls with Rove months earlier and that they involved questions involving his old job at the Miller Center at the University of Virginia.

A senior White House official, speaking on condition that he not be identified, said that Rove called Zelikow on behalf of a neighbor in Washington; the neighbor was in his nineties and had been a senior lawyer at the State Department at the end of World War II and had retained his files from negotiations over postwar economic recovery plans for Europe. He thought the Miller Center would want to talk to the man and see his files.

Zelikow said he instantly understood the potential appearance problem of any contact with Rove, so he cut the conversation short and referred Rove to the Miller Center. He said he had no further contact with Rove beyond the one exchange.

The reporter wrote a modest article for the *Times* about the contacts between Zelikow and Rove. Kean and Hamilton were interviewed for the story. Both said they knew nothing about the phone calls between Zelikow and Rove's office and seemed surprised by the news. But they said they accepted Zelikow's explanation that the contacts were innocent.

The article was not published in a crush of other stories at the time about the deteriorating situation in Iraq. So the reporter pulled the story back, asking for more time to see if there was evidence of contacts between Zelikow and Rove beyond the one exchange. There was no evidence at the time of Zelikow's continuing contacts at the White House with Rice.

The phone logs maintained by Karen Heitkotter showed that there were several phone calls from Rove to Zelikow's office telephone number over a four-month period in 2003—at least two in June and two more in September. The logs do not show Zelikow's calls out, nor would they show any calls on Zelikow's cell phone, on which he relied for most of his outgoing calls.

The General Services Administration, which maintains some of the telephone records from the 9/11 commission, would not release records showing the specific telephone numbers called by Zelikow on his cell phone. But the records do show frequent calls to phone numbers in area code 202, which is Washington, that begin with the prefix 456-. That prefix is exclusive to phone numbers at the White House. (In fairness to Zelikow, many if not most of those calls were almost certainly routine; he had frequent contact with White House lawyers over the commission's document and interview requests.)

Zelikow later insisted that regardless how many conversations he had with Rove, he was careful never to discuss the business of the 9/11 commission with him. Zelikow said he understood that would create an appearance problem. But White House officials contradicted Zelikow. A senior White House official familiar with Rove's memory of the contacts with Zelikow said there had been "ancillary conversations" about the workings of the commission.

OFFICE OF POLITICAL AFFAIRS
The White House
AUGUST 2003

K arl Rove had a surprisingly modest office on the second floor
of the West Wing. Alberto Gonzales and Margaret Spellings,
President Bush's domestic policy aide, were at opposite ends
of the same hallway, with much nicer corner offices. Scott McClellan,
the president's press secretary, had an office that was nearly twice as
large downstairs on the first floor, close to the Oval Office.

But despite everything else that he had accomplished in a career in
Republican politics, including electing a president and helping orches-
trate the GOP takeover of Congress, Rove insisted he was not one to
concern himself with the square footage of the office space he controlled. He had more important things to worry about in 2003, including
the work of the 9/11 commission. He would have been a fool not to keep
an eye on the commission, given the potential trouble it could create for
Bush on the eve of his reelection campaign—a campaign that would be
centered almost entirely on the president's record on terrorism.

Certainly the commission and its staff had a sense of being watched
by Bush's political guru. Some of the Republican commissioners had
heard from GOP friends that Rove had ordered up secret opinion polls
on the commission's visibility—and, as important, its credibility—with
the public.

John Lehman, whose support for John McCain in the 2000 election
had cost him most but not all of his friends in the Bush administration,
had heard that Gonzales's stubbornness in his negotiations with the
commission on legal issues was choreographed by Rove. Lehman said
Rove viewed the commission's work as a "mortal threat" to the president's reelection hopes in 2004.

"Absolutely Rove was very much involved," Lehman said. "Gonzales cleared everything with Rove." Lehman said he was told by Republican friends that "Rove was the quarterback for dealing with the commission."

The White House always denied it. Senior administration officials insisted that Rove was never as concerned about the 9/11 commission as the commissioners clearly wanted to believe. In modern American politics, there had never been anybody quite like Karl Rove—Darth Vader meets George Gallup, a political strategist who inspired fear, respect, and loathing in equal measure. Rove's formidable reputation meant that his hand was seen in many political disputes in which he actually had no involvement at all. Many Democrats tried to flatter themselves in the belief that Rove was obsessed with their every move—if Rove was targeting you, you must be important. In truth, Andy Card said later, Rove was never obsessed with the 9/11 investigation. He had too much else to worry about as the presidential campaign approached.

Still, it was hard for Tom Kean to forget that it was Rove who first approached him about running the commission. And Rove was part of the internal debates in the White House throughout 2003 and 2004 over whether to share documents with the commission and authorize interviews. Rove's office did do some polling about the commission; White House officials acknowledged that Rove's office conducted at least two polls that gauged the public's interest in the work of the 9/11 commission. In a GOP survey in early 2004, respondents were asked which of several news stories they were paying closest attention to. Among the possible choices: Martha Stewart's insider-trading case, Enron's collapse, and the 9/11 commission's investigation. The poll suggested that the commission's work was not high on the public's list of priorities, which was a relief at the White House.

Rove was among Kean's growing number of detractors in the White House. In many ways, it seemed, the White House should have been grateful to Kean, given his adamant early refusal to consider issuing subpoenas against the administration; a subpoena battle was a nightmarish thought among the president's aides. In an election year, could Bush afford a court battle in which he was seen as fighting to withhold subpoenaed information about his own performance on terrorism?

But in a White House that demanded total loyalty from within the GOP, that saw loyalty to the president as the same thing as loyalty to the party, Tom Kean was trouble.

Certainly Gonzales had come to believe that. In Gonzales's meetings with Kean and Hamilton, it was Kean who was adamant that the White House needed to turn over documents and make officials available for interviews. Kean was always much more agitated than Hamilton, sometimes coming close to raising his voice. Card, who had tried to convince Kean in their first meetings in 2002 to "stand up" for the president, was disappointed to see that Kean usually would not.

There was "angst that some of us were feeling about Tom Kean," Card said. "Is he a friend? Who is defending us over there? Who is looking out for us?"

The anger with Kean had spread to the White House press office, where Kean was seen as trying to resurrect a long-dormant political career at the expense of the president who had given him the honor of running the 9/11 commission. In the press office, Kean was referred to—out of earshot of most reporters, of course—as "the Has-Been."

The White House found that its best support on the commission came from an unexpected corner—from Lee Hamilton, the panel's top Democrat. Hamilton, they could see, was as much a man of the Washington establishment as he was a Democratic partisan. Probably more so.

Hamilton understood the prerogatives of the White House—in particular, the concept of executive privilege—in a way that Kean did not or would not. Cheney and Rumsfeld, Hamilton's old friends, let others in the White House know that Hamilton could be trusted.

"I came to really respect Lee Hamilton," Card would later say. "I think he listened better to our concerns than we had expected and maybe even heard our concerns better than Tom Kean." He said Hamilton was a "better listener than Tom Kean. I think Tom Kean had a tendency to speak before he absorbed everything that had been said."

In many ways, the White House came to see Kean as disloyal, effectively operating as one of the commission's Democrats, while Hamilton was a de facto Republican.

Kean and Hamilton could see that for themselves.

"I think the White House believed Lee was more reliable than I was," Kean said later. "They thought I was volatile." Hamilton thought that Gonzales in particular trusted him more as a go-between. "I think Gonzales felt I was the more reliable channel to convey the White House's feeling to the rest of my commission," he said.

Dan Marcus, the general counsel, recalled a funny, if slightly awkward, moment during the investigation when a CIA official arrived for a private interview with commission investigators and explained that she had once lived in Indiana, that Hamilton had been her congressman there, and how much she admired him.

Jim Thompson, the former Illinois governor, told the woman with a wry grin that it was not surprising she held Hamilton in such esteem. "Well, he *is* a Republican," Thompson said. The crack produced knowing laughter among the commission staff in the room.

At the White House, the other Democrats who had been on the commission from the start were considered partisans who could not be trusted, especially Richard Ben-Veniste and Tim Roemer. Jamie Gorelick seemed to be less partisan, more reasonable, but her connections with the Clinton administration made her suspect, too. The commission's new arrival, Bob Kerrey, was an uncertain commodity; the White House took some comfort in his past antagonism toward Clinton.

As THEY came to office in 2001, Bush and his White House treated John Lehman like a "pariah" because of his support for John McCain in the presidential election in 2000.

"They wouldn't touch me in the transition, even for a briefing, because I had been with McCain," he said. "I knew they hated me." If McCain had defeated Bush for the nomination and gone on to become president, Lehman would likely have been in line for a top cabinet job, maybe defense secretary or director of central intelligence. But in the Bush administration, he was a nonentity.

Outside the Bush White House, no one ignored John Lehman like that. He was described by friends and enemies alike as a force of nature. In his twenties, he was a brash top aide to Henry Kissinger in the National Security Council in the Nixon administration. In 1981, when Lehman was thirty-eight, Ronald Reagan named him navy secretary. Lehman oversaw a massive buildup of the fleet, which grew by more than a hundred warships during his six years in the Pentagon.

He also engineered the unthinkable at the navy—he forced the retirement of Admiral Hyman G. Rickover, the legendary if self-worshipping father of the nuclear navy; Rickover's cultlike following had allowed him to avoid normal retirement rules.

As he prepared to pack up his office in 1982, Rickover took the opportunity to go to Reagan and warn him that Lehman was a "pissant" and "goddamned liar" who knew "nothing about the navy." Lehman wore Rickover's insults as a badge of honor. After the Reagan administration, Lehman earned a fortune as an investment banker in New York.

The Bush White House's suspicion of Lehman began to lift several months after he joined the 9/11 commission. He was proving to be of help to the White House on the investigation when it came to Iraq. As much as anybody on the commission, Lehman was willing to listen to the administration's arguments about the possible links between al-Qaeda and Iraq and why the invasion of Iraq had been justified, in part, by Saddam Hussein's purported collaboration with Osama bin Laden.

There had been undeniable contacts over the years between al-Qaeda and Iraq. Saddam's intelligence agencies had approached bin Laden's representatives in the 1990s "if for no other reason than they really worried about these guys," Lehman said. Ultimately, he said, the Iraqis believed al-Qaeda was "a major threat to Saddam" and needed to be closely monitored in the guise of working together. There was solid evidence to show that Iraq had also provided al-Qaeda with weapons training over time.

Lehman was open to conversation at the White House about its theories, promoted most heavily by Paul Wolfowitz at the Pentagon, that the ties between Iraq and the terrorist network went well beyond weapons training. In 2003 and 2004, Lehman was given frequent meetings at the Pentagon and the White House, including with Cheney, Card, Rumsfeld, and Wolfowitz.

The White House was trying to cheer Lehman on, to urge him to keep asking questions that might cement in the public's mind the idea that Saddam Hussein was al-Qaeda's patron—more ominously, that Iraq's rumored stockpiles of weapons of mass destruction might eventually end up in bin Laden's hands for use against the United States.

The White House told Lehman it could not share with him every bit of intelligence it had to demonstrate al-Qaeda's ties with Iraq—the material was just too closely held, too classified—but he should take it on faith that the intelligence existed. He could "take it to the bank." He remembered Wolfowitz telling him, "Just wait until you see the evidence we've got."

"I got that line from everybody I talked to: 'Wait and see, just wait until you see the evidence,'" Lehman said. It would take almost a year for him to understand fully how wrong the administration had been about Iraq and al-Qaeda. "I think they were all drinking their own bathwater," Lehman said later.

— 27 —

OFFICES OF THE DIRECTOR OF CENTRAL INTELLIGENCE
CIA Headquarters
Langley, Va.
SEPTEMBER 2003

In the fall of 2003, Lee Hamilton wanted to see George Tenet, and the former congressman was invited to join Tenet for breakfast at CIA headquarters in Langley. The two men had known each other for a quarter century, since Tenet's days as a junior staffer on Capitol Hill, and they had always gotten along. Hamilton had always admired Tenet's gruff, slap-on-the-back charm and his ability to turn potential adversaries into members of his admiration society. Hamilton had barely sat down before Tenet answered the most important question that Hamilton was there to ask.

"Lee, you're not going to get access to them," Tenet blurted out before either man had taken a mouthful of his breakfast. "It's not going to happen. Meeting adjourned."

Tenet had gotten advance warning of why Hamilton was there—to request access on behalf of the commission to senior al-Qaeda terrorists captured after 9/11. At the top of Hamilton's list were Khalid Sheikh Mohammed, the mastermind of the 9/11 plot, known throughout the intelligence community as "KSM"; and Ramzi bin al-Shibh, the young Yemeni who was the plot's middleman in Germany. Both men had been captured in Pakistan and were then being held, it was reported, in secret prisons that the CIA had established in Eastern Europe and Southeast Asia. The conditions of their confinement and the methods of their interrogation were a mystery at the time outside the CIA, although no one assumed they were being treated with kid gloves.

Apart from Osama bin Laden himself, it was unlikely that anyone knew more than KSM and bin al-Shibh about the logistics of the 9/11 plot, how it was financed, and if foreign governments had provided assistance to the hijackers.

The head of the commission's "plot" team of investigators, Dieter Snell, a former assistant United States attorney in New York who had helped prosecute Ramzi Youssef, the 1993 World Trade Center bomber, insisted that there be face-to-face interrogations of al-Qaeda suspects in American custody.

Snell was described by Justice Department colleagues as a true by-the-book prosecutor—an exceptionally decent and honest lawyer who was wedded to rules and regulations, sometimes to the point where he could appear inflexible. Snell joked that it was part of his heritage. He had been raised by German-born parents in New York City, and German was the language spoken in his home; Zelikow could see how that would be of value when it came time for the commission to consult German prosecutors about their monitoring of the al-Qaeda cell in Hamburg that had carried out the attacks.

At the Justice Department, Snell was seen as more insistent than other prosecutors in bringing an indictment only if there was near 100 percent certainty of a defendant's guilt. He did not want to go to trial unless he was convinced that he would, and should, win. His dedication to protecting the innocent was admired by defense lawyers in New York City.

And even though this was not a criminal prosecution, he seemed determined to try to bring the same standards to the evidence and proof before the 9/11 commission. Snell knew that testimony from key witnesses like the al-Qaeda detainees would have value only if they were questioned in person, with investigators given the chance to test their credibility with follow-up questions. The face-to-face interrogations would be especially important in situations in which the al-Qaeda members were giving conflicting testimony.

Hamilton had gone to see Tenet to make the case.

"It's just not going to happen," Tenet repeated, trying to preempt Hamilton from asking any more questions on the subject of the captured terrorists and their whereabouts. "Not even the president of the United States knows where these people are," he said. "And he does not have access to them. And you're not going to get access to them." Hamilton could see this was a "bright line" for Tenet. The conversation was over.

THE COMMISSION had first requested information about the detainees in June 2003, when it put in a written request to the CIA, FBI, and Pentagon for "all reports of intelligence information" from a list of the key captured al-Qaeda suspects. There was no request for the full interrogation reports; the commission wanted only the information the terrorists had revealed about the 9/11 plot and their activities before the attacks.

Within months, the commission had begun to receive partial interrogation reports reflecting interviews with some of the detainees. But Snell and the others on the team could see that partial reports were inadequate; they addressed few of the questions that the "plot" team needed to answer. The CIA and Pentagon interrogators were not focused on 9/11 and al-Qaeda's activities before the attacks; their focus, understandably, was on learning what future attacks al-Qaeda was planning and trying to preempt them.

Despite Hamilton's unsuccessful lobbying effort with Tenet, Snell continued to press the commission to demand access to the detainees. "They're the only people who really know what happened" on 9/11, he said. Snell had gone so far as to offer to fly anywhere on Earth wearing a blindfold if that was what it took to protect the secrecy of the CIA's interrogation sites. There was an offer to question the detainees by videoconference, or to observe questioning through one-way glass. Tenet, with the blessings of the White House, rejected all of the commission's proposals.

MIKE JACOBSON could tell that dealing with Snell, his new boss on the commission, was not going to be easy. From his years as an intelligence analyst at the FBI, Jacobson knew that the 9/11 commission was making a mistake if it tried to bring courtroom standards of proof to the investigation. Gathering information about al-Qaeda and other shadowy terrorist networks was like doing a jigsaw puzzle, albeit with the understanding that important pieces of the puzzle had been lost long ago and were irretrievable. The 9/11 commission was not like a criminal prosecution; there was never going to be 100 percent proof of anything. If the CIA waited for guilt beyond a reasonable doubt to move against the country's enemies, it would never act against anyone (and the agency was commonly accused of inaction anyway, of course).

In his first weeks on the commission, Jacobson was still trying to figure out what to make of the astonishing documents that he had uncovered buried in the FBI's files in Washington and San Diego.

During the congressional investigation into 9/11, where he had worked until he was hired by the commission in 2003, it was Jacobson who had uncovered the evidence to suggest that two of the 9/11 hijackers—Nawaf al-Hazmi and Khalid al-Mihdhar—had a support network in Southern California, a network that appeared to be connected somehow to the government of Saudi Arabia. Jacobson knew how explosive that might be.

He had been frustrated at how much more was left to do when the congressional investigation shut down in 2003. He was convinced that FBI officials had tried to hide much of the evidence in its files that was connected to the two hijackers, and he knew there was much he probably still had not seen.

He wanted the commission to press the Saudi government for access to Omar al-Bayoumi, the Saudi middleman in San Diego who had befriended the two hijackers, and even more importantly to Fahad al-Thumairy, the former Saudi diplomat in Los Angeles. Both Bayoumi and Thumairy were back in Saudi Arabia. Thumairy was not at home by choice; he had been banned from resuming his diplomatic duties in the United States because of his alleged ties to terrorists.

With Dana Lesemann's firing, Jacobson had lost his most knowledgeable ally in the hunt for new information in San Diego. But he had eager new allies when Zelikow assigned Raj De, the young Harvard Law School graduate, and Hyon Kim, a former FBI lawyer who had also worked on the Senate Intelligence Committee, to the "plot" team.

As De and Kim listened to Jacobson offer a primer on the mysteries of San Diego, they could see few innocent explanations for why so many Saudis and other Arab men living in Southern California had come forward to try to help the two hijackers—to help them find a home, to set up bank accounts, to travel.

At first, Jacobson and the others found the FBI to be as uncooperative with the 9/11 commission as it had been in the congressional investigation. It was painfully slow to meet the commission's initial request for documents and interviews. Had Robert Mueller learned nothing from the congressional inquiry, which ended with a recommendation that the government seriously consider breaking up the FBI?

Jacobson knew that the cautious Snell would never join any sort of formal protest over the FBI's obstruction—that would have been too confrontational for the hypercautious Snell—so they went around him to Jamie Gorelick. She was among the most approachable of the commissioners, and she knew the FBI from her years at the Justice Department. Gorelick went to see Mueller personally to complain. She warned him that he was fast losing the goodwill of the commission. If Mueller wanted to save the FBI, he needed to listen and cooperate.

JACOBSON AND the others had an ally in John Lehman. Just as he was worried about ties between Iraq and al-Qaeda, Lehman was also concerned about a Saudi tie to the 9/11 plot itself. He thought it was clear early on that there was some sort of Saudi support network in San Diego that had made it possible for the hijackers to hide in plain sight in Southern California.

He was especially intrigued by the thousands of dollars' worth of "charity" checks that had been signed by the wife of the Saudi ambassador to Washington and how that money had ended up in the bank accounts of the men in Southern California who had befriended Hazmi and Mihdhar.

Lehman was convinced that Princess Haifa, the ambassador's wife, had no idea where the money was going to end up. She had simply signed checks that had been put in front of her by the radicals who worked in the embassy's Islamic affairs office in Washington. Lehman said it was well-known in intelligence circles that the Islamic affairs office functioned as the Saudis' "fifth column" in support of Muslim extremists.

When he went to the White House to talk about a possible connection between Iraq and al-Qaeda (a conversation the White House was eager to have), Lehman also brought up Saudi Arabia (a conversation the White House never wanted to have).

Lehman was struck by the determination of the Bush White House to try to hide any evidence of the relationship between the Saudis and al-Qaeda. "They were refusing to declassify anything having to do with Saudi Arabia," Lehman said. "Anything having to do with the Saudis, for some reason, it had this very special sensitivity."

He raised the Saudi issue repeatedly with Andy Card. "I used to go over to see Andy, and I met with Rumsfeld three or four times, mainly to say, 'What are you guys doing? This stonewalling is so counterproductive.'"

Of the leaders of Saudi Arabia, Lehman said, "Everybody knows that they've got a pact with the devil." The Saudi royal family held on to power through its alliance with leaders of the extremist, anti-Western Wahhabi branch of Islam, and for years, Wahhabi imams had been "telling Saudis that it's their duty to go and kill Americans," Lehman said.

So was it surprising, he wondered, if a low-level Saudi diplomat and others connected to the Saudi government had agreed to help out two men tied to al-Qaeda after they landed in California? Lehman was not necessarily alleging that Saudi officials, either in Riyadh or San Diego, knew the details of the 9/11 plot. But he believed they did know that Hazmi and Mihdhar were "bad guys" who intended to harm the United States. "The bad guys knew who to go to to get help," he said.

— 28 —

K STREET OFFICES OF THE
9/11 COMMISSION
Washington, D.C.
DECEMBER 11, 2003

M ike Scheuer wanted to be under oath. So many people were lying, were spinning—even former colleagues at the CIA, the institution he loved no matter how often and enthusiastically it had tried to humiliate him. He did not want there to be any question about his truthfulness. So bring out a Bible and swear me in, send me to jail if I'm lying, he challenged them.

Scheuer made the request to be sworn in almost as soon as he took a seat in the conference room in the commission's K Street offices on Thursday, December 11. It would be the first of three long, private interviews with the commission. He sat across the table from Alexis Albion, the commission's investigator who had spent weeks reviewing Scheuer's files at the CIA. Scheuer had been the first director of the agency's Osama bin Laden unit—"Alec Station," it was called—after it was created in 1996.

"I'd prefer to testify under oath," he explained to Albion and the others, tugging at thick glasses that gave him the look of a bookish scholar—albeit a scholar, they all knew, whose mission was to kill the person who was the focus of all his research. "I'm not going to tell you anything I can't document."

In case his memory failed him, Scheuer had brought documents, too. He clutched a loose-leaf notebook with about five hundred pages of the most important e-mails, cables, and memos from his years in the search for bin Laden.

He tried to hand over the notebook to Philip Zelikow, who was at the session; but Zelikow declined, saying it needed to pass through the CIA's declassification process before it could be accepted by the commission.

"All right, sir," said Scheuer, whose father was a marine and who spoke with an almost rigid politeness, full of "sirs" and "ma'ams."

Albion and the others were surprised by Scheuer's request to be sworn in. Zelikow had asked to be sworn in for his awkward interview several weeks earlier. Other than Zelikow, no other witness during the investigation had requested an oath—no surprise, since it opened a witness to a possible perjury charge. Scheuer did not realize it, but with or without an oath, he had had plenty of credibility with Albion and the others long before he walked through the doors on K Street.

Among some of the commission's staffers, Scheuer had a nickname: "the Prophet." More than anybody else in the CIA, and much earlier, Michael Scheuer had understood the danger that Osama bin Laden posed to the United States. For four of his twenty-two years at the CIA, until he was ousted from the bin Laden unit and banished to a small cubicle in the agency's library in 1999, he had done little but think of ways to capture or, preferably, kill bin Laden.

George Tenet could point to the creation of the unit in 1996 as early evidence of the CIA's commitment to dealing with the threat of bin Laden. It was a "virtual station," which meant it functioned like an overseas CIA post, with a specific foreign target, but was physically located inside the United States. In part to inspire out-of-the-box thinking, its offices were away from the agency's headquarters in Langley. They were put in a nearby office complex in northern Virginia, close to the sprawling Tysons Corner shopping center. Scheuer liked the location. "It was a good idea because it kept us away from the crap" back at Langley, he said.

Within a year, the unit had determined that bin Laden was much more than a terrorist financier; he was organizing military-style terrorist attacks against the Untied States and its allies.

"By 1997, we had more information on al-Qaeda than we had on terrorist groups we had been collecting against for twenty years," he said. "And it's not because we were great at it. We did some very good operations, but we had a couple of walk-ins that were just golden, because they not only corroborated what we had collected, they added to it."

He was referring, specifically, to the most important of the "walk-in" al-Qaeda defectors—Jamal Ahmed al-Fadl, a Sudanese-born Arab who had been a trusted lieutenant of bin Laden's in Khartoum, the Sudanese capital. Bin Laden had lived in Sudan from 1991 to 1996. Fadl defected to the United States in late 1996 with a wealth of information about al-Qaeda, its organization and its plans.

If Scheuer had a message for the 9/11 commission in his interviews, it was this: He believed the CIA had done an extraordinary job tracking bin Laden since the mid-1990s, and there had been real, if missed, opportunities to capture or kill him during the Clinton administration. What had been lacking for so many years was the bravery, both at the White House and within the CIA, needed to get bin Laden, said Scheuer.

"I think what's going to come out eventually is that there's never been a lack of intelligence," he said. "The intelligence has been good on this issue."

The CIA's files were full of evidence of Scheuer's personal obsession with al-Qaeda. The sign-in sheets from Alec Station showed he often entered his offices at 4:30 in the morning and left long after his children—including his son, Alec, whose name was given to the unit— had gone to bed.

Scheuer explained that he first came to realize that bin Laden was a "truly dangerous, dangerous man" after reading his fatwa—his declaration of war—against the United States in August 1996. The fatwa condemned the Saudi royal family for having allowed American troops to be stationed in the kingdom, home to Islam's holiest sites, and called for a Muslim war to drive out the Americans.

Scheuer remembered very clearly sitting at his desk at Alec Station one morning in September 1996, reading through the twelve-page translation of the fatwa and thinking, My God, it sounds like Thomas Jefferson. This was not a "rant" by some crazed religious fanatic. Instead, the fatwa read like "our Declaration of Independence—it had that tone. It was a frighteningly reasoned argument." It contained none of the usual Islamic extremist rhetoric about the dangers of "women in the workplace or X-rated movies."

Instead, it was a clear statement of how a generation of Muslims was outraged at the Western exploitation of Arab oil, at American support for Israel, and, most important, at the presence of infidel American troops in the land of the prophet Muhammad. "There was no ranting in it," Scheuer said of the fatwa. "These were substantive, tangible issues."

Early on, it was tough for Scheuer and his colleagues to convince senior officials in the Clinton administration that bin Laden posed a threat that was worth much of their time. "They could not believe that this tall Saudi with a beard, squatting around a campfire, could be a threat to the United States of America," Scheuer recalled.

It was a tough argument to make even among some of his superiors at the CIA. In December 1996, Alec Station prepared a fifty-paragraph memo, based on information from Fadl, about bin Laden's efforts to acquire weapons of mass destruction, including a nuclear device. Fadl described in alarming detail how bin Laden had sought out scientists and engineers to help him obtain enriched uranium and then convert it into a weapon.

Scheuer sent the memo to Langley, urging that it be distributed widely throughout the agency. Terrorists with nuclear weapons? It was too terrifying to contemplate. "We'd never seen anything like this," Scheuer said.

But his superiors at CIA headquarters refused, saying the report was alarmist and wouldn't be taken seriously; they agreed to circulate only two paragraphs from the report and only if they were buried in a larger memo. "They thought it was impossible for a terrorist group to have weapons of mass destruction," Scheuer said. It took almost a year for Alec Station to have the full report distributed within the agency. After 9/11, Fadl's information about bin Laden's nuclear plans was confirmed by documents seized from al-Qaeda's former hideouts in Afghanistan.

But if the files of Alec Station were a tribute to Scheuer's commitment to the mission, Albion and the others knew that they were also evidence of failure. It may have been an impossible job to begin with, but Scheuer had failed to convince his superiors at the CIA and further up the chain of command—at the Pentagon, the State Department, the White House—of the bin Laden threat.

Scheuer's passion may have been part of the problem. His father was a marine, he was educated by Jesuits, and it showed. He was committed to his mission to the point of what some of his colleagues saw as zealotry. It could be offputting. His eyes almost glowed with passion; it had made many of his colleagues at the CIA uncomfortable.

They caustically dismissed Scheuer and his team of about twenty analysts, most of them women, as the "Manson family," a description that infuriated Scheuer, who knew how much his colleagues, especially the women, had sacrificed for their work. "We had marriages break up, we had people who delayed operations they needed," he said. "People were working sixteen, seventeen hours a day, some of them seven days a week for years."

Scheuer explained to Albion and the others that he was eager to cooperate with the investigation because he expected the commission to demand accountability of government officials who had failed to do their jobs before 9/11, who had ignored the clear warnings of catastrophe. Alec Station had done its work. Others had not.

"You need to look to see what people did or did not do to protect America," he said, looking at Albion for some recognition that she agreed with him. He wanted these people fired, maybe prosecuted.

"I am big on personal accountability. I'm not sure we could have stopped this attack, but I know for a fact that we didn't do everything we could. I do think that if we had killed bin Laden in the desert, this never would have happened," he said of 9/11. "If you find something wrong that I did, then tell me, accuse me or fire me, but I'm not the only guy around who deserves that kind of scrutiny."

At the top of the list of culprits, he said, was Richard Clarke, the White House counterterrorism czar. Scheuer insisted that Clarke had repeatedly foiled the CIA's plans during the Clinton administration to kill bin Laden and his henchmen in their sanctuary in Afghanistan.

He believed Clinton himself had been eager to kill bin Laden. Scheuer disdained Bill Clinton for his personal conduct—"the nightmare of the kind of guy you don't want your daughter to bring home"— but he admired Clinton's cold-bloodedness on the question of al-Qaeda. Scheuer was certain that Clinton would have been overjoyed if someone had brought the news that bits and pieces of bin Laden's flesh had been found strewn across the desert after a missile attack. "Clinton was ruthless, and that was fine by me," Scheuer said.

But the man who filtered the information that had gone to the Oval Office, Clarke, had suppressed it, or so Scheuer believed.

"Clarke scared people at the upper levels of the agency," Scheuer said, describing how Clarke would try to intimidate CIA officials who brought plans to the White House for missile attacks on bin Laden and his compound. Clarke, he said, would sneer at them as thinly veiled and possibly illegal assassination plans.

To Scheuer, Clarke "talked a big game" about killing bin Laden, but he would not take the risk of supporting a plan to carry it out that might fail and tarnish Clarke's golden career.

Scheuer had believed that several of the capture plans developed by his unit would have worked if someone had shown the guts to act on them.

The best of the plans, which Scheuer described as "the perfect operation," was drawn up in 1997 and 1998 and called for Afghanistan tribal leaders working with the CIA to snatch or kill bin Laden in a nighttime raid on Tarnak Farms, his training camp near Kandahar. If bin Laden had been captured, the plan was for the tribes to turn him over—days or weeks later—to the United States. Through satellite surveillance and other intelligence sources, the CIA had managed to map out Tarnak Farms; Scheuer and his colleagues had a good idea where bin Laden and his wives slept at night in the camp. The operation was reviewed by the Pentagon, which found the plan remarkably well crafted. Scheuer said that one of the CIA top field officers working in Afghanistan gave the plan a 50 percent chance of success—about as good as it gets for a covert operation. And it was remarkable in its "plausible deniability" for the United States.

"It was the perfect capture operation because even if it went completely wrong and people got killed, there was no evidence of a U.S. hand," Scheuer said.

But for reasons that Scheuer did not understand at the time, the operation was called off and eventually abandoned. He had been convinced that it was Clarke's doing. "The reason we didn't go after him had nothing to do with whether the operation would work; it had much more to do with the agency being frightened by Clarke," he said. (To his dismay, Scheuer learned later from the commission that it was someone else, not Clarke, who called off the mission.)

There was another clear shot at bin Laden in February 1999. That month, bin Laden was located in the southern deserts of Afghanistan as he paid nightly visits to royal visitors from the United Arab Emirates, a Persian Gulf nation that was supposed to be a close ally of the United States. The UAE entourage was in Afghanistan to hunt a prized migratory bird known as the bustard. This was no ordinary "Huck and Tom" hunting party, Scheuer said. It was led by a prince who had traveled to Afghanistan aboard a C-130 cargo plane that was part of the UAE royal family's fleet. The hunting party had "huge fancy tents, with tractor trailers with generators on them to run the air-conditioning."

"And so once the camp was up and running, we established over the course of a week the pattern of bin Laden's visits—he would come for evening prayers or he would come for dinner and stay for evening prayers," Scheuer said.

But even though Scheuer believed the CIA had another clear shot at bin Laden and urged a quick missile attack—"the collateral damage was basically just a prince and his entourage"—the missiles were never launched. The commission would later determine that the idea was considered but abandoned because the White House (Scheuer assumed again it was Clarke) worried that the prince's death would destroy American relations with the UAE and damage its ties elsewhere in the Persian Gulf. In hindsight, that was not an unreasonable fear.

Like others, Clarke saw Scheuer as "dysfunctional" and a "tantrum thrower" whose difficult personality undermined his effectiveness. There was no little irony that the two men in the federal government who best understood the al-Qaeda threat hated each other.

"Fine that you came to the same conclusion that we all came to, fine that you're all worked up about it, and you're having difficulty getting your agency, the rest of your agency, to fall in line, but not fine that you're so dysfunctional within your agency that you're making it harder to get something done," Clarke said of Scheuer in an interview with *Vanity Fair* magazine.

Scheuer had no way of knowing it as he spoke to the 9/11 commission, but the truth about the decision to call off his plans to kill bin Laden was much more complicated than he knew.

Scheuer thought that George Tenet—his boss and, he believed, friend—had supported the capture-or-kill plans. He thought Tenet had been their strongest champion when he got in front of Clinton. In fact, as Scheuer later understood it, Tenet had "betrayed" him. The commission was learning that it was Tenet who, more than anyone else, had canceled some of Scheuer's daring plans. Not Clarke.

It was a startling discovery for Scheuer, who had always thought of Tenet as a patron in his years at the agency. "He's the hardest man in the world to dislike," Scheuer said. "I remember the day my dad died, and he came down to my office to offer his condolences. He just came in and sat down and said, 'I'm sorry to hear about your father. If you want to take the day off, go ahead and do it.'"

But Scheuer later came to see that Tenet had been a disaster as director of central intelligence. He believed that Tenet had genuinely understood the al-Qaeda danger but, like Clarke, was never brave enough to stake his reputation on a plan to kill bin Laden. Tenet would not take the risk that the operation would go badly and he would be left to explain what had gone wrong. Tenet would not fight. Fighting meant that he would make enemies, and George Tenet never wanted to make an enemy.

"You didn't hear one bad thing about Tenet from anybody," Scheuer said. "And if there's a definition of a bad DCI, that's it."

Scheuer was outraged that so many good opportunities to capture or kill bin Laden had been missed, and his frustration boiled over later in 1999. He committed what amounted to professional suicide: He went outside his usual chain of command and sent an e-mail directly to Tenet and most of Tenet's deputies on the seventh floor at CIA headquarters that listed the ten things that needed to change at the CIA if it was ever to succeed in ending the threat from al-Qaeda.

Within days, Scheuer found himself called into the offices of Tenet's deputy, Jack Downing, and fired from Alec Station. Downing, he said, made no reference to the e-mail, but it was clearly responsible for what was happening. Scheuer's e-mail was seen as outrageous insubordination.

"You're off balance, you're burned out," he remembered Downing telling him.

"You're nuts, Jack," Scheuer replied. "Do you want this problem with al-Qaeda resolved or don't you?"

Scheuer was transferred back to CIA headquarters and given a cubicle in the agency's library. He was made, effectively, a junior librarian and given almost nothing to do. He was despondent. He tried to telephone Tenet to discuss what was left of his career at the agency. Tenet, he said, would not call him back.

THE CAPITOL

JUNE 11, 2002

Tim Roemer sensed that Dick Clarke knew much more than he was saying. It was June 2002, nine months after the 9/11 attacks, and Roemer was still in Congress, finishing out his sixth and final term in the House; he had announced plans to give up his seat and retire from Congress the next year. He was among several House members and senators who had gathered on this late spring morning in a high-security conference room in the Capitol—one used by the House and Senate intelligence committees for classified CIA briefings—to hear from Richard Clarke, who was then still at the White House. Clarke had been called as a witness before the joint congressional investigation into the failures of the nation's spy agencies before 9/11.

At the time, Roemer, a member of the House Intelligence Committee, did not know Clarke except by reputation. Clarke proved himself to be a riveting witness as he fielded questions from lawmakers for nearly six hours behind the closed doors of the hearing room. He was intelligent, articulate, seemingly candid in discussing his own failings as White House counterterrorism czar. Still, Roemer sensed that Clarke was being coy about certain questions—especially about President Bush and Condoleezza Rice. Clarke had been at the White House on the morning of September 11; he had been there throughout the spring and summer of 2001, when the government was being flooded with warnings of an imminent terrorist attack. So if anyone knew whether Bush and Rice had reacted appropriately to the threats reaching the Oval Office before 9/11, it was Clarke. Yet in front of these lawmakers, Clarke seemed unwilling to make any judgments about the president and Rice. He was certainly volunteering little about his bosses. He was still on the NSC's payroll. Perhaps it was understandable that Clarke would want to hold his tongue for now.

Roemer figured that Clarke's files at the NSC might answer the questions that were suddenly being asked by Democrats that spring about the pre-9/11 performance of the Bush White House; the first news reports about the existence of the August 6, 2001, PDB and its warnings about domestic hijackings had appeared in May 2002. But Clarke's paper trail was beyond the reach of Congress, Roemer knew; the White House was well within its constitutional rights to deny National Security Council files to Congress, even if the files involved a turning point in American history like 9/11. By its very nature, the NSC existed to offer advice to the president, and presidential advice was precisely what executive privilege was supposed to shield from outside scrutiny.

For that reason, the White House had also made clear that Condoleezza Rice, as national security adviser, would never testify before the joint congressional inquiry. That her deputy Clarke was being allowed to go to Capitol Hill to answer some questions—behind closed doors, with all of his responses considered classified—was a concession by the White House. The White House had insisted that Clarke not be called a "witness" by the lawmakers since that would suggest his comments amounted to testimony; they agreed to refer to him instead as a "briefer." For the same reason, he was not placed under oath. And because what Clarke was telling the lawmakers in June 2002 was classified, Roemer could not discuss it outside the conference room without risking prosecution.

K STREET OFFICES OF THE 9/11 COMMISSION
WASHINGTON, D.C.
DECEMBER 18, 2003

A year and a half later, Roemer found himself back in a Washington conference room with Clarke, but now both men were out of government. And Clarke's story, Roemer suspected, was about to create a political firestorm for the Bush administration unlike any it had ever experienced.

One of Roemer's final acts in Congress was to make sure he was named to the 9/11 commission as one of its five Democratic members. Roemer had been a sponsor of the bill that created the commission and one of the legislation's most aggressive advocates on the Hill. Like others involved in the congressional investigation, Roemer was convinced that the full truth about September 11 could only be told by an independent, bipartisan commission with subpoena power and the willingness to use it. He knew that the commission, unlike Congress, might actually get the PDBs and the files from the NSC, including Clarke's.

The first of Clarke's private interviews with the 9/11 commission was scheduled for mid-December, in the commission's offices on K Street.

Under his recusal agreement with the commission, Philip Zelikow was not supposed to be involved in questioning Clarke on any issue involving the 2001 transition. He had reason to dread what Clarke was about to tell the commission: It was Zelikow, after all, who had been the architect of Clarke's demotion in the early weeks of the Bush administration, a fact that had never been aired publicly.

For weeks ahead of the private interviews, Zelikow continued his campaign to disparage Clarke and his credibility, telling the commission's investigators that Clarke was known in the White House for having a "weak grasp of the truth." Zelikow had succeeded in convincing the rest of the staff that Clarke needed to understand that he was under threat of perjury at his private interviews. He made it clear that "Clarke was somebody who ought to be under oath," said Dan Marcus, the general counsel. And Clarke was sworn in before the first interview.

The questioning of Clarke was left mostly to Marcus, who knew Clarke slightly from their days together in the Clinton White House. Despite Zelikow's claims, Marcus had never heard Clarke described as a liar. Instead, he believed that Clarke was an exceptionally talented bureaucrat whose career had been hindered by his ego and prickliness. "He was not as effective as he might have been as counterterrorism coordinator because he antagonized so many people," Marcus said. "People really hated him."

IT TOOK only minutes for Marcus and the others who participated in the first interview to realize what a spectacular witness Clarke was going to be—and what damage he might do to Bush and Rice if he gave the same testimony in public.

"Here was a guy who is totally unknown outside the Beltway, who had been a Washington bureaucrat all of his life, who turns out to be a dynamite witness," Marcus said later.

Clarke told the story that would later become familiar to the public, but it was shocking to Marcus and others who were hearing Clarke's words for the first time. How the president and Rice had all but ignored the terrorism threats during 2001. How Rice rebuffed his requests to brief Bush on al-Qaeda throughout that year. How he had been demoted in the first weeks of the presidency.

He said that Rice and her deputy Stephen Hadley had seemed determined instead to focus on their "vestigial cold war concerns" like the Anti-Ballistic Missile Treaty with Russia. Marcus remembered being amused by one particular remark from Clarke, who, as the world was about to learn, spoke in perfectly formed sound bites. "My favorite line was how people like Rice and Hadley were preserved in amber from the cold war," Marcus recalled.

Clarke claimed that Rice, in her early briefings as national security adviser in 2001, had given him the impression that she had never heard the term *al-Qaeda* before (something she would later strenuously and effectively deny). He said he told her directly that al-Qaeda had cells within the United States.

Perhaps most startling of all, Clarke would also reveal that President Bush had been determined within hours of the 9/11 attacks to try to link them to Saddam Hussein. Clarke recalled being in the Situation Room on the evening of September 12 when Bush approached him.

"Look, I know you have a lot to do and all," the president said, according to Clarke's account. "But I want you, as soon as you can, to go back over everything, everything. See if Saddam did this. See if he's linked in any way."

Clarke said he told the president that the issue had already been researched extensively and there was no evidence of a close working tie between Iraq and al-Qaeda.

That was not what Bush wanted to hear, Clarke said.

"Look into Iraq, Saddam," the president repeated testily before walking away.

Clarke explained to Marcus and the others that since leaving the White House, he had been at work on a book about his years in government; it was scheduled to be published in 2004, in the midst of the presidential election. Marcus could just imagine the impact the book might have if it included any of the details that Clarke had just shared with the commission.

"Could we see an advance copy of the book?" Marcus asked.

Clarke replied, seemingly without much concern, "Oh sure, just talk to my publisher."

OFFICES OF THE 9/11 COMMISSION
New York, N.Y.
SEPTEMBER 2003

John Farmer's worry bordered on panic by September 2003. There was so much to do on the commission and so little time left. There were moments when Farmer felt himself close to despondent. He told his wife that fall that joining the 9/11 commission might have been "the biggest mistake in my professional life—I really thought this was going to be a disaster."

He was leading the team of investigators responsible for the detailed chronology of the events of September 11—what had happened to the four hijacked planes that morning and, after they crashed, how rescue efforts had been carried out at the World Trade Center and the Pentagon. At every turn, it seemed, government agencies were trying to stonewall his part of the commission's work.

He was getting nowhere in his negotiations with New York City over access to much of its documentation on the rescue effort at ground zero, especially the tapes of the 911 emergency calls that morning; Mayor Bloomberg's staff was defiantly uncooperative throughout the investigation. But at least in New York, much of the rescue effort at the World Trade Center had been documented elsewhere, if only by the nonstop presence of reporters and camera crews at the site for months after the attack. There was no shortage of witnesses in lower Manhattan or at the Pentagon. (There was no similar struggle for information from the local police and fire departments in northern Virginia that had handled the rescue effort at the Pentagon, no surprise since Farmer's teams had found their response was performed with impressive speed and competence on 9/11; there was nothing to hide.)

There was a much bigger problem in Washington with the FAA and NORAD, the key federal agencies involved in responding in real time to the hijackings. There was no substitute to the records locked away in their files, and Farmer was convinced that both of the agencies were holding back evidence about what had happened in the skies on September 11.

Earlier in the year, Farmer had joined with some of the Democratic commissioners in urging Tom Kean and Lee Hamilton to reconsider their decision not to issue blanket subpoenas to federal agencies for documents and interviews.

Farmer thought Kean and Hamilton had made a potentially disastrous mistake; if subpoenas had been issued to the FAA and the Pentagon from the start, there would have been time to go to court to enforce them. "The agencies would know that they couldn't run out the clock," he said. But by fall, the clock was ticking down; the commission was scheduled to shut down in May. There would be almost no time left to litigate.

The FAA had insisted in August that it had turned over all the material that the commission had asked for in its document requests earlier that summer. But Farmer found that impossible to believe. The commission had requested every imaginable bit of evidence from FAA files about the agency's actions on September 11, including tapes of communications among its managers and air traffic controllers and every logbook and computer entry that referred to the FAA's contacts with the Defense Department about the four hijacked planes. The document requests were broadly worded to make it clear that the FAA should hold back nothing that might apply to the investigation. If there was any question about the relevance of a document or tape, it should have been turned over.

But much of the material that Farmer had expected from the FAA was not in the boxes of evidence that the agency had provided to the commission. There were few of the tapes or transcripts he had expected to see. There was none of the detailed records of the presumably panicked communications that morning within the FAA.

In September, he and his team organized interviews at the FAA air traffic control centers on the East Coast and the Midwest that had dealt with the hijackings. Farmer assigned himself to the Indianapolis office. He was only a few hours into the interviews before he realized just how much evidence the FAA had held back. The unionized employees in the Indianapolis office seemed eager to blow the whistle on FAA headquarters in Washington. The Indianapolis workers made it clear that there was extensive information the commission had not seen, including tape recordings of conversations between the individual air traffic controllers and the hijacked planes.

Farmer was told that FAA headquarters had apparently decided to provide the commission only with the agency's "accident package." It was the term used to describe an edited FAA summary of the evidence the agency had gathered in an investigation—in this case, the investigation of the FAA's own performance on September 11. The commission had not been provided with the much larger "accident file," which would have the full body of evidence about the FAA's actions during the terrorist attacks. Other members of Farmer's team were hearing the same story that same day at other FAA air traffic centers they were visiting.

Farmer was furious, and he called Dan Marcus in Washington to tell him what the staff had discovered. FAA headquarters in Washington was contacted within hours to explain itself, and officials there were surprisingly quick to admit that the FAA held back information that the commission was entitled to see. It was unintentional, they insisted. Within days, several boxes of new material arrived at the commission's offices from the FAA, including the full library of air traffic control tapes.

But Farmer was not satisfied. This was becoming personal for him and his team; they could imagine how they and the commission would be treated by history—and by the growing circles of conspiracy theorists—if it was later found that they had missed important clues about 9/11. It was time for the commission to begin issuing subpoenas, he felt, and the panel should start with the FAA. At least if there were subpoenas, Farmer and the others could hold their heads high and say that at least they tried to get the evidence.

He asked Kean and Marcus for permission to address the commissioners to make the case for a subpoena, and he was given the chance at a meeting of the full commission on October 14.

"My team and I have lost confidence in the FAA," he told the commissioners. "We do not believe we have time to take any more chances on the possibility that they will act on good faith." He said he thought "there is no choice other than a subpoena."

His request gave the Democratic commissioners the ammunition they had been seeking for months to call again for blanket subpoenas on the Bush administration—not just on the FAA, but on the White House and every other executive branch agency.

"This is exactly why we should have subpoenaed everything in the first place," said Jamie Gorelick.

But Kean and Hamilton were still skeptical. To them, even the word *subpoena* still sounded unnecessarily confrontational. Wide-ranging subpoenas might shut down all cooperation from the Bush administration, they argued again. Slade Gorton recommended a compromise that the Democratic commissioners accepted: Subpoena only the FAA for the moment, but issue a stern public warning to the White House that more subpoenas on more agencies might soon follow.

Gorton signaled that he would break with his fellow Republicans and join the Democrats in voting for subpoenas if it came to that. When it did, he was as good as his word.

In a statement the next day, the commission announced the FAA subpoena—its first subpoena of any type—and warned the White House and other agencies that the commission's "document requests must be taken as seriously as a subpoena." Other agencies, it continued, "must review the efforts they have made so far to assure full compliance. In the absence of such assurances, additional subpoenas will be issued."

LATER THAT month, Farmer and his team traveled to NORAD's regional command center in Rome, New York. Farmer found it a grim place, a grime-colored aluminum bunker that was about all that was left of Griffiss Air Force Base, which had been a major American installation for B-52 bombers during the cold war. With NORAD's mission scaled back after the Soviet Union's collapse, Griffiss was decommissioned, although the regional NORAD command center remained open to keep a watch on the skies.

On September 11, 2001, the Rome base in upstate New York known formally as the Northeast Air Defense Sector, or NEADS, had been responsible for trying to coordinate the military's response to the hijackings.

Farmer's day at Rome began with a tour of the command center. He could see the dozens of desks stuffed with electronic equipment and blinking radar monitors where NORAD workers kept watch on air traffic across much of the United States. He asked his tour guide if any of the conversations in any of the stations had been tape-recorded; the commission had received no such tapes.

The guide answered innocently enough, "Oh sure, yes."

Farmer was startled. He asked a few more questions and discovered that it was not just some of the air traffic monitoring stations that had been taped on September 11. "They all had been taped," Farmer said. "We didn't have any of it." He could see for himself that in one corner of the room there were several old-fashioned Dictaphone tape recorders; they had recorded all of the communications in the room on the day of the attacks.

To Farmer's mind, this was far more serious than the situation with the FAA.

"What NORAD had done was egregious," he said. By withholding the tapes, NORAD had effectively denied the commission the true story of the military's response on September 11—of how a group of young Arab men with minimal pilot training had managed to foil every element of national security and kill thousands of Americans within the country's borders. "Those tapes told the story of the air defense better than anything else that anyone could have given us," he said.

Farmer cut the tour short and announced angrily that he was leaving immediately to fly to New Jersey to see Tom Kean, who agreed to rearrange his schedule to meet with Farmer in the president's offices at Drew as soon as he landed.

"Listen, we have to subpoena this stuff," he told Kean. "We may not get it, but if we don't try to get it, how can you explain to the public that we have done our job?"

Farmer knew it was going to be much harder to convince the full commission to issue a subpoena to the Defense Department than to the FAA. The FAA had no obvious constituency on the commission or with the public. Farmer knew the commissioners would be much warier of plunging into a fight with the Defense Department and Secretary Donald Rumsfeld, one of Washington's best bureaucratic infighters.

"When you're talking about subpoenaing the DOD, the room goes quiet," Farmer recalled. Kean did not give his immediate support to a subpoena; the decision of issuing a subpoena to the Pentagon would have to be left to the full commission.

Farmer did not tell Kean at the time, but he had decided that if the commission did not back up his request for the NORAD subpoena, he would resign. "I would have quit if we didn't," he said. "I felt we were becoming a laughingstock."

Farmer and his team felt there was another stumbling block: Philip Zelikow. During the debate over the FAA subpoena, Zelikow was overseas, leading a commission delegation to the Middle East and Afghanistan, so he was not actively involved in the discussion. But he was back in Washington by late October, and Farmer and his team had reason to fear that Zelikow would try to block their efforts to issue a subpoena to the Pentagon.

It was yet another issue of Zelikow's conflicts of interest. Zelikow made no secret that he had good friends on Rumsfeld's staff, most importantly Steven Cambone, the undersecretary of defense for intelligence, who was Rumsfeld's most trusted aide. Dan Marcus, the general counsel, had found it distasteful the way Zelikow would "flaunt" his closeness to Cambone.

Although there had been no direct confrontations between Farmer and Zelikow before this, many on the staff felt a clash between them was inevitable.

Because he worked out of the New York office, Farmer was mostly spared face-to-face encounters with Zelikow. But he had heard all of the stories from Washington about Zelikow's efforts to shield his friends in the White House and elsewhere in the government from the commission's scrutiny. He had heard the stories about Zelikow's unauthorized telephone calls with Karl Rove and his contacts with Condoleezza Rice, and he was shocked by them, too.

But unlike so many others in the commission, the strong-willed Farmer seemed ready to do battle with Zelikow. Other people on the staff were clearly terrified of Zelikow and his tirades, especially after the abrupt firing of Dana Lesemann, the last person to really stand up to him. But Farmer liked to remind his team's investigators that he came from an Irish family and he knew how to brawl. "It doesn't really bother me," he said.

Farmer went down to Washington to get an initial reading of Zelikow's intentions on the NORAD subpoena. Zelikow seemed to suggest he would support the subpoena, although the support was obviously lukewarm. "He was hard to read," Farmer said.

He recalled that almost as soon as he returned to New York, there was an urgent call from Dan Marcus in Washington, warning him that Zelikow was maneuvering to derail the NORAD subpoena and that Rumsfeld's office had hurriedly tried to arrange a meeting for the defense secretary with the commissioners to dissuade them.

"You'd better get down here," Farmer remembered being told by Marcus. "It's all unraveling. Philip is undoing this."

Farmer rushed back to Washington to meet with Zelikow again—this time to confront him. He was joined in Zelikow's office on K Street by Dana Hyde, a former congressional staffer who was a Washington-based member of Farmer's team. She was even more outraged by what appeared to be Zelikow's effort to protect his friends in the Defense Department.

"We can't do our job if you frustrate us," Hyde said, clearly furious with Zelikow.

Farmer joined in. "What's going on?" he asked Zelikow angrily. "I thought you were supporting this subpoena. Now I hear otherwise. What's going on?" He insisted to Zelikow that he be allowed to make a presentation to the commissioners before they voted, just as he had before the vote on the FAA subpoena.

Zelikow refused. "I represent the staff," he said. "I will represent your views." His face had turned the crimson color that the staff in Washington had seen before in moments of his most extreme rage. Zelikow was furious to be challenged like this by Farmer and others who supposedly worked for him.

"It's beyond our pay grade at this point," he told Farmer and Hyde, explaining that there was nothing more to talk about. "It's been taken to a higher level."

Farmer was getting angrier. "I don't see this as something that can be past our pay grade. We need this subpoena. We're not getting cooperation."

Farmer stormed out of Zelikow's office. Would he follow through on his promise to himself to resign?

Memories of this confrontation differed sharply between Zelikow and members of Farmer's team, another reflection of just how poisonous the relationship had become between Zelikow and many of the commission's best investigators—how much distrust there was of Zelikow's motives. Zelikow insisted later that he had never stood in the way of a subpoena and shared Farmer's suspicions about the truthfulness of NORAD's leaders. He did not deny there had been a confrontation with Farmer, however. "We did have concerns about timing and tactics." he said later, without elaboration. "Tension was building to a breaking point." Although Farmer's team suspected that Zelikow had arranged the last-minute Pentagon meeting with Rumsfeld in an effort to sabotage the subpoena, Zelikow said he did not recall having anything to do with organizing the meeting; it remains unclear who did. In this case Marcus, who was often so suspicious of Zelikow, stood by Zelikow's account. Marcus said he did not recall the telephone call to Farmer urging him to return to Washington. Nor, he said, did he believe Zelikow tried to derail the NORAD subpoena because of his friendship with Cambone, or for any other reason.

On November 5, 2003, the day before the commission's scheduled vote on the subpoena, Hamilton and Gorton went to the Defense Department for the meeting with Rumsfeld. Deputy Defense Secretary Paul Wolfowitz and Cambone sat in. Rumsfeld, as charming and agreeable as anyone in Washington when he wanted or needed to be, insisted he was unaware of the problems between the commission and NORAD. He vowed to get them resolved. If NORAD had held back any evidence from the commission, it would be turned over immediately, he promised. Surely there was no need for a subpoena, he said. Hamilton left the meeting convinced that he could rely on the word of his old friend. He would defy the other Democrats and vote against a subpoena.

"I've known Don Rumsfeld for twenty, thirty years," Hamilton explained to the other commissioners. "When he said, 'I'm going to get that information for you,' I took him at his word."

But Gorton thought that NORAD, like the FAA, deserved no more of the commission's patience. "I was outraged with NORAD and the way they had operated," he said. He suspected that NORAD officials had knowingly made false statements to the commission. "Even if it wasn't intentional, it was just so grossly negligent and incompetent," he said.

When the commission met the next day, Gorton announced that he would join with the Democrats, apart from Hamilton, to subpoena NORAD.

Since Hamilton intended to vote against the subpoena, the decision came down to Kean, who knew that this might be seen as a turning point for the commission—the first time he and Hamilton had disagreed on any substantive issue. It pained him a little to think of any crack in the perception of his partnership with Hamilton. There was a danger in that, he thought. But he voted for the subpoena. He, too, was convinced that NORAD was trying to hide something. The subpoena on NORAD, approved by a commission vote of six to four, was announced later the next day. Hamilton called his friend Rumsfeld to break the bad news.

THE TAPES from NORAD showed up about a month later, and the commission needed several more weeks to prepare comprehensive transcripts; NORAD had not prepared transcripts itself.

The tapes showed what Farmer had expected and feared—that NORAD's public statements about its actions on 9/11 had been wrong, almost certainly intentionally.

This was not the fog of war. This was the military trying to come up with a story that made its performance during 9/11 look reasonably competent, when in fact the military had effectively left the nation's skies undefended that morning.

A central element of the NORAD cover story, repeated over and over after 9/11, was that air force jet fighters had heroically chased United 93. Had it not crashed in Pennsylvania because of the struggle between the hijackers and passengers, the United plane would have been blown out of the sky before it reached its target in Washington, NORAD had wanted the public to believe.

But the tapes made it clear that every element of the story was wrong. NORAD knew nothing about United 93 until after it had already plunged to the ground. The tapes showed that NORAD was not notified until 10:07 a.m. that United 93 had been hijacked; the plane crashed at 10:03. Farmer believed that it was "99 percent" certain that Defense Department officers knew they were lying when they made the statements to the commission, sometimes under oath.

If it was not perjury, it was arrogance, Gorton suspected when the staff's results were presented to him. He thought that the generals, with all of those stars and ribbons on their chests, felt that they had no special responsibility to go back and be certain that their public statements about 9/11 were true. "I just don't think they cared," he said. "They didn't regard this as very important. And they are responsible for a lot of the conspiracy theories that we have to deal with to this day."

I⊤ was an endless discussion on Farmer's team: Were the generals and colonels at NORAD and the Pentagon intentionally misleading the commission? Was this perjury? Miles Kara was a retired Army intelligence officer who had worked as an investigator in the Pentagon's inspector general office before joining Farmer's team on the 9/11 commission. Kara respected his new colleagues on the commission but thought they were too quick to assume the worst about the military. He understood the gargantuan bureaucracy that is the Defense Department, how much stress the men and women at the top of it felt constantly. He thought the uniformed officers he dealt with in the investigation were, by and large, telling the truth about September 11 as best they understood it— phenomenally muddled as it was.

John A. Azzarello, a former federal prosecutor from New Jersey and another member of Farmer's team, reflected the more widely held, and more cynical, view among the team's investigators. Azzarello believed that the false statements from military officers and FAA officials might easily rise to the level of perjury, and that they needed to be reviewed outside the commission, preferably by the Justice Department. "I certainly felt we had been misled and lied to," he said. "This was potential criminal activity." And he too became convinced that Zelikow was doing what he could to shield the Defense Department from the investigation. That became apparent to Azzarello, he said, when Zelikow failed for weeks that spring to act on a memo sent to him by Farmer's team, urging the full commission to consider a criminal referral. "He just buried that memo," Azzarello said. A version of the memo was finally presented to the ten commissioners at their very last meeting that summer, too late to have an impact on the writing of the commission's final report. And when the commissioners finally did agree on a last-minute referral of the allegations, it was not to prosecutors at the Justice Department. It was to the offices of the inspectors general at the Pentagon and the FAA, which do not themselves have the ability to bring criminal charges.

For his part, Zelikow later insisted that Azzarello misunderstood what happened that spring, and that others in the commission's Washington office—not Zelikow—had been responsible for any delay in acting on the team's memo. "I was then, and remain to this day, deeply disturbed about the apparent conduct of certain officials, especially some particular USAF officers assigned to NORAD," Zelikow said. He described Azzarello as an "excellent, hard-working staffer" but said he was "party to relatively few of the conversations or e-mail exchanges on this. So on this issue, and perhaps some others, he may have misunderstood or not been directly aware of my actual role."

Again, it was almost impossible to sort out the truth. Farmer supported Azzarello's account of what had happened; he and Azzarello later became named partners in the same law firm in Chatham, New Jersey. Dan Marcus, the commission's general counsel, largely supported Zelikow. On these issues involving the military, Marcus said, Zelikow did not "pull his punches."

Azzarello admitted that he had more reason than others on the Farmer team to feel strongly about all of this—to take this personally. His brothers-in-law, John and Tim Grazioso, both employees of the financial services firm Cantor Fitzgerald, had worked and died together in the North Tower of the World Trade Center on September 11. Their survivors included their widows and a total of five children, ranging in age from ten months to twelve years old. Azzarello's wife, Carolee, had agreed to allow him to take a job on the 9/11 commission, so long as she never, ever, had to hear about his work. "I think you should do this," he remembered being told by Carolee. "But frankly, if the government failed, I don't want to hear about it from you."

— 31 —

CIA HEADQUARTERS
Langley, Va.

If a newspaper is judged by its readership, the president's daily brief is the most exclusive in the world. It almost certainly has the smallest circulation. Copies of the PDB are distributed by the CIA every day except Sunday to the president, the vice president, and the secretaries of state and defense. It contains what is supposed to be the most important and sensitive information gathered overnight by the nation's spy agencies. The information is so classified that the president and other "subscribers," as they are sometimes known, generally do not keep copies of the PDB for themselves. As soon as they have finished reading, they are expected to hand the PDB back to the CIA briefer so it can be returned to Langley the same morning.

President Bush was never known to be much of a reader—he preferred to receive intelligence reports through face-to-face meetings—so the length of the PDBs was cut back in the Bush administration to no more than ten pages. President Clinton, by contrast, was a voracious reader. He would read as many pages as were put in front of him, and his copy of the PDB would often be returned to the CIA covered with his scrawled notes; passages that interested him would be circled, with questions scribbled in black or blue ink in the margins. The CIA would try to get the questions answered for a subsequent briefing. Bush would usually hand back his copy of the PDB with no markings at all.

In the Bush White House, the PDB was usually made up of a few one- or two-page articles, each focusing on a different national security issue; the articles were printed on heavy paper and taken into the Oval Office in a leather binder that was known as "the Book." Every morning at about 8:15, Monday through Saturday, Bush was presented with the PDB by the CIA's "presidential briefer"—an invariably sleep-deprived intelligence analyst whose sole job at the agency was to prepare the PDB and organize the president's briefing each morning. The briefer offered a short verbal summary of each article as it was handed to Bush.

George Tenet, the director of central intelligence, had not attended the briefings during the Clinton administration. But Bush had wanted Tenet to be there, and Tenet was pleased to have daily access to the president and the chance to bond with him. Tenet liked to say that he provided "color commentary" to the president as the briefing went along. When Bush was traveling, the CIA briefer went with him, and Tenet sometimes participated in the briefing by a video hookup.

It was clear to Tom Kean and the other commissioners early in the investigation that the panel would need to see the PDBs—maybe all of them from the Bush and Clinton administrations. Certainly the commission would need to see the PDBs that referred to al-Qaeda and terrorist threats. It was the best way to gauge exactly what Bush and Clinton knew before 9/11 about Osama bin Laden and his terrorist network, whether the two presidents had been well served by the CIA, and whether they reacted responsibly to the intelligence they were given. Kean knew better than to make any sort of public analogy to the Watergate investigations, but he was reminded of the famous question posed by Senator Howard Baker about Richard Nixon: "What did the president know, and when did he know it?"

If Bush and his aides refused to turn over the PDBs and this became a fight, Kean thought, the White House had no one to blame but itself.

Before 9/11, it was well-known in Washington that the president received a daily intelligence briefing. But the existence of the actual document known as the PDB was less well-known. Kean was told that before 9/11, the name itself—"president's daily brief"—was considered classified.

The White House had helped create a furor over the PDBs, especially among the 9/11 families, when it refused to give a detailed response to news reports in May 2002 that suggested that Bush and others in the administration had received—and ignored—specific warnings before 9/11 about al-Qaeda's plans to carry out hijackings, possibly within American borders. The most damaging leak was to CBS News, which reported on May 15, 2002, that a daily briefing presented to Bush a few weeks before the attacks warned him specifically about the threats of a domestic hijacking by al-Qaeda.

The CBS story startled the White House, especially after it was picked up by other news organizations, including reliably conservative newspapers and magazines that had given Bush mostly unquestioned support since 9/11. There was special alarm among Bush's aides over the stark front-page headline in the otherwise Bush-friendly *New York Post*: 9-11 BOMBSHELL: BUSH KNEW. The White House press secretary, Ari Fleischer, called the *Post*'s editor to complain.

Instead of releasing the PDB or at least offering a detailed explanation of what was in the document, the White House chose to have National Security Adviser Condoleezza Rice hold a news conference at the White House in which she raised as many questions about the August 2001 briefing as she answered.

It would later become clear to many of the commission's members and its staff that she had tried to mislead the White House press corps about the contents of the PDB. She acknowledged that Bush had received a briefing about possible al-Qaeda hijackings, but she claimed that the PDB offered "historical information" and "was not a warning—there was no specific time, place, or method." She failed to mention, as would later be clear, that the PDB focused entirely on the possibility that al-Qaeda intended to strike within the United States; it cited relatively recent FBI reports of possible terrorist surveillance of government buildings in New York.

The commission was bolstered in demanding access to the PDBs because of what became known on the panel as "the Woodward factor." Even as the White House had refused to share the PDBs with the commission, senior administration officials had begun to share information from the briefings, if not the actual documents, with Bob Woodward of *The Washington Post*. Woodward had mostly removed himself from day-to-day reporting at the *Post,* devoting himself instead to his best sellers about what went on in Washington's corridors of power. The White House had given Woodward extraordinary access to Bush and his senior aides for Woodward's November 2002 book, *Bush at War.* The book described the actions of the Bush White House in the immediate aftermath of the 9/11 attacks and was mostly flattering in its portrayal of the president.

The White House did not welcome all of Woodward's reporting. A few days after Rice's news conference, Woodward and his colleague Dan Eggen published a front-page article in the *Post* that revealed the full, alarming title of the August 6, 2001, PDB—"Bin Laden Determined to Strike in U.S."—and quoted "knowledgeable sources" as saying that the PDB made it clear that al-Qaeda was determined to "bring the fight to America."

The article seemed a direct challenge to Rice's credibility. It noted that despite her claim at the news conference, the information in the PDB was not solely historic; it noted her failure to make it clear that the document referred specifically to domestic terrorist threats. The article also cited an intriguing error made by Ari Fleischer, who told reporters after Rice's appearance at the White House press room that the title of the PDB was "Bin Laden Determined to Strike the United States." As Woodward noted, Fleischer had left out the title's all-important preposition—"in" the United States.

The commission debated for months in early 2003 how to go about making a formal request for the PDBs. The White House had refused to make them available to congressional investigators about 9/11, citing executive privilege. The PDBs had never been made available to Congress in any fashion. In more than three decades in Congress, including his tenure as chairman of the House Intelligence Committee, Lee Hamilton had never seen one.

Alberto Gonzales had made it clear in his very first meeting with Philip Zelikow that the commission would not get them, either, and he repeated the denial in his later meetings with Kean and Hamilton.

But Kean and Hamilton would have to try, if only to preserve the commission's credibility; they needed to demonstrate that it had at least attempted to see every important document in the government's files related to al-Qaeda and 9/11. Like Kean, Hamilton could also see that the PDBs were becoming the "holy grail" for the 9/11 families and for the press corps. If the commission ended its investigation without reviewing them, "that would be the only thing the press would be interested in," said Hamilton. It seemed as if no other evidence unearthed by the commission mattered; if the commission did not see the PDBs, it would be seen in history as having failed.

The decision was made to hold off on requests for the PDBs until the commission had gone through several other rounds of document requests with the White House and had built up some sort of track record with Gonzales and his deputies.

When the request was finally made for the PDBs themselves in late summer 2003, it was to the CIA—the agency that wrote and kept custody of the PDBs—instead of to the White House. Dan Marcus and the commission's other lawyers felt it would be easier to get a court to enforce a subpoena against the CIA than against the president, if it came to that.

The request was not as wide-ranging as it might have been. It was not for the full library of PDBs from the Clinton and Bush administrations. Instead, the commission requested PDB articles from 1998 on that made mention of the following: al-Qaeda; domestic terrorist threats; terrorist plots involving airlines used as weapons; and intelligence involving Afghanistan, Pakistan, Saudi Arabia, Sudan, Yemen, and Germany. Mohammed Atta and many of the other 9/11 hijackers had met as students in Hamburg.

Through Gonzales, the White House responded in September: No, there would be no inspection of PDBs, not even brief excerpts of them.

Gonzales offered what he said was a compromise—a briefing for all ten commissioners about the "contents" of the PDBs. Kean and Hamilton wondered what that meant. Was Gonzales suggesting that he would share details verbally about what was in the PDBs about al-Qaeda? Kean and Hamilton agreed to the briefing, reluctantly, with no promise that it would satisfy the commission's demands. Their wariness was justified. The briefing was held on October 16, 2003, in the same reading room in the New Executive Office Building where the commission's staff reviewed other documents, and it was comically inadequate.

The White House lawyers offered an overview of the PDBs: a general description of what the documents were, how they were prepared, the choreography of the CIA's morning briefings in the Oval Office. The lawyers disclosed that about three hundred PDBs from the Clinton and Bush administrations contained the sort of information about al-Qaeda and other terrorist groups that the commission was looking for.

And that was where the briefing stopped. The White House lawyers went silent. They said they were barred from saying anything more. They refused to answer any other questions about what might actually be in the hundreds of PDBs. It was the equivalent of a book reviewer promoting a new book because it had many interesting pages, with no other hint at what might be on those pages.

"This is ridiculous," Jim Thompson, the former Illinois governor, could be overheard grumbling.

The commissioners were seething. If the briefing was meant to placate them, it had done the opposite; it was one more bit of proof of Gonzales's ham-handed strategy in dealing with the investigation. If anything, the commissioners were now more anxious to see the actual PDBs. Thompson and the other Republicans felt a special snub from Gonzales and his team. They were effectively being told by a Republican White House that it did not trust them with classified information.

After the White House had wasted their time yet again, the commissioners wanted the PDBs themselves. "We were not going to take no for an answer," said Thompson.

The negotiations between the commission and Gonzales went on for two more weeks, without any sign of agreement. Gonzales was his usual obstinate self, and Kean's patience had run out. Hamilton was always amazed by Kean's willingness to keep negotiating "until hell freezes over." It finally had.

THE NEW YORK TIMES had a long-standing request to interview Tom Kean at Drew University; he was more likely to speak openly there. Washington really did seem to be enemy territory to Kean. He invited a reporter from the paper's Washington bureau up to New Jersey in late October.

His offices took up much of the second floor of Mead Hall, a Greek Revival–style mansion that dated from the 1830s and was the sort of ornate pile that Kean's aristocratic ancestors would have called home. The interior decoration of the president's office reflected Kean's whimsical sense of humor. Near his desk was a life-size cardboard cutout of Sarah Michelle Gellar, the actress from the television series *Buffy the Vampire Slayer;* a blue Drew T-shirt was pulled over the cutout. Kean had become a *Buffy* fan after watching the show at the urging of students. At one corner of the room was a water bowl for Kean's champion border terrier, Willie, who greeted guests to Kean's office with an excited shower of licks. It occurred to the reporter that Fala must have served the same purpose in the White House for Kean's distant cousin FDR.

It was not clear if Kean had an agenda for the meeting; the commission's battles over the PDBs were not public at that point. But his agenda became clear within minutes.

Only a few days earlier, the commission had issued its first subpoena (to the FAA). Was the commission having trouble obtaining evidence from other government agencies? Was it possible there would be other subpoenas?

"Yes," Kean said somberly. "We're having trouble with the White House." The reporter leaned over to check his tape recorder to make sure it was working. From his tone, Kean seemed ready to drop a bombshell on the White House.

He revealed that the commission was in a battle with the White House over intelligence briefings—he was careful never to say "president's daily brief" or "PDB" because he believed the terms were secret—and it was now a possibility that the commission would need to slap a subpoena on the White House.

His language was remarkably direct.

"Any document that has to do with this investigation cannot be beyond our reach," he said. "I will not stand for it."

The reporter called editors at the Washington bureau of the *Times* and urged them to make space for an important story that weekend. The article, which had the headline 9/11 COMMISSION COULD SUBPOENA OVAL OFFICE FILES, was the lead story on page one in the paper on Sunday.

The interview infuriated the White House, especially after potential Democratic presidential candidates seized on Kean's remarks to accuse the White House of hiding evidence about 9/11. "After claiming they wanted to find the truth about September 11, the Bush administration has resorted to secrecy, stonewalling, and foot-dragging," said Senator Joseph Lieberman of Connecticut, one of the Democrats hoping to challenge Bush in 2004. "They have resisted this inquiry at every turn."

The White House could not allow the perception that Bush was stonewalling the 9/11 investigation to go unchallenged, and the decision was made to have Bush himself address the issue. He met with the White House press corps in the Oval Office the day after the story. They asked about Kean's complaints.

"You're talking about the presidential daily briefing," Bush said. "It's important for the writers of the presidential briefing to feel comfortable that the documents will never be politicized and/or unnecessarily exposed for public purview.

"Now having said that," he continued, "I am—we want to work with Chairman Kean and Vice Chairman Hamilton. And I believe we can reach a proper accord to protect the integrity of the daily brief process and, at the same time, allow them a chance to take a look and see what was in the—certain—the daily briefs that they would like to see."

Kean knew that Bush's comments had changed everything. First of all, by using the words *presidential daily briefing*, Bush had effectively declassified the name of the document, or so Kean believed. So now Kean could say specifically what it was that the commission wanted to see. More significant, Bush had now made a public vow to work to allow the panel to see at least some of the PDBs. Intentionally or not, he had undermined his loyal counsel, Gonzales, who had been so insistent that the PDBs would never be revealed to the commission.

Bush's aides had little choice but to try to negotiate this out. Gonzales notified Kean that the White House had a new proposal: Kean and Hamilton and two staff members would be allowed to review twenty "core" PDBs that mentioned al-Qaeda or had other information that met the commission's criteria for relevance. And then one of the four members of the review team would be allowed to read through the full universe of PDBs to determine if any needed to be moved to the "core" pile.

The commission met on November 6 in Washington and rejected the offer as painfully inadequate. There was a vote to subpoena the PDBs. The vote failed, but it received the support of all the Democrats except Hamilton, who, characteristically, wanted to continue the negotiations.

Kean and Hamilton went to see Gonzales and Andy Card, Bush's chief of staff, the next day with a counterproposal: that two of the four members of the review team be allowed to look over the larger universe of PDBs. Hoping to stem the tide of headlines about White House "stonewalling," the White House reluctantly agreed.

"We expect the terms of this agreement will provide the commission the access it needs to prepare the report mandated by our statute, in a manner that respects the independence and integrity of the commission," Kean and Hamilton said in a press release.

Two of the commission's Democrats, Tim Roemer and Max Cleland (who was in his final weeks on the commission), were beside themselves with anger over the compromise and expressed it to any reporter who called. They believed all ten commissioners needed to see all of the PDBs. Many of the 9/11 family advocates were equally furious with what they saw as the commission's capitulation. "A limited number of commissioners will have restricted access to a limited number of PDB documents," the Family Steering Committee said in its own statement. "The commission has seriously compromised its ability to conduct an independent, full, and unfettered investigation."

The families were startled by one more announcement from Kean and Hamilton. They revealed the names of the other two members of the review team. One was Jamie Gorelick, a choice the families did not consider controversial. But the other was Philip Zelikow. None of the other Republican commissioners was eager to make the commitment of time that would be required for the review. So Kean and Hamilton thought that Zelikow was the logical choice for the job given his wide-ranging knowledge of national security issues.

The families took the Zelikow choice as one more bit of evidence that the commission was doing the bidding of the Bush White House.

"How much more Zelikow do we have to take?" asked Kristen Breitweiser, one of the Jersey Girls. Her view was shared by several members of the commission's staff, who said the selection of Zelikow to review the most secret intelligence files in the White House would give him yet another opportunity to protect Bush and Rice from scrutiny, or at least create that perception. Said Dan Marcus: "If we were going to have a staff person do this, Philip was not the right person."

— 32 —

ROOM 5026
New Executive Office Building
Washington, D.C.
DECEMBER 2003

Tom Kean could not deny the thrill of this. He took a seat in the reading room in the New Executive Office Building in early December and was handed the sheaf of PDBs from the Clinton and Bush administrations. Here in his hands were the documents that the White House had been so determined for so long to keep from him. Lee Hamilton liked to refer to the PDBs as the "holy of holies"—the ultimate secret documents in the government—and Kean assumed that must be the case.

"I thought this would be the definitive secrets about al-Qaeda, about terrorist networks and all the other things that the president should act on," he said. "I was going to find out the most important things that a president had learned." He assumed they would contain "incredibly secretive, precise, and accurate information about anything under the sun."

Each PDB was only several pages long, so Kean could read through months of them in a stretch of a few hours.

And he found himself terrified by what he was reading, really terrified. Here were the digests of the most important secrets that were gathered by the CIA and the nation's other spy agencies at a cost of tens of billions of dollars a year.

And there was almost nothing in them.

"They were garbage," Kean said of the PDBs. "There really was nothing there—nothing, nothing." If students back at Drew turned in term papers this badly researched, "I would have given them an F," he said.

There were "snippets of information" in the PDBs about al-Qaeda and other terrorist groups. Occasionally, there was something intriguing, maybe a report of a bin Laden sighting somewhere or a tip from Israel's Mossad or Britain's MI-6 or another foreign spy agency on what sort of attack al-Qaeda might be planning next. But there was usually little context for these nuggets, and the PDBs often did little but repeat what had already appeared that morning on the front pages of *The Washington Post* and *The New York Times*.

Kean pointed that out to one of his White House minders who accompanied him to the reading room. "I've read all this," he told the minder in astonishment. A lot of the information in the PDBs and other supposedly top-secret intelligence reports had already been revealed by the nation's big news organizations. "I already knew this."

"Oh, but you're missing the point," the minder replied. "Now you *know* it's true."

It occurred to Kean that this might be the commission's most frightening discovery of all: The emperors of espionage had no clothes. Perhaps the reason the White House had fought so hard to block the commission's access to the PDBs was that they revealed how ignorant the government was of the threats it faced before 9/11. Kean could understand their fear. Imagine the consequences if al-Qaeda and its terrorist allies knew how little the United States really knew about them.

JAMIE GORELICK, who along with Philip Zelikow was given access to the larger universe of PDBs, was more impressed by the documents than Kean had been. Or at least she was less unimpressed. She knew the Bush administration was right to complain that much of the intelligence in the PDBs in the months before 9/11 was maddeningly nonspecific about a possible date or place of an attack. Some of the intelligence in the PDBs was "paltry"; sometimes the information contradicted itself from one day to the next, Gorelick said.

But she was astonished by the sheer volume of the warnings. Flood, cascade, tsunami, take your pick of metaphors. She could see that in the spring and summer of 2001, there was a consistent drumbeat of warnings, day after day, that al-Qaeda was about to attack the United States or its allies. It was clear to Gorelick that the CIA had gone to President Bush virtually every morning for months in 2001 to give him the message that the United States needed to be ready for a catastrophic terrorist strike. And from what she was reading, no one ruled out the possibility of a domestic attack.

"Something is being planned, something spectacular," she said, summarizing what the president had been told by George Tenet and what Bush should have read in the PDBs. "We don't know what it is, we don't know where it is, but something is happening."

She said CIA analysts were trying to tell Bush, as bluntly as they could, that the threat in those months was "the worst thing they've ever seen—an unprecedented threat," worse than the threats before the millennium.

Gorelick read the August 6 PDB for the first time and could see that the concluding two paragraphs in the twelve-paragraph document referred specifically to current threats to Americans—within American borders. In New York City, no less.

After noting unconfirmed 1998 reports that Osama bin Laden had intended to hijack an American passenger plane, it read:

"FBI information since that time indicates patterns of suspicious activity in this country consistent with preparations for hijackings or other types of attacks, including recent surveillance of federal buildings in New York.

"The FBI is conducting approximately 70 full-field investigations throughout the U.S. that it considers bin Laden-related. CIA and the FBI are investigating a call to our embassy in the UAE in May saying that a group of bin Laden supporters was in the U.S. planning attacks with explosives."

She read those passages again and was struck by the use of verbs. They were almost all in the present tense—"indicates," "is conducting," "are investigating." How could those warnings be considered "historical"?

To her surprise, Gorelick had found that she and Zelikow worked well together. After he was hired as executive director, Gorelick was told by friends who knew Zelikow that she would need to "wield a two-by-four to hit him over the head so that he does what you want rather than what he wants." Like the other Democrats, she had worried about all of his friendships at the Bush White House, especially with Rice.

But on this sensitive assignment, Zelikow did not seem to be pulling any punches, she said. And Zelikow treated Gorelick with deference. He clearly respected her intelligence. For sheer brainpower, she might have been Zelikow's equal among the commissioners. And he saw her as even-tempered and collegial—certainly easier to deal with than Richard Ben-Veniste or Tim Roemer, who could be openly confrontational with Zelikow. Gorelick found that Zelikow's encyclopedic knowledge of national security issues—not just about al-Qaeda—was invaluable in the search through the PDBs.

"He had been through all the CIA documents, and so he had terrific context," she recalled. "I would say, 'Where does this come from?' And he would give me the background on it." They sat together in the reading room in the New Executive Office Building for days, passing the PDBs between them.

Gorelick and Zelikow agreed that about fifty of the more than three hundred PDBs were directly relevant to the investigation and should be added to the twenty or so in the White House's "core" pile, which would allow Kean and Hamilton to read them as well. They provided the list of the additional fifty to the White House.

But Alberto Gonzales's office said that was impossible; under the agreement with the commission, the White House had expected that no more than one or two of the larger universe of PDBs would be transferred to the "core" pile. Fifty? There was no chance of that, Gonzales told the commission.

He also balked at the detail in the ten-page report written by Gorelick and Zelikow for the full commission that summarized what they had found in the PDBs; the report included headlines from many of the briefings, as well as virtually all of the language from the August 6 PDB. The White House said it had expected the report would be no more than a page or two—certainly not ten pages, certainly not with the damning detail from the August 6 PDB. Gonzales refused to allow the document to circulate to the other commissioners.

The commission was fed up with Alberto Gonzales. Kean had begun referring to Gonzales and a few others at the White House who were involved in negotiations with the commission as "control freaks." By now, it was impossible to mention Gonzales's name among the commissioners without hearing a growl of anger or exasperation. It was January; the commission was scheduled to begin its high-profile, televised public hearings within weeks, at which cabinet officers from the Bush and Clinton administrations would be called to testify. The deadline for the final report was only four months away. And the commissioners still had not had full access to the most important documents they needed to see.

Once again, Republicans appeared even angrier with Gonzales than the Democrats. It was time to threaten a subpoena again, and this time the commission was serious enough that it authorized Dan Marcus to hire an outside constitutional expert to draw up a subpoena and prepare for what would likely be a historic courtroom showdown with the White House.

Marcus himself wanted to avoid a subpoena. He thought the commissioners were kidding themselves, that whatever the political pressures, the White House would stand up to the subpoena threat and continue to withhold the PDBs. If the commission went to court to enforce a subpoena, the clock would run out on the investigation before the court case was anywhere near a resolution.

"It would have been Armageddon," he said. "Even though we had a good legal argument, the subpoena would have been a disaster for us because we could not have won the litigation in time to get the PDBs."

Still, he had to be ready for Armageddon, so he retained Robert Weiner, a noted Washington appellate lawyer and former colleague from the White House Counsel's Office in the Clinton administration, to help prepare for the court fight.

The decision was made not to subpoena the PDBs themselves, but instead to demand access to the voluminous notes taken by Gorelick and Zelikow. Their careful notes referred to all of the most important information from the PDBs, and Marcus and Weiner assumed a federal judge would be far more likely to uphold a subpoena for the commission's own notes than one for the PDBs themselves. The commission was prepared to issue the subpoena in early February.

Zelikow had a last-ditch plan to preempt the subpoena. Working virtually nonstop over two days, he prepared a seventeen-page, seven-thousand-word document that broadened the original report on the PDBs he had written with Gorelick. Zelikow knew that much of the material the White House found most alarming in their original report was actually available in other, much less classified documents—especially the SEIBs, the intelligence summaries that were more widely circulated within the government.

By cleverly cross-indexing his report with the SEIBs and other documents, Zelikow argued that the ten commissioners would see all the information they needed to see, and they could avoid a potentially disastrous court battle with the White House.

Whatever his interest in protecting friends in the Bush administration, Zelikow was as furious as the commissioners about the way the White House had handled this. He said later that Gonzales's "trench warfare" in dealing with the commission was shockingly self-defeating, if only because it made the PDBs seem more important than they were. "The PDBs had become superimportant politically because of the mystique they had acquired in the public eye," in part because the White House had struggled so long to keep them under wraps, he told a Harvard researcher.

Feeling beaten down by the long negotiations with the White House, Gorelick read through Zelikow's report and agreed that it could serve as the basis for a compromise with the White House. Under pressure from Andy Card and others at the White House to preempt a subpoena, Gonzales agreed as well.

Kean and Hamilton released a public statement on February 10 announcing the compromise and said that "we are confident that the commission has obtained an account of all the PDBs that relate to the al-Qaeda threat and the events of September 11."

Many of the 9/11 family groups were outraged by this new compromise; it was even clearer now that only Gorelick and their nemesis Zelikow would ever see the full library of PDBs; the other commissioners would see only an edited version of what Gorelick and Zelikow chose to show them.

By early 2004, however, the families' struggles with the commission seemed a minor story to the Washington press corps; reporters wanted to focus instead on what they saw as the real headline—the growing hostility between the 9/11 commission and George Bush's White House and its implications for Bush's reelection.

With the PDB issue settled, Kean and Hamilton prepared for their next struggles with the White House: first to find a way to force Condoleezza Rice to answer the commission's questions in public, and then to persuade Bush and Cheney to meet with all ten commissioners to answer their questions. Gonzales had reluctantly agreed to make Rice available for a private question-and-answer session with the commission. But he insisted she would never testify publicly. He said Bush and Cheney might answer a few questions privately, but certainly not from all ten commissioners.

OFFICE OF THE SPEAKER
House of Representatives
JANUARY 27, 2004

T he otherwise infuriating battle over the PDBs had a silver lin-
ing for the commission: It made it easier for Kean and Hamilton to argue for more time to finish the investigation. They
could blame White House stalling for the need for an extension.

It was clear by the end of 2003 that the commission could not meet its
original deadline to issue a final report—the following May—and Kean
and Hamilton began polling the other members and the staff about how
much more time might be needed.

Any change in the deadline required new legislation, so the commission would need support from Republican congressional leaders and
the White House. And Kean and Hamilton were certain it would be a
tricky negotiation, if only because 2004 was a presidential election year,
in which the outcome might be determined in part by the commission's
conclusions about George Bush's performance in dealing with terrorists.

Gorton and Roemer called for an extension of at least six months,
which would push the release of the report past the November elections.
But Kean and Hamilton doubted that the White House and Republican lawmakers would ever permit such a lengthy extension, fearing that
parts of the report damning to Bush would be leaked throughout the fall
in an effort to damage his reelection campaign.

Kean's political instincts also told him that it was best to get the report
out before the election anyway. He wanted the commission's recommendations to become an issue in the presidential campaign; he wanted the report
to become a political football. He saw that the report might set off a campaign season "bidding war" between Bush and his Democratic contender
to adopt the commission's recommendations as their own.

In a statement to reporters on January 27, Kean and Hamilton made
the formal announcement that the commission needed more time. They

said the commission had gathered most of the documents it needed and completed most of its interviews. But they said the panel still needed an extra sixty days to complete its report, pushing the deadline to July. They said they were aware of the political implications of the request but that "the right course is simply this: Put aside the politics and just ask for the time we really need."

As expected, there was no enthusiasm at the White House for a delay. But Bush's aides feared a new, ugly round of headlines about how Bush was failing to cooperate with the investigation, so they agreed to the extension. Andy Card and Karl Rove figured that if the report was issued in July, they would still have time before election day to organize an effective response to any criticism of Bush. The Senate Republican leadership signed on quickly to the deal.

But Dennis Hastert, once again, was furious with the commission. The White House had reached the deal on the extension to July without getting his okay.

"The commission is a creation of Congress, and the Congress is not consulted about when the commission goes out of business?" Hastert said angrily to one of his top aides, clearly feeling snubbed once again. "That's not right."

He decided he would single-handedly block the extension. He had the enthusiastic support of some conservative news outlets, notably the editorial board of *The Wall Street Journal,* which put the headline THE 9/11 AMBUSH on top of an editorial that savaged the commission: "The membership and behavior of the current 9/11 commission have always looked like a political crackup waiting to happen. Now the commission, which was supposed to report in May, is asking for more time." The editorial writers said that "our sources tell us the real problem is that Democrats have held up drafting the final report with the excuse that some document might materialize that changes the entire picture."

On the commission, some Democrats wondered if Hastert was really doing the dirty work of the White House in trying to block the extension. If Hastert's contempt for the commission was being stage-managed by anyone at the White House, it was assumed on the commission to be Dick Cheney. The vice president was a frequent, if rarely announced, visitor to the Speaker's office.

One theory, and it made as much sense as any, was that Hastert also felt personally insulted by the commission—both that it was ignoring him and that it was insulting the institution he ran. The latter was undeniably true. During the course of the investigation, members of the commission frequently sneered at any mention of Congress and its "dysfunctional" oversight of intelligence and law enforcement agencies. Hastert was tired of it.

He made his true feelings known when he agreed to be interviewed on February 5 by Michael Smerconish, a conservative radio talk-show host in Philadelphia. The Speaker bluntly accused Democrats on the commission of leaking classified information that was intended to tarnish the administration in the run-up to the election.

"I think there's a belief that they would like to drag this thing out and drag it out and then have death by a thousand cuts," Hastert said angrily. "There are Democrats on this thing that are leaking things already. They will leak it all the way to the election and make it a political issue."

Kean figured that he would have to intervene to try to make peace with Hastert, no matter how distasteful that would be. His view of Hastert was shaped in part by Hamilton, and Hamilton's contempt for the Speaker—as expressed behind the closed doors of the commission—was almost palpable.

But Kean knew that the commission needed the extension; there was no hope of finishing the final report by May. So he and Hamilton organized a meeting on the Hill with Hastert, Tom DeLay, and other House Republicans on March 2.

The meeting began badly. The House was enemy territory for the 9/11 commission. Kean said he could not remember who started hurling insults at the meeting. But he remembered the insults:

"You're hurting the troops."

"You guys are doing this without consulting us—and we created you!"

"Who do you think you are?"

The venting reflected months of House Republican anger over the commission, and Kean was reminded again of what a mistake it had been to not open a line of communication earlier.

He was pleased that Hastert and DeLay had said little in the unpleasantness of the first few minutes of the meeting. At one point, he turned to Hastert, hoping to make the personal connection he should have made months earlier with the Speaker. After all his years in the statehouse in Trenton, Kean understood that political deals were often clinched by a tiny kindness, a small remark that reminded his opponents that "I am not the devil."

"You know, Mr. Speaker, you and I have a lot in common," Kean said. "You were a high school history teacher?"

"Yes," Hastert replied.

"And so was I," Kean said, reminiscing about his two-year stint as a teacher at St. Mark's, the Massachusetts prep school that he had attended as a student. "And you were a wrestling coach?" he continued.

"Yes," Hastert said, clearly softening. "Yes, I loved that."

"And so was I," Kean said.

Kean could not say if the fond reminiscences of two old high school wrestling coaches were what got the 9/11 commission more time. But Hastert walked out of the meeting that afternoon to announce that he and Kean had worked out the final details of the two-month extension. He told reporters that he was reluctant to do it, but it was "apparent they couldn't get their work done" any other way.

THE INSULTS headed Congress's way from the commission did not stop. If there was one conclusion that the commissioners agreed on virtually from the first day of their investigation, it was the need for Congress to remake itself when it came to intelligence and national security. The House and Senate intelligence committees were poorly informed and, often, poorly led. The committees lacked budget authority over the CIA and other spy agencies; control over the budgets fell instead to the appropriations and armed services committees. The commission's staff determined that eighty-eight committees and subcommittees in Congress had oversight responsibilities for the newly created Department of Homeland Security, which effectively meant that an agency to deal with domestic terrorist threats after 9/11 had no clear point of contact in the House or Senate.

Slade Gorton had served on the Senate Intelligence Committee in the early 1990s and found it a dismal experience. There was little in the way of true oversight of intelligence agencies because the agencies would share so little of what they knew. He quit the committee in frustration "because I felt it was a useless exercise—I never felt I was being told anything that I hadn't learned in *The Washington Post*."

— 34 —

THE SITUATION ROOM
The White House
FEBRUARY 7, 2004

For all of Hollywood's efforts to depict it as the high-tech nerve center of American power, the White House Situation Room was actually an unremarkable-looking place, a reminder of just how small the West Wing really was. The name was a misnomer. At five thousand square feet, the "Sit Room" was not a single room; it was a cramped suite of rooms in the West Wing's basement, with a wood-paneled conference room at its core. Even though it was supposed to be the White House equivalent of the Pentagon's war room, most of the telephones and electronic equipment in the Situation Room were years out of date. The "watch officers" who manned the room round-the-clock sat in front of computers with old-fashioned tube monitors. In fact, apart from the computers and touch-tone phones, surprisingly little had changed in the Situation Room since it was opened during the Kennedy administration. President Kennedy was alarmed to discover after the Bay of Pigs disaster that there was no central office in the White House to gather intelligence in a crisis. So one was created, literally under Kennedy's feet, in the basement.

Condoleezza Rice knew how the symbolism of the Situation Room would work to her advantage on February 7, 2004, the day of her long anticipated private meeting with the 9/11 commission. For all that Rice might be criticized for the foreign policy she had helped George Bush craft after 9/11, no one was better in the White House at managing its presentation.

The Situation Room might be "uncomfortable, unaesthetic, and essentially oppressive," as Henry Kissinger had once said of the place (he had spent too many long nights there in the Nixon and Ford administrations), but the 9/11 commissioners were obviously impressed with the setting as they filed into the conference room, their eyes darting around the walls, looking for evidence of all the history that had taken place there.

"It was a small, plain conference room," said Dan Marcus, the general counsel, who would lead the questioning of Rice. "But it has a mystique."

This was where Lyndon Johnson had spent hours poring over maps of Vietnam, personally selecting bombing targets in the paddy fields off the Mekong River; where Jimmy Carter's closest aides had agonized at news of the failed rescue of American hostages in the U.S. embassy in Tehran in 1980; where Richard Clarke had directed the government's response on the morning of September 11. (The commission's staff had been told that when Clarke's deputies refused his orders to evacuate the room—another hijacked plane was reported to be bearing down on the White House—they passed around a yellow legal pad; everyone wrote down their names so that recovery teams would know how many bodies to search for.)

"I'd like to welcome you to the Situation Room," Rice began. Her head turned slowly around the table; she looked each of the commissioners squarely in the eye. That dazzling smile. "I've been looking forward to this."

It was a Saturday. Rice had agreed to meet with the commissioners over the weekend, when she would have more time and when more of the out-of-town commissioners could get to Washington to participate.

Under the ground rules that the commission had established with the White House a year earlier, the questioning of senior Bush aides was to be officially described as a "meeting" instead of an "interview"; the White House felt "interview" sounded too formal and prosecutorial. And the rules for the "meeting" with Rice were even more stringent than those for other top administration officials.

Unlike cabinet officers, Rice and her predecessors as national security adviser generally never testified before Congress or anywhere else— exceptions had been made in cases involving allegations of criminal activity—and the Bush administration was not about to set a new precedent. Rice would meet with the 9/11 commission, but there would be no recording of the interview; she would certainly not be placed under oath. The interview was supposed to be limited to two hours, although it lasted four.

Philip Zelikow was at the session, although under his new recusal rules, he could not participate; he sat glumly listening to Marcus open the questioning.

Several of the commissioners had not met Rice before, and they marveled at her ability to take command of a room so effortlessly.

So much was appealing—dazzling really was the word—about Condoleezza Rice. The magic began with that name; her music-loving parents named her for the Italian musical term *con dolcezza*, which translates as "with sweetness." She had style, she had brains, she had "rock star" charisma worthy of a Kennedy. Rarely had fashion writers at *The Washington Post* used up so much ink to catalog a public figure's wardrobe. It was all combined with a compelling life story that had taken Rice from a childhood in segregated Birmingham, Alabama, where one of her childhood playmates was a victim of the city's infamous 1963 church bombing, to the campus at Stanford University, and then to the White House.

It was that inspiring biography that may have shielded Rice from some of the harshest attacks leveled at the administration after things started going so badly in Iraq following the 2003 invasion. Few Democrats, especially the mostly doughy white males who then ran the party in Congress, were eager to be seen attacking such an accomplished black woman. To her credit, Rice seemed determined to stop anyone from seeing her as some sort of affirmative action prize.

So how were the Democrats on the 9/11 commission going to ask the question that was on all their minds: Had Condi Rice simply failed to do her job in the spring and summer of 2001, when the government was flooded with warnings of an imminent terrorist attack and apparently did so little to respond to them?

Rice seemed unaware of what Richard Clarke had told the commission's investigators a few weeks earlier—that she, in particular, had ignored the warnings. Was she aware that Clarke was about to publish a book that was going to make that case publicly? There were even more sensitive questions about Rice's truthfulness in her public statements after 9/11, especially about her assertions of what Bush had known about al-Qaeda threats before the attacks.

Privately, some of the Republican commissioners had the same questions about Rice's performance, although they knew they would face the wrath of the White House and congressional Republicans if they dared ask them in public. Better to leave those questions to the Democrats.

Kean did not want to single her out for blame in the final report, "but obviously Rice bears a tremendous amount of responsibility for not understanding how serious this threat was" in the months before 9/11.

John Lehman had worked in the National Security Council under Henry Kissinger, and he knew that had it been Kissinger and not Rice at the NSC in the summer of 2001, much more would have been done to respond to the CIA's frantic warnings about an imminent al-Qaeda strike. Kissinger would have paid much more attention. "I have no doubt that he would have," said Lehman. He thought Rice was no more culpable for inaction than other senior aides to Bush, including Donald Rumsfeld and George Tenet, and the president himself. But he did think that Rice, like the others, had failed to understand that the world had changed radically in the eight years that Republicans had been out of power at the White House—that terrorism was the great and growing threat of the new century. She was focused instead on missile defense, U.S.-Russian relations, the purported threat posed by Saddam Hussein's Iraq. "What I don't understand is how it was that they had totally left terrorism out of their grand strategy," he said of the White House team.

Slade Gorton said Rice and others in the White House had somehow come to the conclusion that they had "all time in the world" to deal with the al-Qaeda threat—that Osama bin Laden and his henchmen were just "a bunch of people off in a cave." It did not seem to matter that from the moment Bush and Rice arrived at the White House in 2001, the CIA was telling them precisely the opposite.

"Hindsight is always twenty-twenty," said Gorton. But in failing to act on what it was being told in the spring and summer of 2001 by the CIA and by its staff, especially by Clarke, the Bush White House was "spectacularly wrong," Gorton said. "They screwed up."

THE DEMOCRATS understood that they were on treacherous ground in trying to question Condoleezza Rice's competence.

Jamie Gorelick did not like the idea of attacking the first woman—and the first black woman at that—to hold the job of national security adviser.

Gorelick had been the first woman herself in many of her high-powered jobs in government. But she thought that anyone who had closely reviewed Rice's performance in 2001 had reason to question her competence. "I think most people did," Gorelick said. "That was my question."

Gorelick was struck by the comparisons between what Rice had done at the NSC in 2001 and what Sandy Berger had done in the run-up to the millennium, the last time there had been such a sustained drumbeat of intelligence warnings of a terrorist strike against the United States.

As the commission's staff had learned, Berger had organized almost daily meetings at the White House in December 1999 at which the attendance of every cabinet secretary with national security duties, as well as George Tenet and FBI director Louis Freeh, was mandatory. Berger demanded that they "shake the trees" within their agencies every day for the smallest bit of evidence about al-Qaeda plans. There had been nothing like that in the months before 9/11.

Gorelick thought it obvious that much would have shaken loose had there been a similar effort in 2001, especially at the FBI and CIA. The arrest of Zacarias Moussaoui. The Phoenix memo. The CIA's belated watch listing of Nawaf al-Hazmi and Khalid al-Mihdhar. It would not have been so difficult in August 2001 for someone to connect those dots.

It seemed to Gorelick that Rice had "assumed away the hardest part of her job" as national security adviser—gathering the best intelligence available to the White House and helping the president decide how to respond to it. Whatever her job title, Rice seemed uninterested in actually *advising* the president. Instead, she wanted to be his closest confidante—specifically on foreign policy—and to simply translate his words into action. Rice had wanted to be "the consigliere to the president," Gorelick thought.

Domestic issues seemed to bore her. Her deputy, Stephen Hadley, had told the commission something remarkable in his private interview the month before: He and Rice had not seen themselves as responsible for coordinating the FBI and other domestic agencies about terrorism. But if they weren't responsible, who was? There was no separate domestic security adviser in the White House. They had just demoted Clarke.

Bob Kerrey was initially less critical of Rice than other Democrats on the commission. "There was a lot of sympathy that flowed to Condoleezza Rice. She's black, she's female, she's got this phenomenal demeanor, she stays on message," he said.

Yes, Rice should have "rattled his cage" and forced Bush to concentrate on the intelligence about an imminent terrorist threat in 2001. But he believed Bush could not duck ultimate responsibility for what went wrong in the White House that spring and summer. "He's the president," said Kerrey. "I don't think you can lay this at Condoleezza Rice's door."

As the investigation went on, though, Kerrey listened more closely to the way Rice described her job, and he began to reconsider. He began to view Rice much more harshly. Under the White House ground rules, Rice's private interview with the commission could not be recorded or transcribed, so he could not remember her exact words. But Kerrey recalled a comment that Rice made about her responsibilities as national security adviser—and how troubling her description was. She said something like, "I took the president's thoughts, and I helped the president describe what he was thinking," Kerrey remembered.

Kerrey thought it was a rare, unguarded acknowledgment from Rice, and it captured what she had done wrong as national security adviser. Kerrey agreed with Gorelick: Rice's job was not simply to repackage and prettify the thoughts of a president whose understanding of national security issues was limited enough in 2001. Her job was to wake up in the morning, review the raw intelligence presented to the White House by the government's spy agencies and the Pentagon, and then advise the president what to do. Condi Rice had turned the definition of her job on its head.

THE QUESTIONING of Condoleezza Rice in the Situation Room was polite but pointed.

Some of the first questions focused on Richard Clarke. Rice seemed to be suggesting that if there was a failure at the White House to respond to terrorist threats, the responsibility could be laid at Clarke's door, not hers.

Clarke and his Counterterrorism Strategy Group were the "nerve center" for dealing with the threats, she said. She suggested that she deserved credit for simply agreeing in early 2001 to keep Clarke on the NSC staff in the Bush administration. The decision was "not uncontroversial" since "Dick is someone who broke china," she said. She acknowledged that she had removed him as a de facto member of the Principals Committee, but she suggested that was "sound policy making," since everyone else of Clarke's rank reported through the next rung of policy making—the Deputies Committee. If Clarke was unhappy about any of these changes, "he never told me," she said.

Richard Ben-Veniste wanted to question Rice about the August 6 presidential daily brief; it seemed to some of the other commissioners that the August 6 PDB was becoming an obsession with him. Certainly the White House thought he was obsessed with it—and with every other bit of evidence the commission could turn up that might embarrass Bush. Away from reporters, Ben-Veniste's name was invoked often at the White House, and never with affection.

Andy Card, Karl Rove, and others in the White House thought Ben-Veniste was struggling to re-create the glories of his early career. He wanted to bring down another president; Richard Nixon had been the first. Ben-Veniste's shining moment in the public eye had been in the 1970s, when he was the pugnacious young lawyer on the Watergate special prosecutor's team; he was thirty-one years old when Nixon resigned.

Ben-Veniste had become so well-known by the 1970s that he found himself immortalized in *The Incredible Hulk* comic books; he was the inspiration for the series' crusading prosecutor "Ben Vincent." (Ben Vincent aided the Hulk in ousting the treacherous Man-Beast from the White House, which the latter had occupied.)

After Watergate, Ben-Veniste insisted he would be happy to be rid of his celebrity status. "I never saw myself as the Jean-Paul Belmondo of the legal profession," he said. But with his appointment to the 9/11 commission a quarter century later, Ben-Veniste again seemed to revel in the spotlight.

If he had learned nothing else from Watergate, he knew a "smoking gun" when he saw it, and Republicans sensed that Ben-Veniste believed the August 6 PDB was just that.

Ben-Veniste was still among the commissioners who had not been allowed to see the actual PDB before he was invited to the Situation Room for the interview with Rice in February 2004. But he had an idea of what was in the PDB: Its frightening title, "Bin Laden Determined to Strike in United States," had been revealed in news reports.

Over the course of the commission's investigation, no document or any other piece of evidence took on anything like the significance, real or imagined, of the August 6 PDB.

Long before it was made public, it was assumed by President Bush's detractors, including many of the 9/11 family groups, that the PDB would turn out to have been a clear warning to Bush that al-Qaeda was about to launch a terrorist attack within American borders involving hijackings.

The White House had no plans to ever make the PDB public. But after word of its existence was leaked, White House aides, Rice chief among them, wanted people to assume that it was a much less ominous document that drew together a long history of al-Qaeda plots and suggested only that Osama bin Laden hoped to attack on American soil someday, possibly by hijacking planes. It contained no up-to-date evidence of a plot, Rice said repeatedly.

The truth, as it finally turned out, was somewhere in the middle. There were slightly more than 470 words in the entire PDB—it is not possible to say exactly how many words since four short passages in the PDB have never been declassified—and they left no doubt that bin Laden was indeed determined to kill Americans within their borders. It cited reports dating back to 1997 that bin Laden and his aides intended to "bring the fighting to America" and that the 1999 millennium plot may have been part of al-Qaeda's plan to strike on American soil.

From what they had learned about the PDB, the commission's staff knew that Rice had been misstating its contents for the better part of a year. They knew that despite her claims, it did contain some fresh intelligence in 2001 to suggest an ongoing al-Qaeda hijacking plot, possibly one directed at buildings in New York.

In preparation for the meeting in the Situation Room, some of the commissioners and staff had gone back and reread a copy of the transcript of Rice's White House news conference from Thursday, May 16, 2002, when she had gone before the White House press corps to respond to the initial leaks about the PDB.

In hindsight, the transcript is a remarkable document. To many of the commission's staff, it offered proof of how, to Condoleezza Rice, everything is semantics. A threat is not a threat, a warning is not a warning, unless she says it is. The word *historical* appeared to have an especially broad definition to Rice. To her, a warning that was a few weeks or months old was of relatively little value because it was "historical."

At the time of her news conference, no reporter had a copy of the PDB or knew about its title. CBS had broken the story of its existence but had few details of what was actually in the document. So the White House press corps would have to trust Rice's description of what was in it.

She described the PDB as a "warning briefing but an analytic report" about al-Qaeda threats and said that it contained "the most generalized kind of information—there was no time, there was no place, there was no method of attack" mentioned apart from a "very vague" concern about hijacking. "I want to reiterate," she said. "It was not a warning."

Ben-Veniste would learn by the spring of 2004 that all of that was wrong; the PDB would later be shown to refer to the scores of ongoing FBI investigations of al-Qaeda threats, as well as reports of recent efforts by terrorist groups to carry out surveillance of the New York skyline. It was certainly more than "historical."

Her most astonishing claim in the news conference was one that was replayed again and again on the network news broadcasts that night. Asked if 9/11 didn't represent an intelligence failure by the administration, she replied almost testily, "I don't think anybody could have predicted that these people would take an airplane and slam it into the World Trade Center, take another one and slam it into the Pentagon—that they would try to use an airplane as a missile."

Over time, Ben-Veniste learned that the nation's intelligence agencies had predicted exactly those things before 9/11.

Rice's news conference came eight months after the attacks. Yet she was suggesting that in all that time, no one had bothered to tell her that there were indeed several reports prepared within the CIA, the FAA, and elsewhere in the government about the threat of planes as missiles. Was she really suggesting that no one informed her that in the Moussaoui case, an FBI agent had warned specifically in August 2001 that he might be involved in a plot to "crash a plane into the World Trade Center"? Had no one told her in all those months that the Department of Defense had conducted drills for the possibility of a plane-as-missile attack on the Pentagon? Had she forgotten that when she and President Bush attended the G-8 summit in Italy in July 2001, the airspace was closed because of the threat of an aerial suicide attack by al-Qaeda?

Like Ben-Veniste, Tim Roemer made it his goal to get the August 6 PDB made public and to prove once and for all that Condoleezza Rice and her White House colleagues had a concept of the truth about 9/11 that was, at best, "flexible."

To Roemer, Rice had long ago passed the "threshold" between spin and dishonesty. "She'd lost credibility with me," he said. The question among the Democratic commissioners was whether anybody would be brave enough to go public to question Rice's competence and her honesty.

— 35 —

26 FEDERAL PLAZA
New York, N.Y.
JANUARY 21, 2004

I t seemed like a good omen for Thomas Pickard, the accountant-
turned–FBI agent who ran the bureau as its acting director in the
months before 9/11. The 9/11 commission was not requiring him
to travel down to Washington for his interview. Instead, the commission's staff agreed to meet with him in its New York offices, which were
in the same sprawling government building in lower Manhattan—the
Jacob K. Javits Federal Building at 26 Federal Plaza—where Pickard had
spent so many of the best years of his career. The FBI's New York field
office was in a separate wing of the Javits Building, reached through a
different elevator bank.

For Pickard, it was comforting simply to do it in New York. This was
home. He still spoke with the heavy accent of his childhood neighborhood in Woodside, Queens; he could sound more like a New York City
cop than a suit-and-tie agent of the FBI. He returned to New York after
retiring from the bureau in 2002 and was now security director of phar-
maceutical giant Bristol-Myers. Pickard had been Louis Freeh's top deputy when Freeh resigned abruptly in June 2001 as FBI director, leaving
Pickard to run the bureau until Robert Mueller's arrival in September.

Few FBI officials welcomed the invitation to be questioned by the
9/11 commission. Within the bureau, it was assumed—feared—that the
commission would try to punish the bureau for its pre-9/11 blunders
by recommending that it be broken up, with terrorism investigations
turned over to some new domestic equivalent of the CIA.

But by the time he took a seat in a commission's conference room
for his interview on January 21, 2004, Pickard felt almost relieved to be
answering these questions. Yes, the bureau had made mistakes, terrible
mistakes, before 9/11. Pickard was not going to defend them. The "FL,"

the "fuck-ups list," as it was known at FBI headquarters in Washington, was long: Zacarias Moussaoui, the Phoenix memo, the failure to detect the two hijackers who had lived under their own names in San Diego in the home of an FBI informant.

Pickard had lost sleep for months after 9/11 because of the blunders. Especially about Moussaoui. It still seemed unimaginable that no one had told him—or anybody else at the senior ranks of the FBI in Washington— about Moussaoui until the afternoon of September 11. "It all haunts me," Pickard said. "I'll take that to my grave."

The first time he heard about Moussaoui was during a hastily arranged 3:00 p.m. conference call on September 11 with FBI supervisors from around the country. The sheepish Minneapolis supervisor mentioned that some Muslim extremist "nut" had been arrested at a flight school out there a few weeks earlier. Was it possible that the "nut" was tied to the terrible events of that morning? asked the Minneapolis agent.

But if the FBI failed before 9/11, Pickard knew that it had not failed alone. The bureau was only one agency of the Justice Department, all of it overseen by the attorney general. Why weren't people asking more questions about Attorney General John Ashcroft and his failures in the spring and summer of 2001 as the nation's chief law enforcement officer?

Pickard took his seat across the conference table from Mike Jacobson and Caroline Barnes, two former FBI analysts who were now working on the staff of the 9/11 commission. Both Jacobson and Barnes had worked on counterterrorism cases during their bureau careers, and they knew all too well how the FBI had largely ignored domestic terrorist threats before 9/11.

The interview did not begin well. The commission's investigators asked Pickard if they could tape-record the interview. That was fine with Pickard, as long as he could have a copy of the tape. Jacobson and Barnes knew that Zelikow would never approve of it, so they declined. Both sides would have to depend on the accuracy of their handwritten notes in remembering the remarkable things that Pickard was about to say.

Pickard did not consider himself a whistle-blower. Certainly not. He had seen too many whistle-blowers torn apart in his long years at the FBI. He knew and had always liked Coleen Rowley, the Minneapolis agent who had gone public with her account of the FBI's disastrous performance on Moussaoui. She was one of a trio of women whistle-blowers who had been named *Time* magazine's "Persons of the Year" in 2002. (The others blew the whistle at Enron and WorldCom.) But Rowley also saw her career at the FBI and many of her friendships there destroyed by her disclosures.

Pickard was by nature a cautious, conservative man, entering the FBI in 1975, three years after the death of J. Edgar Hoover, whose influence was still everywhere to be seen at the bureau.

In part because his accounting background was so valuable in a complex criminal case, Pickard found himself attached early in his career to headline-grabbing investigations, including ABSCAM, in which members of Congress were caught accepting bribes from a phony Arab sheikh. Later, as a supervisor for "national security" cases in New York, Pickard had a hand in the investigations of the 1993 bombing of the World Trade Center and the 1996 explosion of TWA Flight 800 near Long Island.

Pickard would later find himself on a first-name basis with the mastermind of the 1993 bombing of the World Trade Center, Ramzi Youssef. Youssef was captured in Pakistan two years later and brought to the United States for trial. Pickard would take visitors to go see "Ramzi" defend himself in the federal courthouse in lower Manhattan. Youssef had asked to serve as his own lawyer, and when he saw Pickard enter the courtroom, he would stop and welcome his distinguished visitor from the FBI. "He'd just call me Tom," said Pickard.

For Pickard, Youssef—whose uncle, Khalid Sheikh Mohammed, was the mastermind of 9/11—offered a frightening introduction to the sort of sophisticated terrorist threat that the United States now faced. Youssef was intelligent, poised; he spoke English with a British accent, and his vocabulary and grammar were better than many of the New Yorkers on his jury.

"My God," Pickard recalled thinking at the time, "this is what we're up against? If there are a lot more like this, we're in trouble."

In the spring and summer of 2001, Pickard could see that John Ashcroft had no similar interest in the terrorist threat faced by the United States.

The relationship between Ashcroft and Pickard had been difficult since they talked for the first time in December 2000, when Bush announced that he was nominating Ashcroft as attorney general. Pickard, then

Louis Freeh's deputy, was responsible for the nominee's security detail, and within hours of Bush's announcement, the FBI learned of threats against Ashcroft.

Ashcroft was a hero in the most conservative circles of the Republican Party—and a lightning rod for liberals—for his absolutist views on abortion and gun control; he was fiercely opposed to both. His selection for Bush's cabinet was seen as an effort to placate the religious conservatives who had helped Bush eke out his election victory.

"The threats started right away," said Pickard, recalling how he had called Freeh and said, "I think we should put a protection detail on Ashcroft."

Freeh did not want to make the call to Ashcroft himself. "Why don't you call him?" Freeh told Pickard, warning his deputy that Ashcroft had a reputation for being unpleasant. "I understand that he's testy to deal with."

"Gee, thanks," Pickard replied with annoyance.

Pickard had found it a pleasure to deal with Ashcroft's predecessor, Janet Reno. She was popular with the FBI's rank and file, especially the agents in her security detail. "She was *so* nice," Pickard said. "The agents loved working with her. She was very good about making sure that they got something to eat. If it was the holidays, she wanted to make sure they got home to their families." Reno's modest apartment in downtown Washington was a two-minute walk from the FBI, and Pickard was called over one day to see her there. He was startled to arrive at the building and find no agent on duty in the lobby. "So I draw my weapon, thinking that there's something wrong," Pickard said. "I knock on the door. I go inside. Reno is there. She's making chicken soup because the agent is not feeling well."

Pickard remembered his exasperation. "You know, Ms. Reno, if he's not feeling well, we can call another agent," he told her.

Given Freeh's warning, Pickard made the call to Ashcroft with trepidation. But he had no choice. "I called Ashcroft's office and finally got through to him and explained about how we were getting these threats," Pickard said.

"Who is making these threats?" Ashcroft asked.

"We're just getting anonymous threats. There are letters coming in. There's e-mail coming in," Pickard replied, thinking that Ashcroft would welcome the FBI's concern for his safety. "We're responsible for your personal protection. I recommend we put a security detail on you and your family, until we can sort this out. I can have a team there tonight at your residence. They'll want to meet you and your family members so they can recognize them. They'll want to look through your house and determine a room where you could go and be safe if something should happen. And then they'll come back in a couple of days for a further security survey. Check the locks and alarms."

Ashcroft cut him off. "That's all fine, but they're not coming in my house."

Pickard wasn't sure Ashcroft had heard him properly; the idea here was to protect Ashcroft and his family. "I didn't know what to say," Pickard recalled. "So I went through it again, thinking maybe we had a poor connection."

Ashcroft was growing angry. "You don't understand," the nominee barked. "They're not coming into my house. They're not meeting my family."

Pickard was growing perplexed—and just as angry as Ashcroft. "I said, these guys are risking their lives to protect you," he told Ashcroft.

Ashcroft ended the conversation: "Well, that's the way it's going to be."

Ashcroft had finally arrived at the Justice Department in February, confirmed after a bruising confirmation battle in which all but eight of the Senate's Democrats voted against him, and the relationship between the new attorney general and the FBI grew even more difficult.

Whatever Ashcroft's odd behavior, he had reason to be wary of the FBI. On his first day in his new offices, literally within hours of his swearing-in, Ashcroft was informed that a veteran FBI counterintelligence agent, Robert Hanssen, was about to be arrested as a Russian spy; the FBI argued that the investigation was so sensitive—Hanssen's betrayal lasted more than twenty years—that Ashcroft could not be told about it until he had assumed his duties at the department. Six weeks later, the FBI notified Ashcroft's office that it had failed to provide defense lawyers for Timothy McVeigh, the Oklahoma City bomber, with potentially exculpatory information from FBI files, which meant that McVeigh's execution would have to be delayed at least one month, and maybe much longer. Then Freeh resigned in June, pointedly giving no advance warning to Ashcroft.

But if Ashcroft was worried about the FBI, the FBI was growing equally alarmed about the new attorney general and his peculiar behavior.

Because federal tax laws require officials who travel in government cars from their homes to pay some taxes for the service—about $4,500 a year in Ashcroft's case—Ashcroft declared that he would not ride in a government car from home in the morning. He walked, while armed FBI agents rode in the car beside him.

Ashcroft's fixation on his personal privacy only intensified. That winter, an obviously pregnant Justice Department lawyer was forced to fly to Missouri, where Ashcroft had kept a home, during a storm to obtain his signature on a document to authorize a special intelligence wiretap. CIA director George Tenet was traveling, so Ashcroft's signature was required. The lawyer knocked on his door and was amazed when Ashcroft did not invite her in. For the next thirty minutes, the big-bellied Justice Department lawyer remained on the porch, in the bitter cold and rain, while he read the wiretap application. He would not invite her in. The story quickly made the rounds at the FBI. "It was just so weird," Pickard said.

To Pickard and other senior officials at the FBI, Ashcroft made it clear he had two priorities as attorney general: supporting the agenda of the National Rifle Association (NRA), a major backer of Ashcroft in his political career, and ending the court disputes that had delayed the execution of McVeigh. In the Senate, Ashcroft had been a passionate champion of restoring the federal death penalty, and Pickard could see that Ashcroft was "dying to be the first attorney general to pull the switch."

Pickard thought Ashcroft's obsession with the logistics of putting McVeigh to death were perplexing, given Ashcroft's very public devotion to the nonviolent tenets of his Christian faith. Pickard said he was startled to attend meetings in Ashcroft's office at the Justice Department in which prayers were said.

"I found it astonishing," he said, recalling how he and another senior FBI official, Ruben Garcia, walked into Ashcroft's office to "find him standing there by himself, his arms outstretched to his sides, praying. So Ruben and I just bowed our heads until he finished." As Ashcroft concluded his prayer, Pickard and Garcia weren't quite sure what to do. "But we're both good Catholics, so we started making the sign of the cross, just as the good nuns had taught us to do."

At the same time, Pickard could see, Ashcroft had no interest in many of the other issues before the Justice Department, including dealing with terrorist threats. The CIA was warning of an imminent attack, probably overseas, but the agency made it clear to Pickard that there was no assurance it would not occur in the United States. Yet Ashcroft suggested the topic was of little interest to him. In May, Ashcroft released an agencywide statement listing his ten priorities for the Justice Department; terrorism was not on it. Pickard was in his office when Dale Watson, the bureau's executive assistant director for counterterrorism, walked in, exasperated.

"Did you see this?" he said in a disgusted tone, holding a copy of Ashcroft's statement. "Nothing about terrorism."

Pickard found it hard to believe that Ashcroft's office had accidentally left terrorism off the list, given how focused the rest of the government was on the threat. "If he didn't think about it, his staff should have," Pickard recalled thinking.

After Freeh's resignation in June, Pickard said he had resisted Ashcroft's request that he lead the FBI until a new Senate-confirmed director was in place. The two men had continued to battle regularly since Ashcroft's arrival at the Justice Department.

"I told him, 'Look, you can pick somebody else, and I'll do whatever they want,'" Pickard said. "I was already well past retirement age." Working directly for Ashcroft for several more months was "the last thing I needed," Pickard thought.

But Ashcroft insisted. "No, no, no, I want you to stay," he told Pickard. "And I want to meet with you once a week. I want to know what's going on in the FBI." Pickard agreed, warily.

Ashcroft made new attempts to assert control over the famously independent bureau. He ordered Pickard never to give a briefing on Capitol Hill or go to the White House without his approval. He told him that the FBI should never issue a press statement without approval from the Justice Department.

Pickard flinched at the orders, but he was in no position to argue. He gave Ashcroft the first of his weekly briefings in June. Before the meeting, Pickard sent an agenda to Ashcroft's office of the issues to be discussed. Terrorism was the number one item on the list. By the time of the first briefing, the CIA's warnings about an al-Qaeda attack were dire; they were reported to be the most serious and most convincing warnings of a terrorist strike since the millennium. So Pickard figured it was the first issue he should discuss with Ashcroft. During the briefing, Ashcroft suggested he knew little about al-Qaeda, so Pickard offered a primer on the terrorist network and its murderous history. "I told him about al-Qaeda and bin Laden, a little history about the World Trade Center bombing and East Africa."

Ashcroft listened, but he seemed far more intrigued by other items on the agenda, especially the latest on the FBI's efforts to end delays on background checks for gun buyers. Pickard said that over the course of the summer, most of his contacts from Ashcroft involved problems with the background check system, which was administered by the bureau. Ashcroft's interest was obviously prompted by complaints to his office from the NRA's lobbyists, Pickard figured. "He was like their poster boy," Pickard said of Ashcroft's relationship with the gun group. "People would get denied when they tried to buy their guns, and then the NRA would call him, and then I'd hear about it."

Pickard opened the next briefing, on July 12, 2001, with the latest on the CIA warnings about an al-Qaeda attack.

"We're at a very high level of chatter that something big is about to happen," Pickard began. "The CIA is very alarmed—"

He had barely begun the presentation when Ashcroft jumped in angrily. "I don't want to hear about that anymore," he said. "There's nothing I can do about that."

Pickard was dumbfounded; the attorney general didn't want to hear anything more about threats of an imminent terrorist attack? Yes, the warnings pointed to an attack overseas. But how could Ashcroft be so sure that the attack might not happen here?

"Mr. Attorney General, I think you should sit down with George Tenet and hear right from him as to what's happening," Pickard said.

"I don't want you to ever talk to me about al-Qaeda, about these threats," Ashcroft said. "I don't want to hear about al-Qaeda anymore."

Pickard thought the situation was absurd. Ashcroft was not interested in terrorist threats? Shouldn't the FBI and the other law enforcement agencies that answered to Ashcroft—the Immigration and Naturalization Service, the Border Patrol, the Marshals Service—be readying themselves for the possibility of an attack?

Pickard was furious. With his retirement so close, he figured he had nothing to lose and would make his anger clear to Ashcroft. "I got up out of my chair, and I got in his face," Pickard said. "And he got in my face." According to Pickard, others in the room watched, astonished at what they were seeing—the makings of a street brawl between the two most powerful men in federal law enforcement. (Aides to Ashcroft said later that nothing like that happened and have disputed much of the rest of Pickard's account, including his description of Ashcroft praying in his office.)

As Pickard and Ruben Garcia left Ashcroft's office, Garcia turned to Pickard. "I thought you were going to kill him," Garcia said. "You jumped out of the chair so fast, I could see your gun." Like other FBI agents, Pickard usually wore a gun beneath his jacket while on duty. "I thought you were going to use it," said Garcia.

Within days of the July 12 briefing, Ashcroft offered a final demonstration of his lack of attention to terrorism. In its annual budget request, the FBI had asked for a sizable budget increase for only one of its divisions—counterterrorism. But on July 18, Ashcroft sent a letter to Pickard saying the request had been turned down and that several FBI divisions faced budget cuts, including counterterrorism. Pickard contacted Ashcroft's office to ask if he might appeal. Ashcroft agreed. Pickard sat down "with the assistant directors that July and decided that we would appeal only the terrorism cuts—that's the only thing we're going to appeal because it's the most important thing. We'll drop everything else." He would not hear back from Ashcroft for several weeks.

Pickard slept on his couch at FBI headquarters on the evening of September 11, 2001; the skies over the Potomac were still gray with smoke from the Pentagon. His wife came into Washington to bring him a change of clothes. The next morning, Pickard's secretary walked into his office, a sly smile on her face. She flipped a copy of a letter from Ashcroft onto Pickard's desk. It was a denial of his request for more money for the counterterrorism division. The letter was dated September 10, 2001. "I just threw it aside," Pickard remembered. "I couldn't think about it."

As Pickard told his remarkable story to the 9/11 commission investigators, Jacobson and Barnes eyed each other nervously. Were they really hearing this about Ashcroft? Was it possible that the attorney general had simply ignored terrorist threats in the summer of 2001—that he had just been too bored by the subject to mobilize the Justice Department for an imminent attack? Pickard spoke with conviction about what had happened, and he had details, and Jacobson and Barnes had little doubt that he was telling the truth.

— 36 —

K STREET OFFICES OF THE
9/11 COMMISSION
Washington, D.C.
JANUARY 14, 2004

Mike Hurley, the Team 3 leader, and his colleagues wondered if Sandy Berger was ill. Berger had arrived in the commission's offices on K Street on January 14, 2004, for what was scheduled to be an all-day interview, a preview of testimony that Berger was scheduled to give at a public hearing that spring. Hurley's team wondered if the interview should be called off. Berger looked terrible. His hands were shaking badly, and the tremors only seemed to grow worse as the interview went on. At one point, he had to hold one hand down with the other to stop the shaking.

Every half hour or so, Berger would ask that one of the commission staffers go out to the street and buy him a large cup of coffee from the nearby Starbucks. "It's like he's chain-drinking the coffee," one of the Team 3 investigators said later. It was one cup after the other. Berger ignored the sandwiches that had been brought in for the session; he nibbled on the corner of one of the home-baked cookies that Alexis Albion had provided that morning.

If this was a display of nerves, it was especially odd to see it from Berger. Whatever his private insecurities, he was known in the Clinton White House for his gruff, good-humored cool in most public settings; he had always been a natural on the Sunday television talk shows for just that reason. Now he was nothing but nerves—caffeine-jangled nerves at that.

Hurley and the others did not know it at the time, but Berger had reason to be panicked. He had learned weeks earlier that he was under criminal investigation by the Justice Department over the theft of classified documents from the National Archives—specifically, several copies of Richard Clarke's secret 2000 after-action report on the millennium terrorist threats. Berger knew that at the Justice Department, a few prosecutors who ultimately answered to the Bush White House were reviewing evidence that had the potential of destroying his reputation and ending his career—even of sending him to prison.

To THE ARCHIVES staff, there was no doubt about what Berger had done. They believed they had proved the thefts conclusively during his fourth and final trip to the archives three months earlier—on October 2, 2003—to review the Clinton White House's intelligence files. He was preparing at the time for his interviews with the 9/11 commission.

Suspicious that he had taken something in his earlier trips in 2002 and 2003, Nancy Kegan Smith, the senior archivist for White House documents, had gathered the classified files that were supposed to be presented to Berger in October and numbered the back of each document in a light pencil. The files that Berger had reviewed in his earlier visits were mostly uncataloged; they were so highly classified that only a few archives workers would have had the security clearance needed to prepare an index. So if Berger had taken something in his earlier visits, the archives might never be able to document exactly what was missing.

As Smith had feared, Berger took the bait during the October visit. In his search of the files that day, Berger found two more copies of Clarke's 2000 report, and he set them aside to be stolen. The staff suspected in his earlier visits that he used his frequent trips to the men's room to hide stolen documents in his clothes. And the pattern repeated itself in October. He began visiting the bathroom frequently, every thirty minutes or so, even though the archives staff knew that Berger did not have much to drink that day.

During one of his bathroom visits, most of Smith's colleagues hurriedly went through a stack of documents that Berger had just reviewed, checking to see if anything was missing. She started counting: Documents 213, 214, 215, 216 . . .

Document 217 was missing; it was yet another copy of Clarke's 2000 report. Dismayed, Smith and her colleagues quickly printed another copy of it. When Berger returned from the bathroom, Smith presented him with the new copy.

"We apparently forgot to give you this document," she told Berger, trying to hand him another copy of Document 217.

He looked at it. "No, I think I've already seen it," he replied.

Smith insisted that he take another look at it; she told him the archives had a method of tracking the documents that Berger had been given during his visits. She said she needed to feel confident that Berger, as President Clinton's liaison to the 9/11 commission, had seen all of the documents in the archives' possession.

In fact, Smith was giving Berger a final test, setting a final trap. Would he steal this copy as well?

Berger said later he should have realized at that moment that the archives staff was on to him. Why else would Smith be making a special effort to present him with, of all documents, yet another copy of Clarke's report? "The bomb should have burst in the air," he said later. "But obviously it did not."

Berger stole that copy, too. He used the same method for the theft. He asked Smith for a few minutes of privacy, claiming that he needed to make a phone call. Smith left the room and went to a nearby desk that shared the same telephone lines. She could see that Berger had lied; he was not using the phone in her office—the line on the phone did not light up. She rushed back to her office to try to catch him in the act. But she was nearly "mowed over" by Berger as he charged out the door for the bathroom again.

The archives staff did a final tally and determined that all three copies of Clarke's report, plus the extra copy that Smith had presented to him, were gone. "The staff and I were almost physically ill," Smith said.

At about 6:00 that night, Berger told Smith that he wanted to leave for the day; he was exhausted.

"I just can't do this anymore, Nancy," he told Smith. "My mind is a dishrag."

She did not feel she had the authority at that moment to confront Berger and accuse him of stealing classified documents. But she apparently did not want to contemplate the idea that Berger would return to the archives and steal more from the White House files. She suggested that he take a walk and try to finish up the rest of the documents.

Berger agreed reluctantly. But rather than walking the hallways of the archives, he left the building altogether. He walked out of the north entrance of the archives onto Pennsylvania Avenue. He had the four copies of Clarke's report and about fifteen pages of his notes from the visit stuffed in his pockets. He crossed Pennsylvania Avenue to a construction site on 9th Street.

252 / PHILIP SHENON

He pondered his options. Did he really want to walk back into the archives with the stolen documents? Did he want to risk two more opportunities for detection—as he walked back in and walked back out?

Why don't I put these documents in a place where no one can see them? he thought. It was, he acknowledged later, a "logical impulse in a totally illogical context." The construction site was ringed by a wire fence. It was twilight. He emptied his pockets and folded the papers into a V shape. He placed the folded documents beneath a trailer on the site.

His self-described "craziness" grew worse. He now had five copies of Clarke's 2000 report—four he had stolen that day and one taken during an earlier visit. After he returned to the construction site later that night to gather the documents, Berger drove back to his downtown office and used scissors to cut up three of the copies of Clarke's report into small pieces, which he placed in his office trash can. He still had two other copies of the report; he did not need five.

THAT WEEKEND, Berger learned that he had been found out. He got a call at home from Smith on Saturday, October 4. The archives staff had spent most of Friday and Saturday morning trying to figure out what to do, and the decision was made to have Smith phone him and question him directly about the thefts. She told him that at least three of the documents that he had reviewed were missing. Did he have them? Could he look for them?

Berger was petrified. He initially tried to pretend he was indignant with Smith and her staff, accusing the archives of losing the documents and of trying to blame him for the loss. She urged him to keep looking.

"I hope you can find them because if not, we have to refer this to the NSC," she said ominously. The NSC—the White House, in other words—had formal control over the archives, and National Security Adviser Condoleezza Rice's staff would have to be notified about what had happened. Smith urged Berger to go to his office to search.

Berger got into his car and drove to downtown Washington, his mind a blur of panicked thoughts. Should he admit what he had done? Would he be prosecuted? Could he convince the archives not to reveal to the Justice Department what he had done? He could only imagine what the Bush White House would do with this, how Bush's aides would wait for just the right moment to leak it. Berger was going downtown with the intention of rummaging through his trash can. He hoped that perhaps the trash had not been picked up since Thursday, that the pieces of the documents he had cut up with scissors might still be there. If he could present the documents to the archives, even in pieces, perhaps he would be treated less harshly. His heart sank when he entered his office; the trash can was empty. He tried to find a telephone number for the waste disposal company that picked up the trash in the office building. No luck.

Later that night, Berger spoke by phone with another senior official of the archives.

"I think I solved the mystery," he said, trying to sound unconcerned, as if this were all an understandable, innocent mistake. "I found two documents"—the pair of copies of Clarke's after-action report that he had not destroyed. The archives was welcome to come pick them up, he announced.

The archives felt it had no choice but to notify the White House about what had happened. On Sunday, the archives called the White House and asked to speak to someone at the NSC. An NSC lawyer provided the archives with the names of lawyers at the Justice Department who would need to be contacted about a criminal investigation of Berger. Berger had already called his own lawyer.

DESPITE THE CAFFEINE buzz that only increased the shaking of his hands, Berger was able to answer questions coherently during the January interview at the commission's offices. Berger took a little comfort from the fact that the commission's staff seemed to know nothing about what had happened at the archives.

He had gone into the meeting with several "talking points." He wanted to make it clear to the commission and its staff that he believed Bill Clinton had taken al-Qaeda seriously, as seriously as any other national security threat, and that the Clinton White House had done what it could to try to kill Osama bin Laden. Not wound or capture him. Clinton had given explicit authority to the CIA to kill bin Laden, Berger said. "He wanted him dead."

The remark created confusion among some of the members of Team 3. Was this just bluster on Berger's part? In interviewing George

Tenet's deputies at the CIA, the commission's staff had been told again and again that the agency had not been authorized to kill bin Laden and his henchmen—that the CIA had instead been given a confusing set of presidential orders that allowed for bin Laden's capture, but not his death. Within the CIA, the common wisdom was that overly cautious lawyers at the White House or at Janet Reno's Justice Department were wary of anything that resembled an assassination order.

Told of the CIA complaints, Berger looked confused. No, he assured the commission's staff, there was an explicit, if highly secret, order given by Clinton to the CIA in late 1998 to kill bin Laden. It was part of a so-called memorandum of notification, or MON, involving Afghanistan. MONs were top-secret orders prepared by the White House to authorize covert operations abroad by the CIA. "There is paperwork," Berger said. "Keep looking for it."

Berger also wanted to overcome any perception that Clinton had been hindered in dealing with al-Qaeda because of his many personal scandals, in particular the furor over Monica Lewinsky. Berger said it was remarkable how little Clinton allowed the scandals to affect his performance as president, most impressively in the summer of 1998. On August 7, the American embassies in Kenya and Tanzania were blown up by al-Qaeda followers, killing 224 people, including 12 Americans. That same month, the Lewinsky scandal was at its height, with Clinton scheduled to testify before a grand jury on August 17 about his relationship with the former intern. A special prosecutor, Kenneth Starr, was only weeks away from presenting a report to Congress that was expected to accuse Clinton of several impeachable offenses, including lying about his relationship with Lewinsky. (Starr's report was finally released to the public on September 11, 1998, exactly three years before the attacks on the World Trade Center and the Pentagon.)

After the East Africa bombings, Clinton weighed a military response to the attacks targeting al-Qaeda and its sponsors in the African nation of Sudan. Clinton's political advisers worried that the attacks, especially if they failed to kill bin Laden, would be perceived as an effort by Clinton to divert attention from Lewinsky. But Berger said Clinton refused to allow any political considerations to be factored into the response to the attacks. The commission's staff had heard this from others around Clinton, including Defense Secretary William S. Cohen, the cabinet's sole Republican. "We're going to get crap either way," Berger recalled Clinton saying. "So you should do the right thing."

Berger said there was another important way of measuring the commitment of the Clinton White House to dealing with terrorism. "Look what we did with Dick Clarke," he reminded the commission's staff. An otherwise midlevel career bureaucrat in the NSC, Clarke had become a formidable power in his own right during the Clinton administration, with almost instant access to the Oval Office. The Counterterrorism Strategy Group, which Clarke led, bypassed the usual reporting lines in the White House. The CSG reported directly to Berger's so-called Small Group, which was made up of Cohen, Secretary of State Madeleine Albright, Janet Reno, and a tiny number of other senior officials cleared to know the most secret information about the government's counterterrorism efforts. The decision to grant so much authority to Clarke had come at an institutional cost to Berger, who often had to spend much of his workday in the West Wing trying to soothe the egos of others in the government who were offended by the sharp-elbowed Clarke.

Berger explained that during the transition between the Clinton and Bush administrations, he had tried to impress upon his successor, Condoleezza Rice, how dangerous bin Laden was. He recalled how he made a special effort to drop in on the introductory NSC briefing that Clarke gave to Rice, his new boss, about al-Qaeda. Berger said he wanted to signal, by his presence at the briefing, the severity of the threat. "You know, Condi, you'll be spending more time on terrorism in general— and al-Qaeda in particular—than anything else," he recalled telling her. He was never sure he got his message across to Rice or the other members of the transition team, including her counterterrorism adviser, Philip Zelikow.

OFFICES OF THE DIRECTOR OF CENTRAL INTELLIGENCE

CIA Headquarters
Langley, Va.
JANUARY 22, 2004

Rudy Rousseau thought George Tenet looked tired, as tired as he had ever seen him.

"He just didn't look well," said Rousseau, a twenty-year veteran of the CIA who was leading the DCI Review Group; Tenet had set up the group shortly after 9/11 to reconstruct the agency's work over the years on al-Qaeda and prepare for the inevitable investigations that would follow.

Rousseau joined Tenet in the director's seventh-floor conference room at CIA headquarters on January 22, 2004, the first of three days that Tenet would set aside for private interviews by the 9/11 commission. Tenet would also be called to testify at two of the commission's public hearings later in the year.

The wood-paneled room could have passed for one of the more modest corporate boardrooms on Wall Street, apart from how the walls were decorated. There was a framed government-issue photograph of President Bush on one wall, next to digital clocks that showed the time in Kabul, Baghdad, and other global hot spots. Another wall was covered with plaques with the logos of the CIA and the government's fourteen other spy agencies, including the NSA and the Defense Intelligence Agency. Tenet's title was "director of central intelligence," not "director of the CIA." He was supposed to supervise the work of all of the government's spy agencies, not just the CIA, although it was increasingly clear to the staff of the 9/11 commission that his real powers did not extend much beyond the gates of Langley.

As in any reasonably equipped corporate boardroom, Tenet's conference room had flat-screen monitors that were supposed to allow him and his deputies to keep an eye on the television networks and beam in their colleagues from around the globe for videoconferences. "The truth is the damn stuff never worked, so we mostly gave up on it," said Rousseau.

Tenet took a seat at the long, rectangular table at the center of the conference room. His aides thought it was remarkable that he was able to set aside most of a day for the commission; Tenet and the agency were overwhelmed at that moment with the deteriorating situation in Baghdad. Eight months after the invasion, there were clear signs of an insurrection in Iraq. That morning, the Knight Ridder news service had reported that CIA officers in Iraq had issued new warnings to the Bush administration that the country might be headed toward civil war; the White House, which refused to apply the term *civil war* to what was happening in Iraq, was furious with the agency over the article.

Tenet had insisted on all-day, almost all-night cram sessions to prepare himself for the interview with the 9/11 commission. "He spent an enormous amount of time mastering an enormous amount of material," Rousseau said. "George is very intense, and this was very personal."

That meant sessions on the weekend—and until midnight during the week—to review the vast archives of material on the work of the bin Laden unit and the various, failed plans to capture or kill Osama bin Laden. There were mountains of paperwork for Tenet to look over, much of which he had never seen before. It occurred to Rousseau that Tenet was being obsessive in the preparation. "He tried to master too much material," he thought later.

Tenet wanted specifically to master what had happened in Kuala Lumpur in 2000 with Nawaf al-Hazmi and Khalid al-Mihdhar and why the CIA had apparently failed for so long to alert anyone that the two hijackers had later entered the United States from Asia. Like almost everyone else at the agency, Tenet seemed to understand that the CIA's failure to watch-list the pair after their arrival in California was the agency's Achilles' heel—the one horrendous blunder that could sink the CIA.

On the other side of the conference table, Richard Ben-Veniste took a seat alongside Philip Zelikow and several of the commission's investigators from Team 3. As Zelikow had recommended, Tenet was sworn in for the interview. Tenet, not realizing there was anything unusual about the oath, did so without protest.

If anyone had protested, Zelikow was ready to make a strong argument why Tenet needed to testify under threat of perjury. The CIA's record was full of discrepancies about the facts of its operations against bin Laden before 9/11, and many of the discrepancies were Tenet's.

The interview with the commission started going badly almost immediately, although Tenet appeared not to understand that. (It was only long after the commission had gone out of business that Tenet realized, angrily, that it had been playing "stump the dummy" with him.)

The problem was Tenet's memory. It was incredibly faulty, or so he seemed to be trying to suggest. As he was led through the chronology of the CIA's struggles with al-Qaeda since the 1990s, he kept falling back on the same answers:

"I don't remember."

"I don't recall."

"Let me go through the documents and get back to you with an answer."

Tenet remembered certain details, especially when he was asked the sorts of questions he was eager to answer—about how he had battled budgetary restraints throughout the 1990s, about how prescient many of the CIA's analysts had been about the al-Qaeda threat.

But on so many other questions, his memory was cloudy. The closer the questions came to the events of the spring and summer of 2001 and to the 9/11 attacks themselves, the worse his memory became.

It wasn't just details that Tenet claimed he could not remember. He could not recall entire meetings and key documents. The commission's staffers eyed one another warily as Tenet claimed that he could not remember anything of what was discussed at his first meeting with George Bush after Bush's election in 2000. That seemed especially suspicious given how eager Tenet was at the time to try to hold on to his job in the transition from the Clinton to the Bush administration. The commission's investigators thought it would have been one of the most important meetings of Tenet's career—essentially a job interview with the new president of the United States.

Tenet could not remember exactly what he had told Bush in the morning intelligence briefings at the White House in the months before 9/11, a time when his "hair was on fire," the memorable phrase he uttered in the interview to describe the frenzy over the threat reporting in 2001.

Zelikow said there was no one "a-ha moment"—no one set of questions or answers—when he began to question seriously whether Tenet was telling the truth under oath. It was the cumulative "I don't recall" and "I don't remember" responses that did it for Zelikow—Tenet's "inability to recall or add much to our understanding of many critical episodes." Zelikow said later that "we just didn't believe him."

The former prosecutors among the ten commissioners had seen this before. Tenet was like a grand jury witness who had been too well prepared by a defense lawyer. The witness's memory was good when it was convenient, bad when it was convenient. Unless the witness had something to say that would bolster the defense case, the witness would say nothing, blaming a faulty memory.

THE OTHER CIA officials in the room would say later that Tenet's memory was no better or worse in his meetings with the 9/11 commission than usual.

Rousseau believed Tenet was telling the truth throughout the interviews. He acknowledged that it was a shame that Tenet did not remember more—"It wasn't good that he doesn't remember"—about some central moments in the CIA's battles against bin Laden. But to Rousseau, it was a miracle that Tenet's memory was not more faulty given the whirlwind of his tenure at the CIA. "I'm surprised he remembered as much as he did," said Rousseau.

Tenet's loyal aides were furious when they were told later that Zelikow had reported back to the commissioners that Tenet had, essentially, perjured himself. Given the thousands of documents, the millions of words of e-mail, that passed through Tenet's office in any given week, was it a surprise that his memory sometimes failed him? Rousseau wondered. As director of central intelligence, Tenet went to upward of twenty meetings a day; was he supposed to remember them all? "It's outrageous to suggest the DCI held back," said John Moseman, Tenet's former chief of staff. "I attended every prep session, and every meeting with the commission, open and closed. The DCI, and those of us supporting him, provided an enormous amount of information. Neither he, nor we, held information back. At no time did any commissioner or member of the commission's staff tell the DCI that they thought he was not being fully candid. To suggest so now is not honorable."

Rousseau was indisputably right about one thing: By early 2004,

George Tenet was dead tired—physically exhausted. Apart from the president and Defense Secretary Don Rumsfeld, Tenet was under pressure like no man in Washington. Not only was the war in Iraq going badly, Tenet was also faced with multiple investigations of why the intelligence that took the nation to war—the intelligence that he had presented to the president about Iraq's weapons programs—had been so wrong. Unlike Bush and Rumsfeld, Tenet gave himself no chance for rest. He had aged visibly in the job. (Between his insistence on a full night's sleep and his extended ranch vacations in Texas, the president almost always looked well rested; and the astonishingly youthful-looking seventy-one-year-old Rumsfeld seemed incapable of showing fatigue no matter how long his workday.)

Sleep deprivation was a frequent topic of conversation among people who worked in the executive offices at the CIA, just as it was at the Pentagon and the White House and other agencies where round-the-clock workdays were common. It occurred to many of Tenet's deputies, just as it occurred to aides to the administration's other true workaholics, that a little more sleep and a lot more time at home would have resulted in better decisions.

Tenet rose before dawn every day so he was ready at 6:15 to climb into an armored SUV for the ride to the White House, where he conducted a final read-through of the PDB before it was presented to Bush. The workday would not end until after he had reviewed a copy of the PDB for the next day's Oval Office briefing; it arrived on a classified fax machine in Tenet's home at about 11:00 p.m. He would read it through and call in to Langley if he wanted changes. REM sleep was almost impossible for Tenet, since the phone tended to ring in the middle of the night with news of some disaster somewhere in the world.

Rousseau could see that Tenet was growing more and more tired as the questioning from the commission went on in the conference room. He worried that Tenet was setting a trap for himself because of his fatigue.

"I thought he was pushing it," he said. During a break in the afternoon, Rousseau took Tenet aside in the hallway outside the conference room.

"George, you're getting tired, you're going to make mistakes," Rousseau told his boss. "This needs to end."

Tenet warily agreed. He returned to the conference room, made excuses, and told Ben-Veniste and the commission's investigators that they were welcome back, anytime, for more questions.

The commission's delegation returned to their offices alarmed by Tenet's claims of a faulty memory.

If Zelikow needed any more evidence of what was wrong at the CIA, he now had it in Tenet's seeming inability to tell the truth under oath. It soon became common wisdom on the commission's staff—and among most of the ten commissioners—that George Tenet was, at best, loose with the facts. At worst, they thought, he was someone flirting with a perjury charge. Even Tom Kean, who found it difficult to say anything critical of anyone, began to accept the common wisdom. Tenet was a witness who would "fudge everything."

WHATEVER HIS memory problems, Tenet had a good answer to a question that had perplexed many on the commission's staff: If he had truly warned President Bush every day for months before 9/11 that al-Qaeda was about to launch a catastrophic attack, why didn't the White House do more to respond, especially within American borders?

Tenet explained that his contacts with the White House were limited mostly to Bush—at the morning intelligence briefing—and Condoleezza Rice and Chief of Staff Andy Card. As director of central intelligence, he looked mostly to threats abroad; he would not have had daily contact with the FBI or other domestic agencies. He would have had much more contact with the Pentagon, especially over the situation in Iraq and Afghanistan, and with the State Department. And he was confident in the summer of 2001 that the Pentagon and State Department were fully mobilized for the terrorist attack he was certain was coming. "Ships were being put out to sea, embassies were being put on heightened alert," Tenet said. "I could see what I could see."

He could only assume the FBI and the other domestic agencies were being mobilized for a possible al-Qaeda strike as they had been in the past—through the National Security Council. That had certainly been true during the millennium threats; in December 2000, Berger and the NSC had daily meetings at the White House with the directors of the domestic agencies, including Janet Reno and Louis Freeh, to insist that they prepare for the possibility of a domestic terrorist attack during the holidays that year. Tenet assumed—he certainly hoped—that the same thing was happening in the summer of 2001, when the threat from Osama bin Laden was far more severe. "I had no reason to believe the domestic side was not fully engaged," he later told colleagues. "I thought Condi had it under control."

STUDIOS OF NBC NEWS
Washington, D.C.
APRIL 4, 2004

The studios of *Meet the Press* were sometimes compared to a confessional, a place where Washington's powerful go early on Sunday morning to acknowledge some weakness, political or otherwise. It was not that they always wanted to confess. But the show's host, Tim Russert, NBC's Washington bureau chief, was better than most other television journalists in the capital at dragging something out of them. Russert was accused of being deferential to Washington's powerful; he was unfailingly polite to his guests. But he was known for the quality of the research behind his questioning. He seemed to relish the chance to confront politicians with a quotation dug out from a years-old newspaper story or some grainy piece of videotape that demonstrated the hypocrisy of their current positions. He tended to ask public officials the questions they did not want to answer.

On April 4, 2004, Tom Kean and Lee Hamilton went on *Meet the Press* and reluctantly acknowledged—in response to Russert's questions—what many on the commission's staff believed had been obvious since the early days of the investigation: The 9/11 attacks could have been prevented. They should have been prevented.

It was a conclusion that Kean and Hamilton had seemed wary of reaching publicly, since it might be seen as an election-year judgment on the Bush administration's performance on dealing with terrorist threats in the months before 9/11. (It might also be seen as a reflection on the Clinton administration's performance, but in the early heat of Bush's reelection bid in 2004, Bill Clinton's presidency seemed a distant memory.)

"Congressman," Russert asked Hamilton, "do you think September eleventh could have been prevented?"

"There's a lot of ifs," Hamilton replied with his usual caution, pausing for a moment to collect his thoughts. "You can string together a lot of ifs." But he had to acknowledge that, "frankly, if you'd had a little luck, it probably could have been prevented."

Kean went through the list of bungled opportunities at the FBI and CIA: Moussaoui; the delays in putting Hazmi and Mihdhar on watch lists after they entered the United States; the decision to call off some of the CIA's more promising capture-or-kill operations against bin Laden.

"There were times we could have gotten him, there's no question," Kean said of bin Laden. "Had we gotten him and his leadership at that point, the whole story might have been different."

Russert then asked Kean and Hamilton an even trickier question— about Philip Zelikow. He raised "the very sensitive issue" of Zelikow's involvement in the investigation and the families' repeated complaints about Zelikow's ties to Condoleezza Rice and his involvement in George Bush's 2000 White House transition team. It was the most public forum in which Kean and Hamilton had ever been asked about the conflicts of interest of the commission's executive director.

Kean insisted that Zelikow had been chosen for the Bush transition team in 2000 because "he was one of the best experts on terrorism in the whole area of intelligence, in the whole country"—not because he was Rice's friend. Kean said that he had not found "any evidence to indicate in any way that he is partial to anybody or anything. In fact, he's been much tougher, I think, than a lot of people would have liked him to be."

Zelikow, he said, "is the best possible person we could have found for the job."

Hamilton agreed. He said Zelikow had "played it right down the line— I found no evidence of a conflict of interest of any kind." It was a judgment that almost no one on the commission's staff would have agreed with.

If there had been any lingering doubt that Zelikow would survive as executive director until the end of the investigation, Kean and Hamilton had put it to rest with their statements of support to Russert on national television. Zelikow would remain in charge.

CAMP DAVID, MD.

Despite his obvious disdain for what was increasingly becoming known as the "mainstream" media, Vice President Dick Cheney had a special relationship with Russert. Certainly he had a respect for the platform that *Meet the Press* offered. It had been the top-rated Sunday morning show for years. Cheney offered Russert arguably the most important exclusive of the newsman's career when, on September 16, 2001, the Sunday after the attacks, Cheney invited Russert to the presidential retreat at Camp David for an hour-long interview. Although the public did not realize it at the time, Camp David often functioned as the "secure undisclosed location" where Cheney worked and lived in the first weeks after 9/11— supposedly an effort to guarantee a smooth transition of power if Bush was killed or disabled in a new terrorist strike on Washington.

It was the vice president's first significant interview after the attacks, and it seemed an obvious effort by the White House to establish an early, and definitive, account of what had happened in the executive branch on the morning of the attacks. It would be the most authoritative account until the 9/11 commission's report was released in 2004.

It was a riveting hour of television. Cheney was characteristically articulate and composed, even as he reviewed the chaos in the White House on the morning of September 11. He described watching television in his West Wing office and seeing the second plane hit the Twin Towers. "Terrorism," he remembered thinking at that moment. "This is an attack."

He described how Secret Service agents hustled him from his office into the tubelike underground bunker beneath the East Wing, the so-called Presidential Emergency Operations Center, or PEOC. The bunker had been built for Franklin Roosevelt during World War II.

"They came in and said, 'Sir, we have to leave immediately,' and grabbed me," he said. "They hoisted me up and moved me very rapidly down the hallway, down some stairs, through some doors, and down some more stairs into an underground facility under the White House." He said that he had been moved to the PEOC because of warnings that another hijacked airplane was headed for the White House.

Russert asked Cheney what was the most difficult decision made during the course of the day.

"Well, I suppose the toughest decision was this question of whether or not we would intercept incoming commercial aircraft," Cheney said, referring to the decision to order military jets to shoot down passenger planes that approached Washington.

Russert followed up: "And you decided..."

Cheney corrected Russert. "*We* decided to do it." He was referring to himself and Bush.

"So if the United States government became aware that a hijacked commercial airliner was destined for the White House or the Capitol, we would take the plane down?" Russert continued.

"Yes," Cheney said somberly. "The president made the decision—on my recommendation." He said that Bush decided that if passenger planes "wouldn't pay any attention to instructions to move away from the city, as a last resort, our pilots were authorized to take them out." Bush relayed the decision to Cheney in one of their telephone calls that morning, Cheney said.

"Now, people say, you know, that's a horrendous decision to make," Cheney continued. "Well, it is."

On the commission, the chronology of events of the morning of 9/11 had been left to John Farmer's team, and the commission's investigators had come to believe that a central element of Cheney's account—the shoot-down order—was false.

The staff was convinced that the "horrendous decision" was not made by Bush; it was made by Cheney, and the vice president had almost certainly made it alone. If Farmer's team was right, the shoot-down order was almost certainly unconstitutional, a violation of the military chain of command, which has no role for the vice president. In the absence of the president, military orders should have been issued by Defense Secretary Rumsfeld, bypassing the vice president entirely.

Apart from Cheney's account, and a later attempt by Bush to back up the vice president, there was no evidence to suggest that Bush had weighed in on the shoot-down order before Cheney had issued it. And there was plenty of evidence to suggest that Bush knew nothing about it. "We didn't believe it," Dan Marcus, the general counsel, said of Cheney's account.

Even in moments of crisis, the White House keeps extraordinary records of communications involving Bush and his senior staff; every phone call is logged, along with a detailed summary of what happened during the call. Many foreign leaders who talk to Bush by phone might be surprised to learn how many other people in the White House are listening in silently.

But for 9/11, the logs offered no evidence of a call between Cheney and Bush in which Bush authorized a shoot-down. And Farmer's team reviewed more than just one set of communications logs. There were seven of them—one maintained by the White House telephone switchboard, one by the Secret Service, one by the Situation Room, and four separate logs maintained by military officers working in the White House.

Many of the people in the PEOC that morning, including Lewis "Scooter" Libby, Cheney's chief of staff, and Cheney's wife, Lynne, took detailed handwritten notes on yellow legal pads about everything that happened, including what they overheard of Cheney's phone conversations; there was no reference to a shoot-down order from Bush. The notes of Ari Fleischer, the press secretary, who was aboard Air Force One with Bush, also showed no reference to an order until several minutes after it had been issued by Cheney.

Joshua Bolten, who was then deputy chief of staff in the White House and was in the PEOC with Cheney, told the commission's staff in an interview on March 18, 2004, that he was so concerned about the shoot-down order that he urged Cheney to take a "quiet moment" to call Bush. Bolten wanted Cheney to make sure the president understood the ominous military order that had just been issued in his name by the vice president. Although Bolten might be too discreet to say so, the commission's staff took his comment to mean that he did not believe Bush knew of the order. (Bolten later suggested that the commission's staff had misconstrued his comments. "I was not concerned that the vice president lacked authority to issue the shoot-down order, but I did want the president to know that the vice president had executed on that authority," he said.)

Farmer's team discovered that the timing of the shoot-down order— and Bolten's recommendation to Cheney to call the president—was memorialized in Libby's notes, which referred to Bolten by his initials.

Libby's entry from 10:15 a.m. to 10:18 a.m. read: "Aircraft 60 miles out, confirmed as hijack—engage? VP? Yes. JB: Get President and confirm engage order."

Marcus thought that, in many ways, it would have been completely understandable for Cheney to issue a shoot-down order without authorization from Bush. Whatever the constitutional issues, it would have been difficult to second-guess Cheney about a decision to save the White House from destruction if a suicide hijacker was bearing down on the capital and there were only seconds to act.

"If Cheney orders a shoot-down of a plane that he thinks is coming at the White House, who'd blame him?" Marcus said. "But his staff was obsessed with showing that he *didn't* give the order."

It was not difficult to imagine why Cheney and his staff would have been determined to rewrite the history of that morning. The White House would have been concerned about any perception that Cheney had usurped presidential power, especially in a crisis. By the start of the 2004 campaign, no one doubted that Cheney was the most powerful vice president in the nation's modern history; Bush's reelection strategists were eager to dispel any notion of Cheney as Bush's puppeteer or Svengali.

Members of the commission's staff suspected that the Russert interview was the moment that the false but well-packaged account was first presented to the public. By then, Marcus said, "they all had their stories straight, and the story was that the president was in charge, was in full communication with the staff," on September 11. Even if it was not true.

Marcus wondered how Cheney and his staff would respond if the commission concluded in its final report that summer that it did not believe the vice president was telling the truth about what really happened that morning in the White House. Cheney, as it turned out, would be furious. He would try to have the report rewritten on the eve of its release.

FEDERAL BUREAU OF INVESTIGATION
Washington, D.C., Field Office
OCTOBER 2003

Maybe you could just mail it in?" the FBI agent asked in October 2003. "You know, snail mail?"

He had that tone of resigned embarrassment that the 9/11 commission's investigators had grown used to when they interviewed FBI employees.

"There really isn't e-mail at the bureau," he said. "I know that's hard to believe."

The agent in the FBI's Washington field office was explaining why, if the commission's investigators wanted him to answer more questions in writing, they should mail them in. The U.S. Postal Service might take a day or two for delivery, he said, but it was the best way of ensuring that the information got to the FBI.

It had come to that. In 2003, nearly a generation after electronic mail had become routine in American businesses and on college campuses and almost everywhere else, the Federal Bureau of Investigation had no functioning internal e-mail system or easy employee access to the Internet. There was no searchable computer database for most FBI case files.

FBI agents might go home at night to find their teenagers playing on their laptops, swapping e-mail messages with school friends, or trading MP3 files. But when the agents went back to work at the bureau the next morning, they were returned to the electronic dark ages. Amy Zegart, a professor of public policy at UCLA who studied the way the FBI managed information before and after September 11, found to her amazement that the bureau's computers were so out of date before 9/11 that it took twelve commands to store a single document. That explained why almost half of all the FBI's records—six billion pages—was still stored on paper. Tom Pickard, the bureau's acting director in the summer of

2001, told the commission that "the FBI computer system was the joke of Washington, D.C.—the FBI knew it, DOJ knew it, and Congress knew it." In the hours after the 9/11 attacks, FBI agents sent around copies of photographs of the suspected hijackers by Express Mail, the U.S. Postal Service's overnight delivery service, because they did not have computer scanners in the bureau's field offices.

It wasn't just the FBI's field agents who were complaining about the bureau's shockingly out-of-date technology. The acting director of the Washington field office, the second largest FBI field office in the country, after New York, told the commission's investigators that he was embarrassed that he had only one way to relay a message across town to FBI headquarters from his desk in an emergency: Pick up the phone and dial. If he wanted to use e-mail or the Internet, he had to walk down the hall. There was only one Internet terminal on each floor of the field office.

The commission's team of investigators focused on the FBI, Team 6, was appalled by what it was discovering about the operations of the FBI, and their surprise went well beyond outdated computer equipment or nonexistent e-mail service. Members of the team found it difficult to describe what they were learning about how dysfunctional the FBI was, especially when it came to terrorism. Words like "incompetent" or "inept" were often used, but they could not begin to capture how far the problems went.

To Team 6, the bureau's great blunders before 9/11—Moussaoui, the Phoenix memo, Hazmi and Mihdhar in San Diego—were all too understandable the more the commission learned about the way the FBI operated; they were typical of the sorts of errors that the bureau was making day after day, especially when it came to counterterrorism. The career path for the bureau's terrorism specialists was considered a backwater.

"It failed and it failed and it failed," Tom Kean said later of the FBI. "This is an agency that does not work." Philip Zelikow agreed. "There were some things about what the FBI had become that were just really indefensible," he said, describing the largely justified conventional wisdom after 9/11 that the FBI was "the poster child for the broken agency."

The investigators on Team 6 were always careful to point out that there were some extraordinary, dedicated people at the FBI—men and women who were as talented as any criminal investigators in the world. The honors list began with the Minneapolis agents who were rebuffed when they tried to warn FBI headquarters about Moussaoui in August 2001, and with Kenneth Williams, the agent in Phoenix who sent a memo to headquarters that July asking the bureau to study why so many young Muslim men were seeking flight training in the United States.

The problem was mostly with the agency's sclerotic, hierarchical bureaucracy in Washington—at its core, unchanged since the days of J. Edgar Hoover—as well as the FBI's unmatched arrogance in dealing with other government agencies.

Its failures were on display most clearly when it came to the threat posed to the United States by terrorist groups.

Hoover may have been the greatest turf fighter in the modern history of the federal bureaucracy. During his nearly half century at the FBI, he maneuvered to ensure that serious proposals for a separate domestic intelligence agency—an American equivalent to Britain's MI-5—went nowhere. If spies or terrorists operated within American borders, Hoover believed it should be the responsibility of the FBI to track them down, just as it dealt with bank robbers and kidnappers and pornographers.

But for FBI agents, the incentive within the bureau for chasing bank robbers and kidnappers was always much greater than for hunting down spies and terrorists. Bank robbers got arrested, prosecuted, and sent to prison every day. Every one of those convictions was a notch on an arresting FBI agent's belt, an easy way of establishing how well the agent was doing the job.

In tracking down spies and terrorists, success could never be so clear. There was no simple way to quantify what the FBI's counterintelligence and counterterrorism agents did for the bureau. The most talented counterintelligence and counterterrorism agents at the FBI might not make a single arrest in their careers. Spies tended to be kept under surveillance, not arrested. Foreign-born terrorists were not seen as much of a problem until the 1993 World Trade Center bombing. And the commission's investigators were startled to discover that even after the 1993 attack, there was no grand rethinking of the FBI's role on terrorism.

In the eight years between the 1993 attempt to bring down the Twin Towers and the 2001 attacks that succeeded in that horrifying goal,

FBI headquarters in Washington produced no analytical reports—not a single one—on the overall terrorist threat facing the United States. Before 9/11, if President Clinton or President Bush wanted a briefing from the FBI on domestic terrorism threats, there was no piece of paper to offer him.

Even though the bureau functioned as the government's domestic intelligence agency, FBI agents "literally didn't write intelligence reports," Zelikow said. Instead, when they completed an interview as part of an investigation, FBI agents prepared a "302," the standard FBI form used to record interview results, and often deposited it in a file cabinet or desk drawer, never to be read again.

Richard Clarke, the former White House counterterrorism czar who had served both Republican and Democratic presidents, told the commission's investigators in his private interviews that the FBI was simply incompetent when it came to terrorism: "I didn't think the FBI would know whether or not there was anything going on in the United States by al-Qaeda." The FBI, he said, was "clueless" on terrorist threats.

Many FBI analysts who were supposed to be terrorism specialists were routinely asked to take up other, unrelated duties. The commission had several tearful interviews with counterterrorism analysts who explained how they were demeaned by their colleagues who handled routine criminal cases. Some terrorism analysts said they were treated as "übersecretaries," asked to man the reception desk while secretaries went to lunch; a few analysts said they were asked repeatedly to empty the trash.

There was plenty of blame to go around for the desperate condition of the FBI in 2001. Surely Attorney General Janet Reno, who had titular authority over FBI director Louis Freeh during the Clinton administration, and President Clinton himself deserved criticism for having failed for eight years to insist on reforms at the bureau.

That point would be noted repeatedly by Condoleezza Rice when she was asked to explain the government's intelligence failures before 9/11. If the bureau was broken, why wasn't it fixed during President Clinton's two terms in office? "I think the question is why, over all of these years, we did not address the structural problems that there were with the FBI," she told the commission. It was a legitimate question.

But many on the commission's staff believed that if one person should be singled out for blame, it had to be Freeh, who ran the bureau from 1993 until June 2001.

While at the FBI, Freeh had seemed nearly immune from criticism. He savored his reputation as the feisty, independent-minded, incorruptible G-man—he began his career as an FBI agent in New York—and he made a special effort to court lawmakers in Congress. Republicans on Capitol Hill had special admiration for Freeh because of his antagonism toward Clinton over a series of Democratic fund-raising scandals. Freeh had let it be known to Washington reporters that he loathed the president. He turned in his White House gate pass as a sign of protest over the conduct of Clinton and his aides, even though that limited his access to the West Wing in the event of a crisis.

But while Freeh's rhetoric on terrorism was always appropriately tough, he never moved the money or people to the FBI's counterterrorism programs that he had so publicly claimed they deserved.

The commission's investigators determined that although the FBI's counterterrorism budget tripled during the mid-1990s, the bureau's spending on terrorism cases remained fairly constant in the four years before 9/11. Money designated by Congress for the counterterrorism investigations was shifted elsewhere by Freeh and his deputies. In Freeh's last year at the FBI, there were twice as many agents working on drug cases as on terrorists. Only about 6 percent of the bureau's personnel were agents involved in terrorism cases. Within the FBI, there were so few translators of Arabic and the other common languages of terrorist groups that more than one hundred thousand hours of intercepted conversations of terrorist suspects had not been translated before 9/11.

Freeh also had to take blame for the disastrous condition of the FBI's technology. He seemed to take pride in his own backwardness when it came to electronics. He had let it be known to his colleagues that he refused to learn how to use e-mail, as if that were some sort of badge of honor; in the military-style hierarchy of the FBI, it seemed to send out the message that no one else should worry about e-mail, either. Ultimately, Freeh had the computer in his office removed because he never used it. That was in stark contrast with the CIA, which, whatever its other organizational problems, had cutting-edge technology.

Freeh's best gift to the bureau may have been the timing of his departure, just three months before September 11. Had he still been at the FBI at the time of the 9/11 commission's investigation, that might well have been reason enough for the commission to recommend that the bureau be broken up. Freeh's presence would have made the bureau an easy target. The commission could have pointed a finger at Freeh, identifying him as the embodiment of all that had gone wrong at the FBI for so many years. Instead, the commissioners faced his replacement, Robert Mueller, who had no responsibility for the bureau's pre-9/11 bungling but was eager to apologize for it.

Even with Mueller in charge, there was still a sense early on among the commissioners that the bureau needed to be overhauled, if not broken up. Leaders of the congressional investigation of pre-9/11 intelligence failures had recommended a sweeping reorganization of the FBI, possibly including creation of an American MI-5 to take over its role on domestic terrorism. John Lehman and other commissioners wanted to seriously consider a recommendation for a separate domestic intelligence agency. He thought it was hopeless to think the FBI could ever do that job properly. At the bureau, "the law enforcement mentality is all there is," he said. "It's like talking to a dog about becoming a cat."

Certainly the staff of Team 6 could see from the early weeks of the investigation that the FBI was incapable of what should be its new, central mission—protecting the United States from another 9/11.

Whatever Mueller's public relations talents, the team's investigators believed that remarkably little had changed in his two years on the job. He had attempted some structural changes within the bureau, including bringing terrorism investigations under the control of FBI headquarters. But the commission's investigators could see that counterterrorism agents and analysts remained second-class citizens within the bureau and that they remained overwhelmed by their responsibilities.

By LATE summer in 2001, John Ashcroft thought he had set the FBI on the right course by picking the widely respected Robert Mueller to replace Louis Freeh. Mueller did not like publicity, which meant that Ashcroft would have no rival in asserting himself as the Bush administration's spokesman on law enforcement issues. There would be none of the traditional headline-grabbing rivalry between the FBI and the Justice Department.

Ashcroft's inner circle of aides at the Justice Department were used to seeing their boss portrayed as a wild-eyed conservative fanatic—a punching bag for Democrats, liberals, and the late night comics. It was a role that the White House seemed grateful Ashcroft had taken on; it drew away criticism that might otherwise have been directed at the president.

And Ashcroft punched back, not so much in person—he seemed decidedly meek in interviews and speeches—as through a high-powered press office run by Mark Corallo, a former army infantryman who became a Republican congressional aide.

With the creation of the 9/11 commission, Corallo readied himself to explain Ashcroft's performance as attorney general in the months before 9/11, and Corallo thought Ashcroft's record would prove to be perfectly defensible.

The Justice Department could not claim that it was on full alert for a domestic terrorist strike in 2001. But Corallo knew that Ashcroft had been told repeatedly by the FBI and CIA that the evidence suggested al-Qaeda would attack overseas. Ashcroft was not privy to the PDBs, so he had not seen the August 6 PDB that warned of domestic threats.

In the summer of 2001, Ashcroft had turned down the FBI's request for a sizable budget increase for its counterterrorism division for the 2003 fiscal year, which obviously looked bad in hindsight. But Corallo argued that had to be seen in the context of the Bush administration's budget request for fiscal year 2002, in which it requested the largest percentage increase in the FBI's counterterrorism budget since 1997.

But if Corallo was beginning to feel sanguine about the 9/11 commission, that the investigation posed no special threat to Ashcroft, he was mistaken. *The New York Times* and other news organizations were about to change that. In early 2004, reporters began to hear the first rumblings, both from the commissioners and from the staff, about what the commission had learned of Ashcroft, especially his apparently bizarre confrontations with Tom Pickard at the FBI. A reporter from the *Times* called David Ayres, Ashcroft's deceptively laconic chief of staff, for comment. If the commission was gunning for the attorney general, it was a front-page story, and Ashcroft deserved the chance to respond. The attorney general responded in a way that nearly tore the 9/11 commission apart.

K STREET OFFICES OF THE
9/11 COMMISSION
Washington, D.C.
MARCH 2004

Stephanie Kaplan, Philip Zelikow's hyperefficient young assistant, had been monitoring the Amazon.com website for weeks for details about Richard Clarke's book. It was clear from the commission's private interviews with Clarke in December and January that his book, *Against All Enemies,* might do damage to the president, Condoleezza Rice, and others in the administration, and Zelikow had reason to worry what it might say about him and the 2001 transition. But Zelikow and others took some relief from the fact that the book's publication date had been set for April 29, more than a month after Clarke's planned public testimony before the commission, which was scheduled for Wednesday, March 24.

In early March, Kaplan came out of her office on K Street, appearing agitated and motioning to her computer monitor.

"You'd better look at this," she told colleagues outside her office. Her monitor flickered with the page on Amazon's website where customers could preorder Clarke's book. "They've changed the publishing date."

The date had been moved up dramatically by Clarke's publisher, the Free Press, which understood the value of releasing their bombshell book on the eve of Clarke's testimony to the commission. The new publication date was March 22, two days before Clarke's appearance. The Free Press had also quietly begun to negotiate with CBS News to promote the book with an interview on *60 Minutes* on the Sunday before his testimony.

Zelikow was incensed, and he knew that Kean and Hamilton would be as well. The commissioners had said repeatedly to the staff that they did not want surprises at their public hearings, at least nothing that would surprise *them.* And Zelikow could only imagine what surprises

Clarke had saved up for his book and, perhaps more important, for *60 Minutes,* easily the most watched and powerful news show on television.

Zelikow went to Dan Marcus and ordered him to ready some sort of legal action against the Free Press to get a copy of the book before the hearing.

"Philip went ballistic," Marcus recalled. "He wanted to subpoena it."

Marcus knew better than to draw up a subpoena or threaten any other sort of legal action. It was a ridiculous idea, he thought. The commission had enough enemies; it did not need to make one out of the publishing industry. How would it look if the commission, unwilling to issue a subpoena to the Bush White House, slapped one on a book publisher instead? That might turn the Washington press corps against the commission as well.

"Yeah, that's just what we need, Philip—a First Amendment battle," he said to Zelikow, scoffing at the idea.

But Zelikow was insistent. "Well, we have subpoena authority," he told Marcus. "And they have no right to withhold it from us."

Marcus called lawyers for the Free Press in New York and its parent company, Simon & Schuster, and had what he described as a polite conversation. He said he did not threaten a subpoena: "I didn't use the 's' word." Instead, he explained that the commission wanted Clarke to live up to a promise, made during his private interviews with the commission, to provide the panel with an advance look at his book. After talking with Clarke, the Free Press agreed to turn over a copy of *Against All Enemies* to the investigation. But the publisher insisted on several conditions, including a promise that the book's distribution within the commission would be limited to three staff investigators who were involved in preparing for the Clarke hearing. Clarke had insisted personally on another condition: Zelikow could not be one of the three. Clarke figured that if Zelikow got a copy, he would immediately share it with Condoleezza Rice and others at the White House or turn it over to a favored reporter to bust the embargo on the book and destroy its news value. "I wanted it in writing that Zelikow wouldn't read it," Clarke said.

Marcus consulted with the commissioners and agreed to the publisher's conditions, over the angry protests of Zelikow. Marcus and others on the staff could not deny that they enjoyed Zelikow's discomfort. Throughout the investigation, Zelikow had insisted that every scrap of secret evidence gathered by the staff be shared with him before anyone else; he then controlled how and if the evidence was shared elsewhere. Now Zelikow would be the last to know some of the best secrets of them all.

The commission was true to its word, and the contents of *Against All Enemies* remained embargoed until the Friday before Clarke's testimony, when CBS issued a press release about its interview with Clarke for that Sunday night and hinted at some of his book's more explosive revelations.

The *60 Minutes* interview was gripping television, with Clarke, who was unknown to the public until that moment, explaining to a wide-eyed Lesley Stahl that Bush and Rice had ignored his urgent warnings throughout the spring and summer of 2001 about an imminent attack. Clarke, as the public could see for itself, was made for television. In part it was his physical presence—his shock of white hair and ghostly pallor, as if he had emerged from years of hiding in sunless back rooms of the West Wing to share the terrible secrets he had learned. But even more, it was Clarke's urgent speaking style. He was merciless about Rice. Like others in the administration, she was obsessed with cold war issues, not with the terrorist threats in front of her. President Bush, Clarke said, had "done nothing" about al-Qaeda before 9/11 and then, after the attacks, tried desperately to link 9/11 to Saddam Hussein to justify an invasion of Iraq.

"I find it outrageous that the president is running for reelection on the grounds that he's done such great things about terrorism," Clarke said. "He ignored it. He ignored terrorism for months when maybe we could have done something to stop 9/11."

The morning after the broadcast, the White House was in a near panic over Clarke. Andy Card said it was always difficult to calibrate panic in the White House; almost every day had some moment of "extreme anxiety," especially after 9/11. But Card could not deny that Clarke's testimony had created genuine alarm within the West Wing. No matter how much the White House press office tried to tear at Clarke's credibility, his allegations were a direct threat to Bush's reelection hopes.

Card said that no person was more upset than Condoleezza Rice, who had never seen her competence or her motives questioned in public like this before. It was the first time that some in the White House had ever seen her express anything like fear.

Rice took to the airwaves herself, granting several television interviews in a matter of days to respond to Clarke. She scheduled her own *60 Minutes* interview for the following Sunday. For someone as self-controlled and diplomatic as Rice, her tone was remarkably angry. Clarke's attack on her was personal, and her counterattack would be personal, too.

"Dick Clarke just does not know what he's talking about," she said. "I really don't know what Richard Clarke's motivations are, but I'll tell you this: Richard Clarke had plenty of opportunities to tell us in the administration that he thought the war on terrorism was moving in the wrong direction, and he chose not to."

The White House onslaught against Clarke was fierce throughout the White House, something Clarke had predicted.

"I assumed they would do everything they could possibly do, and I didn't try to dwell too much on the specifics," Clarke said later. "I kind of thought this was suicide." He had worked in the Bush administration for almost two years before he left the White House, and he said he understood its brass-knuckle tactics. "I wouldn't have been surprised if Karl Rove had broken into my house and strangled me," he said, not entirely in jest.

Dick Cheney joined in the attacks. He went on Rush Limbaugh's radio show and accused Clarke of nursing a "grudge" against the administration after having been turned down for the job of deputy secretary of the new Department of Homeland Security, a job Clarke had indeed wanted. Cheney said that in the Bush White House, Clarke "wasn't in the loop, frankly" and "clearly missed a lot of what was going on" within the administration in responding to terrorist threats. Cheney's remarks had unintentionally proved exactly what Clarke was saying—that his authority was so diminished in the Bush administration that he had no ability to reach the decision makers in the White House when threats emerged.

But even though he knew he would be attacked by the White House, Clarke later said that he had not predicted the attacks would be so ugly or personal. The conservative columnist Robert Novak suggested that Clarke's criticism of Rice was motivated by racism, that he could not tolerate a "powerful African-American woman." Clarke's sexual orientation became part of the attacks. The conservative commentator Laura Ingraham opened an especially unsavory line of criticism on the never married Clarke, asking why "this single man" was such a "drama queen."

Against All Enemies became an instant best seller and was sold to

Hollywood for a film adaptation. The book promised to make Clarke a wealthy man. Still, he thought the publicity might destroy the small security firm, Good Harbor Consulting, that he had set up after leaving the White House. Ahead of his testimony to the commission, he called his two partners in the firm and offered to resign.

As a result of the book, "we're never going to get a government contract—or a contract from anybody who wants a government contract," Clarke warned them. "This is not what you guys signed up for and, therefore, if you want to dissolve the company or if you want to leave it, then you two go ahead without me." He said he assumed that ABC News, which had just signed him up as an on-air consultant on terrorism, would also find a way to get out of the contract. His fears were unfounded. Although Clarke's two partners at Good Harbor "thought I was crazy" to take on the Bush administration, they stayed with him. ABC did, too.

In the hours before his testimony, Clarke had a final decision to make: What would he say in his prepared testimony? The commission had invited him to speak for up to ten minutes before submitting to questioning.

Clarke had prepared a long written statement. But on the eve of his testimony, he decided not to read it at the hearing.

"Don't be some spineless bureaucrat," he told himself. "You've got people in there, in the audience, whose lives have been ruined." He knew that the first several rows of the audience at the hearing would be the family members of 9/11 victims.

"Fuck it," he said to himself. "I'm just going to apologize to them."

— 41 —

OFFICE OF THE COUNSEL TO THE PRESIDENT
The White House
MARCH 24, 2004

I n the hours before Richard Clarke's testimony before the 9/11 commission, Alberto Gonzales was busy at the White House. He was helping to prepare lists of questions for the commission's Republicans to ask Clarke—to destroy his credibility. Gonzales and his staff spoke to Fred Fielding, the former White House counsel, and Jim Thompson, the former Illinois governor. They were seen as the administration's most reliable supporters on the commission. During Clarke's testimony, Fielding and Thompson could be seen standing up from the dais periodically and disappearing to a back room to take phone calls, apparently from the White House. Gonzales's office had also been in contact with the office of Senator Bill Frist, the Republican majority leader, who was prepared to rush to the Senate floor to denounce Clarke and question his truthfulness as soon as the hearing was over.

The White House press office was busy, too. The morning of the hearing, it had authorized Fox News to reveal that Clarke was the formerly anonymous "senior administration official" who had given a briefing to reporters in early August 2002 to defend President Bush's terrorism record. It was the sort of insider "background" briefing that White House officials in all administrations gave to reporters in exchange for a promise that their names would not be revealed. During the briefing, Clarke did what he had been ordered to do by the NSC: He offered a qualified defense of the Bush administration's efforts against terrorist threats before 9/11. When the attacks happened, he said, Bush had been moving to "a new strategy that called for the rapid elimination of al-Qaeda."

What Clarke said to the reporters was true: A new antiterrorism plan was being developed in the White House before 9/11. What Clarke failed to mention in the briefing was that the White House had moved so slowly that the plan was not ready for the president's approval until after 9/11. Nor did Clarke mention his belief that Bush and Condoleezza Rice had ignored dire terrorist threats throughout the spring and summer.

In agreeing to allow Fox News to reveal that Clarke had given the 2002 briefing, the White House was attempting to paint him as a liar—a one-time Bush defender who had become a Bush critic in order to sell a book.

Clarke had been asked by Rice to give the 2002 briefing to rebut charges in a damning *Time* magazine cover story days earlier that reported that the White House had ignored calls to get tough on al-Qaeda before 9/11. The magazine's cover bore an ominous image of the Twin Towers, as seen through a pair of binoculars, set beneath the head-line "The Secret History: Nine months before 9/11, the U.S. had a bold plan to attack Al Qaeda. It wasn't carried out until after the towers fell." Clarke knew that although the magazine's story was mostly true—the "bold plan" was essentially his, after all—he was expected to spin the facts to try to knock down the story's larger theme of the White House as negligent. And Clarke did what he was told to do, even if the spin took him perilously close to dishonesty, albeit the sort of dishonesty practiced every day in official Washington.

The White House decision to reveal Clarke's involvement in the 2002 briefing was denounced by Democrats as a dirty trick; Clarke had given the briefing on the assumption that his anonymity would be protected forever. But dirty trick or not, the White House got what it wanted. Clarke's credibility was now open to question, with Fox leading the charge against him. His words from two years earlier might have been "spin," but the White House knew that subtlety might be lost on a national audience that would wonder why Clarke was defending Bush in 2002 only to turn around and try to destroy the president two years later.

Zelikow got hold of a copy of the briefing transcript a few minutes before the hearing, and he was thrilled by what he was reading. Maybe this would be enough to end the Dick Clarke "circus," he said.

"Does it get any better than this?" he asked gleefully to one of the Team 3 investigators at the thought that Clarke was about to be savaged on national television.

With all of the frenzy created by his *60 Minutes* interview and the release of the book, Clarke's appearance before the 9/11 commission had turned into a true Washington spectacle.

It was one of those moments in the capital when anyone of importance in the city was in front of a television set. The audience in the hearing room of the Senate's Hart Office Building, just down the street from the Capitol dome, was packed with the family members of 9/11 victims, curious congressional aides, reporters, and anyone else who could squeeze in.

Clarke entered the hearing room and took his seat at the witness table. Tom Kean asked him to stand and be sworn in. As Clarke raised his right hand, scores of cameras began clicking, the flashes popping, as photographers maneuvered to find the one image that captured the best of all Washington dramas—the former White House insider turned whistle-blower. It was being compared by reporters to the sort of drama that John Dean's testimony provided in Watergate or Lieutenant Colonel Oliver North's testimony offered in the Iran-Contra affair.

Clarke took his seat. Kean invited Clarke to give an opening statement, asking him to limit it to the preagreed ten minutes. The witness would not need nearly so much time.

"Thank you, Mr. Chairman," Clarke began.

"I have only a very brief opening statement. I welcome these hearings because of the opportunity they provide to the American people to better understand why the tragedy of 9/11 happened and what we must do to prevent a reoccurrence. I also welcome the hearings because it is finally a forum where I can apologize to the loved ones of the victims of 9/11. For those who are here in the room, to those who are watching on television, your government failed you. Those entrusted with protecting you failed you. And I failed you. We tried hard. But that doesn't matter. Because we failed. And for that failure, I would ask, once all the facts are out, for your understanding and for your forgiveness. With that, Mr. Chairman, I'll be glad to take your questions."

There was silence for a moment. Then it was replaced by gasps and then sobs from many of the family members in the audience. An apology? An admission of error? It was the first apology that the 9/11 families had heard from anybody of importance in the Bush administration. What Clarke had done seemed such a simple act, really. It was a request for forgiveness from someone who had reason to know what the government had done, and not done, to try to prevent something like 9/11. Even if Clarke's apology was rehearsed, even if the White House was right and his motivations were entirely cynical, this was the moment of catharsis that many of the wives and husbands and children of the victims had been waiting for. Lorie Van Auken, one of the Jersey Girls, tried not to cry, but she could feel the tears streak down her face.

At each public hearing, the commission varied the order in which the commissioners asked questions, and Clarke was fortunate in his lineup. The more harshly partisan Republicans were further down the list, which meant that the early, sympathetic questioning from Democrats would be the focus of the initial reports on CNN and the other television networks, as well as on the Associated Press and Reuters wire services. More than any other news organizations, the AP and Reuters shaped the agenda for how a story was covered by the rest of the Washington press corps, since their initial dispatches were read by assignment editors across the country within a few minutes of any important event.

The first questioner was former Democratic congressman Tim Roemer, who was eager to have Clarke repeat his attacks on Bush and Rice. Roemer asked Clarke to compare the Clinton and Bush administrations in the urgency with which they treated terrorism threats.

"My impression was that fighting terrorism in general and fighting al-Qaeda in particular were an extraordinarily high priority in the Clinton administration, certainly no higher a priority," he said. "I believe the Bush administration in the first eight months considered terrorism an important issue but not an urgent issue."

When Bush came to office in 2001, he said, "George Tenet and I tried very hard to create a sense of urgency by seeing to it that intelligence reports on the al-Qaeda threat were frequently given to the president and other high-level officials. And there was a process under way to address al-Qaeda. But although I continued to say it was an urgent problem, I don't think it was ever treated that way."

He explained his decision to step down as counterterrorism director in 2001: His warnings about the dangers posed by Osama bin Laden were being ignored.

"This administration, while it listened to me, either didn't believe me that there was an urgent problem or was unprepared to act as though there were an urgent problem," Clarke said. "If the administration doesn't believe its national coordinator for counterterrorism when he says there's an urgent problem, and if it's unprepared to act as though there's an urgent problem, then probably I should get another job."

A dramatic apology? The contrast of the "extraordinarily high priority" given to terrorism in the Clinton administration versus Bush's attitude that terrorism is "not an urgent issue"? Clarke was making it easy for the reporters in the hearing room to write their stories that morning.

Slade Gorton was up next in the questioning. His tone, as usual, was significantly less partisan than that of some of the other Republicans. He was polite; there was no sarcasm. And he obtained an important concession from Clarke, one that was surely welcomed at the White House. If all of Clarke's recommendations had been followed in the Bush White House before the attacks, Gorton asked, "is there the remotest chance that it would have prevented 9/11?"

Clarke: "No."

Gordon: "It just would have allowed our response after 9/11 to be perhaps a little bit faster?"

Clarke: "Well, the response would have begun before 9/11."

Clarke was not conceding that the attacks had been fated to happen. It seemed clear to Clarke and others that if the FBI and CIA had done their jobs properly before 9/11, at least some of the hijackers could have been captured before the attacks. The statement was welcomed, nonetheless, at the White House as at least a partial exoneration for the West Wing.

RICHARD BEN-VENISTE opened his questioning with praise for Clarke's apology: "I want to express my appreciation for the fact that you have come before this commission and stated in front of the world your apology for what went wrong. To my knowledge, you're the first to do that." There was wild applause for Clarke from some of the 9/11 families.

Then it was Jim Thompson's turn for questions. The mood in the room chilled instantly. Thompson was about to remind the audience why he had been so feared in his years as a federal prosecutor. Before Thompson's election as Illinois governor, he had been the United States attorney in Chicago. In courtrooms in Chicago, he was renowned for his ability to take apart a defense witness on cross-examination. His questioning of Clarke had that same caustic tone.

Thompson raised his arms slightly above the dais. In his left hand he held up a copy of Clarke's freshly published book. In his right hand was a copy of the 2002 briefing transcript that was being distributed by Fox News. There was a contemptuous scowl on Thompson's face.

"Mr. Clarke, as we sit here this afternoon we have your book and we have your press briefing of August 2002," he began. "Which is true?"

Clarke did not flinch at the allegation that he had lied. A tough prosecutor was up against an even tougher witness.

"I think the question is a little misleading," Clarke began, explaining that what he had done in the 2002 briefing was a routine effort by a presidential aide "to try to explain that set of facts in a way that minimized criticism of the administration."

He continued: "I was asked to make that case to the press. I was a special assistant to the president. And I made the case I was asked to make."

Thompson tried again: "Are you saying to me that you were asked to make an untrue case to the press and the public and that you went ahead and did it?"

Clarke: "No, sir. Not—"

Thompson: "What are you saying?"

Clarke: "Not untrue. Not an untrue case. I was asked to highlight the positive aspects of what the administration had done and to minimize the negative aspects of what the administration had done. And as a special assistant to the president, one is frequently asked to do that kind of thing.

"I've done it for *several* presidents."

The last remark produced roars of knowing laughter in the audience, as well as among some of the commissioners. Clarke was expected to "spin" for Republican presidents, just as he had "spun" for Democrats before that, and a veteran Chicago pol like Jim Thompson understood that as well as anyone. Nobody bought Thompson's claims of naiveté. The audience was with Clarke.

But Thompson kept pressing the point: "What it suggests to me is that there is one standard—one standard of candor and morality for White House special assistants and another standard of candor and morality for the rest of America. I don't get that."

Clarke replied: "I don't think it's a question of morality at all. I think it's a question of politics."

The remark brought a new burst of supportive applause from the audience for Clarke. Thompson, seeming to realize that he had asked one too many questions, appeared flustered.

There was another series of attacks from John Lehman, another Republican commissioner. He opened his questioning by referring to Clarke as "Dick," as if they were long-lost friends, and noting that they had worked together in government dating back to the Reagan administration. "I have genuinely been a fan of yours," said Lehman. It was the sort of syrupy praise that, in Washington, at least, tends to suggest that a witness is about to be torn to bits.

"You've got a real credibility problem," he told Clarke. He suggested that the attacks on Bush in *Against All Enemies* were part of a cynical marketing campaign by his publishers and that Clarke had provided contradictory testimony in his hours of private interviews with the commission.

"This can't be the same Dick Clarke that testified before us, because all of the promotional material and all of the spin in the networks was that this is a rounding, devastating attack, this book, on President Bush. That's not what I heard in the interviews," Lehman said. "I hope you'll resolve that credibility problem because I'd hate to see you totally shoved to one side during a presidential campaign as an active partisan selling a book."

Beyond suggesting that Clarke was perjuring himself, Lehman was apparently repeating the allegation by the White House that Clarke's book was an effort to curry favor from Democrats and win Clarke an invitation to return to work at the White House if Senator John Kerry, the Democratic presidential nominee, ousted Bush in November.

Clarke dealt first with the allegation that he was lying:

"As to your accusation that there is a difference between what I said to this commission in fifteen hours of testimony and what I am saying in my book and what media outlets are asking me to comment on, I think there's a very good reason for that. In the fifteen hours of testimony, no one asked me what I thought about the president's invasion of Iraq. And the reason I am strident in my criticism of the president of the United States is because by invading Iraq—something I was not asked about by the commission, but something I chose to write about a lot in the book—by invading Iraq, the president of the United States has greatly undermined the war on terrorism."

Then he dealt with the politics: "I've been accused of being a member of John Kerry's campaign team several times this week, including by the White House. So let's just lay that one to bed. I'm not working for the Kerry campaign."

He continued: "The White House has said that my book is an audition for a high-level position in the Kerry campaign. So let me say here, as I am under oath, that I will not accept any position in the Kerry administration, should there be one—on the record, under oath."

Lehman seemed taken aback. Once again, Clarke seemed to have the upper hand.

After the hearing, Clarke was swarmed at the witness table by dozens of the family members of 9/11 victims. Many wanted to embrace him, choking back tears as they thanked him for his apology.

BEYOND HIS attacks on the president and Rice, Clarke's public testimony was significant in resolving one of the lingering mysteries about the government's response to the 9/11 attacks—why dozens of members of Osama bin Laden's extended family living in the United States had been allowed to evacuate the United States on special charter flights within days of the attacks.

When the evacuations were revealed weeks after the fact, the White House had been unable to come up with a coherent explanation for why they had been allowed to take place and who had authorized them. The evacuation of bin Laden's family inspired many of the most persistent of the conspiracy theories heard after 9/11. Was there some secret agreement between the Bush White House and the Saudi government to ferry terrorists, some of them bin Laden's kin, out of the United States? The conspiracies were the focus of books and of Michael Moore's incendiary documentary *Fahrenheit 9/11*.

Clarke revealed in his testimony that he was responsible for the evacuation flights. He had made the decision to allow the bin Ladens to leave after consulting with the FBI.

"The Saudi embassy had apparently said that they feared for the lives of Saudi citizens, because they thought there would be retribution against Saudis in the United States," Clarke said. "The Saudi embassy, therefore, asked for these people to be evacuated—the same sort of thing that we do all the time in similar crises, evacuating Americans."

He asked that the FBI review the names on the passenger manifests before the flights to be certain none of the passengers were terrorist suspects.

"The FBI then approved—after some period of time, and I can't tell you how long—approved the flight. Now, what degree of review the FBI did of those names, I cannot tell you. How many people there were on the plane, I cannot tell you. But I have asked since, were there any individuals on that flight that in retrospect the FBI wishes they could have interviewed in this country? And the answer I've been given is no."

AFTER CLARKE's testimony, Zelikow was agitated. He saw Ben-Veniste call over Raj De, one of the young staff investigators, to ask De to quickly gather some research material for use in the questioning of another administration official that afternoon. As a commissioner, Ben-Veniste saw nothing wrong in asking for help from the staff in the middle of a public hearing. There was no time to leave the dais and do it himself.

By early 2004, the relationship between Zelikow and Ben-Veniste had become poisonous. Zelikow thought Ben-Veniste, in particular, was trying to make use of the commission's supposedly nonpartisan staff for blatantly partisan purposes. He thought Ben-Veniste wanted to turn De into his "personal 'oppo' researcher" in trying to savage Bush administration witnesses.

Zelikow pulled De aside a few minutes later.

"What are you doing," he demanded.

"I'm doing some work for Richard," De replied.

"You know this isn't the Democratic National Committee," Zelikow sneered.

AMONG NEWS organizations, the reaction to Richard Clarke's testimony was predictable. Conservative newspaper editorial boards and television commentators laid into Clarke, pointing to the August 2002 briefing transcript as proof of his duplicity, even his perjury.

Bill O'Reilly of the popular Fox News show *The O'Reilly Factor* opened his broadcast the night of Clarke's testimony with a statement and a question: "Tonight, Richard Clarke did not tell the truth on at least one occasion. How badly does this damage him?"

But the rest of the Washington press corps seemed to believe that Clarke's credibility was still mostly intact. Certainly his credibility was intact for most of the commission's staff—apart from Philip Zelikow, of course. Warren Bass and the rest of the investigators on Team 3 had read through Clarke's files and knew that his paper trail and e-mail traffic backed up almost every essential assertion in his testimony. Clarke had certainly gotten the public's attention. A poll by the Pew Research Center released the day after Clarke's testimony showed that 90 percent of those surveyed had heard something about Clarke's allegations against the president; 40 percent of them had heard "a lot" about Clarke.

The polling created fresh alarm at the White House. The president's political handlers felt that Bush, his reelection campaign well under way, had to respond to Clarke's accusations of pre-9/11 negligence, albeit without mentioning the former White House aide by name. The political dangers of any further silence by Bush were too great.

"Had I known that the enemy was going to use airplanes to strike America, to attack us, I would have used every resource, every asset, every power of this government to protect the American people," Bush said the next day at a campaign appearance in Nashua, New Hampshire; he was apparently hoping his audience would forget that the August 6 PDB had warned specifically that planes might be hijacked by al-Qaeda within the United States.

Bush then tried to shift the blame to his predecessor. He suggested that Bill Clinton had more explaining to do for 9/11 than he did, noting that the commission was looking at "eight months of my administration and the eight years of the previous administration."

Bush's political handlers feared that Clarke's testimony had guaranteed that it was Bush's eight months—not Clinton's eight years—that would be the focus of what remained of the investigation by the 9/11 commission.

THE PRESIDENT'S RANCH

CRAWFORD, TEX.

On one side of the debate was Alberto Gonzales, David Addington (Dick Cheney's hard-nosed counsel), and the rest of the executive privilege absolutists in the Bush White House.

On the other side of the debate was Condoleezza Rice. She was desperate to be given a chance to clear her name in front of the 9/11 commission.

In the middle was President Bush, who was asked to interrupt a brief spring holiday at his beloved Texas ranch to decide whether Rice could testify publicly before the commission to rebut Clarke's devastating attacks.

For many lawyers who specialize in constitutional issues and the separation of powers, the White House was on firm ground in refusing to allow Rice to testify before the commission—much firmer ground even than in its initial refusals to turn over the PDBs. The doctrine of executive privilege holds that a president must be able to speak freely with his advisers, without fear their communications would be revealed to Congress or anyone else. Although there is no reference to executive privilege in the Constitution and the case law on the issue is ambiguous, the Supreme Court has recognized that the privilege exists for presidents and their senior advisers. And no one met the definition of senior presidential adviser better than Rice; the national security adviser is the highest-ranking official in the executive branch, apart from the chief of staff, who does not require Senate confirmation. The concept, which Congress has accepted, is that the national security adviser's job exists to provide confidential advice to the president. National security advisers and their earlier counterparts in the White House have almost never testified before Congress. There have been exceptions, but almost always in proceedings in which there were allegations of criminality. In 1980, Jimmy Carter's national security adviser, Zbigniew Brzezinski, testified to the Senate about allegations of wrongdoing by Carter's brother Billy in his lobbying for the government of Libya.

From his first meetings with Kean and Hamilton, Gonzales had been uncompromising on the point, as firm as on any issue in his tortured negotiations with the 9/11 commission. While Rice would meet informally with the commission, just as she met routinely with members of Congress, there would be no public testimony from her, Gonzales told them. "I'm sure you understand that this is not negotiable," he said to them more than once.

But in the panicked aftermath of Clarke's testimony and his book, everything was negotiable, including the question of Rice's testimony. Senior White House officials said that Rice grew uncharacteristically frantic. They said she went to Bush and pleaded to be allowed to testify. "Condi desperately wanted to do it," Andy Card said.

She certainly tried to make her case on television. On Monday,

March 22, she appeared on the morning news programs of ABC, CBS, NBC, and CNN and was interviewed later in the day by Sean Hannity of Fox News to rebut Clarke's charges. But the many interviews in the wake of Clarke's testimony, including her own interview on *60 Minutes* the Sunday after Clarke, seemed to have backfired on Rice. By accepting almost every invitation she received from television networks to respond to Clarke, Rice left the impression that she would answer any question put to her by a television reporter but was ducking the questions of the official government commission that was trying to understand how the 9/11 attacks happened.

Kean and Hamilton had stepped up the pressure on Rice, saying in interviews that Clarke's allegations needed to be answered, and they needed to be answered—in public and under oath—by Condoleezza Rice.

As usual, Gonzales would not budge. White House colleagues said that he felt his own credibility rested on holding firm in refusing to make Rice available for public testimony to the commission. He had already been forced to make concessions on the PDBs, despite his earlier insistence that the commission would never see any of them. Would he now have to reverse himself on Rice, on an issue of executive privilege that was far more important?

The answer, as it turned out, was yes. The political pressure on the White House was too great, and Rice's persuasive powers with the president were more than a match for Alberto Gonzales's. Rice was as strong-willed as any member of the White House staff. Gonzales was strong-willed until the president told him otherwise.

Karen Hughes, the former White House communications director and one of Bush's closest advisers from Texas, acknowledged that political necessity overwhelmed any sense of constitutional principle when it came to Rice's testimony.

"The president recognized that the debate about the process—about who and how and where and whether it was public or private or sworn or unsworn—was overwhelming the facts of the matter," she said at the time. Hughes said Bush had told his aides, "Let's figure out how we can do this."

Bush made the announcement himself after he returned to the White House from Texas a few days later. He revealed that Rice would testify in public and under oath before the commission. And he announced an additional White House reversal: He and Cheney had agreed to meet in private with all ten members of the commission.

"I've ordered this level of cooperation because I consider it necessary to gaining a complete picture of the months and years that preceded the murder of our fellow citizens on September 11," Bush said in a brief appearance before White House reporters. "Our nation must never forget the loss or the lessons of September 11, and we must never assume that the danger has passed."

The commission had received a letter from the White House, signed by Gonzales, a day before the president's announcement. The letter disclosed the reversal on Rice's testimony and on the commission's meeting with Bush and Cheney. Dan Marcus, the commission's counsel, was delighted—and astonished—by what he read. He marveled at the nearly complete collapse of every executive privilege argument that Gonzales had been making for a year.

THE RICE hearing was scheduled for Thursday, April 8. Even after the furor over Clarke's testimony, this was almost certain to be the dramatic high point of the commission's public hearings. Washington was abuzz with speculation about what might happen when Rice was finally forced, under oath, to explain what had happened on September 11 and in the months leading up to the attacks. No one understood the event's importance better than Richard Ben-Veniste, the veteran Watergate prosecutor, who had seen how disclosures made during televised hearings had pulled the final pillars out from under Richard Nixon's presidency.

So there was astonishment among the other commissioners when they received an e-mail from Ben-Veniste on April 1 in which he said he regretted that he would have to miss Rice's testimony:

"I will not be able to attend the Rice hearing, as I am scheduled to be in a trial and the judge will not permit me to be absent."

There was a second e-mail from Ben-Veniste about an hour later: "April Fool."

— 42 —

ROOM 216
Hart Senate Office Building
APRIL 8, 2004

Condoleezza Rice almost never let her nerves show. Maybe it was all the years of training as a little girl, the choice of childhood hobbies—ice-skating, concert piano—that demanded rigidly disciplined public performances, usually solo performances at that. But this once, Rice did look anxious, her posture a little too erect, her smile frozen in place. Her eyes swept back and forth across the audience as she marched into the Senate hearing room where all of Washington seemed to have gathered to judge her. She knew that much of the country, and for that matter the world, was watching, too; major television networks were carrying her testimony live, interrupting their big-profit game shows and talk shows, something almost unheard of in the years since network news divisions were forced to turn a profit. She could see Philip Zelikow, a friendly face, on the dais, which doubtless offered a little comfort.

The logistics of the room, which normally served as the hearing room for the Senate Intelligence Committee, worked to her benefit. The witness table was set well below the platform where the commissioners sat, which gave the appearance of a modern-day Star Chamber. That had worried the commission's staff throughout the investigation; some had wondered if the commission should find a different room for the more confrontational hearings. In Rice's case, it was hard not to feel sympathy for this poised, strikingly accomplished African-American woman all alone at the table. She was being looked down on, literally, by nine very white men and one woman who were the personification of the old American Establishment. Behind them sat several of the commission's staff members, most of them white and male. It was a moment like this that reminded Jamie Gorelick why she had been right to push for more women on the commission. A black or Hispanic commissioner would not have hurt, either.

Tom Kean and Lee Hamilton were alarmed about the potential for disaster at the Rice hearing. Richard Clarke's testimony two weeks earlier had produced the first sharp public split on the commission on partisan grounds, the first real threat to the commission's unity since the troubles with Max Cleland. A direct attack on Rice would almost doubtless attract a new round of fierce attacks from Dennis Hastert and other congressional Republicans and from their allies on talk radio and in the press. Kean thought the situation was dangerous, potentially the moment when the investigation might unravel. He had gone to several of the commissioners privately and urged them to try to tamp down any harsh expressions of partisanship during Rice's testimony. The success of the commission, certainly its ability to produce a unanimous report, was at stake. He repeated the plea in a meeting with the commissioners the night before her appearance.

Kean and Hamilton decided that, unlike past hearings, when they allowed other commissioners to lead off the questioning, they would ask the first rounds of questions themselves. The decision worried some of the Democrats, who guessed that Kean and Hamilton might ask soft-ball questions of Rice. They knew Rice could expect a true grilling after that. The decision was made for the commissioners to go in alphabetical order, which meant that Richard Ben-Veniste would come first among the Democrats, and he was easily the most aggressive and prosecutorial in questioning administration witnesses.

Even before asking the first question, Kean and Hamilton also decided that they would make a public statement—to try to establish a tone of nonconfrontation. It was read for the cameras by Hamilton.

"Our purpose is not to embarrass," he said. "It is not to put any wit-ness on the spot. Our purpose is to understand and to inform. Questions do not represent opinions." If the White House had made bad choices in 2001 in dealing with terrorist threats, perhaps that was understandable, Hamilton seemed to be suggesting. "Policy makers face terrible dilem-mas," he continued. "Information is incomplete. The in-box is huge. Resources are limited. There are only so many hours in the day. The choices are tough. And none is tougher than deciding what is a priority and what is not." Some of Hamilton's fellow Democrats winced at the statement, as if the commission were suggesting that Rice had nothing to answer for.

When Kean asked Rice to stand up to take the oath, the room erupted with the now familiar machine-gun rattle of clicking cameras. For the photographers and cameramen, this was the iconic moment of the commission's investigation, even more so than when Clarke had testified. Rice stood up in her demure beige suit, an American flag pin on her lapel, raised her right hand, and swore to tell the truth about what had happened on 9/11. It was the first time a White House national security adviser had been forced to testify like this.

As she put down her hand and returned to the seat, Rice glanced at the clock. It was shortly after 9:00 a.m. Rice had come into the hearing with an important advantage. The commission had promised to limit her testimony to a single appearance, and Rice could feel confident that the ordeal would be over by lunch. The panel had not announced it publicly, but the White House knew that the commission had scheduled its private interview with Bill Clinton that afternoon across town.

Given the time constraints, Rice's strategy was an obvious one, then. She was a fanatical football fan, and on how many Sundays had she watched her beloved Cleveland Browns take a slight advantage on the scoreboard and then try to run out the clock? With the friendly Republican commissioners, she would answer their questions respectfully and give them the chance to follow up. With the more aggressive Democrats, she would try to run out the clock—talk and talk and talk, giving them no chance to ask follow-up questions before the ten minutes that each of the commissioners had been allotted had run out.

Kean invited Rice to present an opening statement. Most of the witnesses before the commission were requested to limit their remarks to a few minutes, with their full written statements introduced into the commission's records. But given the sensitivity of Rice's appearance, Kean and Hamilton did not want to be seen as restricting her ability to make the administration's case.

So Rice began reading her full public statement—ten single-spaced pages, all of it a painfully familiar recitation of what the White House had said in the past about 9/11. The presentation ate up twenty-five minutes before the first question could be asked, a remarkable contrast to Clarke's opening statement, his two-minute apology. Rice made no apology to the 9/11 families because, she suggested, there was nothing to apologize for.

"There was no silver bullet that could have prevented the 9/11 attacks," she said. Long before George Bush came to office, she said, the government had failed again and again to deal with the threat that Osama bin Laden and his terrorist network posed. For almost two decades, she said, "the terrorists were at war with us, but we were not yet at war with them."

Kean asked the first questions, and he surprised and pleased some of the Democrats by opening with an unexpectedly tough one. It was about Clarke and his allegations against Rice. Kean wanted to know how Rice had reacted in January 2001 when Clarke and her predecessor as national security adviser, Sandy Berger, had warned her that al-Qaeda was the most serious threat that she faced in the White House.

"We all had a strong sense that this was a crucial issue," she replied with seeming calm. "The question was, what do you then do about it?" What she had done about it, she said, was to keep Clarke in place at the NSC in early 2001 and to rely on the advice of other experienced holdovers from the Clinton administration, including George Tenet at the CIA and Louis Freeh at the FBI.

Kean followed up with another relatively tough question, asking her about Clarke's charge that the White House had hastily focused on an attack on Iraq after 9/11. Rice denied that there had been any rush to judgment about Baghdad. She ducked Kean's next question, about whether Clarke was telling the truth when he claimed in his book that Bush had cornered him in the White House Situation Room after 9/11 and urged him to look for an Iraqi connection to the attacks. "I personally don't remember it," she replied.

Hamilton opened with a question for Rice about why, if the White House was focused so sharply on the flood of terrorist threats in the summer of 2001, Bush had told Bob Woodward that his blood was "not so boiling" and he had felt no "sense of urgency" about bin Laden before 9/11.

Rice suggested that Bush's answer had been taken out of context— she said he meant to say that he had felt no urgency about a specific plan to *assassinate* bin Laden, as opposed to capturing him or shutting down his network—and that Bush had taken the al-Qaeda threat seriously from the start.

Ben-Veniste was up next. For a veteran prosecutor whose name would be linked forever to the investigation that ended the presidency of Richard Nixon, this was Ben-Veniste's moment again, his chance to try to extract a damaging confession from a hostile witness under oath, with all the world watching.

"Good morning, Dr. Rice," he said, a clear trace of menace in his voice. "Nice to see you again."

Rice smiled slightly. "Nice to see you," she replied.

To no one's surprise on the commission, Ben-Veniste wanted to focus on the August 6 PDB and why the Bush administration—and Rice in particular—had done so little to respond to it and other warnings throughout the spring and summer of 2001. In her private interview two months earlier, Rice had acknowledged being told by Clarke of the existence of sleeper cells of al-Qaeda in the United States, and Ben-Veniste wanted to know if the warning had been passed on to Bush.

"Did you tell the president at any time prior to August 6 of the existence of al-Qaeda cells in the United States?" he asked.

Rice was not going to take Ben-Veniste's bait. Either answer—yes, she did tell the president; no, she didn't—had the potential to suggest that the White House had mishandled the threats. So she was going to run out the clock on Ben-Veniste.

"First," she began, "let me just make certain—"

Ben-Veniste interrupted. "If you could just answer that question."

Rice: "Well, first—"

Ben-Veniste: "Because I have a very limited—"

Rice: "I understand, Commissioner, but it's important—"

Ben-Veniste: "Did you tell the president?"

Many in the audience, especially the family members of 9/11 victims, could see what Rice was doing, her bobbing and weaving, and they applauded Ben-Veniste's insistence that she answer the question.

Rice interrupted again: "It's important that I also address—it's also important, Commissioner, that I address the other issues that you have raised. So I will do it quickly, but if you'll just give me a moment…"

Ben-Veniste: "Well, my only question to us is whether you told the president."

Rice: "I understand, Commissioner, but I will—if you will just give me a moment, I will address fully the questions that you've asked."

She then offered a two-minute digression—two precious minutes from Ben-Veniste's ten-minute allotment—about the origins of the August 6 PDB and why it had been ordered up by Bush and how it offered no specific recommendation to the president about how to deal with al-Qaeda cells.

With his time almost gone, Ben-Veniste could see that if he asked a question that left any hint of ambiguity, Rice would take advantage of it to eat up more time. So he asked as specific a question as he could.

"Isn't it a fact, Dr. Rice, that the August 6 PDB warned against possible attacks in this country?" he said. "And I ask you whether you recall the title of that PDB?"

Rice did not hesitate a moment to answer the question, which made her answer all the more startling to people in the audience: "I believe the title was 'Bin Laden Determined to Attack Inside the United States.'"

There was an audible gasp in the audience as Rice confirmed officially, once and for all, what had long been suspected—that the August 6 PDB was an explicit warning from the CIA, only a month before 9/11, that al-Qaeda was going to try to strike on American soil. The guessing on the commission was that Rice had planned in advance to reveal the title at the hearing, if only because the hearing would offer her the best possible public forum to try to disparage the PDB's importance.

Ben-Veniste tried to cut her off before she could use up more time: "Thank you."

"No, Mr. Ben-Veniste," she tried to continue. "Now, the PDB—"

Ben-Veniste: "I will get into the—"

Rice: "I would like to finish my point here."

Ben-Veniste: "I didn't know there *was* a point." The audience burst into laughter.

Rice: "Given that you asked me whether or not it warned of attacks—"

Ben-Veniste: "I asked you what the *title* was." His tone was one of almost theatrical exasperation, and it produced more laughter in the audience.

By the time Bob Kerrey had the chance to question Rice, he felt he knew exactly what she was up to. Kerrey was a veteran of the Senate, home of the filibuster, and Rice was demonstrating her mastery of the art. Still, he would try to pin her down, and his first question was about her relationship with Zelikow.

"Let me ask you, first of all, a question that's been a concern for me from the first day I came onto the commission, and that is the relationship of our executive director to you," Kerrey said. "Did you ask Philip Zelikow any questions about terrorism during the transition?" Zelikow sat directly behind Kerrey, looking startled by Kerrey's question.

Rice replied, "Philip and I had numerous conversations about the issues that we were facing."

Kerrey pressed her. "Did you talk to him about terrorism?" More specifically, he asked, "Did you instruct him to do anything on terrorism?"

Rice acknowledged that she had asked Zelikow specifically to review Clarke's performance at the NSC, "to help think about the structure" of "Clarke's operations, yes."

Kerrey changed the subject, thinking he had established for the record just how close the ties were between Rice and the commission's executive director. He moved on to the larger issue of what happened in the White House in the months before 9/11.

"You said the president was tired of swatting flies," he said, referring to Bush's famous remark early in 2001 about the need for a wide-ranging government strategy for dealing with al-Qaeda. "Can you tell me one example where the president swatted a fly when it came to al-Qaeda prior to 9/11?"

Kerrey continued before Rice had a chance to answer: "We didn't swat any flies." His voice rose with what seemed to be sincere anger. "How the hell could he be tired?"

Kerrey asked specifically why the White House had not ordered any sort of military response to the al-Qaeda attack in Yemen on the USS *Cole,* which had been bombed only three months before President Bush came to office.

"Why didn't we respond to the *Cole?* Why didn't we swat that fly?"

Rice fell back on the defense that the White House had offered in the past on the *Cole*: that the administration was in the middle of a broad review of counterterrorism strategy throughout 2001. A limited military response against al-Qaeda over the *Cole,* she said, would have been counterproductive, demonstrating American weakness, not strength.

"We simply believed that the best approach was to put in place a plan that was going to eliminate this threat, not respond to it tit for tat," she said. "I do not believe to this day that it was—would have been a good thing to respond to the *Cole,* given the kinds of options that we were going to have."

Kerrey asked her why she didn't act on Clarke's Delenda plan to attack al-Qaeda sanctuaries in Afghanistan in 2001. Clarke had given her a copy of the plan at the White House on January 25, 2001, when he made his initial, urgent request for an early cabinet meeting on the al-Qaeda threat.

"I want to be very clear on this, because it's been a source of controversy," Rice said. "We were not presented with a plan."

"Well, that's not true," Kerrey replied.

He could see that Rice was going to play more of her word games. Clarke had given her a document called the "Delenda plan," and Rice had previously referred to it as the "Delenda plan." But now, she was saying, a "plan" was not a "plan."

"What we were presented with on January the twenty-fifth was a set of ideas and a paper, most of which was about what the Clinton administration had done, and something called the Delenda plan, which had been considered in 1998 and never adopted."

Under her strained definition, a "plan" was now not a "plan" if it was not acted on.

With only a few minutes remaining of his ten-minute allotment, Kerrey tried to move the conversation elsewhere, but Rice wanted to go back again and again to the subject of Clarke and Delenda—and eat up more time.

"Let me move to another area," Kerrey said.

"May I finish answering your question, though?" she asked. "Because this is an important point."

"No, I know it's important, everything that's going on here is important. But I get ten minutes."

Rice: "But since we have a point of disagreement, I'd like to have a chance to address it."

Kerrey: "Well, no, actually, there's going... we have many points of disagreement with Mr. Clarke that we'll have to give a chance."

Rice: "I think—"

Kerrey had had enough.

"Please don't filibuster me, it's not fair," he said with agitation. "It's not fair. I have been polite. I have been courteous. It is not fair to me." Many in the audience applauded Kerrey.

Rice stood her ground. "Commissioner, I'm here to answer your questions. And you asked me a question, and I'd like to have an opportunity to answer it."

Kerrey asked her the circumstances of a White House meeting that she organized with Clarke and Andy Card on July 5, 2001, to discuss how the FBI and other domestic agencies were prepared to deal with what the CIA believed was an imminent terrorist strike. Rice had argued previously that the meeting was proof of how well she had done her job that summer.

"So you have a meeting on the fifth of July where you're trying to make certain that your domestic agencies are preparing a defense against a possible strike—you know al-Qaeda cells were in the United States. You've got to follow up, and the question is: Where was your follow-up? What is the paper trail that shows that you and Andy Card followed up on this meeting?"

"I followed up with Dick Clarke," Rice said, once again suggesting that if anyone was responsible for the failures of coordination among domestic agencies before 9/11, it was Clarke, not her. "I talked to Dick Clarke about this all the time."

Then she returned to the point she had tried to make so often before—that the warnings of an attack were so vague in 2001 that there was little for the FBI and other domestic agencies to respond to. "You have no time, you have no place, you have no 'how,'" she said.

But Kerrey knew that was not true, either. The August 6 PDB had specified that al-Qaeda was considering domestic hijackings and that there were warnings of terrorist surveillance of buildings in New York. There was a place. There was a how.

So Kerrey decided to do something at the hearing that was almost certainly illegal. He was going to take it on himself to reveal classified information—specifically, he was going to read out the most explosive finding in the body of the PDB.

"In the spirit of further declassification, this is what the August sixth memo said to the president, that 'the FBI indicates patterns of suspicious activity in the United States consistent with preparations for hijacking,'" he said, reading directly from PDB. "That's the language of the memo that was briefed to the president on the sixth of August."

By the end of the hearing, it seemed a draw. Democrats could see in it what they wanted—Rice as duplicitous, eager to hide the truth about her performance, and Bush's, before 9/11. Republicans saw her as heroic, valiantly defending the president, giving as good as she got from Ben-Veniste and the other Democratic "bullies." Even if they were confounded by her unwillingness to answer their questions, Democrats could not fail to be impressed by Rice's ability to remain calm even in the midst of fierce questioning. Under the harsh television lights, style really could stump substance. Tom Shales, the television critic of *The Washington Post,* said that "if it were to be viewed as a battle, or as a sporting event, or as a contest," then "Condoleezza Rice won it." Dan Rather, the CBS News anchorman who was disdained by the White House for his perceived antagonism toward the Bush administration, praised Rice's performance as "steady and composed."

If anything at the hearing qualified as truly bad news for the White House, it came in the final few minutes, when Kean closed the hearing by announcing that the commission wanted to see the entire August 6, 2001, PDB declassified and made public. "There was a lot of discussion about the PDB," said Kean. "We have requested from the White House that that be declassified, because we feel it is important that the American people get a chance to see it. We are awaiting an answer on our request and hope by next week's hearing that we might have it."

— 43 —

301 7TH STREET, SW
Washington, D.C.
APRIL 8, 2004

The government office building in southwest Washington, several blocks from the Capitol and about fifteen minutes by cab from the commission's downtown offices, could not have been more anonymous. Suitably, it housed offices for the most faceless of federal agencies, the General Services Administration, which served as the government's real estate broker. In 2003 and 2004, the GSA building at Seventh and D streets also served as overflow offices for the 9/11 commission, housing the teams of investigators who did not require daily access to highly classified documents.

There was a frenzy among GSA employees when they heard the rumor on April 8, 2004, that a celebrity had been seen wandering through their building. People put down their phones and coffee cups, stood up from their desks, and rushed to the hallways to try to find him. Just a glimpse. Maybe a handshake or an autograph? The GSA workers were giddy at the thought that Bill Clinton was there.

The former president was in the building that afternoon for his private interview by the 9/11 commission. Unlike George Bush, Clinton had readily agreed from the start of the investigation to meet with all ten commissioners and answer their questions at length. His aides said Clinton would even have considered public testimony before the commission. But the possibility was never considered seriously, since the panel's Republicans knew Bush would never agree to a public appearance—and that would create the appearance that he, unlike his predecessor, was hiding something.

The commission had tried to keep the Clinton meeting secret, if only to avoid a crush of television cameras and reporters; that explained the decision to conduct the interview at the commission's out-of-the-way offices at the GSA rather than its central offices on K Street.

Two of the Republicans on the commission knew Clinton reasonably well: Tom Kean, who had always liked the former president and once considered Clinton's offer of a cabinet post; and Jim Thompson, who had been Illinois governor when Clinton was his counterpart in Arkansas. The other Republican commissioners had spent the years of the Clinton administration mostly bemoaning his presidency. While in the Senate, Slade Gorton had voted to convict Clinton in his impeachment trial for obstructing justice in trying to cover up about the affair with Monica Lewinsky.

Clinton had a well-deserved reputation for being late for everything, and he was late, about an hour, for his interview with the 9/11 commission.

"It's not my fault," Clinton told Kean apologetically. He said he was well aware of his reputation and had made a special effort to be on time for the commission. The FAA was supposed to have made special arrangements for Clinton's small private plane to land at Washington's close-in Reagan Airport, which had banned most private jets since 9/11 as a security precaution; the airport's flight path was directly along the Potomac and brought planes perilously close to the Pentagon. But someone at the FAA had bungled the request, so Clinton's plane from his new home in New York did not have clearance to land. Given what they now knew about the incompetence of the FAA and its performance on 9/11, Kean and the other commissioners were forgiving. "Welcome to our world," Kean said, chuckling. Some of the commissioners were relieved that Clinton was late. They were pleased to catch their breath after the circus of that morning's public hearing with Condoleezza Rice.

Whatever Clinton's reputation for tardiness and undisciplined work habits, the 9/11 commissioners who did not know the former president were about to learn what it was like to see him at his most impressive. Clinton said he had been up much of the night, in a final push to finish his long overdue memoirs. "I finally got to bed at three a.m.," he told the commissioners. But if Clinton was fatigued, it was impossible to detect from his performance that afternoon. He had obviously done his homework for the session, reviewing all of the counterterrorism material that Sandy Berger had prepared for him to review. Ever the politician, Clinton had also made a special point of learning in advance something about his questioners, including putting names to faces for the three Republican commissioners he did not know.

John Lehman, one of the Republicans, was startled to see Clinton pushing past some of the Democrat commissioners to rush over and say hello.

"He comes over to me and he says, 'Mr. Secretary, how are you? It's good to see you, John,'" said Lehman, remembering how impressed he was that Clinton seemed to know who he was. "And I'd never met him before in my fucking life. He was even more charming than his reputation."

Clinton then turned to "my friend Jim"—Thompson—and explained to the commissioners how, when the two men were governors, they had shared a baby-sitter at a conference of the National Governors Association.

Then the questioning began. For most of the next four hours, Clinton offered a master class in the history of his administration's struggle with al-Qaeda and other global terrorist threats. He offered no apologies for his failure to kill Osama bin Laden, because, he said, he had done everything within his power to accomplish it.

"I wanted to see him dead," Clinton said, repeating the words that Berger had attributed to him.

Even as he defended his own actions at the White House, Clinton impressed the Republicans with his reluctance to criticize Bush for having done too little against bin Laden in the first months of 2001. He refused the invitation of some of the Democrats to attack Bush. Clinton repeated something else that Berger had already told the commissioners: He insisted that his personal scandals and the impeachment battles in 1998 and 1999 had not affected his eagerness to confront bin Laden.

That was where Bob Kerrey stopped him.

Clinton had to be kidding, Kerrey thought. Clinton may have been too self-absorbed to realize it at the time, but on Capitol Hill, the Lewinsky mess and all of Clinton's other sexual and financial scandals had a terrible impact on the ability to rally support for any move against al-Qaeda. Clinton's troubles had certainly hindered Kerrey and his Democratic colleagues in the Senate from trying to support the national security policy of a president who was swamped by allegations of sexual misconduct. A president less hindered by scandal might have been able to mount a determined effort to rally support in Congress to destroy bin Laden's network before it became such a threat, Kerrey thought. Every time Clinton lobbed a cruise missile at bin Laden, the White

House—and Clinton's Democratic allies in Congress—were forced to deny that the attack was an attempt to divert attention from some turn in the Lewinsky scandal.

"I'm willing to accept the fact that it didn't have any impact on you," Kerrey told Clinton. "But it had a big impact on me. It affected my ability to carry out my responsibilities."

The Republicans on the commission were wowed by the former president. Fred Fielding walked up to Kean afterward to say how impressed he had been by Clinton. "And he seems like such a nice man," Fielding said.

Lehman went home to New York and told his wife, Barbara, about Clinton's bravura performance. "I said, 'This guy is really impressive, and he really answered the questions,'" he said.

She looked at him askance, reminding him of all the terrible, insulting things he had said about Bill Clinton during his presidency. "After all you've said about Clinton?" she said. "John, you're a star-fucker."

OFFICES OF THE 9/11 COMMISSION
NEW YORK, N.Y.

Mayor Michael Bloomberg of New York City had found just the right, punchy adjective to describe the 9/11 commission: "ghoulish." It would fit nicely in one of the garish front-page headlines in the city's tabloids. He insisted on one of his weekly radio shows in November 2003 that it was "ghoulish" for the commission to want to review the police and fire department tapes of rescue efforts on the morning of 9/11, as well as the tapes and transcripts of 911 emergency calls. The tapes, he explained, contained the last words of people who died horrifying deaths in the Twin Towers. "I have an obligation to protect the families and their memories to the extent we possibly can," he said, questioning what value the tapes could possibly have to the commission. "I don't know why they don't get on with what they're really supposed to do."

The commission's investigators had difficulty understanding why Bloomberg and his aides were always so antagonistic toward them. Bloomberg was elected and took office after 9/11; if errors were made in the city's emergency planning before the attacks, he had no responsibility for them. Still, Bloomberg seemed eager to do what he could to obstruct the commission's investigation. There was speculation that the mayor had been put up to it by his Republican predecessor, Rudy Giuliani, who might not be so eager to see all of the facts aired, especially given the glory that his performance on 9/11 had otherwise brought him.

The city government was the third and final target of a subpoena from the commission. The subpoena was issued in November 2002 and demanded the emergency tapes and transcripts. But unlike the Pentagon and the FAA, which immediately agreed to comply with their subpoenas from the 9/11 commission, Bloomberg was initially defiant. He said he would go to court to fight the commission.

Bloomberg claimed partial victory in a settlement with the commission two weeks later. The mayor agreed to make all of the material available to the commission, but with the understanding that anyone heard on the tapes would not be identified by name in any public document unless they or their survivors gave approval.

The commission's investigators spent weeks in city offices, listening to the tapes and reviewing transcripts. Bloomberg had not exaggerated the horror of what was in the material. At the same time, they also were proof of the heroism of so many of the city's rescue workers who had rushed into the Twin Towers in the knowledge that they were likely sacrificing their own lives.

What may have worried Bloomberg, and perhaps Giuliani, was something else the emergency tapes demonstrated. They were the clearest evidence obtained by the commission of just how unprepared the city was to deal with a catastrophic terrorist attack—the sort of attack that had been predicted since 1993, when Islamic extremists made their first attempt to bring down the Twin Towers. Eight years later, when the terrorists returned to lower Manhattan and attacked again at precisely the same place, this time with hijacked planes rather than a truck bomb, the city seemed to have been no better prepared.

— 44 —

RIYADH, SAUDI ARABIA

FEBRUARY 23, 2004

For its official visitors, the Saudi royal family maintains a series of palaces in Riyadh, the kingdom's capital, and other cities. They function like four-star hotels, complete with luxury spas and complimentary round-the-clock laundry and room service. For the investigators from the 9/11 commission, there were two drawbacks to using them for their interrogations of Saudi officials in 2004: The phones and rooms were almost certainly bugged by the Saudi spy agencies, and there was no hope of finding alcohol. (The managers at Western-run hotels in the otherwise dry kingdom often kept a secret stash of alcohol for favored guests.) As they contemplated their questioning of Fahad al-Thumairy, the 9/11 commission's investigators joked that they could have used a drink.

Thumairy was the young Saudi diplomat who had worked at the country's consulate in Los Angeles in 2000 and 2001 and who appeared to be a middleman of some sort for Nawaf al-Hazmi and Khalid al-Mihdhar, the two 9/11 hijackers who had lived in San Diego. Mike Jacobson, Raj De, and other investigators on the commission's "plot" team had compiled a long dossier on Thumairy, much of it built on evidence that Jacobson had found buried in FBI files that suggested just how dangerous the Saudi diplomat was.

Although he held a diplomatic passport, Thumairy's principal, official role in Los Angeles was religious; he actually worked for the Saudi Ministry of Islamic Affairs and was the consulate's liaison to the city's huge Saudi-financed King Fahd mosque. He served as an imam at the mosque and had a reputation for extremist, anti-Western views that included calls for jihad. When he tried to return to the United States in May 2003 after a brief trip home, he was detained on arrival at Los

Angeles International Airport and immediately deported; his visa application had been revoked because of concerns at the State Department that he was tied to terrorists.

The evidence gathered by the commission suggested Thumairy had orchestrated help for the hijackers through a network of Saudi and other Arab expatriates living throughout Southern California and led by Omar al-Bayoumi, the seemingly bumbling "ghost employee" of a Saudi aviation contractor. Although Thumairy had denied in previous interviews with the FBI that he knew Bayoumi or the two hijackers, the commission's investigators had found evidence and witnesses that proved he was lying. The commission's investigators had traveled to Saudi Arabia because they wanted to confront Thumairy with his lies.

The most intriguing, potentially damning evidence against Thumairy was found by Jacobson and De in a group of classified FBI reports prepared in 2002. The reports detailed the results of the interrogation of an Arabic-speaking taxi driver from Los Angeles who had been arrested on immigration charges a few months after 9/11. The Tunisian driver, Qualid Benomrare, was linked to Thumairy in the FBI files, apparently because he had done chauffeur work for the consulate.

The driver was shown a series of photographs of young Arab men and asked if he recognized any of them; Benomrare surprised the FBI questioners and quickly picked out the two hijackers—Hazmi and Mihdhar—before realizing what he had done. He then nervously backtracked and denied knowing the pair.

Asked about his ties to Thumairy, Benomrare said that the Saudi diplomat had introduced him before 9/11 to "two Saudis"—young men, he recalled—who had just arrived in the United States and needed help. He drove them around Los Angeles and to the Sea World amusement park in San Diego.

To Jacobson and De, it seemed likely that the "two Saudis" introduced by Thumairy to the driver were the two terrorists Thumairy claimed never to have met. The two terrorists whose photos Benomrare had initially recognized.

Bayoumi had been interviewed in an October 2003 visit to Saudi Arabia by Philip Zelikow and Dieter Snell, the head of the "plot" team. Bayoumi had returned home to Saudi Arabia after 9/11 when it became clear that he was under intense scrutiny by the FBI. He insisted to

Zelikow and Snell that he had no idea Hazmi and Mihdhar might be tied to al-Qaeda, that he had befriended them in accordance with the best traditions of Muslim hospitality. He repeated the unlikely account of how he met the two men in February 2000 by coincidence at a halal restaurant near Los Angeles International Airport.

Thumairy had a problem in insisting to the FBI after 9/11 that he did not know Bayoumi, because Bayoumi acknowledged that he knew Thumairy. Bayoumi said he and the Saudi diplomat had talked on occasion at the King Fahd mosque—"solely on religious matters," Bayoumi claimed.

The commission's interview with Thumairy was scheduled for the middle of the night in Riyadh, traditional work hours for Saudi government officials. They tended to sleep or rest through the day, given the country's harsh daytime temperatures. Thumairy arrived in a conference room at the visitors palace in traditional white robes and headdress.

Given what he knew about Thumairy and his support for violent extremism, Raj De was hesitant to shake his hand. It was like shaking the hand of a terrorist, he thought. De remembered Thumairy as short and slight, with small, dark eyes.

The Saudi government had made the arrangements for Thumairy's interrogation, and Saudi minders joined in on the conversation. They were almost certainly there to make sure Thumairy said nothing that compromised the Saudi government. Although Thumairy must have understood the consequences if he misspoke to the 9/11 commission, he demonstrated remarkable calm at the start of the questioning. He spoke in Arabic through an interpreter at the beginning of the conversation, but later, as the questions from his English-language interrogators became accusatory, he switched to English for his answers.

Thumairy told the story he had told before to the FBI: that he was not a Muslim extremist, that he was not anti-American, and that it was "ridiculous" to try to link him to some sort of Saudi government support network for 9/11.

"I do not know this man Bayoumi," he said. He certainly did not know Hazmi and Mihdhar, the hijackers, he insisted. It was possible, of course, that he had been in the King Fahd mosque at some time when Bayoumi or the hijackers had gone there to worship, but that certainly did not mean he knew them; thousands of Muslims from across Southern California worshipped there.

Raj De interrupted Thumairy. "Your phone records tell a different story," said the young American. "We have your phone records."

Thumairy was silent for a moment. It occurred to De that Thumairy had not expected to be cross-examined like this. Perhaps the Saudi thought he still enjoyed some sort of diplomatic immunity. Maybe he thought his phone records back in Los Angeles were protected from release by some diplomatic nicety? The expression on his face was one of shock.

"I don't know what you're talking about," Thumairy said, agitated.

De explained that the commission had obtained FBI records that documented numerous phone calls between Bayoumi and Thumairy between December 1998 and December 2000. Bayoumi had called Thumairy's home telephone number at least ten times, and Thumairy had called Bayoumi's cell phone and home phone even more often—at least eleven times in December 2000, nine months before the attacks.

"So you still don't remember Mr. Bayoumi?" De asked sarcastically.

Thumairy began to sputter. "I have contact with a lot of people."

K STREET OFFICES OF THE 9/11 COMMISSION
WASHINGTON, D.C.

There was something theatrical about Doug MacEachin, and it was valuable in a career spent mostly as an intelligence analyst at the CIA. He understood that a fine, well-thought-out intelligence report on some esoteric national security issue might go unread at the White House if there wasn't a little something in it to grab a reader. A little stagecraft. He was an intellectual, a true scholar, whose specialty at the CIA had been in Soviet and Eastern European affairs. But he knew that a pithy turn of phrase in a report—or some well-timed bit of profanity uttered at just the right moment during an intelligence briefing—would keep his audience awake and engaged.

The marine veteran certainly saw his life as a performance to be savored. MacEachin was no gray bureaucrat. After his 1997 retirement from the CIA, where he had been the agency's number two analyst, with the title "deputy director for intelligence," he had gone off to live in the south of France, a place full of the fine wines and beautiful women he so admired. He would have happily stayed there under the Mediterranean sun had he not been invited onto the 9/11 commission by Philip Zelikow, who knew him from projects at Harvard's Kennedy School of Government. Zelikow thought MacEachin would be a natural to lead the team that would investigate the history of al-Qaeda and the early efforts of the government to deal with it.

By early 2004, MacEachin had spent nearly a year on the commission with his nose in the files of the CIA and other spy agencies, poring over documents that showed what the agency had known about Osama bin Laden and when. And as a career intelligence analyst, he was offended by what he had discovered about the agency's performance on terrorist threats. There was much to admire in the CIA's files—the work of middle-ranking officers in the United States and abroad who had recognized the al-Qaeda threat and tried to act on it.

But as someone who had made his reputation as an intelligence analyst, MacEachin was shocked that no one at the senior levels of the CIA had attempted—for years—to catalog and give context to what was known about al-Qaeda. No one had made the effort to present the White House and the rest of the government with a comprehensive analysis of the threat that bin Laden had so obviously posed since the early 1990s. It was not just Zelikow on the commission who believed that the CIA's analysts had failed so badly in the months and years before 9/11; it was also MacEachin, who had spent so much of his career at Langley.

MacEachin decided to use a little "wise-ass" theater to make that point clear to the members of the 9/11 commission. He was called before the commissioners at a meeting on February 27, 2004, to discuss the progress of his team's part of the investigation. He opened the session by announcing solemnly that he had just come across a critical intelligence report about al-Qaeda and that he needed urgently to share it with the commissioners. It had been kept from them until now, he said.

He held a copy of the mysterious intelligence report, apparently from the CIA, in one hand. "Commissioners, this is a coincidence, but this is the seventh anniversary of the publication of this really, really critical paper," he said. "It was a paper written on February 27, 1997."

The commissioners could see that the 1997 report was full of graphs and charts and timelines. They documented the early chronology of the al-Qaeda threat: the terrorist group's ties to attacks on Americans in the 1990s, including the shoot-down of two American Black Hawk helicopters in 1993 in Somalia, prompting a firefight in which eighteen American soldiers were killed; bin Laden's efforts in the mid-1990s to buy weapons-grade uranium to build nuclear weapons; his later campaign to merge the efforts of terrorist groups from around the Muslim world. MacEachin had prepared PowerPoint slides of some of the charts from the report, so the commissioners could see more closely what he was talking about.

The report was startling and also, in a way, comforting. It seemed proof that some forward-thinking analysts within the CIA had tried to gather all the known evidence about al-Qaeda in the late 1990s and present it to policy makers to convince them of the need for action—action, presumably, to kill bin Laden and destroy his network long before they would have the chance to carry out 9/11.

"This is wild," Tom Kean said.

"Why don't we have this document?" demanded Jamie Gorelick, startled that she had never heard of it before. "I insist that we get a copy."

"What the *fuck*?" Bob Kerrey said incredulously. He had been deputy chairman of the Senate Intelligence Committee in 1997 and should have seen such a finely crafted bit of intelligence analysis. MacEachin would later recall having to "bring Kerrey down off the ceiling," he was so angry.

Then a devilish smile crossed MacEachin's face. "I lied," he said. "There was no such document." He had written this "report" himself. "But my point is there could have been such a document in 1997," he told the commissioners. There should have been such a report, he said. All of the information in the document was available within the CIA by February 1997, but nobody within the CIA had thought to pull it all together.

It was astounding, MacEachin explained. But for almost four years before 9/11, the CIA had not issued a so-called national intelligence estimate on terrorism. Even after the bombing of two American embassies in Africa in 1998. Even after the bombing of an American warship, the *Cole,* in the port of Aden, Yemen, in October 2000, only eleven months before the 9/11 attacks.

The reputation of NIEs had become tarnished in the aftermath of the Iraq war, when it was discovered that the prewar NIE on Iraq's purported stockpiles of weapons of mass destruction was wrong in almost every essential detail. But for many years before that, NIEs had a different reputation. They were considered the gold standard of American intelligence. They were the trusted, authoritative documents that outlined the best information available to the CIA and the government's other spy agencies about national security threats.

The last full NIE on terrorism had been issued in 1997, and it was mostly an update of what MacEachin thought was an excellent, although incomplete, NIE on the subject two years earlier. The prescient 1995 document was prompted in part by the World Trade Center bombing two years earlier. It predicted that international terrorist groups would attack again on American soil and that the danger would only increase with time. It identified potential targets of attacks, including the White House, the Capitol, and the symbols of capitalism on Wall Street, such as the World Trade Center. The 1997 update mentioned Osama bin Laden only in passing—only a few sentences in a six-page document—and did not include any mention of al-Qaeda by name.

After 1997, the CIA issued a variety of analytical papers about bin Laden and the threat of al-Qaeda, and some of them were reasonably detailed and impressive, MacEachin thought. Information from many of the reports made its way into the president's daily briefs, so they were seen—in bits and pieces—at the White House.

But there was no NIE, and MacEachin thought that helped explain why the response to the 1998 embassy bombings had been so timid—cruise missiles sent against bin Laden's deserted Afghan training camps and against a factory in Sudan that may or may not have produced chemical weapons—and why the attack on the *Cole* in 2000 had gone entirely unanswered by both the Clinton and Bush administrations.

MacEachin thought it was "unforgivable" that there had been no NIE for four years before the 9/11 attacks. He thought that if policy makers had understood that the embassy bombings and the attack on the *Cole* were simply the latest in a long series of attacks by the same enemy, they would have felt compelled to do much more in response.

Instead of providing analysis that gave context to a national security threat, he said, the CIA had turned itself in the late 1990s into a "headline service" that fed small nuggets of intelligence about terrorist threats to policy makers but never made the larger context clear. That gave officials at the White House and elsewhere a chance to duck responsibility when it came to responding to individual attacks. The *Cole* was the most appalling example of it, MacEachin thought. By any standard, an attack on an American warship in a foreign port was a true act of war; it should have demanded an immediate, and devastating, reaction.

Even though it was obvious within days that al-Qaeda was responsible for bombing the destroyer, Clinton was clearly not eager to respond; a response might well have been seen as yet another "wag the dog" moment, this time intended to help Al Gore clinch an election victory the following month. When Bush and his new team came to office three months later, they saw the *Cole* attack as old news; it had happened on Clinton's watch.

It occurred to many on the commission—commissioners and staff alike—that a fierce response to the *Cole* might have preempted or at least delayed the attacks in New York and Washington on September 11. If Clinton or Bush had pounded al-Qaeda's camps in Afghanistan, really turned them into dust, and ordered the FBI and CIA to begin a world-wide manhunt to find bin Laden and his allies, wasn't it just possible that bin Laden might have been tempted to rethink 9/11? Wouldn't that have made the FBI and CIA work harder to coordinate the clues in front of them? The commission's investigation had turned up evidence to suggest that the timing of the 9/11 attacks was decided only in late August 2001. According to the CIA interrogation reports, Khalid Sheikh Mohammed, the mastermind, had told his interrogators that bin Laden might have canceled the 9/11 attacks if he had known about the arrest of Zacarias Moussaoui in August in Minnesota. But bin Laden, like the acting director of the FBI that summer, did not learn about the arrest until after September 11.

The evidence suggested that the lack of an American response to the *Cole* had, in fact, emboldened bin Laden to carry out larger attacks. The commission's investigators came across a chilling intelligence report that quoted an informant as saying in February 2001, four months after the *Cole* bombing, that "the big instructor," probably a reference to bin Laden, had wanted and expected an American counterattack to the attack on the destroyer. If there was no American response to the *Cole*, "the big instructor" planned to launch something deadlier, the report said.

Among the commissioners, no one was more agitated over the *Cole* than Kerrey. He was a navy man, after all. He was confronted in the mirror every morning with the evidence of the sacrifices he had made in his navy service—the missing ten inches of his right leg, blown away by an enemy grenade in Vietnam. He could not understand why an attack on an American warship, why the deaths of those seventeen sailors aboard the destroyer, should ever have gone unanswered. If there had been a fierce American response that targeted bin Laden after the *Cole,* wasn't it just possible that 9/11 might not have happened? He seemed to blame Clinton as much as Bush.

John Lehman took this personally, too. The *Cole* was, in a sense, part of his legacy as Navy secretary. The destroyer was commissioned in 1996, but the budgeting for it had begun more than a decade earlier, when Lehman was running the Navy in the Reagan administration and doing everything in his power to expand the American fleet.

"It's astounding," he said of the decision made early in the Bush administration not to retaliate for the *Cole.* "Nobody doubted it was al-Qaeda," he said. But the neoconservatives who were running the Bush administration were "just besotted" with other national security issues—missile defense, Iraq, North Korea, China, Russia. "They were living in another world; they had their own construction of the world, and the *Cole* was not part of that world. Al-Qaeda was just not part of their threat scenario."

If there had been a response to the *Cole,* "I think it could well have avoided 9/11," he said. "I totally believe that. It would have changed the calculations for Osama."

— 45 —

K STREET OFFICES OF THE
9/11 COMMISSION
Washington, D.C.
JANUARY 2004

Len Hawley, the new arrival on Team 3, could see why the staff of the commission was so frustrated. He could certainly understand why Warren Bass, the commission's NSC specialist, had seemed so close to resigning at the end of 2003. Philip Zelikow's micromanagement meant that the staff had little, if any, contact with the ten commissioners; all information was funneled through Zelikow, and he decided how it would be shared elsewhere. Hawley certainly heard the allegations about Zelikow's partisanship—about how he seemed to be trying to shield Condoleezza Rice and others in the Bush administration from the scrutiny they deserved for 9/11—from Bass and the others on the team.

But Hawley was willing to give Zelikow the benefit of the doubt. Hawley found it hard to believe that experienced politicians like Tom Kean and Lee Hamilton would agree to keep Zelikow on as executive director if his efforts to help the White House were so obvious. Perhaps the problem with Zelikow was not partisanship, Hawley told his new colleagues. Perhaps it was just Zelikow's outsize, abrasive personality. People simply did not like working for him.

At fifty-seven years old, Hawley was older and more experienced than the twenty- and thirty-somethings who populated most of the rest of the commission's staff. He radiated calm, a sense of having seen it all in Washington and in the government. He had one of the most impressive résumés on the staff, certainly the most varied. A West Point graduate and Vietnam veteran, Hawley had spent the first two decades of his career in the army, rising to senior assignments on the Joint Chiefs of Staff and as a professor at the National Defense University. He retired with the rank of colonel and went to work on the staff of the House Armed Services Committee and then in the National Security Council and State Department.

In the Clinton administration, he had been a deputy assistant secretary of state, overseeing diplomatic efforts in war zones like the Balkans, Sierra Leone, and East Timor. He was seen as likely to get a top diplomatic assignment or NSC job if John Kerry was elected president in 2004.

HAWLEY HAD initially been hired to help ease the burden on Warren Bass and other members of Team 3. And he took on other responsibilities, including helping to prepare Zelikow and the commissioners for private interviews with current and former cabinet members ahead of their public testimony. As an early assignment, he was asked to help prepare the commission for its private questioning of former attorney general Janet Reno; she was scheduled to testify in public in March.

Hawley reviewed what was available to the commission about Reno's record at the Justice Department on terrorism. He could see she was praised within the department for her aggressive pursuit of criminal investigations involving al-Qaeda, even as she was criticized elsewhere in the government for her unwillingness to lend legal backing to military and spying operations that might end with Osama bin Laden's assassination. Reno felt the war against al-Qaeda was best handled as a law enforcement operation, with terrorists brought to justice in courtrooms, not executed on the battlefield.

As she took her seat in the commission's conference room on K Street, Hawley and the other staff members could see that Reno's Parkinson's disease had grown worse since her departure from Washington; the shaking of her head and hands had become more violent in the three years since she'd left the Justice Department. (It was certainly much worse than Sandy Berger's shaking during his private interview.)

There were a few routine pleasantries between Reno and Zelikow, who would lead the questioning, before Zelikow launched into what turned into a fierce interrogation. Zelikow made it obvious, at least to Hawley, that he had utter disdain for Reno and her performance at the Justice Department under Clinton, that she was an architect of the Clinton administration's weak-kneed antiterrorism policies.

Zelikow asked none of the questions that Hawley had prepared for the interview, instead pursuing his own—all of them focused on demonstrating that Reno had been disorganized, even incompetent, in her management of the department and in overseeing its part in the war on terror.

Hawley was startled by Zelikow's antagonistic tone. He looked around the room to see if others were as concerned as he was about Zelikow's treatment of Reno. Reno herself seemed unfazed. As was typical of Reno during her tenure as attorney general, when she routinely faced insults from Republicans anytime she testified on Capitol Hill, she gave no sense that she was offended by Zelikow.

The interview was supposed to last about two hours, and Zelikow had monopolized all but the last five or ten minutes of it before turning to Hawley and the other staff members in the room and asking if they had questions. With only a few minutes left, there was little they could do to try to undo the hostile atmosphere established by Zelikow.

After each private interview, the staff was asked to prepare a memo for the records, or MFR, as it was called in the commission, that summarized what had happened; the MFRs were then shared with commissioners and other staff members who had not attended. After the Reno interview, the task of writing the memo fell to Hawley. He decided that he needed to get across to the commission what Zelikow was up to—that his partisanship had been blatantly on display in his questioning of Reno.

So Hawley prepared a memo that, rather than summarizing the interview, was largely a transcript of the harsh questions that Zelikow had asked and the answers Reno had given.

"I don't want anybody reading this memo, commissioner or staff, not to understand what happened," Hawley told colleagues. After the memo was circulated, several people came up to Hawley to report they were offended to see how Reno had been treated by Zelikow. It was a pattern that Hawley would see again and again on the commission. Others would tell him how offended they were by Zelikow and what they saw as his pattern of partisan moves intended to protect the White House in the investigation. But apart from Warren Bass, most would never confront Zelikow themselves. Others on the commission, including some of the commissioners, were frightened of Zelikow.

THE TENSIONS between Zelikow and the rest of the staff kept building in early 2004. Under assault from the 9/11 families and other critics,

Zelikow wanted to find some way to get out in front of the attacks before they did lasting damage to his reputation. One way, he thought, was to promote himself as the face of the investigation during a series of high-profile televised public hearings that the commission planned to hold throughout the winter and spring.

Working from a model provided by the joint congressional 9/11 committee, the commission's teams of investigators were asked to prepare interim staff reports that would be released at the hearings and read out to the audience. Each report was meant to be a summary of the staff's findings on the topic of the day's testimony; the reports helped frame the questions that the commissioners would then ask witnesses. They would also form the basis of chapters of the commission's final report, so they were an important preview of what the commission's final report that summer would say.

Many of the staff reports made headlines; some rewrote elements of the history of 9/11. Reporters first learned to pay close attention to the interim reports after an early public hearing in January 2004, when the staff released a report that amounted to the first authoritative account of what had happened aboard the four hijacked planes on September 11. In chilling detail, the report revealed how the terrorists had used mace and wielded knives—not box cutters or guns, as had previously been reported—to enter the cockpits and take control of the jets. The same report revealed that at least nine of the nineteen hijackers had been flagged as potential security risks by the FAA's computer screening system before they boarded the planes; that seemed to undermine the initial claims from the FBI and CIA that the terrorists had nothing in their backgrounds to arouse suspicion.

Zelikow declared to the staff that he, and he alone, should read out the interim reports before the television cameras at the hearings, depriving the principal authors of their moment in the spotlight. Under his plan, the first thirty minutes or so of each public hearing would be another episode of "the Zelikow Show," as a few of the staffers referred to it disparagingly, with Zelikow reading out the reports that others had written. The staff was furious over Zelikow's proposal, and several of them went to the commissioners; Zelikow was quickly forced to back down. Kean and Hamilton agreed to a compromise in which Zelikow would read the introduction of each staff report, with the report's authors following after him, each reading a portion.

Scott Allan, a young lawyer whose specialty was international law and who had worked with Clinton's United Nations ambassador, Richard Holbrooke, was hired by Zelikow and placed on Team 3. Allan was to focus on the State Department and review the department's archives on terrorism policy before 9/11. His job was made easier by the fact that, unlike so many other federal agencies, the State Department seemed eager to cooperate with the investigation. That was no surprise since the department's records showed that Secretary of State Colin Powell had grasped the al-Qaeda threat in the early months of 2001 and mobilized his department to be prepared for an attack. The records made Powell look good.

Allan was also given the assignment of drafting the interim staff report on the history of American diplomat efforts against al-Qaeda. The report was scheduled to be released at a public hearing in March in which Powell and his Clinton administration predecessor as secretary of state, Madeleine Albright, would testify. Allan went at the assignment with his usual enthusiasm, producing a draft for Zelikow's review that outlined the history of diplomatic efforts to monitor bin Laden's actions in the 1990s and the government's often fruitless efforts to work with Saudi Arabia and other supposedly friendly Muslim nations to rein in al-Qaeda.

Members of Team 3 expected Zelikow to rewrite the report before it was made public. Zelikow rewrote virtually everything that was handed to him—usually top to bottom, often for the better, given his talents as a stylist. But Allan and other members of Team 3 were shocked when they saw what Zelikow handed back.

In a section about bin Laden's actions in the 1990s, Zelikow had inserted sentences that tried to link al-Qaeda to Iraq—to suggest that the terrorist network had repeatedly communicated with the government of Saddam Hussein in the years before 9/11 and that bin Laden had seriously weighed moving to Iraq after the Clinton administration pressured the Taliban to oust him from Afghanistan.

The passages were subtly crafted, with enough qualifiers to allow Zelikow to argue that he was not saying definitively that there was a working relationship between al-Qaeda and Iraq. But his point was clear, and he must have known what impact the passages would have when reporters and the White House got hold of them. He wanted to put the commission's staff on record as saying that there was at least the strong possibility that Osama bin Laden and Saddam Hussein had collaborated to target the United States before 9/11—precisely the argument that the Bush White House had made furiously before and after the invasion of Iraq.

There was nothing like it at all in Allan's original draft. More to the point, Allan knew from his colleagues who had been through the archives at the CIA and the White House that there was no clear evidence to back up the idea of close ties between Iraq and al-Qaeda. The intelligence that did exist was sketchy. Yet Zelikow was coming close to presenting it as fact.

SCOTT ALLAN could barely sleep the next night. He was horrified at the thought that if Zelikow's language was allowed to stand, the report—*his* report—would become an important propaganda tool for the White House and its neoconservative backers in justifying the Iraq war, which was then starting to go so badly. He could just imagine the newspaper headlines: 9/11 COMMISSION FINDS AL-QAEDA–IRAQ LINK.

As one of the younger members of the team, Allan knew it would be useful to have some gray-haired allies when it came time to stand up to Zelikow. And he did. Other members of Team 3 felt even more strongly than Allan did that the Iraq language had to come out, including Len Hawley. In terms of his government service and other accomplishments, Hawley was as close to Zelikow's stature as anyone on the commission's staff. Allan, Hawley, and the others knew they needed to confront Zelikow, to call his bluff. There was little time left. The public hearing with Powell and Albright was only days off. If Zelikow refused to rewrite the report, the staff would have to protest directly to the commissioners.

A final staff editing session on the interim report was called in the conference room at the commission's K Street offices, with Zelikow and the members of Team 3 facing each other across the table. It would be remembered as an all-important showdown for the staff, the moment when they would make it clear that Zelikow could take his partisanship only so far. The staff would not allow him to trade on their credibility to promote the goals of the Bush White House—not in these interim reports, not in the commission's final report later that year.

HAWLEY'S MANNER with Zelikow was diplomatic but direct.

"Philip, we need to talk about the Iraq material that you've put in the report," he said. "What evidence is there to back up what you've written here?" He pointed Zelikow to the sentences about the purported links between Iraq and al-Qaeda.

Zelikow expressed surprise that Hawley saw any problem with the sentences. They argued it out, with Allan, Albion, and Bass joining in the protests over Zelikow's insertions about Iraq. After several heated minutes of debate, Zelikow agreed to reconsider. And within a day or two, he backed down entirely, telling Team 3 that he agreed to leave the issue of al-Qaeda–Iraq ties until a later staff report. The reference to Iraq was replaced by a new, more general reference to bin Laden's thoughts of leaving Afghanistan in the late 1990s for other, now unidentified countries:

"For a time, bin Laden was reportedly considering relocating and may have authorized discussion of this possibility with representatives of other governments," the new, more neutered passage said. "We will report further on this topic at a later date."

The staff suspected that Zelikow realized at the meeting that he had been caught in a clear-cut act of helping his friends in the Bush White House—that he had tried to twist the wording of the report to serve the needs of the Bush administration and its stumbling military campaign in Iraq. Zelikow said later it was nothing of the sort.

BY EARLY 2004, Zelikow had an idea of what people thought of him. He seemed to have fewer and fewer allies on the staff. Even some of the staff investigators who were originally seen as allied with Zelikow appeared to have turned on him. His colleagues said he winced at unflattering stories that had been written about him in *The Washington Post* and *The New York Times* and his "conflicts of interest" with the White House. Kean and Hamilton could see that he felt embattled by the criticism. Zelikow, who was commuting to Washington weekly from Charlottesville, where his wife and children had remained, told the commissioners how eager he was to finish and go home.

Zelikow understood that some of the staff, as well as some of the 9/11 family advocates and more than a few members of the Washington press corps, considered him a White House mole, especially when it came to promoting the war in Iraq and protecting Bush and Rice from the commission's scrutiny. That perception had grown stronger on the staff after the debate over his editing of Scott Allan's staff statement.

But when confronted on the subject, he insisted that his conflicts were no more serious than those of many other academics of his stature at work in Washington. "The commission could have tried to choose an executive director who had few, if any, ties to any of the principal figures in the investigation," Zelikow said. "To get someone with sufficient qualifications, that could have proved rather difficult."

If staff members had felt the commission was not being tough enough on someone like Rice, Zelikow thought there had been plenty of opportunities for them to push back. "There were many wide-open discussions about the performance of all the relevant principals, including Rice," he said. "Written drafts were exchanged many times on all these subjects— thus avoiding the need for direct conversation by people who felt shy.

"When I had a point of view, I had to get in there with my colleagues and defend it, laying out my proposed language and my evidence and arguments for others," he said. "And they had to do the same."

As for Iraq and al-Qaeda, he said that he had simply wanted the commission not to prejudge the issue.

"I wanted to be sure everyone kept an open mind about the evidence until we were ready to come to judgment," he said. "It would be quite wrong to say that I wanted the commission to come to a conclusion that there was a connection between Iraq and 9/11. I had never made that argument." Nor, he said, did he argue on the staff that there was a substantive collaboration between al-Qaeda and Iraq in the years. If some in the commission chose to see his actions on Iraq as partisan, he said, there was little he could do about it.

"That sort of corridor talk is natural," he said. It was one reason "I took care throughout my work at the commission never, in any setting, to express an opinion about the war in Iraq, pro or con."

Still, he did begin to think that he'd made errors in his leadership of the commission. He realized that he may have made a mistake in maintaining his contacts with Rice and with Karl Rove. "If I had realized just how politicized the investigative process would become, I would have been warier about the optics from the start," he said. "I might not have taken the job in the first place."

— 46 —

ROOM 216
Hart Senate Office Building
APRIL 13, 2004

Jamie Gorelick could have kicked herself later. She should have seen what was coming when she walked up to Attorney General John Ashcroft, held out her hand, and tried to say hello. They were together in the private holding room where the commission's witnesses waited to testify.

Gorelick knew Ashcroft, at least casually. She thought she was on a first-name basis, if only because they shared the connection to the leadership of the Justice Department. She had been deputy attorney general in the Clinton administration.

Everybody expected it to be a difficult day for Ashcroft—maybe the day that marked at least the end of his tenure as George Bush's attorney general—but Gorelick figured it might as well begin with a civil tone. In a few minutes, Ashcroft was scheduled to walk into the white marble Senate committee room for his long-awaited public testimony before the 9/11 commission.

"Hello, John," she said, smiling, holding out her hand.

"Hello, Ms. Gorelick," Ashcroft responded coldly, barely raising his eyes to meet hers. The conversation was over before it had begun.

The commission's staff knew something was very wrong as they fanned out across the hearing room that afternoon. They were looking for someone from Ashcroft's staff who had a copy of the testimony he was about to deliver. The commission had asked all witnesses to provide an advance copy of their testimony to avoid surprises.

But Ashcroft's staff had inexplicably failed to comply. Stephanie Kaplan, Zelikow's tough-minded assistant, marched up to Mark Corallo, Ashcroft's resourceful press spokesman, and all but ordered him to turn it over. Ashcroft's testimony was only minutes away. "Where is it?" she demanded. He shrugged.

In fact, copies of the testimony were in the hearing room already. One of Corallo's aides was literally sitting on a pile of them, with firm orders not to stand up and begin handing them out until Ashcroft appeared in the hearing room.

The room was jammed with television cameras, there to record what was being billed as the Washington equivalent of an execution, with the attorney general in the role of the condemned. It seemed finally that the commission had a senior Bush administration official it could hold responsible, at least in part, for what had gone wrong before 9/11.

There had been press leaks to signal what was coming. The week before, an article published on the front page of *The New York Times* previewed the fierce attacks that Ashcroft was expected to face at the hearing.

The commission's staff had come to the conclusion that Ashcroft had done little, if anything, to prepare the department to respond to the cascade of terrorist threats in the spring and summer of 2001; the attorney general had seemed bored by the whole issue of terrorism. The *Times* published another story about Ashcroft on the eve of his testimony after Lowell Bergman, a reporter at the *Times* with exceptionally good sources at the Justice Department, obtained portions of the commission's staff statement about Ashcroft. The statement contained the startling account from Tom Pickard, the bureau's acting director in 2001, about how Ashcroft had ordered Pickard to stop briefing him about al-Qaeda that summer.

IN THEIR "murder board" sessions to prepare the attorney general for his testimony, Ashcroft's aides recommended, first and foremost, that he apologize for nothing. Ashcroft's inner circle had come to see the 9/11 commission as a dangerous adversary; the damning leaks to the *Times* and other news organizations had proved it. They assumed that even a modest concession by Ashcroft that he had paid too little attention to terrorist threats in 2001 would give the commission the opening it needed to finish the job of destroying him.

Pickard's testimony was obviously going to be a problem; he was scheduled to testify just ahead of Ashcroft at the public hearing on April 13, 2004. If pressed, Ashcroft would accuse Pickard of perjury.

But Corallo and others plotting Ashcroft's strategy knew that a strong defense was not as appealing as a strong offense—change the subject from Pickard—and they went in search of evidence in the Justice Department's files that might aid in a counterattack.

They found what they were looking for in a sheaf of classified documents from 1995. They were internal department memos that, Ashcroft would argue, showed that if anyone was to blame for the dysfunction of the Justice Department in dealing with terrorist threats before 9/11, it was not him. It was the fault of the woman who had signed some of the 1995 memos—former deputy attorney Jamie Gorelick.

ASHCROFT WAS away from the Justice Department for nearly a month before the hearing. He had been recuperating from gallstone surgery, and he looked pale and weak as he entered the Senate hearing room. (The public did not know at the time how eventful his postoperative recuperation had actually been; it was later revealed that Ashcroft had received a bizarre hospital visit shortly after his surgery from White House counsel Alberto Gonzales, who sought approval from the heavily sedated Ashcroft for an eavesdropping plan that Ashcroft's aides considered unconstitutional.) Ashcroft walked haltingly, but he also flashed a surprisingly confident smile as he approached the witness table and greeted the Justice Department officials who would sit directly behind him in the audience.

Among them was. Solicitor General Theodore Olson, the Justice Department's chief lawyer before the Supreme Court. Olson's public display of support for Ashcroft was especially valuable since Olson's wife, the conservative television commentator Barbara Olson, had died aboard American Airlines 77, the plane that crashed into the Pentagon.

As Ashcroft raised his hand to be sworn in, Corallo and his deputies went to work, marching toward the press table to hand out copies of the attorney general's testimony. The commission's staff grabbed copies for themselves and for the commissioners and began to page through it hurriedly to see what it was that Ashcroft was about to spring on the panel.

ASHCROFT OPENED his testimony by insisting, as he had so often since 9/11, that he'd had no idea a domestic terrorist attack was coming in 2001, no matter what Pickard and others might have claimed.

"Had I known a terrorist attack on the United States was imminent in 2001, I would have unloaded our full arsenal of weaponry against it, despite the inevitable criticism," Ashcroft testified. "The Justice Department's warriors, our agents and our prosecutors, would have been unleashed. Every tough tactic we had deployed since the attacks would have been deployed before the attacks."

So why was the Justice Department blind to the possibility of attack on September 11? Who was responsible? Ashcroft was going to let the drama build for a minute. He kept reading.

"The simple fact of September eleventh is this: We did not know an attack was coming because for nearly a decade our government had blinded itself to its enemies. Our agents were isolated by government-imposed walls, handcuffed by government-imposed restrictions, and starved for basic information technology. The old national intelligence system in place on September eleventh was destined to fail."

In the most somber tone he could muster, Ashcroft explained that a classified memo distributed within the Justice Department in 1995, during the Clinton administration, had imposed evidence rules in terrorism cases that amounted to the "single greatest structural cause of the September 11 problem." The memo had erected "a wall that segregated or separated criminal investigators and intelligence agents" by barring them from sharing evidence. It was this "wall," he said, that explained why so much had gone wrong at the FBI in 2001, including the botched handling of the Zacarias Moussaoui investigation and the confusion over whether Moussaoui's belongings could be searched.

"Government erected this wall, government buttressed this wall and—before September 11—government was blinded by this wall," Ashcroft continued. "Somebody did make these rules. Somebody built this wall."

Gorelick understood what was coming, and Slade Gorton, sitting next to her on the dais, could see that she was near panic.

This was Ashcroft's "gotcha" moment.

"Although you understand the debilitating impacts of the wall, I cannot imagine that the commission knew about this memorandum," he continued. "So I have had it declassified for you and the public to review. Full disclosure compels me to inform you that the author of this memorandum is a member of the commission."

Ashcroft paused. He did not say the author's name, but he did not need to. Corallo had also provided reporters and others in the audience, but not the commissioners, with a copy of the memo. The eyes of many in the audience turned to Gorelick.

The attorney general was arguing that if anyone within the Justice Department was responsible for September 11, for the dysfunction of the FBI—for Moussaoui, for the Phoenix memo, for the failures in San Diego—and all else that had gone wrong before the attacks, it was Gorelick.

Even Tom Kean, who took pride in the fact that he was not a lawyer, said he understood instantly how unfair this was. During the course of the investigation, Kean had become enough of a student of the FBI and the Justice Department to know that Gorelick's 1995 memo was mostly a restatement of what had been department policy on terrorism cases for years; the first bricks of the so-called wall were put into place in the 1980s as a result of court orders intended to protect civil liberties. "The wall" was largely a legacy of Watergate and the scandals unearthed by the Church committee, when the nation learned of the dangers of providing the FBI and the CIA with too much authority to spy on American citizens. The reasoning for "the wall" came down to this: The bureau's spy catchers and counterterrorism agents faced a much lower burden of suspicion of wrongdoing to obtain court permission for wiretaps and other eavesdropping; if they shared the results of the wiretaps indiscriminately across "the wall," it could disrupt or destroy criminal cases because the evidence would be considered inadmissible. More important to civil libertarians, the wall discouraged government spying in the guise of counterterrorism. Gorelick's memo had reinforced the wall—and after she left the department, the memo was widely misinterpreted by the FBI to bar almost all evidence sharing—but she was not its creator.

Spin was spin, though, and Ashcroft's was brilliantly coordinated. Ashcroft's staff had orchestrated his attack with several House Republicans. Another Democratic commissioner, Bob Kerrey, the former senator from Nebraska, could feel his BlackBerry vibrating in the middle of Ashcroft's testimony.

"Ashcroft was still speaking, and the e-mails were already coming in," he recalled later. "The e-mails said things like 'You traitor, you should be ashamed of yourself for having somebody like Gorelick on the 9/11 commission.' I could see that this was a setup."

Slade Gorton had not been close to Ashcroft during their years together in the Senate; the attorney general was considered something of a loner among his Republican colleagues. "But you could admire John Ashcroft even without agreeing with him because he was principled," Gorton said, adding that Ashcroft never seemed "calculating in any of the positions he took."

But as he listened to the attorney general's testimony and the attack on Gorelick, Gorton realized how wrong he had been about Ashcroft. "I was shocked," he recalled. "This attack was unprincipled. I was just infuriated."

He turned to Gorelick, who had become his closest friend on the commission, and encouraged her to try to stay calm. He could see that she was shuffling through her papers on the dais, "just pawing through all of these papers to find something so that she could answer" Ashcroft's attack.

On the roster of questioners for that afternoon's hearing, Gorton was ahead of Gorelick. He put his hand on her arm and whispered, "Let me do this."

THE COMMISSION's questioning of Ashcroft was awkward, if only because the commission did not have its own copy of the 1995 memo that the attorney general was now suggesting was a major cause of the government's failure to prevent 9/11.

"Could we have it?" Jim Thompson, the Republican commissioner who would be Ashcroft's first questioner, asked with exasperation.

"We'll be glad to provide it to the commission," Ashcroft replied unhelpfully.

Thompson turned his attention instead to Tom Pickard's damning allegation. "Acting Director Pickard testified this afternoon that he briefed you twice on al-Qaeda and Osama bin Laden, and when he sought to do so again, you told him you didn't need to hear from him again. Can you comment on that, please?" he asked.

Ashcroft denied Pickard's account, insisting that he "never" gave such a direction to the FBI to stop briefing him. "I care greatly about the safety and security of the American people and was very interested in terrorism," he insisted.

The next Republican questioner was Gorton. He was furious, and he was determined to show—on behalf of his friend Gorelick—how unfair Ashcroft's attack on her was.

The commission's staff and several of the commissioners knew all about the larger controversy over "the wall." As Ashcroft had read out his prepared testimony, the staff had tried frantically to gather documents to help rebut his attack on Gorelick. They found a valuable Justice Department memo dated August 6, 2001, a month before the attacks, in which Deputy Attorney General Larry Thompson, Ashcroft's number two, had made an explicit order to keep the 1995 regulations in place. On Ashcroft's behalf, Thompson had effectively endorsed Gorelick's rules. Gorton was given a copy a few minutes before he questioned Ashcroft.

Gorton glowered at Ashcroft. "I have here a memorandum dated August 6, from Larry Thompson, the fifth line of which reads, 'The 1995 procedures remain in effect today,'" Gorton said. Ashcroft's Justice Department had had most of 2001 to tear down the wall. So, Gordon asked, "If that wall was so disabling, why was it not destroyed during the course of those eight months?"

Ashcroft insisted that the full Thompson memo had indeed made some changes in the handling of evidence that lowered Gorelick's "wall." Thompson's memo was no endorsement of Gorelick's rules, he suggested, not convincingly.

Gorton kept pressing. "But it was after August 6, 2001, that Moussaoui was picked up and the decision was made in the FBI that you couldn't get a warrant to search his computer," he reminded Ashcroft. So if Thompson had made changes in the procedures "those changes must not have been very significant."

Ashcroft mostly ducked the point. He said the August 2001 memo would not have applied to Moussaoui because it was meant to deal with clear-up criminal cases, not the sort of immigration charges brought against Moussaoui. But wasn't Moussaoui's exactly the sort of case that should have prompted the Justice Department to want to lower the wall before 9/11? Gorton ran out of time to follow up.

ASHCROFT'S CONSERVATIVE supporters on Capitol Hill were ready to help. Within minutes of his testimony, congressional Republicans had rushed to television cameras and issued press releases demanding Gorelick's resignation from the commission.

The commission had another public hearing scheduled for the next day. In the middle of it, Representative James Sensenbrenner of Wisconsin, the fiery chairman of the House Judiciary Committee, put out a statement to reporters that "Commissioner Gorelick is in the unfair position of trying to address the key issue before the commission when her own actions are central to the events at hand." He continued: "I believe the commission's work and independence will be fatally damaged by her continued participation as a commissioner."

Gorelick got news of Sensenbrenner's attack as she sat on the dais. Distraught, she left the hearing room to call Tom Daschle, the Senate Democratic leader, to ask for his help in answering the GOP onslaught. She had never faced criticism like this in her career; she was frightened by it.

Tom Kean followed her out of the hearing room, saw her on the phone, and asked her what she was doing.

"I'm calling Daschle," she said.

Kean tried to comfort her. "You don't need them to help," he said. "You need us to help you. We'll take care of it."

After the hearings, the commissioners gathered in a private room behind the dais. Kean and Hamilton had made it a practice to hold a news conference after each set of hearings, and this seemed to offer the best chance for the commission to step forward to defend Gorelick. The Republicans were just as angry as the Democrats over what Ashcroft had done, maybe angrier.

"There was universal outrage on the part of all ten people," Gorton remembered. "The outcome of Ashcroft's statement was that Jamie Gorelick got nine older brothers." The five Republicans considered whether they should go out together in front of the cameras to defend Gorelick. But Kean and Hamilton decided it was best that the two of them do it alone.

Asked at the news conference about Sensenbrenner's call for Gorelick's resignation, Kean responded with a comment that came across as flip and insulting to the House Judiciary Committee chairman.

"It's sort of a silly thing—silly statement, I thought," Kean said. "Commissioner Gorelick has followed the same rules that every other commissioner has had. She's recused herself from everything that had to do with any action she had. Many members of the commission have served in the government. That's why they're so good and they're so expert in doing their job. They already have knowledge of these areas."

He continued: "She is in my mind one of the finest members of the commission, one of the hardest-working members of the commission, and, by the way, one of the most nonpartisan and bipartisan members of the commission. So people ought to stay out of our business."

Kean walked away from the podium hoping he had calmed the situation with such a vigorous defense of Gorelick. He figured this would blow over. He was wrong.

THERE WAS no joy among Ashcroft's aides as they left the Senate hearing room after the testimony. But there was relief that the attorney general had survived the ordeal.

The White House—the president in particular—had been given advance warning about Ashcroft's testimony. During his intelligence briefing in the Oval Office with FBI director Robert Mueller that morning, Ashcroft had offered Bush a brief summary of what he was planning to say to the commission at the afternoon hearing; he'd mentioned the Gorelick memo. It was not clear that Bush understood all the implications of what his attorney general was about to do. After the hearing, Ashcroft's office received calls of congratulation from the White House. Alberto Gonzales in particular was reported to be thrilled. His aides called the attorney general's office to report that the White House counsel had watched the hearing on television and was so overjoyed at Ashcroft's attacks on Gorelick that he stood up from his desk and started giving high fives to others in the office.

— 47 —

OFFICES OF THE LAW FIRM
OF WILMER CUTLER & PICKERING
Washington, D.C.
APRIL 2004

T he two weeks after John Ashcroft's testimony had been a nightmare for Jamie Gorelick. Ashcroft's attacks were the choicest red meat to congressional Republicans and others who had been looking for months for some way to undermine the commission's credibility. The conservative editorial boards of the *New York Post,* the *Washington Times,* and *The Wall Street Journal* took up the campaign against Gorelick. "Where is the outrage?" the *Journal* asked in an editorial under the headline GORELICK MUST GO. The editorial suggested that the White House would be within its rights to withhold all cooperation from the commission until Gorelick resigned. "From any reasonably objective point of view, the Gorelick memo has to count as by far the biggest news story so far out of the 9/11 hearings," the editorial said. Rush Limbaugh made her the daily target of his radio show. "Who are these Clinton people?" Limbaugh asked the day after Ashcroft's testimony. "Gorelick? Clinton? They are sixties relics. These are people who grew up hating the FBI. These are people who gave police officers the name 'pigs.'"

On Capitol Hill, Majority Leader Tom DeLay and House Judiciary Committee chairman James Sensenbrenner took the lead in the Republican assault on Gorelick. A day after Sensenbrenner's public call for Gorelick's resignation, DeLay made a broader attack on the investigation, sending a letter to Tom Kean that accused the commission of "partisan mudslinging, circus-atmosphere pyrotechnics and gotcha-style questioning." The letter, which noted the "growing concern about the recent revelations" concerning Gorelick, was quickly released to reporters by DeLay's office. With the sort of unsubtle rhetoric that had earned him the nickname "the Hammer," DeLay accused the commission of putting American troops at risk in Iraq and Afghanistan. The commission's tactics "serve as dangerous distractions from the global war on terror," he said. "They undermine our national unity and insult the troops now in harm's way, to say nothing of those who have already given their lives in this conflict."

Even if he felt under siege from fellow Republicans, Kean had to laugh at the way Representative Jack Kingston, a Georgia Republican, phrased his insult: "The September 11 commission is a reunion of political has-beens who haven't had face time since *Seinfeld* was a weekly show."

Gorelick could find no humor in any of it, especially after the death threats. The first was phoned in only minutes after Ashcroft stood up from the witness table. Several of the threats were taken seriously by the FBI; the police in her neighborhood in suburban Montgomery County, Maryland, posted armed officers and a bomb-sniffing dog outside her home. Wilmer Cutler, her law firm, offered to hire private guards to keep watch at her office; she declined. The profanity-strewn hate mail received at her office was "ugly, gross stuff."

The worst moment for Gorelick came when she got a frantic call from her housekeeper, who was in tears. Someone had just called the family's home and asked if Gorelick's two children were there; the caller seemed to know that Gorelick had two young children. The housekeeper, not recognizing the voice on the line, said yes. "Well, tell that bitch that I'm going to wait until she and her husband and her kids are all in the house and then blow it up," the caller said calmly before hanging up the phone. (The call was later traced by police to a pay phone in the Jamaica Plains suburb of Boston; the caller was never identified.) Gorelick called her husband, a pediatrician at Georgetown University Hospital, to rush home (the hospital was much closer to the house) to get the children out "before the bomb goes off."

This sort of personal attack was something new—and, she admitted, terrifying—to Gorelick, arguably the most successful woman lawyer of her generation in Washington. She was a graduate of Radcliffe and Harvard Law School, and her glittering career path included stops at the Pentagon, where she had been the Defense Department's general counsel; the Justice Department, where she had been Janet Reno's top deputy; Wilmer Cutler, one of Washington's most prestigious law firms, where she was reported to be a seven-figure partner; and now the September 11 commission.

At fifty-three, Gorelick was the definition of a Washington insider, a lawyer who had traveled again and again through the city's revolving door of public and private jobs. In the government, her skills as a legal tactician and problem solver impressed everyone from the gruff, cigar-chomping generals she had worked with at the Pentagon to President Clinton. She had a winning personal style that mixed hard-as-nails law-yering with an almost maternal concern for her opponents in a negotia-tion. Other commissioners later recalled how Gorelick had rushed up to put her arm around George Tenet, the former CIA director, as Tenet left the witness table after a day of brutal questioning at one of the commis-sion's public hearings.

Gorelick had brought order to the chaos at the Justice Department in Clinton's second term, forcing the sometimes dithering Janet Reno to set priorities for the department. Reno came to appreciate the orderli-ness of her deputy's mind; Gorelick was a habitual list maker, a fact that was reflected in her speaking style. Even in casual conversation, Gore-lick spoke as if she were reading from a well-written legal brief.

If there was criticism of Gorelick, it was that her political views could shift with the prevailing winds of Washington, that ambition sometimes trumped principle. She was savaged by liberal groups for having drafted the Pentagon's "don't ask, don't tell" policy; gay rights activists and civil lib-erties groups saw the policy as a sellout given President Clinton's campaign pledge to allow gays into the military. The attacks stung Gorelick, whose father, a Russian immigrant, and mother, a first-generation American, were committed to liberal causes in the 1950s and 1960s and took young Jamie along to civil rights demonstrations and peace marches as a child.

She had tasted scandal once before, after it was revealed that Fannie Mae, the quasi-public mortgage finance company where she worked as vice chair after leaving the Justice Department in 1997, was accused of cook-ing its books to produce large bonuses for its executives; Gorelick herself had received millions of dollars in bonuses. Gorelick was never accused of involvement in the wrongdoing, although she dropped any reference to Fannie Mae from her résumé on her law firm's website for a time.

Gorelick was widely seen as a natural candidate to replace Ashcroft as attorney general if John Kerry defeated Bush in the November elec-tion. Her membership on the September 11 commission, and her pol-ished performance when questioning witnesses during the panel's early public hearings, had burnished her credentials for high appointment in a Kerry administration.

But after Ashcroft's testimony, all of that seemed at risk. "This was a very scary time," she said later. "People were whipped up into a frenzy."

Kean and Hamilton's initial efforts to defend her had obviously not stopped the attacks. She decided that she would have to try to defend herself, turning to television news shows and to a classic Washington forum for a public official under siege: the op-ed page of *The Washington Post*. Her op-ed article, entitled "The Truth Behind the Wall," argued that the point of the 1995 memo was to create procedures to encourage information sharing within the Justice Department, not to shut it down. "I did not invent the 'wall,' " she wrote. "I have worked hard to help the American people understand what happened on Sept. 11," she wrote. "I intend, with my brethren on the commission, to finish the job."

But if anything, the attacks grew worse in the days that followed the op-ed, and Gorelick began to draft a resignation letter in her head.

Kean wondered if Ashcroft knew, if he cared, about the "lunacy" that he had unleashed. He responded to Tom DeLay in a letter in which he wrote that the commission's public deliberations might be "pointed, but no more than in the Congress itself—out of debate and discussion, we are convinced, better policies emerge." He also answered DeLay's suggestion that the commission was somehow undermining the morale of American troops. Through an aggressive investigation, the commission was upholding the "tradition of freedom that our troops around the world defend, and we salute them," Kean said.

Still, Kean feared that Ashcroft and his right-wing allies on Capitol Hill might soon get what they wanted: the commission's collapse in partisan sniping.

There was one bit of good news, Kean thought. The ten commissioners were unified in their defense of Gorelick, the Republicans seemingly even more outraged than the Democrats about Ashcroft's attacks. And their eagerness to defend Gorelick had helped them put aside almost all of the divisiveness of the Clarke and Rice hearings. Kean wondered if the commission's newfound unity would be enough to save it given how fierce the attacks had become. People are really out to destroy us, Kean thought to himself.

LUCKILY FOR the commission and for Gorelick, Ashcroft was about to overplay his hand, and he would do it on the eve of the commission's long-awaited interview with Bush and Cheney.

On April 28, the day before the Oval Office meeting, Kean and

Hamilton joined several of the other commissioners on a trip to Tampa to tour the headquarters of the United States Central Command, which was overseeing combat operations in Afghanistan and Iraq. On a military plane on the trip home to Washington, the commissioners began to plot their next steps to try to end the furor over Gorelick.

She and some of the others were taken aback by a recommendation from Hamilton, always the conciliator, to dispatch Gorelick to Capitol Hill to defend herself to the Republicans and try to make peace.

"You've got to be respectful" to men like DeLay and Sensenbrenner, she remembered Hamilton advising the other commissioners. "No matter how much you disagree with them, sometimes you do something you don't like. Maybe we should send Jamie up to talk with them."

Gorton, as angry as any of the Republicans on the commission about the attacks on Gorelick, shot back. "That's the craziest thing I've ever heard of," he told Hamilton. To Gorton, Hamilton was suggesting appeasement to the malicious congressional Republicans who had stirred this up. The congressional critics, he said, "are not men of goodwill." He told Gorelick, "Don't listen to Lee."

As the plane landed back in Washington, Gorelick's BlackBerry went off with an urgent message. Ashcroft had done it again: He had just released a new batch of counterterrorism memos from her Justice Department files and posted them on the department's website. Some of the documents, which had not previously been turned over to the commission, bore her handwritten notes.

Gorelick knew this meant another venomous burst of attacks. Kean and Hamilton recalled that she offered to resign before rushing from the plane to drive home.

"I don't remember what words I used," she said later; she could not recall if she had actually threatened to quit the commission at that moment. "But I left in a huff. I just couldn't stomach this anymore. I just said, 'This is yours to fix.'"

Kean decided that fixing it was his responsibility. He returned to his hotel, the Four Seasons in Georgetown, and called Andy Card at the White House to warn him of the choice that President Bush needed to make by the next morning.

"Andy, I don't know what you think is on the agenda tomorrow," Kean told Card. "But the first thing on the agenda, as far as I am concerned, is the attorney general. It's absolutely outrageous what Ashcroft is doing."

Card hadn't expected this, and he sensed the political danger to the president. He tried to calm Kean down, telling him the president had had no advance warning about Ashcroft's campaign against Gorelick and the commission. As best Card could tell, Ashcroft had told no one in the White House about his plans until the day of his testimony.

Surely, Card said, whatever the commission's differences with the attorney general, it should have no effect on the meeting with the president.

"We're going to have a good meeting, no?" Card asked sheepishly.

Kean considered Card a friend, but his tone grew more threatening. "We are *not* going to have a good meeting with the president, Andy, because every commissioner is as mad as I am," he said.

Card tried to sound conciliatory, but he was angry, too—with Kean and the other commissioners. It seemed to Card that the 9/11 commission was willing to hijack a historic meeting with the president and vice president of the United States for the sake of defending one of their own. In Card's mind, Gorelick had a genuine conflict of interest in serving on the commission, and it was worth airing, even if Ashcroft had raised the issue in such a ham-handed fashion. "I was mad at Kean, I was mad at the commission, because I thought they were defending themselves rather than doing their job," he said. As far as the meeting with Bush was concerned, "it's irrelevant if Jamie Gorelick is attacked or not attacked."

Even so, Card also knew he could not ignore Kean's call. He would have to do something; there was too much riding on the interview with Bush, who had been preparing for days for the interview. Card went to see the president. At the commission, Dan Marcus, the general counsel, had been unable to get White House lawyers on the phone for days because they were so busy preparing Bush and Cheney for the meeting.

"We do our homework," Card said. "Contrary to the myth, the president does a lot of homework."

— 48 —

THE ROOSEVELT ROOM
The White House
APRIL 29, 2004

Tom Kean waited anxiously in the Roosevelt Room, across the hallway from the Oval Office, to see George Bush. The president was known for his obsessive punctuality, beginning and especially ending his meetings on time. So Kean knew he would have to wait only a minute or two before the heavy ceremonial doors to the Oval Office opened and he was ushered in to see the president.

Kean was a politician who prided himself on never raising his voice, never uttering an obscenity, rarely making an enemy. They were qualities that were all the more remarkable given the blood sport that passed for state politics back in New Jersey.

But this morning, Kean was mad, maybe as mad as he had ever been in his public life. And he worried that he was about to lose his temper in front of the president. He hoped that his warning call to Andy Card the night before had done some good. Kean knew that if Bush moved to rein in Ashcroft and his "gang" and tamp down the furor, it might put an end to the smears before they did lasting damage to Jamie Gorelick—and to the commission. Kean thought that beyond worries about her reputation, there was legitimate reason to fear for Gorelick's safety. The death threats had not stopped.

Kean and the other nine members of the September 11 commission had arrived at the White House early that morning and were required, like most other visitors, to pass through security checkpoints; they were swept by metal detectors for weapons. They were met by White House lawyers working for Alberto Gonzales who escorted the commissioners to the windowless Roosevelt Room, which often served as the holding room for visitors before they were invited into the Oval Office.

Kean and Lee Hamilton had been invited to spend a few minutes with President Bush privately before the rest of the commissioners were brought into the Oval Office; White House aides originally hoped a few minutes of small talk between Bush and Kean, who barely knew each other, would establish a friendlier tone for the larger meeting.

But Kean had no appetite for small talk. He and Hamilton had an agenda for his private session with Bush. They wanted to talk to him about Ashcroft, about the need for the president to put an end to the attorney general's campaign against Gorelick. Kean believed that if Bush did not do something that morning about the attorney general, things might quickly turn ugly when the other commissioners arrived in the Oval Office. It was a remarkable thing to ask a president to denounce a member of his cabinet. But Kean feared the meeting might otherwise be a disaster, both for the president and for the commission.

UNTIL THE worrying phone call from Kean the night before, Andy Card had been convinced that the Oval Office meeting would go well. He and others in the White House seemed confident that Bush, who had been in briefing sessions for days to prepare for the meeting, could deal with the commission's questions about 9/11, no matter how tough.

Card knew that in small settings, in private meetings, Bush always defied his critics' lowered expectations; the president invariably proved himself more thoughtful and articulate behind closed doors than his mangled public appearances would suggest. Card had mostly given up trying to defend Bush's awkward performance on the public stage—the president's ever garbled speech, his inappropriate smirks. Bush was just not like that in private, especially in the Oval Office, Card knew. Democrats who met privately with Bush acknowledged it, too.

Even after so many years in public office, maybe Bush still suffered something like stage fright when out in public, aides thought. Card knew the 9/11 commissioners were about to be impressed when they met George Bush in the privacy of the Oval Office. "He's an excellent conversationalist," Card said. "He likes to have conversations rather than performances—without cameras."

THE DOOR opened to the Oval Office, and Kean took a deep breath, readying himself to confront the president.

"Governor, please come on in," Bush said. "Congressman Hamilton, welcome."

The president shook his visitors' hands and thanked them for coming.

And then it happened. Without any prompting from Kean and Hamilton, the president apologized for the actions of his attorney general.

"I didn't approve of this," he said of Ashcroft's attacks on Gorelick. "I *don't* approve of this." Bush had clearly been well briefed by Card on the need for an effusive apology early in the meeting.

Bush referred to what had happened the night before. He told Kean and Hamilton that it had been unfair for Ashcroft to post the Gorelick memos on the Justice Department's website before the documents had been shared with the commission. "That sort of behavior will stop," he pledged.

Kean took another deep breath. He could feel the tension rush out of the Oval Office.

CARD HAD seen it happen so often. Visitors to the White House were invited into the Oval Office and melted at the simple thrill of being there. Hostilities tended to evaporate at the door. It went beyond the normal clichés about the corridors of power; the Oval Office awed and intimidated in equal measure. Card liked to say that "the Oval Office has a way of putting oil on foaming seas." Its magic was clearly working on Kean and Hamilton, who were relieved by Bush's apology and were clearly overwhelmed by the president's hospitality. Card assumed the room would work its magic on the other commissioners as well.

As the others walked in, Bush demonstrated once again just how well he had readied himself for the meeting. Clinton and Bush had the same technique in disarming potential adversaries. Bush welcomed each of the other eight commissioners by their first names, Democrats and Republicans alike, as if they were old friends, when in fact he had never met most of them before. He complimented John Lehman on his tie as the former navy secretary entered the office. As he had with Clinton, Lehman felt himself in the presence of a natural politician who knew how to convert a stranger into an ally. "He looked everybody in the eye," Lehman recalled. "It was all first name."

Bush was joined in the Oval Office by Dick Cheney and Alberto Gonzales. The White House had insisted that the president and vice president be interviewed together by the commission. It was an obvious effort, most of the commissioners assumed, to ensure that the accounts of Bush and Cheney did not differ on the events of 9/11. The commission did not protest the arrangements, even as they became fodder for late night television comics and editorial cartoonists who pictured Cheney as the president's ventriloquist, with Bush propped up in his lap.

Bush and Cheney took their seats in high-backed chairs in front of the fireplace, with the commissioners on couches and chairs in a semi-circle around the president and vice president. Gonzales sat in the background. The Oval Office was at its best. It was a spectacular spring day. The room was bathed in brilliant morning sunlight from the southerly windows, with a view beyond them to the Washington Monument and the National Mall.

Then Bush sealed the deal with the commission: He repeated to all ten commissioners what he had just told Kean and Hamilton about Ashcroft.

He turned to Jamie Gorelick and said he wanted to apologize for the actions of the attorney general, especially the release of the Justice Department memos the night before.

"Jamie, this shouldn't have happened," he said, repeating that the White House had known nothing about Ashcroft's decision to release the documents the night before; Ashcroft had made these mistakes on his own.

Slade Gorton turned to Gorelick and could see the relief on her face; Bush seemed to have defused a political fight that, for her, had turned into a personal crisis. "It blew her away," Gorton said.

Bush's apology to Gorelick was reported to the White House press corps later in the day. Bush dispatched Scott McClellan, his press secretary, to slap down the attorney general at the midday press briefing. McClellan said that Bush was "disappointed" with what Ashcroft had done and that the president's frustration had been relayed to the Justice Department. "The president does not believe we ought to be pointing fingers," McClellan said. "We ought to be working together to help the commission complete its work."

As HE sat in the Oval Office, Gorton marveled at the masterful performance of Bush and his staff. Bush's apology to Gorelick had really cost him nothing—it was clear there was never much of a personal relationship between Bush and his attorney general—and it had all but guaranteed that the meeting would go well for the president.

"They knew exactly how to do this," said Gorton. "They had us in the Oval Office, and they really pulled the talons and the teeth out of many of the Democratic questions." Both the Republicans and the Democrats went easy on Bush, Gorton said; it was three hours of soft-balls, mostly. "Several of my colleagues were not nearly as tough in the White House as they were when we went in that day."

Kean and Hamilton led the questioning at the start. Many of the early questions focused on the detailed timeline of Bush's actions on the morning of the attacks. The president repeated what he had said so many times in the past: that the intelligence in the spring and summer of 2001 had not suggested a terrorist attack on American soil, that the August 6 PDB gave him nothing to act on, that he had not rushed out of the Florida schoolhouse after learning of the attacks that morning because he did not want to panic the kids. He said he had grown used to the grim jokes about *My Pet Goat,* the children's book he had continued to page through before cameras even after he had been told of the attacks on the World Trade Center.

Despite all the speculation that Cheney might feed answers to Bush, the vice president said little in the interview, answering questions only when they were directed at him specifically or when Bush turned a question to him. "There was no puppeteering by the vice president," Gorelick remembered. "He barely said anything."

When Kean and Hamilton were finished, the other commissioners were allotted ten minutes each for their own questions for Bush.

John Lehman thought that he asked some of the tougher questions of Bush during the session, especially about the possibility of Saudi government ties to some of the hijackers. Lehman recalled asking Bush about the news reports that checks for thousands of dollars written by the wife of Prince Bandar, the Saudi ambassador in Washington, might have been funneled to two of the hijackers in San Diego. "He dodged the questions," said Lehman.

When Tim Roemer's questioning started to go beyond his allotted ten minutes, Kean interrupted, reminding Roemer of the time limit. But Bush cut off Kean, turning to Roemer.

"This is the Oval Office, I make the rules," the president said. "Tim, go on to your next question." Roemer, who would have been expected to be one of the toughest Democratic questioners at the meeting, was charmed by Bush, too.

The commissioners had gone into the room assuming that the meeting would not last much more than about ninety minutes, the time limit suggested informally by Gonzales's office. They did not know that the White House had made a decision in advance to allow the meeting to go on until the commissioners had run out of questions. It would allow Bush to say truthfully on the campaign trail that he had answered every question posed to him by the 9/11 commission. The president's schedule had quietly been cleared for the first half of the day.

The open-ended schedule ended up doing public relations damage to the commission, since the meeting went on past noon, when Hamilton and Bob Kerrey had other long-scheduled appointments across town and had to excuse themselves. Hamilton was scheduled to introduce the prime minister of Canada at a luncheon speech. Several conservative news organizations seized on the idea that Hamilton and Kerrey had snubbed the president after they were seen leaving early from the White House. The headline on the front page of the *New York Post* reveled in alliteration: DEM DUO DISSES DUBYA IN OVAL OFFICE WALKOUT.

The meeting, which had seemed to be such a risk for Bush, was an unalloyed victory for the president. After it was over, Bush called reporters into the Oval Office to savor the moment.

"I'm glad I took the time," he said. "This is an important commission, and it's important they asked the questions they asked so that they can help make recommendations necessary to protect our homeland." That afternoon, the commission put out a statement praising Bush and Cheney for having been so "forthcoming and candid."

Card went up to Bush afterward to ask him how the meeting had gone.

"You know," Bush said, "it was kind of fun."

— 49 —

THE NEW SCHOOL
New York, N.Y.
MAY 18, 2004

BUNKER BARBS STING HIZZONER (*New York Daily News*, JUNE 16, 1998)

BUNKER MENTALITY—RUDY'S AND SADDAM'S (*Daily News*, JUNE 17, 1998)

GIULIANI'S SKY BUNKER (*New York Post*, JUNE 8, 1999)

The headline writers in the New York tabloids were merciless in 1998 after it was revealed that Mayor Rudolph Giuliani was building a forty-six-thousand-square-foot high-tech emergency command center for himself and his top aides. "The Bunker," as the tabloids dubbed it, seemed the supreme example of how Giuliani's ego and arrogance knew no bounds after four years in office. "Has Rudy finally gone too far?" *New York* magazine asked on its cover after the once secret plans for the construction of the command center leaked out. WABC Radio mocked Giuliani with a name-that-bunker contest for its listeners. Among the most popular entries: "Rudy's Nuclear Winter Palace" and "The Nut Shell."

While much of the criticism focused on the $15 million cost of the command center, almost as much was directed at its planned location. It was being built in, of all places, the World Trade Center complex, site of a terrorist bombing only five years earlier and almost certainly still on top of the list of likely terrorist targets in the city. Giuliani had rejected proposals that he place the command center across the East River in Brooklyn or Queens, where it might be less of a target. He wanted it in Manhattan and thought he had found the perfect location in a building in the World Trade Center complex known as WTC 7. It was close to City Hall and across Vesey Street from the Twin Towers. While "bunker" suggested an underground compound, this would be "the bunker in the sky"—on the twenty-third floor, with panoramic views out onto lower Manhattan.

Even if the mayor could not be talked out of putting the command center in Manhattan, some of his deputies tried to convince Giuliani that it was a mistake to put it on such a high floor of the building. What if the electricity went out and the elevators stopped working? What if there was a fire or a water shutoff? Giuliani's former director of emergency operations, Richard Sheirer, told the 9/11 commission that he had thought the command center should have been placed in a "hardened" site much closer to the ground.

"I did not agree with it simply because it was on the twenty-third floor of a building," the severely overweight Sheirer deadpanned in his testimony to the commission. "Do I look like a guy who wants to walk up twenty-three flights?"

So what happened on September 11 was all too predictable. Giuliani never managed to get to the command center in the chaos of the attacks that morning. By about 9:30 a.m., before either of the Twin Towers collapsed, everyone in the command center was ordered to evacuate to the street because of fears that more hijacked airplanes were heading for Manhattan. The crisis center was shut down because there was a crisis. In a final bit of irony, it was determined that a fire that later destroyed WTC 7 on September 11 was probably caused by the rupture of the building's special diesel fuel tanks; the tanks had been installed to provide emergency power to the mayor's command center.

On September 11, with the command center shut down, Giuliani and his top aides were left with no obvious place to gather away from City Hall. That left the mayor on the street, resulting in the heroically iconic image of the soot-covered Giuliani leading hundreds of other New Yorkers to safety as he walked north through the gray clouds of debris unleashed by the collapse of the Twin Towers.

In all the hero worship of Rudy Giuliani after 9/11, why didn't people remember what had happened within the city's government in the years before the attack? It was a question that John Farmer and others on his team of investigators on the 9/11 commission—Team 8, the emergency response team—asked themselves over and over during the investigation. In the public's desperation to make Giuliani a global hero after

9/11, they had forgotten that the Giuliani administration was, in many ways, shockingly ill-prepared for the attacks.

But would the ten commissioners be brave enough to say that out loud, to risk the vengeance of Giuliani and his adoring public? Farmer had reason to be skeptical. This was Rudy Giuliani they were talking about—"America's Mayor," "Mayor of the World." It was one thing for the commission to take on the FAA or the Pentagon; finally, to the public, these were faceless Washington bureaucracies.

But would the commission be willing to take on the most popular political figure in the country—the president-in-waiting, it seemed? By 2004, it was almost crass to refer to New York City's former mayor as some mere politician. "Rudy" was a hero, the embodiment of everything Americans wanted to believe about themselves after 9/11.

Giuliani was scheduled to testify before the commission in May 2004, when the panel would return to New York for its final public hearings in the city. It was being billed by Giuliani's critics, and he still had a few left who were brave enough to speak out, as a showdown that might finally establish the truth about Giuliani.

Farmer and his team always qualified their criticism of the former mayor. There was no doubt that Giuliani had performed heroically on the morning of September 11 and in the days and weeks that followed. On the day of the attacks, when the government in Washington was all but shut down and the president of the United States had disappeared into the skies aboard Air Force One after fleeing that elementary school in Florida, Giuliani was the face of calm and courage. If Bush was nowhere to be seen, Giuliani was everywhere. He comforted a traumatized city—and, it was no exaggeration, the nation and the world. The unflattering parts of Giuliani's reputation as mayor—his well-documented vindictiveness and egomania, his bouts of puritanical intolerance—seemed to have been entombed in the dust at ground zero, as if they had never been all that important to begin with.

But Farmer and his team believed that Giuliani's brave performance after the attacks should not lead the commission to whitewash his record before then. The city had been warned for years to prepare itself for a catastrophic terrorist attack that might take thousands of lives. The most terrifying of the warnings was delivered to the city on February 26, 1993, when a 1,200-pound bomb hidden in a rented Ryder van was detonated in a parking garage beneath the World Trade Center. Six people died;

more than one thousand people were injured; the Twin Towers suffered hundreds of millions of dollars' worth of damage, with smoke damage up to the ninety-third floor.

Giuliani was elected mayor the following year, and he seemed well suited to the job of rethinking the city's preparations for a terrorist attack. He had some background on the issue from his years in federal law enforcement, both at the Justice Department in Washington during the Reagan administration and later as United States attorney in Manhattan. But as mayor, Giuliani was obsessed with street crime, not terrorism. And as Farmer and his team began to review the history of the 1993 attack and what had happened as a result, they were startled to discover how little Giuliani's administration had done to ready the city—and specifically the police and fire departments—in case terrorists struck again.

The foolish decision to place his emergency bunker on a high floor in a building in the shadow of the Twin Towers was only the most obvious of the failures.

Giuliani created an Office of Emergency Management in 1996 to try to end the generations-long turf wars between police and firefighters over how they should coordinate operations in a crisis and who should take command. But on September 11, the confusion was everywhere; the police and fire departments set up separate command centers and had difficulty talking to each other.

Even more troubling, the city's basic emergency radio networks malfunctioned in the hours after the planes struck the towers, and it should not have been a surprise. In responding to the 1993 bombing at the World Trade Center, firefighters who entered the Twin Towers discovered that their analog radios did not function well in such massive concrete-and-steel buildings; the radio frequencies used by the fire department were overwhelmed.

Eight years later, the radio problems had still not been solved. The commission's investigators were certain that the radios were responsible for the deaths of many of the 343 firefighters lost at the World Trade Center on September 11. Because their radios did not work, many firemen inside the Twin Towers did not hear evacuation orders until it was too late to get out. An electronic "repeater" system that was installed in the World Trade Center after 1993 specifically to boost radio signals in an emergency was never turned on by fire chiefs in the North Tower on 9/11. The chiefs believed, mistakenly, that the system was broken. If it had been turned on, the lives of many firefighters in the tower almost certainly would have been saved; they would have known to flee.

Farmer and his team wrote up their findings in staff statements that were scheduled to be made public in the commission's final pair of New York hearings—on May 18, when Giuliani's former police and fire commissioners had been called to testify, and the next day, when Giuliani himself would be the commission's star witness. The staff reports were blistering in their findings about the city's performance on 9/11. After distributing drafts of the statements to the commissioners, Farmer heard back from several of them; they were dumbfounded to discover how vulnerable New York had been on 9/11. They said they intended to ask tough questions of Giuliani.

MORE THAN the other commissioners, John Lehman had reason to be disturbed about what Farmer's team had uncovered about Rudy Giuliani. New York was Lehman's adopted home. He had moved to the city from Washington after stepping down as navy secretary in the Reagan administration. He had raised his children in Manhattan. The only other commissioner who lived in New York, Bob Kerrey, was a much more recent arrival to the city.

On the eve of the first hearing in New York, Farmer met with the commissioners to remind them that they needed to be careful; they needed to remember where they were.

"Welcome to New York," he told them. "It's not Washington. It's different here. You know that."

This was a tougher city; politics were nasty in Washington, of course, but at least in the capital there was usually a patina of formality and courtesy, however thin, layered onto the partisan savagery. None of that in New York. After their first difficult public hearing in New York more than a year earlier, the commissioners should have known what they faced. The debates over 9/11 were much more visceral in New York than in Washington; so many more people had died at the World Trade Center than at the Pentagon.

Farmer told the commissioner that they should ask tough questions, but they should be careful not to give a platform to Giuliani and his loyalists to counterattack; John Ashcroft's campaign against Jamie Gorelick would look like a "garden party" by comparison. The city's take-no-prisoners tabloid newspapers were Giuliani's defenders, and they could be expected to weigh in to defend him if the commission's questioning of the former mayor became too fierce.

Farmer's team had worked up long lists of questions for the commissioners to ask Giuliani and his former deputies—pages and pages of questions about the "sky bunker," about the radios, about the confusion and miscommunication between the police and fire departments, about the 911 telephone operators who had told people trapped in the World Trade Center to stay put in their offices until help arrived, guaranteeing their deaths. Most of the commissioners seemed to be listening to Farmer as he warned them again to watch their rhetoric during the hearings. All except Lehman, apparently.

THE NEW YORK hearings were held, at Bob Kerrey's invitation, in the central auditorium at the New School in Greenwich Village. The scene outside the Tishman Auditorium on West 12th Street was chaotic, with row upon row of television cameras capturing the scene. An unusually large number of the 9/11 families showed up for the hearings, including many of the widows, widowers, parents, and children of New York City firefighters and police officers who had died in the World Trade Center. They knew that the hearings offered their best, and perhaps only, chance to hear Giuliani and his top aides questioned aggressively about the city's inadequate emergency plans before 9/11. Someone had draped a huge banner that read NEVER FORGET across a building near the auditorium.

Farmer's team opened the first day of hearings with a riveting video re-creation of the morning of the attacks. It included the remarkable images caught by Gédéon and Jules Naudet, French filmmakers and brothers, of American Airlines Flight 11, the first plane to hit the World Trade Center, as it plunged into the North Tower and exploded in a fireball. The video re-creation was produced for the commission by Allison Prince, a veteran documentary maker who had spent weeks in the city's archives scouting for previously unseen videos that, while not graphic, captured the horrors of the day.

Then the first witnesses were sworn in, including Bernard Kerik, who had been the city's police commissioner on 9/11, and Thomas Von Essen, who had been the fire commissioner. Both Kerik and Von Essen had left their city jobs to sign on as partners at Giuliani's newly opened and wildly successful private consulting firm. Both men read out statements defending the actions of the police and fire departments on September 11.

JOHN LEHMAN would later say that he was certain he had been set up by Kerik and Von Essen on behalf of Giuliani. He suspected they had come to the hearing with a script. They were waiting for the right question from one of the commissioners that would allow them to launch a pre-scripted fusillade of insults back at the commission, turning the hearing into an us-versus-them fight that the city's tabloids would devour.

Since he was as much a New Yorker as anyone on the commission, Lehman should have known that he was taking a terrible risk when he opened his questioning of Kerik and Von Essen with a direct attack on the city's emergency response on 9/11:

"I'm aware of the history and of the traditions and of the politics that have shaped the public service agencies in this city over many, many years, and I agree with you all that we certainly have the finest police and fire departments, Port Authority police, anywhere in the world," Lehman began. "They're the proudest.

"But pride runneth before the fall," he continued. "And I think that the command and control and communications of this city's public service is a scandal."

Many in the audience, especially the families of the dead firefighters and police, began to cheer Lehman. There was applause. Kean had to call for quiet in the audience.

The anger in Lehman's voice grew as he described the city's emergency response system on September 11 as "not worthy of the Boy Scouts, let alone this great city."

He said it was a "scandal" that the city had not bought adequate radios. "I think it's a scandal that the fire commissioner has no line authority. It's a scandal that there's nobody that has clear line authority and accountability for a crisis of the magnitude that we're going to have to deal with in the years ahead. It's a scandal that after laboring for eight years, the city comes up with a plan for incident management that simply puts in concrete this clearly dysfunctional system."

Farmer winced at the intensity of Lehman's attack. This was just what he had warned the commissioners against. He knew too well what was going to happen next. Kerik and Von Essen would counterattack. The hearing would be portrayed on television that night and in the newspapers the next day as a screaming match between the commission and the heroes of 9/11. Any hope of forcing Giuliani to answer hard questions the next day had evaporated. The dynamic would now turn in Giuliani's favor.

Von Essen led the attack on Lehman, with a tone that suggested Lehman and the 9/11 commissioners had somehow defiled the graves of the firefighters who died in the Twin Towers.

"I couldn't disagree with you more," he said, glowering at Lehman. "I think that one of the criticisms of this committee has been statements like you just made, talking about scandalous procedures and scandalous operations and rules and everything else. There's nothing scandalous about the way that New York City handles its emergencies. We had strong leadership with the mayor. We had strong leadership with the fire commissioner, and the same with the police commissioner.

"You make it sound like everything was wrong about September eleventh or the way we function," he continued. "I think it's outrageous that you make a statement like that."

Just as some of the family members had cheered Lehman, now others in the audience cheered Von Essen.

The tabloid reporters in the audience were scribbling furiously in their notepads. The clash between Lehman and Von Essen and Kerik had lasted only a few minutes. But this story—Lehman and the 9/11 commissioners versus Giuliani and his men—wrote itself. And to make sure the point was not lost on anyone, Kerik and Von Essen went to the streets after the hearing and began giving interviews for the television cameras in which they stepped up their attacks on Lehman and the other commissioners:

"It's almost pitiful that this is what he had to stoop to in order to get his name in lights," Kerik told the *Daily News*. Von Essen described Lehman's questioning as "despicable" and said: "If I had the opportunity, I probably would have choked him because that's what he deserved."

LEHMAN WAS the host at a dinner for the commissioners that night at his apartment on the Upper East Side, overlooking Central Park. It was meant to be a relaxing evening ahead of Giuliani's testimony the next day. But Jim Thompson, the former Chicago prosecutor and Illinois governor, and therefore veteran of the toughest sort of local politics, had a sense of what was coming for Lehman and the commission after Lehman's outburst at the hearing that morning. He walked up to Lehman at the dinner.

"What...the...fuck?" he said with exasperation.

Lehman tried to smile.

THE TABLOID headlines were worse than Lehman and the other commissioners could have imagined. INSULT! screamed the front-page headline in the *Post*. Beneath the headline was an image of a fireman at ground zero, kneeling as if in prayer, next to a smaller headline: "Memo to 9/11 Commission: This Man Is a New York Hero, Not a Boy Scout." The *Daily News* was no kinder, with one columnist urging Lehman to "get down on his hands and knees and beg forgiveness of the public servants he insulted if he wants to preserve a scrap of his reputation. If he wants to be able to walk the streets of New York. If he wants the 9/11 Commission ever to be taken seriously."

IT WAS never clear that the events of the day before were stage-managed by Rudy Giuliani and his allies. But the former mayor arrived for his testimony on May 19 looking supremely confident. He was joined by his adoring new wife, Judith Nathan Giuliani, who rarely took her eyes off Giuliani, as if there were some magnetic field that kept her gaze locked on her husband.

If anyone was still billing the hearing as a showdown between Giuliani and the 9/11 commission, they were mistaken. The battle was over before it had begun, with Giuliani the winner. The tabloid attacks on Lehman that morning had cowed the other commissioners. They were frightened. They had seen what happened when Lehman dared to take on Giuliani's deputies; imagine the wrath they would face if they took on Giuliani himself.

The hearing was a Rudy Giuliani lovefest. In his testimony, Giuliani retold the story of his actions on the morning of September 11. It was gripping even for those in the audience who had heard him tell it so many times before. He described approaching the Twin Towers to see people throwing themselves from the top floors, choosing to die in the fall rather than in the fire or the rubble.

"All of us kept looking up, kept looking up, because things were falling," Giuliani said. "I realized that I saw a man, it wasn't debris, that I saw a man hurling himself out of the 102nd, 103rd, 104th floor. And I stopped, probably for two seconds, but it seemed like a minute or two, and I was in shock."

He acknowledged, without detail, that "terrible mistakes" were made on 9/11. But the "blame should be clearly directed at one source and one source alone—the terrorists who killed our loved ones."

Many of the questions directed at Giuliani by the commissioners barely qualified as softballs, they were so gentle. The long list of tough questions that Farmer's team had drawn up was forgotten

"I salute you," said Richard Ben-Veniste in opening his questioning of Giuliani. "Your leadership on that day and in the days following gave the rest of the nation, and indeed the world, an unvarnished view of the indomitable spirit and the humanity of this great city."

Tom Kean described Giuliani as a "great, great leader to take charge of a terrible, terrible event."

Branded by the tabloids that morning as a traitor to the city in which he lived, John Lehman joined in the adulation of Giuliani. On September 11, he said, "there was no question to the world that the captain was on the bridge."

The families of the dead firefighters and police, the ones who had come to the hearing to see Giuliani finally called to account for the city's failures in planning for a terrorist attack, were enraged as they listened to Giuliani being showered with praise. But initially the families muffled their anger; it showed only in their faces.

That changed when Giuliani, being questioned by Slade Gorton, suggested that the problem with the fire department's faulty radios did not explain why so many firemen had died on September 11. He suggested that the firemen had *chosen* to remain in the North Tower, despite evacuation orders, because they wanted to help with the rescue. "Their willingness, the way I describe it, to stand their ground and not retreat," he said.

That was too much for many of the families of the firemen. To clear his own conscience, or to duck the blame for the faulty radios, Giuliani seemed to be suggesting that their fathers and sons and brothers had chosen to die.

"Talk about the radios!" a man in the audience screamed out, interrupting Giuliani.

Another voice yelled out from among the families: "Put one of us on the panel—just one of us!"

Kean tried to interrupt the protesters. "You are simply wasting time at this point, which should be used for questions," he said.

The questioning turned to Lee Hamilton, who said he had no questions but wanted to say that "it's important that I simply express to you my appreciation not just for your leadership—you've heard a lot of that this morning—but also because of the cooperation you've given this commission and the candor with which you've responded this morning."

"Stop kissing ass!" one of the family advocates screamed out at Hamilton. "Three thousand people are dead!"

There was another voice: "Give me two minutes to rebut him—two minutes to ask a couple of real questions."

And another: "My brother was a fireman, and I want to know why three hundred firemen died. And I've got some real questions. Let's ask some real questions. Is that unfair?"

Another family member spoke up for Giuliani from the audience: "You know what? My brother was one of the firemen that was killed, and I think the mayor did a great job, so sit down and shut up."

WHEN IT was over, Kean and Hamilton realized that the Giuliani hearing had been a "low point" for the commission. It was a moment when the commission had abdicated its responsibility to ask tough questions. "It proved difficult, if not impossible, to raise hard questions about 9/11 in New York without it being perceived as criticism of the individual police and firefighters or of Mayor Giuliani," Kean and Hamilton later wrote. "To those assembled in our hearing audience, it seemed that there was no middle ground: Either the response to 9/11 was heroic and as good as it could have been or it was a terrible failure, and individuals had to be blamed."

— 50 —

OFFICES OF THE DIRECTOR OF CENTRAL INTELLIGENCE
CIA Headquarters
Langley, Va.
JULY 2, 2004

Bill Clinton was ready to kill Osama bin Laden in late 1998; there wasn't any doubt. Even Philip Zelikow, who had been so critical of the Clinton administration for dealing with terrorism as a law enforcement problem rather than a dire threat to national security, could see that Clinton had done it. He had effectively signed bin Laden's death warrant.

The proof was in a one-page document found by the commission, almost by accident, in the files of the National Archives in the late spring of 2004. The document had been drafted just before Christmas 1998, a part of a so-called memorandum of notification; MONs were special, highly classified documents signed by the president that made changes that granted authority to the CIA for covert operations. This MON, sent by Sandy Berger to Clinton on Christmas Eve 1998, gave the CIA authority to kill Osama bin Laden.

The exact wording of the MON remains classified, but Zelikow said later that the one-page document amounted to the "operative language" in the MON—it was the page of instructions about how to carry out the mission. It was the "kill authority," Zelikow later said. "According to one of the administration's lawyers, it was one of the most sensitive and extraordinary documents signed out during President Clinton's time in office."

The December 1998 MON replaced an earlier one that had directed the CIA, through its allies among tribal leaders in Afghanistan, to capture bin Laden but barred them from killing the al-Qaeda leader, except in self-defense. Frustrated by the fruitless search for bin Laden after the August 1998 embassy bombs, Clinton agreed in the new MON to give the tribes the authority to kill bin Laden if his capture seemed impossible. Clinton's aides justified what might be perceived as the assassination of bin Laden. They argued that because the al-Qaeda leader posed an imminent threat to the United States and its citizens, his death would be seen as self-defense—and justified under international law.

As a historian, Zelikow was thrilled by the discovery, even if it tended to bolster the idea that Bill Clinton was more determined to destroy al-Qaeda than Zelikow's friends in the Bush White House wanted to believe.

The Christmas MON resolved an important mystery that had been percolating throughout the investigation: the question whether Clinton had given legal authority to the CIA to kill bin Laden. For months, George Tenet and the others at the CIA had suggested that there was no lethal authority, or at least that the authority was so muddied up by legalisms that effectively there was no authority to kill bin Laden. Tenet had insisted in his private interviews with the commission that "the White House did not authorize a straight kill operation," Zelikow said. CIA agents in the field in Afghanistan had clearly felt that they did not have the authority.

But senior Clinton administration officials, Sandy Berger in particular, had insisted that there was a direct order and that the commission needed to keep digging to find it.

Zelikow and others on the commission's staff would later conclude that the key one-page document they found in the archives had not been withheld intentionally from the commission; it was just so highly classified and tightly held that there would have been few copies of it to find.

During the commission's investigation, inspection of the MONs was left mostly to Alexis Albion, who found it a challenge to understand them since so much of the language was so heavily lawyered. But that was not the case with this one-page document. She agreed with Zelikow: It was written in stark language. It included a list of instructions that were to be read to Afghan tribal leaders as they prepared to try to take bin Laden into custody. It was very clear to Albion and Zelikow that the president was telling the tribal leaders they could kill bin Laden.

The wording had been revised to remove any doubt among CIA officers in the field and the tribal leaders that "if a capture operation is not feasible, you may conduct an operation to kill him," Zelikow recalled. "There were no euphemisms in the language."

So why had Tenet and others insisted in all of their interviews with the commission that there was no such order, no such explicit author-ity? The one-page document appeared not only to have received Tenet's blessing; it appeared to have been written at his request following con-versations between himself and Berger. The commission needed to talk to Tenet again to find out why, once again, his memory appeared to be so cloudy on this and so many other issues. Zelikow asked for another private interview with Tenet.

THE INTERVIEW was scheduled for July 2, 2004, again in Tenet's confer-ence room on the seventh floor at CIA headquarters. Tenet was wary of being interviewed by the commission privately for a third time. He called Jamie Gorelick, an old friend, and others to find out what Zelikow and the commission were up to. She assured him that Zelikow just had a few follow-up questions; there was nothing for him to worry about.

But in fact, for Zelikow, Albion, and others on the commission, this interview was a final test of Tenet's credibility. Now they had the Decem-ber 1998 document. Would Tenet still claim that he knew nothing about a document that gave explicit authority to the CIA to kill bin Laden?

Zelikow and Albion took their seats around Tenet's conference table. It was only two days before the Independence Day holiday weekend, and Tenet looked, as usual, as though he needed a long vacation—drawn, exhausted. Still, he put on his best smile, welcoming the commission's investigators back to the CIA even if he had reason to believe they meant him ill.

Zelikow said he wanted to discuss the Christmas 1998 MON.

"What are you referring to?" Tenet replied.

Zelikow explained that the commission had found the one-page doc-ument of instructions that gave direct authority to the CIA to kill bin Laden through the Afghan tribes. That seemed to conflict with Tenet's insistence through all the months of interviews that there had been no such authority.

"I'm not sure I know what we're taking about," Tenet replied. He said he knew nothing about the one-page document. He suggested he was aware of a separate draft of the MON, dated December 21, 1998, that had no explicit lethal authority.

Zelikow tried explaining again what the commission had found. There was a December 24 revision of the MON, apparently requested

by Tenet himself, that gave the CIA precisely what it needed: the authority to kill Osama bin Laden. The revision included the one-page "kill"
authorization. Surely Tenet remembered it?

Tenet smiled and repeated his reply: He was not sure what Zelikow
was referring to. Perhaps Zelikow had a copy to show him? Zelikow did
not; the MON was so highly classified that he had no authority to travel
with it, even the few miles from downtown Washington to the CIA.
"Well, as I say, I don't know what you're talking about," Tenet said.

Zelikow and Albion looked at each other across the table in disbelief.
It was the last straw with Tenet, the final bit of proof they needed to demonstrate that Tenet simply could not tell the truth to the commission.

Zelikow later insisted that the realization was long in coming, but he
said he concluded that Tenet's "memory lapses" were not that. This final
interview seemed to prove it. Zelikow said he "slowly came to conclude
that George had decided not to share information on any topic unless
we already had documentary proof, and then he would add as little as
possible to the record."

It was only later that Tenet would learn how Zelikow and others on
the commission had, behind his back, accused him of lying—of perjury,
essentially, since he had been under oath at each of his private sessions.

In the case of the Christmas MON, for example, he told colleagues
he was telling the truth when he said he did not remember it—he had
been on his Christmas vacation with his family when it had been signed
by Clinton and when its message was transmitted to CIA operatives and
tribal leaders in Afghanistan.

And although Zelikow and the commission tried to portray the 1998
MON as a clear-cut authorization to kill bin Laden, it was apparently
clear-cut only for a specific group of bin Laden's potential assassins. In
February 1999, another MON went to Clinton that granted lethal authority to the insurgent Northern Alliance in Afghanistan. But in that case,
Clinton had gone out of his way to cross out the key language allowing
bin Laden to be killed if necessary. Clinton would later tell the commission he could not remember why he had given authority to take bin Lad-
en's life to the Afghan tribal leaders but not to the Northern Alliance.

LIKE ALMOST everybody else on the commission who knew George
Tenet, Tim Roemer liked him. But like so many others, Roemer felt he

could not trust him. After investigating the 9/11 attacks for almost three years nonstop—first on the joint congressional committee when he was still a member of the House and now on the 9/11 commission—Roemer was even more confounded by how poorly Tenet had done his job at the CIA in the months before 9/11.

Roemer had heard Tenet's excuses for why he did not act on the reports in mid-August 2001 within the CIA about Zacarias Moussaoui's arrest in Minnesota—how Tenet figured that since it was an FBI domestic case, surely the FBI had it under control. Roemer thought it was a lousy explanation. Tenet knew as well as anyone how dysfunctional the FBI was in terrorism investigations; certainly he knew that in August 2001, the FBI was under temporary leadership—Robert Mueller's arrival was still weeks away—and that FBI headquarters would need some prodding. "The report about Moussaoui shoots up the chain of command at the CIA like the lit fuse on a bomb, but Director Tenet never picks up the phone to call the FBI about it?" Roemer said.

Roemer thought the world might be a very different place if that single, simple phone call had been placed—if Tenet had telephoned Tom Pickard, the acting FBI director, who at that moment was ignorant of Moussaoui's arrest, to tell him that the CIA was ready to help out on the case. Roemer said he was astonished when he learned that Tenet went to a Principals Committee meeting at the White House on terrorism on September 4 and said nothing about Moussaoui then, either. "If the system is blinking red, why don't you bring it up?" Roemer asked.

Roemer had heard all of the criticism within the commission, certainly from Zelikow, about Tenet's credibility. But Roemer wanted to withhold judgment about Tenet; it was a serious matter, of course, to accuse a senior government official of lying under oath. That changed for Roemer on April 14, when Tenet appeared at the second of his two public hearings before the commission and was being questioned about the events of August 2001.

Roemer wanted to know about Tenet's discussions that summer with President Bush about terrorist warnings, especially the period around August 6, when Bush received the now-famous PDB at his Texas ranch that detailed domestic terrorist threats. What had the CIA told Bush in the weeks before 9/11 about a possible al-Qaeda attack?

Roemer: "You see him on August sixth with the PDB—"

Tenet: "No, I do not, sir. I'm not there."

Roemer: "Okay. You're not the—when do you see him in August?"

Tenet: "I don't believe I do."

Roemer: "You don't see the president of the United States once in the month of August?"

Tenet: "He's in Texas, and I'm either here or on leave for some of that time. So I'm not here."

Roemer: "So who's briefing him on the PDBs?"

Tenet: "The briefer himself. We have a presidential briefer."

Roemer: "So—but you never get on the phone or in any kind of conference with him to talk, at this level of high chatter and huge warnings during the spring and summer, to talk to him, through the whole month of August?"

Tenet: "Talked to—we talked to him directly throughout the spring and early summer, almost every day."

Roemer: "But not in August?"

Tenet: "In this time period, I'm not talking to him, no."

To Roemer and many in the audience, it seemed like a bombshell. For a full month in what was being called "the summer of threat," the CIA director was not in contact with the president? It was all the more alarming given the repeated claim by Bush and Condoleezza Rice that the president depended principally on Tenet for his information about terrorist threats. It was true that by August, the terrorist threat appeared to have diminished. But there was still clearly a threat; the August 6 PDB talked about recent evidence of terrorist surveillance of the skyline of New York, after all. Wouldn't Tenet want to follow up with Bush on the information in the PDB at some point in the month?

But if Tenet was insisting that there had been no briefing, Roemer was in no position at the public hearing to pursue it. He moved on to a different question.

Roemer was startled that evening to learn that the CIA's press office had been calling reporters to correct the record. Tenet had misspoken. He *had* briefed Bush in August 2001. Twice. He had flown to Waco, Texas, the airport closest to the president's ranch in Crawford, on August 17 to brief the president personally about intelligence issues; it was Tenet's first visit to Bush's ranch. And then he briefed Bush again in Washington on August 31. In its call-out to reporters, the CIA did not disclose the subject of either of the conversations between the president and Tenet.

ROEMER WAS furious with Tenet. Either Tenet's memory was faulty to the point of dementia or he had lied, hoping that no one would learn what had been discussed between him and Bush on August 16 and August 31. The Texas briefing was especially perplexing. How do you claim to forget flying halfway across the country to brief the president of the United States at his Texas ranch in the middle of August? "It's probably 110 degrees down there, hotter than Hades," Roemer said. "You make one trip down there the whole month and you can't remember what motivates you to go down there to talk to the president?"

By now, Roemer felt he was entitled to assume the worst about Tenet's veracity—and the worst about what had actually happened in August between him and the president. He suspected that Tenet had gone to Texas specifically to talk to Bush about the domestic terrorists, to press upon him that he needed to pay attention to the sort of information that was in the August 6 PDB.

Tenet has since given conflicting accounts about what happened at the meeting at Bush's ranch, suggesting at times that the conversation with the president had nothing to do with the August 6 PDB. In his 2007 memoirs, *At the Center of the Storm*, however, he seems to link the PDB to his visit to the ranch, noting that "a few weeks after the Aug. 6 PDB was delivered, I followed it to Crawford to make sure the president stayed current on events." Tenet wrote that it was his first visit to Bush's ranch, which had made the trip especially memorable: "I remember the president graciously driving me around the spread in his pickup and my trying to make small talk about the flora and fauna, none of which were native to Queens." (Tenet was raised in the New York City borough.) If Roemer's suspicions were right, that meant that the CIA had warned Bush not once but at least twice in August 2001 that al-Qaeda was planning to attack in the United States. The second time had been face-to-face with Tenet in the brutal summer heat of central Texas.

— 51 —

J. EDGAR HOOVER FBI BUILDING
Washington, D.C.
APRIL 2004

FBI director Robert Mueller understood that the commission, or at least its staff, was gunning for the bureau. He knew the commission's team of investigators focused on the FBI's disastrous pre-9/11 performance—Team 6—included former bureau employees who were all too aware of the bureau's failings. And he was right to be worried. Most of the team was convinced that the bureau needed to be overhauled, maybe even broken up and replaced by an American MI-5. As they set to work in the spring of 2004 to draft recommendations for the commission to endorse in its final report, they thought they had the commissioners behind them. John Lehman in particular had talked openly of the need for a separate domestic spy agency to replace the FBI. At the start of the investigation, Lehman had thought "it was a no-brainer that we should go to an MI-5."

But members of Team 6, as well as the commissioners, had no idea what they were up against in Mueller. He was determined to keep the bureau intact, and he still had plenty of weaponry at his disposal—his tenacity, most importantly. It was painful for a man as shy as Mueller to contemplate, but he and his aides knew that a full-court, in-your-face lobbying effort by the FBI director might make the difference with the commissioners who seemed most determined to break up the FBI.

By the spring of 2004, Mueller had been at the bureau for more than two years, and he had come to understand the mystique that the FBI still had. He could see that no matter how well its pre-9/11 failures were documented, no matter how poorly it continued to do its job after 9/11, the FBI was an institution that still managed to inspire the respect of much of the public, even if it did not deserve it. Hollywood was part of the reason; the arbiters of popular culture continued to celebrate the bureau, to want to assume the best about it. In the years after the 2001 terrorist attacks, CBS television alone launched four weekly series about the heroic exploits of FBI agents.

Mueller did not talk about it openly, but his deputies say he was also aware of how much fear the FBI continued to inspire among Washington's powerful and how, even after 9/11, that fear dampened public criticism. Members of Congress who might otherwise describe themselves as champions of civil liberties shrank at the thought of attacking the FBI. Why make an enemy of an agency that has the power to tap your phones and harass your friends and neighbors? For many on Capitol Hill, there was always the assumption that there was an embarrassing FBI file somewhere with your name on it, ready to be leaked at just the right moment. More than one member of the 9/11 commission admitted privately that they had joked—and worried—among themselves about the danger of being a little too publicly critical of the bureau.

MUELLER'S LOBBYING campaign with the 9/11 commissioners could not have been more aggressive. He was in their faces, literally. The commissioners said later that it was a remarkable thing to have the director of the FBI announce that he was ready to open his schedule to them at a moment's notice. He would return phone calls within minutes. He would meet the commissioners whenever and wherever they wished— breakfast, lunch, dinner, at the FBI's expense, of course. If a commissioner wanted to meet with Mueller in Washington, he would volunteer to drive across town to do it. Dan Marcus, the commission's general counsel, referred to it as "Mueller's dog-and-pony show." For some of the commissioners, Mueller's lobbying got to the point of near harassment. Tom Kean told his secretaries at Drew University to turn away Mueller's repeated invitations for a meal.

At some point, Mueller decided to take the biggest possible risk with the commission—"to go for broke," one of his top aides at the bureau later said. Mueller could see that the lobbying was paying off. The commissioners were becoming his friends and admirers. So he agreed to open the commission's case files to the investigation, virtually all of them. He directed his staff to open up a special office at FBI headquarters on Pennsylvania Avenue and provide the commission's investigators with electronic identification cards that allowed them instant access to the building. They could come and go as they pleased. Computer terminals were placed in the commission's room that allowed the investigators to have direct access to the FBI computerized case files, such as they were.

In the minds of the commissioners, Mueller was creating a clear—and, in terms of the FBI's survival, essential—distinction between himself and his CIA counterpart, George Tenet. While Philip Zelikow was reporting back to the commission about Tenet's duplicity and his unwillingness to answer basic questions, the commissioners were seeing Mueller for themselves. And they clearly loved the attention he was lavishing on them.

Slade Gorton would later agree with the statement that Mueller's lobbying prevented the FBI from being dismantled, that Mueller had "saved the FBI." He was a fresh face within the federal government, and he was saying the right things about the need to reform the bureau. "Mueller was a guy who came in new and was trying to do something different, as opposed to Tenet," said Gorton. It was a pleasure to deal with Mueller, who seemed so eager to cooperate. Tenet? "The president should have fired George Tenet in the first week after 9/11 and started all over," Gorton said.

Mueller also benefited from a decision that Lee Hamilton had made. Hamilton had been calling for years for a shake-up of the intelligence community and the creation of a national intelligence director, a super-spy to oversee the workings of all of the nation's agencies, including the FBI. That meant a major overhaul of the CIA.

Whatever the failings of the FBI, Hamilton believed that the government could not afford to overhaul two major institutions—the CIA and the FBI—at the same time, especially in what was being described as a time of war. If only one could be shaken up, Hamilton felt it should be the CIA, not the bureau. This was, then, a zero-sum game. "Mueller had made a very favorable impression on the commission, and on me," Hamilton said later. "We were recommending major changes in the intelligence community. And I, among others—maybe more than others—believed that the system can only stand so much change."

At oxford, Dame Eliza Manningham-Buller had charmed an audience in the role of fairy godmother in a school production of *Cinderella*. Her colleagues at MI-5, the British domestic spy agency, said there was still something of a fairy godmother about her as she went about her job in 2004. It was as if there were some magic wand that allowed her to dispel all self-doubt in the face of the terrorists who, she was certain, were walking the streets of Britain, waiting to attack. Dame Eliza had led MI-5 as its director general since 2002, a job that made her the person most responsible for preempting terrorism on British soil.

If the pressures of such a thankless job weighed on her, Dame Eliza did not let it show. She carried out her duties with the air of the supremely confident aristocrat she was. Effortless self-confidence had been bred into her; her father was a viscount and had been Britain's lord chancellor in the 1960s. She had hobnobbed with royalty since childhood. In the British press, there were frequent, if obvious and sexist, comparisons between Dame Eliza and "M," the spymaster played most recently by Dame Judi Dench in the James Bond movies; friends said that Dame Eliza was far more collegial than Dame Judi's M. (And unlike M, who ran a fictional version of MI-6, the British equivalent of the CIA, Dame Eliza had spying responsibilities that were mostly domestic, not foreign.)

Dame Eliza had arrived in Washington in early 2004 to help play fairy godmother once more—this time for her new friend at the FBI, Bob Mueller. She would try to help grant Mueller his wish to prevent the 9/11 commission from breaking up the bureau. Since the FBI had responsibility for domestic counterterrorism, Mueller amounted to Dame Eliza's closest counterpart in the American government, and the two had bonded since 9/11. The ties had grown closer after the Iraq invasion in 2003, when it became clear that British support for the war would make Britain an almost certain target for new al-Qaeda attacks.

During one of her regular trips to Washington, Dame Eliza rearranged her schedule to permit a visit to the 9/11 commission's offices for an interview. She took a seat in the conference room on K Street—and instantly took command of her audience. She set about dismantling the idea that the United States could have its own MI-5.

"It just wouldn't work for you," she told the commissioners. "The United States is too large."

Dame Eliza said that in a country as physically small as Britain, with less than a quarter of the population of the United States, it was much easier for a central spy agency to maintain close ties with local police departments and keep watch on the population. There were fewer than sixty chief police constables in all of Britain, and she said she knew them all by name. She reminded the commissioners that there were also important civil liberties differences between Britain and the United States. The United Kingdom had no written constitution and far more limited guarantees of personal privacy. The level of electronic surveillance carried out by MI-5 would raise severe constitutional issues if the United States government tried to carry out something similar.

One of the commissioners pointed out the relative success that MI-5 had in dealing for generations with the Irish Republican Army. Why couldn't that success be repeated with Muslim extremists who might now be in the United States?

"It's not a good comparison," Dame Eliza explained. "First, IRA terrorists were not suicidal. Second, IRA terrorists didn't deliberately target women and children. And third, the IRA all came from one place—one island, a sort of game farm," where British secret agents could mix far more easily with the community and target and capture—or kill—the terrorists.

The commissioners could not determine if Dame Eliza was trying for a bit of dark humor with the reference to a "game farm." She said it with a straight face.

In April, Mueller was called to testify publicly before the commission. He might have expected that it might be the showdown in which he would be asked to explain, in excruciating detail, how the FBI had blundered so often before 9/11—the familiar roster of Zacarias Moussaoui, the Phoenix memo, the disasters in San Diego. Instead, he was welcomed as a hero.

Tom Kean: "I came to this job with less knowledge of the intelligence community than anybody else at this table. What I've learned has not reassured me. It's frightened me a bit, frankly. But the reassuring figure in it all is you, because everybody I talk to in this town, a town which seems to have a sport in basically not liking each other very much—everybody likes you, everybody respects you, everybody has great hopes that you're actually going to fix this problem."

John Lehman: "I'd like to echo the encomiums of my colleagues about how good the process has been working with you from the first time you got together with us a year and a quarter ago. It's been a very— very much of a two-way dialogue. You've clearly listened to us, and you've taught us a good deal."

Richard Ben-Veniste joked about Mueller's aggressive lobbying campaign—and praised it. "Let me first echo the comments of my colleagues on this commission, say how much we appreciate not only the time that you've given us, but the interactive nature of our relationship with you. You have been responsive to our questions. You've come back. Sometimes you've come back and showed up when you weren't invited. But we appreciate that." The audience laughed.

Mueller smiled. "I don't recall that occurrence."

Slade Gorton hinted at what the outcome might have been for the FBI—its dismantling—without Mueller's lobbying: "Mr. Mueller, not only have you done a very aggressive and, I think, so far a very effective reorganization of the FBI, you've done an excellent job in preempting this commission."

— 52 —

K STREET OFFICES OF THE
9/11 COMMISSION
Washington, D.C.

L loyd Salvetti liked to say that he ran "the best museum you've never seen." It was the CIA's own museum at the agency's headquarters in Virginia. And like the rest of the CIA compound, it was not open to the public. After a thirty-two-year career at the agency that included stints undercover in Europe and an assignment on the National Security Council in the 1990s, Salvetti was given his last assignment at the CIA as director of its Center for the Study of Intelligence. The center functioned as the CIA's internal think tank and history department. It was also responsible for the museum, which boasted spyware artifacts that included a KGB-designed umbrella that doubled as a weapon (poison pellets were released from the tip) and a spy camera disguised as a matchbox; Kodak had built the miniature camera at the CIA's request in the 1960s. Other items went much further back into the intelligence history, including one of the Enigma code machines used by the Germans in World War II. The cracking of the Enigma codes was considered one of the Allies' great intelligence coups.

Salvetti had been recruited for the 9/11 commission by Philip Zelikow; they had been colleagues together on the NSC. Considered a Renaissance man among spies, Salvetti took on a variety of assignments in the investigation. He formed a close friendship with Lorry Fenner, the air force intelligence officer, if only because both had scholarly backgrounds; she held a PhD in history from the University of Michigan.

In June 2004, Fenner needed Salvetti's help, albeit quietly. As a career military officer, she was not comfortable breaching the chain of command and did not feel comfortable approaching Zelikow directly about her dilemma with the NSA terrorism archives. This was not her job. Reviewing the NSA documents had nothing to do with her formal

duties on the commission; her team was focused on the overall structure of the intelligence community, not the details of the government's
surveillance of al-Qaeda. But she trusted Salvetti, and with only weeks
left in the commission's investigation, she wanted to share her growing
alarm that the NSA documents were going unread.

Since December, she had spent several days in the NSA reading room
in downtown Washington, two or three hours at a time. And the more
she read from the NSA files, the more worried she became about what
the commission had missed. She was especially worried about the files she
had seen that seemed to suggest the relationship between al-Qaeda and
Iran, and between Osama bin Laden and the Iranian-backed terrorist
group Hezbollah.

The NSA files were tough reading. They were densely written and
were often cross-referenced with other documents not immediately
available to the commission because they were still back at the agency's
headquarters at Fort Meade in suburban Maryland. They would be made
available if the commission wanted to see them, but it would take time
to retrieve them.

When she saw the first of the material about Iran and al-Qaeda,
Fenner hoped that someone had already been through all of it—that
she was duplicating someone else's effort on the commission. Maybe her
alarm was unwarranted, she thought, "but I thought that I'd still better
tell somebody." She wanted Salvetti to be a second set of experienced
eyes to help her look over what she was finding, someone "who would
know more than I would."

At her urging, Salvetti walked over to the NSA's reading room and
began to read some of the files that Fenner had set aside for him. It was
not long before he could see that Fenner's worries were well-founded. The
NSA files were a gold mine, full of critical information about al-Qaeda
and other terrorist groups dating back to the early 1990s—material that
the commission should have read through months earlier. Salvetti knew
nothing about the detailed links between Iran and al-Qaeda, for example,
and he feared no one else at the commission did, either.

"Holy moley," he said to himself, almost smacking his forehead as
he read through the first of the documents and saw how important they
were. "You come away with the inference that there was an implicit collaboration between the jihadists and elements of Hezbollah and Iran."

But what should he and Fenner do? The commission's final report was supposed to be completed within days: "It was the eleventh hour."

That al-Qaeda had contacts with Iran and Hezbollah had been reported for years. There were well-documented communications between al-Qaeda and Iranian and Hezbollah officials when bin Laden's network was based in Sudan in the mid-1990s.

But the NSA files suggested that the ties were much more direct than had been previously known, and much more recent. Alarmingly, they showed that Iranian authorities had helped facilitate the travels of several of the 9/11 hijackers in the year before the attacks. There was nothing to suggest that Iran or Hezbollah leaders had knowledge of the 9/11 plot. But there was plenty of evidence to show that they had made special arrangements to allow many of the 9/11 hijackers to visit or pass through Iran.

According to the files, at least eight of the fourteen young Saudi men who were "muscle" hijackers on the 9/11 flights traveled through Iran between October 2000 and February 2001, when the plot was well advanced. In November, three of the young Saudis, who had obtained American visas only the month before, flew together from Saudi Arabia to Beirut and then on to Iran; the NSA files showed that an associate of a prominent Hezbollah official was on the same flight and that other senior Hezbollah figures were closely monitoring the travels of the three young Saudis. Later that month, two more of the "muscle" hijackers flew to Iran. There were similarities to the discoveries being made in the commission's "plot" team about the Saudi expatriates in San Diego and the help they provided to Nawaf al-Hazmi and Khalid al-Mihdhar. If these connections between the 9/11 terrorists and Iran and Tehran's allies in Hezbollah were all a coincidence, it was a remarkable one.

Salvetti thought that Doug MacEachin, the veteran CIA analyst, needed to see this, too. From his work on the commission, MacEachin was the commission's best historian on al-Qaeda. The NSA documents would mean even more to him than to Salvetti or Fenner. After a short visit to the NSA reading room, MacEachin was just as alarmed as they were.

"This is trouble," he said. "We've got to call Hayden." He was referring to General Michael Hayden, head of the NSA. The commission would need to organize a trip as soon as possible to the NSA's headquarters to review the rest of the material.

To his credit, Zelikow immediately understood the implications of what Fenner had discovered: A huge archive of the intelligence community on al-Qaeda and terrorist threats had not been adequately reviewed. And he understood there was almost no time left to do it. He helped organize an early morning trip that weekend by Salvetti, MacEachin, and others to the NSA's headquarters in Maryland to begin poring over the files. The group left before 7:00 a.m. and stayed virtually all day.

They were escorted to a reading room at NSA headquarters to find huge piles of documents—the raw material on which the reports in the agency's downtown reading room in Washington were based—and set to work. "There were stacks and stacks of paper," MacEachin recalled. He sat himself at a table and began to read. "I was angry that I hadn't seen this before," he said.

The next morning at the commission's offices at K Street, the group began to organize the material they had gathered from the NSA that weekend and hurriedly wrote new passages of the final report. With so little time left, the passages might raise as many questions as they would answer. And at a time when the Bush administration seemed eager to engage in saber rattling with Iran, the staff could see the dangers of overstating what they had found about ties between al-Qaeda and Tehran. The Bush administration had gone to war in Iraq the year before based on faulty intelligence; Fenner and her colleagues did not want to see the same thing happen with Iran.

"There is strong evidence that Iran facilitated the transit of al-Qaeda members into and out of Afghanistan before 9/11, and some of these were future 9/11 hijackers," MacEachin and the others wrote, documenting the NSA reports about the movements of the 9/11 hijackers in and out of Iran before the fall of 2001. "We believe this topic requires future investigation by the U.S. government."

What was left unsaid in the report, although the staff knew it perfectly well, was that the NSA archives almost certainly contained other vital information about al-Qaeda and its history. But there was no time left to search for it. Zelikow would later admit he too was worried that important classified information had never been reviewed at the NSA and elsewhere in the government before the 9/11 commission shut its doors, that critical evidence about bin Laden's terrorist network sat buried in government files, unread to this day. By July 2004, it was just too late to keep digging.

— 53 —

K STREET OFFICES OF THE
9/11 COMMISSION
Washington, D.C.
JUNE 2004

Philip Zeikow came out of his K Street office and went down the hallway to the secure phone-fax machine, the so-called STU-III. The phone, which looked like an ordinary office telephone in many ways, was a model designed by the National Security Agency to scramble phone calls; the call was unscrambled by an STU (Secure Telephone Unit) at the other end of the line. The STU-III was used by the commission's staff for phone calls that involved discussions of classified information.

Zelikow was calling the CIA. It was not clear why he believed that the conversation would not be overheard, or why he did not care if it was. Some of the commission's staffers later saw his carelessness as a final bit of evidence that Zelikow believed that, ultimately, his authority on the commission was unchecked.

And the call *was* overheard by one of the commission's young staff members, who was startled by what he could make out of Zelikow's end of the conversation.

Zelikow had called CIA headquarters to conduct an interview with one of the agency's analysts who had prepared the August 6 PDB. He wanted to know about the origins of the PDB. And from what the young staffer heard, Zelikow's questions were leading ones, designed to bolster the White House account of where the document had come from and why it had been written for President Bush in the first place.

With the deadline looming for the final report, Zelikow understood the implications for the White House and Condoleezza Rice if the commission concluded that the PDB was ordered up from within the CIA—not at Bush's request—and that it was some sort of desperate, last minute effort by the agency to warn Bush of the potential for a domestic terrorist attack that summer.

Among other things, that would undermine Rice's sworn testimony in April. She had insisted that the PDB had been written specifically in response to questions raised by President Bush and reflected no new evidence of an imminent domestic threat.

The young investigator who overheard the conversation could not make out every bit of what Zelikow said. But it was clear to him that Zelikow was pressuring the CIA analyst to accept Rice's version of events. He was trying to get the analyst to say that the intelligence in the document was mostly "historical," the word Rice used so often in trying to downplay the PDB's significance.

Whatever Zelikow's intentions in making the call, it seemed a violation of several internal commission rules, including a requirement that significant interviews be conducted in the presence of at least two staff members. With the phone call, Zelikow was conducting a private inquiry into the origins of what was, without doubt, the most controversial document in the investigation.

OVER THE MONTHS, the staff members who were most worried about Zelikow's partisanship had set up a back-channel network to alert the Democratic commissioners when they thought Zelikow was up to no good. Tim Roemer said he often got phone calls late at night or on weekends at home from staffers who wanted to talk about Zelikow. "It was like Deep Throat," Roemer said.

So word of Zelikow's phone call to the CIA quickly reached Richard Ben-Veniste, arguably Zelikow's harshest critic among the Democrats. He had been suspicious of Zelikow from the day of their first meeting in January 2003, worried that Zelikow's close ties to Rice and the White House would undermine the investigation. For Ben-Veniste, Zelikow's unauthorized call to the CIA—in what seemed an obvious last minute effort to diminish the importance of the August 6 PDB—was the last straw.

Ben-Veniste's Washington law firm was only a block from the commission's offices on K Street. During his next visit to the commission's offices, he confronted Zelikow, demanding to see the transcripts of all the interviews with the CIA analysts who had helped prepare the August 6 PDB. "Let me go back and see the interviews," he insisted.

With a condescending tone that reflected his disdain for Ben-Veniste, Zelikow explained matter-of-factly that there weren't any transcripts,

Ben-Veniste recalled. Apart from Zelikow's one telephone conversation, none of the CIA analysts involved in the August 6 PDB had ever been questioned in any sort of detail about the document. Certainly not in the detail that would justify a transcript.

After months of battles with Zelikow, it was hard for Ben-Veniste to be shocked by almost anything he did. But the staff could see that Ben-Veniste was genuinely startled. He and other Democrats had made it clear that they believed the August 6 PDB was a vital document—at the very least, a clear warning to President Bush only weeks before 9/11 that al-Qaeda intended to strike within American borders.

Now he was learning that Zelikow and the staff had made no special effort to talk to the people at the CIA who knew the most about the PDB—the analysts who had written it. "Well then, Philip, *I* will interview them," Ben-Veniste declared.

Zelikow would later remember placing the call on the secure phone line to the CIA analyst, but he rejected any suggestion that he was trying to pressure the analyst to say anything at all. He said the call was made as part of his effort to prepare a summary for the commissioners of what was known about the August 6 PDB. "If we had sought to arrange a personal interview, it would have taken time to schedule it," he said. "So CIA folks suggested the phone call for the discussion." He noted that at least one of the authors of the August 6 PDB had been interviewed in April 2004, which demonstrated that questions about the memo had not been ducked earlier in the inquiry, whatever Ben-Veniste's suggestion. It is not clear, however, how much of that earlier interview focused on the August 6 PDB, and how much focused on other PDBs and other issues.

BEN-VENISTE HAD found himself dispirited by the end of the commission's investigation. He was under almost constant attack by Republican lawmakers and conservative editorial page writers and television commentators, depicted as the Democrats' most partisan "attack dog" on the commission. Like some of the other Democrats, he found it frustrating to work under Lee Hamilton, who had proved so unwilling to lead the Democrats into combat with the Bush White House.

Still, he felt he had no choice but to mount one last battle with

Zelikow—and possibly with the commission—to get to the truth about the August 6 PDB.

It was early July. The final report was only days away from being sent to the publisher, and Zelikow told Kean and Hamilton that the commission should resist Ben-Veniste's demand to interview the PDB authors. He got backing from some of the Republican commissioners, who argued that Ben-Veniste was engaged in some sort of last-gasp effort to rewrite the report to make it overstate the importance of the August 6 PDB and embarrass the White House. Zelikow told the commission that he had been advised by the CIA that the analysts who wrote the PDB were reluctant to be interviewed and that the interviews would interfere with important counterterrorism work being done at the CIA that summer. "The CIA was pleading with us not to do this, since the career people involved in preparing and presenting PDBs would be intimidated, disrupting the sense of confidentiality and candor they considered essential for the PDB process," Zelikow said.

As often happened, it was Kean, not Hamilton, who came to Ben-Veniste's defense. Ben-Veniste's admiration for Kean, for Kean's genuine desire to prove the value of bipartisanship and for his honesty, had grown stronger. Kean sided with Ben-Veniste against the other Republicans. If Ben-Veniste felt that an important avenue of investigation had not been pursued, he should be allowed to pursue it, Kean declared. "We should let Richard do this," he said. The time was short, though; Ben-Veniste understood that the interviews would have to be done quickly. And the Republicans insisted that Ben-Veniste be accompanied by a Republican to the interviews. Jim Thompson, who had become slightly more engaged with the commission in its final weeks, was chosen to sit in.

To THE PUBLIC, they could be identified only as "Barbara S." and "Dwayne D." They were veteran CIA analysts who, in the summer of 2001, wrote and edited the president's daily brief. They had written the August 6 PDB, and after 9/11, they were quietly celebrated within the agency as heroes. The document was gravely flawed—it made reference to seventy ongoing FBI al-Qaeda investigations in the summer of 2001, most of which did not exist—but at least it was tangible proof that the CIA was aware of the possibility that bin Laden was eager to strike within American borders. At the White House, it was widely assumed that when the existence of the PDB was leaked to reporters in the spring of 2002, the leak came from the CIA.

Colleagues said that Barbara S. and Dwayne D. were as confused—and later appalled—as anyone over the repeated claims by Rice and others at the White House that the August 6 PDB was simply a "historical" overview of domestic terrorist threats. It was certainly not meant to be, they said. It was meant to remind President Bush that al-Qaeda remained a dire threat in August 2001 and that a domestic attack was a distinct possibility, no matter what he was hearing elsewhere. At the CIA, no one trusted the FBI to know if al-Qaeda had sleeper cells within the United States. If the FBI was not reporting a domestic threat, no one should assume that it did not exist.

Barbara S. and Dwayne D. came to the commission's K Street offices for the interviews on Tuesday, July 13. Despite Zelikow's earlier claim that they had been reluctant to be interviewed, Ben-Veniste found the two analysts willing, even eager, to answer his questions about the PDB. They were proud of their work. As he listened to their answers, Ben-Veniste came quickly to understand what Zelikow had been so nervous about: They were contradicting Condoleezza Rice. Despite Rice's claim that Bush had effectively ordered up the PDB, supposedly a sign of how concerned the president had been about terrorist threats that summer, Barbara S. and Dwayne D. said the PDB was ordered up "in-house" at the CIA in hopes that the White House would pay more attention to the threat. Bush had indeed asked his intelligence briefers several times during 2001 about the possibility of a domestic strike by terrorists. But he had not directed that a special PDB, or any other sort of intelligence report, be prepared. The White House might try to portray it as a subtle distinction, but to Ben-Veniste and other Democrats on the commission, it was important. The most detailed warning to the president about domestic threats that summer had not been ordered up by the president. It had been ordered up within the CIA to remind the president that the threat was still out there.

Barbara S. and Dwayne D. acknowledged that the PDB was "historical" to the extent that it did outline the history of threat reporting involving bin Laden going back to 1997. But the concluding paragraphs of the PDB were meant to tell the president that the threat was current. The president, they said, should have taken no comfort from the passages in the document—written in the present tense—that referred to "patterns of suspicious activity in this country consistent with preparations for hijackings or other types of attacks, including recent surveillance of federal buildings in New York."

"That's not historical," scoffed Barbara S. She and Dwayne D. agreed that when they wrote the report in early August 2001, the threat of a domestic terrorist attack by al-Qaeda was "current and serious."

Over Zelikow's objections, Ben-Veniste insisted that the material from Barbara and Dwayne be placed prominently in the final report. The negotiations over how it would be worded were tortured, but Ben-Veniste finally agreed to this paragraph:

During the spring and summer of 2001, President Bush had on several occasions asked his briefers whether any of the threats pointed to the United States. Reflecting on these questions, the CIA decided to write a briefing article summarizing its understanding of this danger. Two CIA analysts involved in preparing this briefing article believed it represented an opportunity to communicate their view that the threat of a Bin Ladin attack in the United States remained both current and serious. The result was an article in the August 6 Presidential Daily Brief titled "Bin Ladin Determined to Strike in US."

— 54 —

K STREET OFFICES OF THE
9/11 COMMISSION
Washington, D.C.

JUNE 2004

B y June, Philip Zelikow acknowledged the truth of it; certainly he could not stand in the way of the truth being told. In the early days of the investigation, he had pushed for the commission's staff to try to find evidence linking al-Qaeda and Baghdad. He pushed so hard that even some of the less suspicious investigators on the commission became alarmed that Zelikow was doing the bidding of the White House, trying to help the Bush administration justify the war in Iraq.

But with only weeks left in the investigation, Zelikow agreed that the evidence was just not there. Certainly there had been contacts over the years between Osama bin Laden and the Iraqis. Most tantalizing, the commission's staff found intelligence reports that a senior Iraqi spy made visits to bin Laden's sanctuary in Sudan in the mid-1990s in which the Iraqi met with the al-Qaeda leader. It appeared from the reports that bin Laden had asked for Iraq's help during that time period in establishing terrorist training camps in Iraq and obtaining weapons.

But the intelligence suggested bin Laden's interest in Saddam Hussein went unrequited; the Iraqi leader mostly did not reply to al-Qaeda's overtures. The intelligence showed that when bin Laden wanted to do business with Iraq, Iraq did not want to do business with al-Qaeda. Among intelligence analysts, it was assumed that Saddam Hussein saw bin Laden, who was crusading for an overthrow of secular government in the Muslim world, as a threat to his own very brutal and very secular rule in Iraq.

The commission's staff believed that it had debunked, once and for all, the widely circulated intelligence report about the so-called Prague meeting—a supposed encounter in the Czech capital between a senior

Iraq spy and Mohammed Atta, the 9/11 ringleader, on April 9, 2001. The report had been circulated by the Czech intelligence service and embraced by the Bush administration—Vice President Dick Cheney in particular—to suggest an Iraqi link to 9/11. But the commission's staff was convinced that the Prague meeting never happened; the CIA and FBI had reached the same conclusion. The Czech report was based on a single, uncorroborated witness account. There were extensive phone and travel records to show that Atta was in Virginia on April 4 and then traveled to Florida, where he was seen on April 11. His cell phone was used in Florida several times on April 6, 10, and 11, as well as on April 9, the day Atta was supposedly in Prague.

The staff's conclusion that there was not a working relationship between al-Qaeda and Iraq had the makings of a political firestorm for the White House—as dire a threat to George Bush's reelection hopes in November as any the commission would pose at the end of its investigation.

By June 2004, the situation for American troops in Iraq had grown even worse. Insurgent groups had stepped up their violence throughout the country. The previous few months had been especially grisly for Americans and Iraqis alike. After four American military contractors were ambushed as their convoy passed through the Iraqi city of Fallujah on March 31, their charred bodies strung up on a bridge over the Euphrates, the Pentagon responded with an assault on the city that had left twenty-seven American soldiers dead. The chaos in Iraq was driving down Bush's poll numbers and, by definition, his hopes for reelection. By June, with only five months left before the November elections, polls showed that the president was viewed favorably by about only half the public.

The administration's initial justification for the war, its claim that Iraq had been secretly stockpiling weapons of mass destruction, had been proved disastrously wrong a year earlier, within weeks of Saddam Hussein's ouster. No chemical, biological, or nuclear weapons were ever found. The administration then struggled to shift the argument, suggesting that the war was justified instead because Hussein had been collaborating for years with bin Laden—that the Iraqi leader was a patron of the man behind 9/11. It was a constant refrain in the speeches of both Bush and Cheney throughout 2003 and 2004. "The liberation of Iraq is a crucial advance in the campaign against terror," Bush said aboard the aircraft carrier *Abraham Lincoln* in May 2003; it was the speech in which he stood beneath a banner that read MISSION ACCOMPLISHED and prematurely declared an end to major combat operations in Iraq. "We have removed an ally of al-Qaeda and cut off a source of terrorist funding."

But now, to the horror of Bush's reelection team, the 9/11 commission was about to knock down that justification for the war as well. There was no close link between al-Qaeda and Iraq. Even if he wanted to, there was little Zelikow could do to rescue the administration now.

The results of the commission's investigation of the al-Qaeda–Iraq ties and the Prague meeting were supposed to be released in a staff statement at the panel's final public hearings, scheduled for June 16 and 17 in Washington. If Zelikow tried to tamper with the report now, he knew he risked a public insurrection by the staff, with only a month left before the commission's final report was due.

The staff's findings about the tenuous relationship between al-Qaeda and Iraq were contained in a single paragraph, found at the bottom of page five of the sixteen-page staff report entitled "Overview of the Enemy" that was made public at the June hearing. The paragraph read:

> Bin Ladin also explored possible cooperation with Iraq during his time in Sudan, despite his opposition to Hussein's secular regime. Bin Ladin had in fact at one time sponsored anti-Saddam Islamists in Iraqi Kurdistan. The Sudanese, to protect their own ties with Iraq, reportedly persuaded Bin Ladin to cease this support and arranged for contacts between Iraq and al Qaeda. A senior Iraqi intelligence officer reportedly made three visits to Sudan, finally meeting Bin Ladin in 1994. Bin Ladin is said to have requested space to establish training camps, as well as assistance in procuring weapons, but Iraq apparently never responded. There have been reports that contacts between Iraq and al Qaeda also occurred after Bin Ladin had returned to Afghanistan, but they do not appear to have resulted in a collaborative relationship. Two senior Bin Ladin associates have adamantly denied that any ties existed between al Qaeda and Iraq. We have no credible evidence that Iraq and al-Qaeda cooperated on attacks against the United States.

Within minutes of the release of the report, the Associated Press and Reuters carried their first bulletins, setting the tone for what would become a nightmarish day of news coverage for the White House. An early story by the normally sober AP began with a stark first sentence: "Bluntly contradicting the Bush administration, the commission investigating the September 11 attacks reported Wednesday there was 'no credible evidence' that Saddam Hussein had ties with al-Qaida.'" The revised story later in the day was even worse for the White House. "Already in question, President Bush's justification for war in Iraq has suffered another major setback," it began. "An independent commission threw cold water Wednesday on the administration's insistent claims of a link between Saddam Hussein and al-Qaida."

Senator John Kerry of Massachusetts, Bush's Democratic opponent in the November elections, saw the opening that the commission had given him. He quickly released a statement to reporters: "The president owes the American people a fundamental explanation about why he rushed to war for a purpose that it now turns out is not supported by the facts."

AT THE WHITE HOUSE, no one was reading the news coverage more closely, or with greater fury, than Dick Cheney. He seemed instantly to grasp the political danger posed by the commission's findings on Iraq and how they were being conveyed to the public. He was incensed by the banner front-page headlines the next morning in *The Washington Post* (AL QAEDA–HUSSEIN LINK IS DISMISSED) and *The New York Times* (PANEL FINDS NO QAEDA-IRAQ TIE). Cheney had a special loathing for the *Times,* in part because its editorial board, unlike the *Post*'s, had so fiercely opposed the Iraq invasion and the conduct of the American occupiers.

Reminded of why he had tried to block creation of the 9/11 commission in the first place, Cheney decided to go public with a counterattack. The attack would be targeted not at the commission, at least not directly, but at the reporters and headline writers who had dared to accurately describe the commission's findings. He singled out the *Times* in an interview the next day on the financial cable news network CNBC.

The veteran political reporter and CNBC anchor Gloria Borger had known the vice president for decades and could see that the normally imperturbable Cheney was visibly upset: "Mr. Vice President, I don't think I've ever seen you, in all the years I've interviewed you, as exercised about something as you seem today."

She was right, said Cheney.

"What *The New York Times* did today was outrageous," he said. "They do a lot of outrageous things. But the headline? 'Panel Finds No Qaeda-Iraq Tie.' The press wants to run out and say there's a fundamental split here now between what the president sad and what the commission said" about al-Qaeda and Iraq. "There's no conflict," he declared.

He said that reporters, including those at the *Times,* had confused the question of whether there was an Iraqi tie to September 11 with the larger issue of whether a relationship existed between al-Qaeda and Saddam Hussein. Cheney said the commission "did not address the broader question of a relationship between Iraq and al-Qaeda in other areas, in other ways."

President Bush joined in from the West Wing, telling White House reporters after a cabinet meeting that "the reason I keep insisting that there was a relationship between Iraq and Saddam and al-Qaeda" is "because there was a relationship between Iraq and al-Qaeda."

There was an Alice in Wonderland quality to the White House response to the conclusions of the commission's staff. The president and vice president were trying to pretend, at least publicly, that the report did not say what it clearly said—that the commission had found no convincing evidence of a "collaborative relationship" between al-Qaeda and Iraq after bin Laden returned to Afghanistan in the 1990s.

Cheney went one step further in this parallel universe of spin. He wanted to revive a theory that even Bush had repeatedly knocked down: that Iraq was involved in the 9/11 attacks. In his CNBC interview, Cheney said that whatever the commission's conclusion, he still would not rule out the possibility that Saddam Hussein was tied to the 2001 attacks; he still did not rule out the possibility that the Prague meeting had occurred. "We don't know," he said when asked about an Iraqi link to the 9/11 attacks. "What the commission says is that they can't find any evidence of that. We had one report which is a famous report on the Czech intelligence service. And we've never been able to confirm or knock it down."

Borger put it to Cheney: "Do you know things that the commision does not know?"

"Probably," replied Cheney.

KEAN, HAMILTON, and several other commissioners were alarmed at the prospect of a public debate with the White House over al-Qaeda and Iraq. And they began to equivocate about the meaning of the words in the staff report. Some of the Republican commissioners all but dis-owned the staff report in interviews after the hearing, seeing the damage it might do to Bush's reelection hopes. Kean and Hamilton asked Doug MacEachin, the principal author of the report, and his team to go back and determine if they had missed evidence tying Iraq and al-Qaeda. Was it possible that Cheney was right, that the intelligence showed a closer link? "We really need to nail this," Hamilton said sternly to MacEachin. Kean and Hamilton also issued a public challenge to Cheney. If he "probably" had information that the commission lacked, the vice presi-dent needed to hand it over in a hurry. "I would like to see the evidence that Mr. Cheney is talking about," Hamilton told reporters.

— 55 —

HARVARD UNIVERSITY
Cambridge, Mass.
JUNE 2004

P hilip Zelikow had hired Harvard historian Ernest R. May as a consultant to the 9/11 commission. A specialist in foreign policy and the workings of the federal government, the courtly, seventy-five-year-old Harvard professor was a friend and mentor of Zelikow's from their years together at the university's Kennedy School of Government. Throughout the spring and early summer of 2004, May paid regular visits to the commission's offices in Washington to review early drafts of chapters of the final report. May, the author or editor of more than a dozen books himself, was struck by the quality of the writing and editing in the chapters he saw; it was a tribute to his protégé Zelikow.

May could see that this was not going to be just another gray, bureaucratic government report that would go unread, gathering dust on a bookshelf. The commission's staff did a little research on the subject: Since 1965, there had been 640 federal blue-ribbon commissioners on one subject or another, and almost all of their public reports were impenetrable. But not this one. The 9/11 commission report was going to work as literature. The writing was elegantly spare, a result of a directive from Lee Hamilton that adjectives and adverbs be avoided whenever possible to avoid the appearance that judgments were being made. "Go to the facts," he said. Among the commissioners and staff, "Go to the facts" became a mantra whenever there were debates over the wording of a passage. "Democrats pushed for adjectives to support President Clinton, while Republicans pushed for adjectives to support President Bush," Hamilton said later. "It was such a minefield that we finally cut all adjectives and ended up with a sparse narrative style." Some of the draft chapters, especially the chapters detailing events in the air and on the ground on the morning of September 11, read like a taut, well-paced thriller.

The commissioners appreciated May's perspective. He was not quite an outsider; he had been brought in by Zelikow in the early weeks of the investigation in 2003. But unlike Zelikow and the rest of the commission's staff, May had not lived and breathed the investigation every day for more than a year. Although he spoke often by phone to Zelikow, he visited Washington only sporadically. And unlike so many of the staff, he was not intimidated by Zelikow.

As the investigation was coming to an end, May told Zelikow something that he almost certainly did not want to hear. He was troubled by much of what he was reading. He thought the report was incomplete in many ways. It was a report that was being censored—*had* to be censored, probably—to achieve unanimity between a group of harshly partisan Democrats and harshly partisan Republicans. But what he was reading went beyond a balancing act to satisfy partisans. The 9/11 commission's report was skirting judgments about people who almost certainly had some blame for failing to prevent September 11. That included two presidents and their top advisers. The commission's judgments about Bush and Clinton and their senior aides were overly forgiving—"indulgent," May said—and veiled many of their failures at the White House in dealing with terrorist threats. To achieve unanimity, there was little accountability.

THE FRIENDSHIP between May and Zelikow perplexed some of the commission investigators. In temperament, they were opposites. Like Zelikow, May had family roots in Texas; he was from Fort Worth and still spoke with a slight drawl. Like Zelikow, May had headed west to California for college. But unlike his protégé, the courtly May had allowed some of the easygoing charms of the Texas plains and Pacific coastline to rub off on him. May earned his PhD in history, as well as his bachelor's and master's degrees, at UCLA; it was not a university that bred the sort of Ivy League pomposity that May would encounter through much of the rest of his career at Harvard. The commission's staffers figured that May was willing to overlook Zelikow's prickliness because the younger historian was so well-read, hardworking, and willing to share credit. They taught classes together at Harvard and had collaborated on *The Kennedy Tapes,* the book about the Cuban missile crisis that was turned into the 2000 Hollywood movie *Thirteen Days* starring

Kevin Costner. Friends said May found it a heady thing to see his name in the screen credits with Costner's.

May thought that Zelikow was often unfairly criticized. The two men met when Zelikow was a graduate student at the Fletcher School of diplomacy at Tufts University and he took a course offered by May at Harvard. Zelikow was May's "prize student," and after Zelikow left the NSC in the first Bush administration, he was recruited by May to join the faculty at Harvard. "I can only say that Philip and I have managed harmonious cooperation over many years," May said. "We have had our differences but never serious ones."

After he was approached by Kean and Hamilton in January 2003 about running the investigation, Zelikow immediately telephoned May to discuss whether he should take the job. May was at home in Cambridge, Massachusetts, not far from his office on the Harvard campus, and he remembered that the call lasted more than an hour, with the two men agreeing that it was an extraordinary opportunity to try to produce a "professional-quality narrative history" of a watershed moment in American history, "on a par at least with Pearl Harbor."

After Pearl Harbor, both men knew, there had been no similar effort to explain the disaster to the public. There was an effort at accountability in the Pearl Harbor investigations—the navy's fleet commander in the Pacific and his army counterpart were both relieved of their commands in disgrace—but there had been no effort to put the 1941 attacks in historical context and explain the forces that had led the Japanese to launch a surprise attack and why the military had left itself so vulnerable. As a historian, it was exciting, May remembered, to think of producing a report that would remain *the* reference volume on the September 11 attacks and that would be "sitting on the shelves of high school and college teachers a generation hence."

Zelikow initially wanted May's advice on how the final report should be structured, and they went to work, secretly, to prepare an outline. May was given a desk in Zelikow's office on K Street in Washington, which he used on his occasional visits from Harvard. By March 2003, with the commission's staff barely in place, the two men had already prepared a detailed outline, complete with "chapter headings, subheadings, and sub-subheadings."

He and May proposed a sixteen-chapter report that would open with a history of al-Qaeda, beginning with bin Laden's fatwa against the United States in 1998. That would lead to chapters about the history of American counterterrorism policy. The White House response to the flood of terrorist threats in the spring and summer of 2001 were left to the sixth chapter; the events of September 11 were left to the seventh chapter. Zelikow and May proposed that the tenth chapter be entitled "Problems of Foresight—And Hindsight," with a subchapter on "the blinding effects of hindsight."

Zelikow shared the document with Kean and Hamilton, who were impressed by their executive director's early diligence but worried that the outline would be seen as evidence that they—and Zelikow—had predetermined the report's outcome. It should be kept secret from the rest of the staff, they all decided. May said that he and Zelikow agreed that the outline should be "treated as if it were the most classified document the commission possessed." Zelikow came up with his own internal classification system for the outline. He labeled it "Commission Sensitive," putting those words at the top and bottom of each page.

Kean and Hamilton were right to be wary. When it was later disclosed that Zelikow had prepared a detailed outline of the commission's final report at the very start of the investigation, many of the staff's investigators were alarmed. They were finally given copies of the outline in April 2004. They saw that Zelikow was proposing that the findings about the Bush administration's actions before 9/11 would be pushed to the middle of the report, which meant that readers would have to go searching for them past long chapters of al-Qaeda history. Many assumed the worst when they saw that Zelikow had proposed a portion of the report entitled "The Blinding Effects of Hindsight." What "blinding hindsight"? They assumed Zelikow was trying to dismiss the value of hindsight regarding the Bush administration's pre-9/11 performance. A few staffers began circulating a two-page parody of Zelikow's effort entitled "The Warren Commission Report—Preemptive Outline." The parody's authorship was never determined conclusively. The chapter headings included "Single Bullet: We Haven't Seen the Evidence Yet. But Really. We're Sure."

AFTER THE FINAL public hearings in Washington, the commission had only a month to finish the report. Although there was a legal deadline of July 26 to release the report, Kean wanted it out at least a few days earlier. The Democratic National Convention in Boston, at which Senator John Kerry would be anointed as his party's nominee, was scheduled to open on July 26, and Kean and Hamilton wanted to avoid competition with the convention as a news story. So the release date was set for Thursday, July 22.

The body of the report was mostly written by late June. The interim staff reports released throughout the public hearings provided discrete, well-written chapters about the history of the attacks and the chronology of al-Qaeda, as well as a detailed analysis of the failures at the FBI, the CIA, and elsewhere that prevented the government from foiling the attacks.

Whatever May's criticisms of the final report, he mostly did not share them with others on the staff. There was not much point in that. He talked directly to Zelikow, who, more than anyone else, controlled what the final report would say.

May's complaints centered on the lack of judgments in the report, both about people and about institutions. Within the staff, Zelikow tended to take the blame for the perception that the report was going easy on his friends in the Bush White House. But May believed that the report was going soft on Clinton, too, and on a generation of American policy makers who had failed to prepare the nation for the potential of domestic terrorist threats.

"The report is probably too balanced," May later wrote in a remarkably candid assessment of the work of the commission in *The New Republic* magazine a year later. It was true for agencies and people. If an institution was criticized in one sentence, it would be praised in the next. "Individuals, especially the two presidents and their intimate advisers, received even more indulgent treatment," he said. "The text does not describe Clinton's crippling handicaps as leader of his own national security community. Extraordinarily quick and intelligent, he more than almost anyone else had an imaginative grasp of the threat posed by al-Qaeda. But he had almost no authority enabling his to get his government to address the threat."

As for Bush, May appeared less critical of the president himself than of Condoleezza Rice and Bush's other top aides in the White House.

May had come to his own conclusion about the central dispute between Richard Clarke and Condoleezza Rice over the performance of the Bush White House in 2001. It may have infuriated Zelikow to hear it, but May was certain that Clarke was right. Clarke's assertion that the Bush White House failed to make terrorism an urgent issue before September 11, despite all of the threats of an imminent attack, was "manifestly true," May thought. (He believed the same criticism could be made of the Clinton White House.) May thought the report was being written to avoid "even implicit endorsement of Clarke's public charge." The staff was never certain May understood that it was his protégé Zelikow who had worked so hard to undermine Clarke and his allegations against Rice. May would later say that he had crafted language endorsing Clarke's views on Bush but that "people with better partisan antennae," including a prominent Democrat on the staff, urged him not to put it in the final report. They thought the language was "potentially inflammatory," he said, "and I accepted their judgments."

May thought the commission had made a serious mistake in its decision not to demand access to al-Qaeda terrorists in American custody. The interrogation reports that had been provided to the commission by the CIA and Pentagon were incomplete and poorly written. And the fact that the information had almost certainly been obtained under "coercive questioning"—techniques that the Bush administration's critics would later describe as torture—diminished their value even more, as many on the staff knew. May tried to read each and every one of the interrogation reports, and "what impressed me overall was the poor quality of the summaries as historical evidence." May felt that the commission had also compromised its promise to tell the full story of the 9/11 attacks by its refusal to tackle the issue of how American support for Israel and repressive Muslim regimes in Saudi Arabia, Egypt, and Pakistan had "fed the anger that manifested itself on September 11." But May was told that the commissioners believed questions about Israel and Saudi Arabia were too controversial to be addressed in the final report. "Composing a report that all commissioners could endorse carried costs," May wrote.

Surprisingly, criticism of the commission for failing to "name names" and hold individuals accountable for 9/11 was also being made at the place where many of the "names" presumably worked: the Bush White House. In the spring of 2004, Richard A. Falkenrath, a former Harvard colleague of Zelikow and May's, was in his final weeks on the White House staff. He had joined the White House in 2001, initially on Rice's staff, and was made a special assistant to Bush for homeland security after 9/11. Falkenrath was diplomatic enough not to say it loudly while he was still on the White House payroll, but he could see that the 9/11 commission was doing a disservice to the nation by failing to identify officials in the Bush administration—and the Clinton administration—who had left the nation vulnerable to attack on 9/11. (Falkenrath never said so publicly, but colleagues suspected he was talking specifically about Rice and, to some degree, Clarke.) The failure to name names, he believed, was "exactly the wrong message to send to future government officials and the people who train them."

After leaving the White House and joining a Washington think tank, Falkenrath surprised—and, many suspected, outraged—Zelikow by writing a savage critique of the commission's report and having it appear where it would almost certainly cause Zelikow discomfort: the scholarly journal *International Security,* published jointly by Harvard and MIT. Falkenrath has since insisted that his criticism was not directed personally at Zelikow and May and that he respects both men. But since his former Harvard colleagues were the architects of the report, Zelikow and May may still have winced at Falkenrath's accusation that the commission had endorsed a "no fault" theory of government in which individuals were not held responsible for their actions, no matter how catastrophic. He said that the commission's report instead offered an "imprecise, anodyne and impersonal assignment of responsibility for the U.S. government's failure to prevent the 9/11 attacks."

In fact, "government is not a 'no fault' business," Falkenrath wrote. "When the government fails to act in situations in which it has a legal authority to do so, it is almost always because specific and identifiable officials made a decision, formally or informally, not to act."

MUCH OF THE REST of the commission's staff would have agreed with the sorts of criticisms that May and Falkenrath were making. But with only weeks left in the life of the commission, they were so exhausted and so beaten down by months of working under the autocratic Zelikow that they had no energy left to conduct a larger fight over the report. Zelikow had been so effective in stovepiping the work of the commission that few of the teams of investigations knew exactly what the other teams had uncovered in their months of digging. That helped explain why the NSA terrorism archives had gone mostly unread until the final days of the investigation—almost certainly the commission's most grievous failure in its research. In the final days of the investigation, the teams of investigators were focused almost entirely on making sure their own part of the story of 9/11 was being told accurately and hoping that their findings would be reflected in the commission's final recommendations. Many of the teams were girding themselves for a final showdown with Zelikow to make sure the truth was told.

K STREET OFFICES OF THE
9/11 COMMISSION
Washington, D.C.
JUNE 2004

I t's too Clarke-centric," Philip Zelikow barked to Warren Bass and the other members of Team 3. Bass and the others were writing the portions of the final report that would deal with arguably the most sensitive issue of all before the commission: Had the Bush White House bungled terrorism warnings in 2001? Who was telling the truth: Richard Clarke or Condoleezza Rice? There was no doubt that Zelikow stood with his friend Rice. "We need balance," he declared.

Even after a year of battling Zelikow, Bass was still fuming. He tried never to raise his voice to Zelikow, but it was becoming harder and harder. Why hadn't he resigned when he had the chance? Bass asked colleagues. It was now the late spring of 2004, and he was explaining to Zelikow again that no matter how eager Zelikow was to knock down Clarke's credibility, the former White House terrorism czar had left behind a vast documentary record of what had gone so wrong in the months before 9/11. Bass had the backing of everyone on his team who knew what was in the NSC records, notably Mike Hurley, the team's leader. And it was not just Clarke's records. The other members of the NSC staff who worked with Clarke supported his account in their own interviews with the commission. They had all been alarmed at the slowness of Bush and Rice to respond to the threats in 2001. So had the CIA and the State Department.

The commission's staff had conducted a memorable private interview on January 21, 2004, with John McLaughlin, Tenet's deputy during the summer of 2001. He described how there had been "great tension" at the CIA—near panic, others at the agency would say—over what seemed to be the refusal of the White House to deal with warnings of an imminent terrorist attack in 2001. The White House had just seemed unwilling to believe there was a problem—or at least no problem that required imme-diate attention, and certainly no problem on American soil. McLaugh-lin was a member of the White House Deputies Committee, made up of the number two officials at major agencies, and the commission's staff had come across slides from a briefing that the CIA had given to the committee that April. The message was stark. The slides described al-Qaeda as "the most dangerous group we face" and that its focus was "on attacking U.S." The commission was told that Michael Scheuer and his replacement at Alec Station had both threatened to resign from the CIA in the summer of 2001 and go public as a protest over the White House's stunning lack of interest in dealing with the threats.

So Bass and his colleagues wondered: How did Zelikow propose to balance all of *that* out? There was a large documentary record to back up Clarke and his colleagues. There was little to support Rice.

Well, Zelikow explained, there were Rice's own words. She had given public testimony to the commission, and there was her four-hour private interview with the commissioners in the White House Situation Room in February. He never said so explicitly, but Zelikow made clear to Team 3 that the commission's final report should balance out every statement of Clarke's with a statement from Rice. The team should leave out any judgment on which of them was telling the truth.

Zelikow had some support from Dan Marcus, the commission's gen-eral counsel, who thought that Team 3 tended to make Clarke, unde-servedly, "into a superhero." Marcus felt that the commission's final report "needed to point out some of the limitations and flaws in Clarke's performance." Marcus could see that Team 3's wariness of Zelikow was no longer being hidden; they were openly suspicious of his motives. "In a sense, they overreacted to Philip because they were so worried about him they pushed and pushed and pushed, and sometimes they were wrong," said Marcus.

Members of Team 3 tried to console themselves with the thought—the hope, perhaps—that the public would read between the lines of the report and understand that Clarke was mostly telling the truth, that Rice often wasn't, and that the White House had left the country vulnerable to a clear-cut threat of terrorist attack in September 2001. But the results of the team's work were some of the most tortured passages in the final report, especially in the description of the performance of the NSC in the first months of the Bush presidency. It was written almost as point, counterpoint—Clarke says this, Rice says the opposite—with no conclusion about what the truth finally was.

ALEXIS ALBION, the team's CIA specialist, was having her own final showdown with Zelikow, with the same partisan overtones.

Earlier in the year, the staff had been asked by Hamilton to compile a roster of how often Clinton and Bush had addressed terrorist threats in their speeches and other public remarks before 9/11—al-Qaeda threats in particular. There could be no exact comparison, since Bush had been in office only eight months before the attack, compared with Clinton's eight years. But it would give the commission some idea of the relative priority that the two presidents had given the issue, at least in terms of their public declarations.

The staff uncovered dozens of instances in which Clinton addressed terrorism, which he described as "the enemy of our generation." He referred to it in each of his State of the Union addresses to Congress. In a speech to open the General Assembly of the United Nations in 1999, Clinton said antiterrorism efforts were "at the top of the American agenda and should be at the top of the world's agenda." Clinton often warned that stateless terrorist groups like al-Qaeda might be on the verge of obtaining chemical and biological weapons. (He rarely referred to Osama bin Laden by name, which he told the commissioner was intentional—an effort to avoid enhancing the al-Qaeda leader's stature.) Bush, by comparison, almost never mentioned terrorism in his public speeches, and that was true both on the 2000 campaign trail and after he became president. When Bush did refer to it, it was usually in the context of the dangers of state-sponsored terrorism and how it demonstrated the need for a missile defense system against rogue states like North Korea, Iran, or Iraq.

Albion and others on her team could see that such a direct comparison between the two presidents would annoy, maybe even infuriate, the Bush White House. In a report that otherwise was not going to apportion personal blame for 9/11, a statement that suggested President Bush demonstrated little public curiosity about terrorism would be seen as the report's most direct personal criticism of him. Still, Albion felt strongly that the comparison needed to be in the report. Obviously, what the president of the United States chose to talk about in his public remarks mattered. It set the agenda for the rest of the government and for the press.

Zelikow insisted that it come out—all of it. He was adamant.

"This is totally unreasonable," his colleagues remembered him almost yelling at Albion and the others. "This is unfair." Unfair to President Bush, of course. "He hadn't been in office long enough to make a major address on terrorism," Zelikow said, defending Bush. "We cannot do this." Zelikow's anger was so off the scale on this issue that some of the staff members wondered if this was simply a show on his part to intimidate them into backing down.

Albion argued back. "Philip, it's reasonable to balance out the two presidents" in their public comments on terrorism, she said. "I'm surprised you consider this such a big issue." During the cold war, wouldn't it be fair to judge two presidents about how they publicly measured the national security threat posed by Communist armies, how often they talked about it?

Marcus, the general counsel, sided with Albion and the others. He thought it was one of Zelikow's most overt displays of his partisanship, of his desire to protect the administration. Obviously it was significant if Bush, who was now claiming that he had been gravely worried throughout 2001 about terrorist threats, never bothered to mention it in public during that same period. "You'd think he would say something about it once in a while, right?" asked Marcus.

Zelikow was not backing down, and the comparison between Bush and Clinton came out of the final draft over the objections of the staff. He bristled at the suggestion that he was trying to do a final favor to the White House. He said that "playing it straight" also meant that "if I bent over backwards to be tough on the Bush administration, just to show off, it would be another form of bias."

Albion later got a small dose of revenge. She figured, correctly, that in the chaos of the final days of writing and editing the report, Zelikow would not pay much attention to the drafting of footnotes. So she wrote footnotes that summarized the comparisons between Bush and Clinton and snuck them in.

Chapter 6, footnote 2: "President Clinton spoke of terrorism in numerous public statements.... Clinton repeatedly linked terrorism groups and WMD as transnational threats for the new global era."

Chapter 6, footnote 164: "Public references by candidate and then President Bush about terrorism before 9/11 tended to reflect... [his concern with] state-sponsored terrorism and WMD as a reason to mount a missile defense."

FOR MIKE JACOBSON, Raj De, and the other members of the "plot" team who felt strongly that they had demonstrated a close Saudi government connection to the two hijackers in San Diego, their opponent in revealing the full story was not Zelikow. It was Dieter Snell, the hypercautious prosecutor who was their team leader.

Jacobson and De felt they had explosive material on the Saudis: the actions by Omar al-Bayoumi, the Saudi "ghost employee" who played host to the two hijackers in San Diego, and Fahad al-Thumairy, the shadowy Saudi diplomat in Los Angeles. Jacobson and De had documentation of the unusual cash transfers from the wife of the Saudi ambassador in Washington to the family of another mysterious Saudi who was tied to al-Bayoumi. They were especially excited by the discovery of the FBI files on the taxi driver who had worked for Thumairy in Los Angeles and had initially identified the photos of Nawaf al-Hazmi and Khalid al-Mihdhar.

But after presenting Snell with their final drafts outlining their findings, Jacobson was alarmed to get a phone call close to midnight on one of the final nights of editing. Snell and Zelikow were in the office, rewriting the report. Snell had presented an alternative draft of the chapter, and it removed virtually all of the most serious allegations against the Saudis. Jacobson called De, and they both rushed back to the offices on K Street.

Snell made clear that he was not going to stand for a final report that made allegations that could not be backed up conclusively. From his long career as a prosecutor, he knew that an allegation based on partial evidence should not be made at all, he said. Snell was widely admired by the commissioners for his dedication to the truth. His caution had obviously served him well as a prosecutor. But members of his team believed that the level of proof he was demanding on the 9/11 commission would exonerate the guilty.

In front of Zelikow, Jacobson and De tried all of the arguments they had been using for months—how it was "crazy" to insist on 100 percent proof of guilt when it came to a terrorist network like al-Qaeda or the workings of an authoritarian regime like Saudi Arabia's. The commission was not a trial jury; there was no "reasonable doubt" requirement. Couldn't he see that by removing this material from the report, he was effectively telling the public that Saudi Arabia had done nothing wrong, when in fact there was every reason to fear what Saudi officials had done? But Snell was determined.

Zelikow seemed sympathetic to some of the arguments being made by Jacobson and De; he, too, initially had grave suspicions about the Saudis. But at this late hour, his role was as mediator between Snell and the staff. There were only days left before the entire report had to be at the printers. Short of resigning and removing their names from the report entirely, Jacobson and De had to compromise, and much of their most damning material was moved to the report's footnotes. It was in the report, but readers would have to find it to decipher it in the tiny type of the footnotes.

W. W. NORTON & COMPANY has long been one of the nation's most distinguished publishing houses. The employee-owned company, founded in the 1920s, was the principal American publisher of Sigmund Freud and the British philosopher Bertrand Russell. It prided itself on working with some of the country's best scholars. It was Zelikow's principal publisher at the Miller Center of Public Affairs at the University of Virginia. Zelikow's résumé listed eight books published by Norton that he had either edited or written.

It was Zelikow's idea in the early days of the investigation, endorsed enthusiastically by Tom Kean, that the commission find a private publisher to release the report on the day it was made public in Washington. That way, the report would be instantly available in bookstores around the country. The government's official printer, the Government Printing Office, would take days to distribute even a small number of the reports and would likely need to charge as much as $65 a copy to recoup its costs. Kean left it to Zelikow to conduct the review to decide which private publisher would be best. The idea was to find a publisher that would agree to the commission's strict security arrangements and would publish the report at a reasonable price. Although the research behind the book was prepared at the taxpayer's expense and it was a public document, the publisher could keep all profits from the book. The publisher would make no payment at all to the commission.

Zelikow approached three publishers: Times Books, an imprint of Henry Holt & Company that published some books in collaboration with *The New York Times;* PublicAffairs Books, which specialized in current events and public policy; and Norton. After hearing their proposals, Zelikow urged the commission to select Norton, saying it offered the best package to the commission. Norton agreed to publish the book for a retail price of $10, which other publishers acknowledged was reasonable for a book that was expected to be at least five hundred pages long; Norton readily agreed to meet all of the commission's secrecy requirements. Several commissioners said they only learned of Zelikow's connections to Norton long after the contract was signed. Zelikow said there was no conflict of interest in the commission's choice, since he had long ago waived royalties from his earlier Norton-published books.

K STREET OFFICES OF THE
9/11 COMMISSION
Washington, D.C.
JULY 2004

H ere's to the attorney general!"
In the weeks after the commission released its final, unanimous report, the commissioners and the staff gathered at a
few dinners and parties to celebrate their accomplishment. And at more
than one of the gatherings, wineglasses were raised in a toast—to Attorney General John Ashcroft. And it was only half in jest.

Jamie Gorelick was right to grimace at the toasts; the death threats were
over, but the Ashcroft attacks had complicated, perhaps destroyed, any hope
she had of Senate confirmation as attorney general or any other cabinet job if
John Kerry was elected president that November. Gorelick could not deny,
though, that Ashcroft's attack on her had unified the 9/11 commission. It
had been seen as an attack on the full commission, and the ten of them had
bonded in a way that made it impossible for any of them to seriously consider standing in the way of a unanimous report. Some of the closest friendships on the commission, between Gorelick and Slade Gorton, certainly
between Tom Kean and Lee Hamilton, had been made across party lines.
"John Ashcroft did us a huge favor in trying to break us up," Gorton said.

KEAN AND HAMILTON went into the final deliberations over the report
with trepidation. They assumed that some issue would rise up at the last
minute to destroy the bipartisanship solidarity that the Ashcroft furor
had helped create. There were several potential land mines—maybe
the wording of the passages about al-Qaeda and its purported links to
Iraq, maybe something about the way Bush and Clinton were described,
maybe something about the report's treatment of American relations
with Saudi Arabia or Israel.

But to the relief of Kean and Hamilton, the other commissioners seemed to be as eager as they were to find agreement. Gorton said the unity had much to do with the personalities of Kean and Hamilton, who were so unusual in politics—they never forced their own views on the other commissioners. They would sit and listen to others speak for hours, never interrupting, during the editing of the report. "They were trusted figures," said Gorton. "You just didn't want to disappoint them." He thought there would not have been a unanimous report if Henry Kissinger and George Mitchell, with their forceful personalities and partisan loyalties, had remained on the 9/11 commission. With Kissinger and Mitchell, "all of the air would have been sucked out of the room in the first half hour," he said.

Another force had cemented the group's unity: the power of the report's writing. For many of them, it was a thrill to be associated with a document that was obviously so powerfully written and might have such impact, that would be read by their children and grandchildren. By the end of the investigation, they knew their own legacies were tied up in the commission and its final report. Whatever their other accomplishments in life, it occurred to many of them that their affiliation with the 9/11 commission would be remembered as the most important public service of their lives. The commission would show up in the first few sentences of their obituaries. For Slade Gorton, Bob Kerrey, and Tim Roemer, the 9/11 commission had brought them nearly as much fame as their long political careers. Richard Ben-Veniste had tasted nothing like this sort of fame since Watergate. For Jim Thompson, the 9/11 commission was a welcome distraction from his troubles in the Conrad Black criminal investigation back in Chicago. No great glory would come to the commissioners from a divided commission. Unanimity would cement their place in history.

GEORGE TENET LOST. Robert Mueller won. It was almost that simple. With surprisingly little debate at the end of their deliberations, the commissioners decided that they would recommend the elimination of Tenet's job—director of central intelligence—and that two jobs be created in its place: CIA director, to run the agency, and director of national intelligence, a new cabinet-level superspy. The DNI would have no day-to-day responsibilities at the CIA; instead, the DNI would provide oversight for all of the government's spy agencies, including the CIA, the NSA, and the counterintelligence divisions within the FBI.

The recommendation reflected the view, widespread among the commissioners, that the 9/11 attack proved that when it came to intelligence gathering and counterterrorism, no one was "in charge." The record, they said, showed that Tenet had been either unable or unwilling to provide oversight to the rest of the government's spy agencies and force them to cooperate on dealing with the al-Qaeda threat. If Tenet saw the recommendation as a personal insult, he was right to. By the end of the investigation, many of the commissioners spoke with open disdain of Tenet. At the CIA, the recommendation for a DNI was seen largely as Zelikow's doing, the culmination of his efforts to breed contempt within the commission for Tenet and the workings of the agency.

By the end, Tenet seemed to understand how harshly the 9/11 commission would treat his leadership of the agency. Earlier in the year, he had heard rumblings that the commission was going to call for his dismissal, and he had called Andy Card at the White House for help. Card called Kean, who was startled.

"You know, the president likes George," Card said. "Please don't do this."

Kean stopped him. "It's not true, Andy," he assured Card. "We're not calling for Tenet's resignation. We're not calling for anybody's resignation."

CIA colleagues thought that the imminent release of the commission's report had something to do with the timing of Tenet's announcement on June 3, 2004, that he was resigning from the government. "George Tenet did a superb job for America," President Bush said the next day "It was a high honor to work with him."

For every insult hurled Tenet's way by the commissioners, there was a statement of effusive praise for FBI director Mueller. For all of its astounding failures before 9/11, for all of the evidence that things had changed little at the FBI despite Mueller's promises, the commission would recommend that the bureau stay intact. Team 6, the commission's team of investigators that focused on the FBI, had felt strongly that the bureau needed to be overhauled, certainly when it came to combating terrorism. So they were appalled when they learned what changes the commission would recommend for the bureau—almost none. Several used the word *whitewash* when they saw a draft of the commission's recommendations to be included in the final report. When it came to deciding what reforms were needed at the FBI, "we defer to Director Mueller," the draft said.

Caroline Barnes, the former FBI counterterrorism analyst on the team, gulped when she read it. Defer to Mueller? Change nothing? She and others on Team 6 felt they had to appeal this; the commission had to be tougher on the FBI and on Mueller. As he had throughout the investigation, Zelikow had essentially barred most of the staff from any direct access to the commissioners. Everything had to go through him. If Barnes was going to make a protest to the commission, she would have to do it where Zelikow would not see it. So she cornered Jamie Gorelick in the ladies' room. Barnes had always found Gorelick much more approachable than the other members of the commission.

"Jamie, you know that the staff is very uncomfortable with what you're recommending at the FBI," Barnes said.

She worried that Gorelick might brush her off, that Gorelick would say it was too late to make any changes in the final report. In fact, Gorelick seemed concerned by what she was hearing from Barnes. She told Barnes that regardless of Zelikow's rules, she would arrange for all the members of Team 6 to come and brief the full commission before the FBI recommendations were approved.

The briefing took place, and the final report's language on the FBI was toughened, if only slightly. The wording in the draft that most upset Barnes and the others—the statement that the commission would "defer" to Mueller's judgment—was edited out of the report. But the commission's larger recommendation, that the FBI remain intact, survived in the final draft, albeit with a call for the bureau to make new efforts to promote the work of agents and analysts who specialized in tracking down terrorists. The nation could no longer afford to have the FBI treat counterterrorism agents—like the ones in Minneapolis or Phoenix who might have stopped 9/11 if anyone in Washington had paid attention—as second-class citizens.

KEAN AND HAMILTON had been saying it for more than a year. And in the final weeks of the investigation, they said it again. They wanted no "finger-pointing" in the final report. They were aware of criticism from within the staff, certainly from the 9/11 families, that the report was failing in a basic mission of accountability. Certainly, Kean and Hamilton sensed that the Washington press corps and pundits wanted individuals held responsible for the 9/11 attacks. Depending on the politics of the editorial writer or columnist, it was a roster that tended to include some assortment of Bush, Clinton, Rice, Berger, Ashcroft, Reno, Freeh, and Tenet.

But Kean and Hamilton believed an effort to assign blame to individual government leaders would tear the commission apart. They had hired Zelikow to run the investigation with the knowledge that he was close to many people at the center of it—that he was not likely to agree to savage Rice and his other friends and patrons in the White House who had been in charge on September 11. They kept Zelikow in place even after they learned that his conflicts of interest were far graver than they knew at first: his role in the Bush transition team in demoting Clarke, his role in drafting the "preemptive war" strategy for the White House, his surreptitious phone calls to Karl Rove and his meetings with Rice. Kean and Hamilton believed that the government's structure for dealing with terrorist threats was dysfunctional, dangerously so, and incompetently run. Reforming it was far more important than singling out individuals for what had gone so wrong on that terrible morning in September 2001. What was more important? they asked. Trying to humiliate Condoleezza Rice and detail her failings at the White House in the spring and summer of 2001 or obtaining a unanimous final report that recommended the overhaul of the government's spy agencies? They were convinced it was the latter.

"I get a lot of nasty comments about that because people wanted us to point the finger at Bill Clinton or George Bush or Dick Clarke or Condi Rice," Hamilton said. "But if we had begun coming up with a list of bad actors, it would have blown the commission apart and it would have blown any credibility we had.

"If we had a paragraph saying Condi Rice really screwed up, that's all *The New York Times* would have written about," he continued. "That level of personal accountability would have been a total dead end—there's no end to it."

With a unanimous report, Kean and Hamilton also wanted to prove something that they had stood for throughout their careers and that seemed to have been forgotten in American politics in the new century: that it was still possible for loyal Republicans and loyal Democrats to agree on what was best for national security. After 9/11, both believed that bipartisan cooperation in dealing with terrorist threats might be all that stood between the United States and another attack. If there was one thing that terrorism experts who came before the commission agreed upon, it was the inevitability of another major attack on American soil. Maybe by al-Qaeda again, maybe by some other band of terrorists who hated Americans nearly as much. And next time, Kean and Hamilton knew, terrorists might find a method of attack—germs, chemicals, nuclear devices—that would kill even more people than had four hijacked jetliners turned into missiles.

Kean and Hamilton had settled on a useful catchphrase in describing what had gone wrong before 9/11. There had been a "failure of imagination" by the government as a whole—not so much by individuals who worked in the government—to prepare for the threat that Osama bin Laden posed.

Much as the staff felt beaten down by Zelikow, so did the other Democratic commissioners. By the end, they had given up the fight to document the more serious failures of Bush, Rice, and others in the administration in the months before 9/11. Zelikow would never have permitted it. Nor, they realized, would Kean and Hamilton. The Democrats hoped the public would read through the report and understand that 9/11 did not have to happen—that if the Bush administration had been more aggressive in dealing with the threats flooding into the White House from January 2001 through September 10, 2001, the plot could have been foiled. The Clinton administration could not duck blame for having failed to stop bin Laden before 2001. But what had happened in the White House in the first eight months of George Bush's presidency had all but guaranteed that nineteen young Arab men with little more than pocket knives, a few cans of mace, and a misunderstanding of the tenets of Islam could bring the United States to its knees.

THE PHONE call came during the final weeks of the commission's investigation, and it was from the Justice Department's criminal division—specifically, the division's office of counterespionage.

It was a courtesy call, but hardly a routine one. It was a quiet, lawyer-to-lawyer warning to the commission's general counsel, Dan Marcus, that he should be aware that the department had opened an investigation into whether the 9/11 commission had mishandled classified information. The request for the criminal investigation had come from the CIA.

To Marcus's astonishment, the focus of the investigation was Zelikow.

There was no allegation that Zelikow had intentionally leaked information to reporters or anyone else. But the Justice Department was reviewing allegations that Zelikow had been careless in the handling of information from secret documents gathered by the commission, especially in his e-mail exchanges with others on the commission, including e-mails sent overseas.

Zelikow would later say that he knew nothing about the investigation as it was going on—that he was never contacted by the Justice Department or FBI, that no one had raised it to him when he underwent questioning for additional government security clearances after leaving the 9/11 commission. "In 2005, my security clearances were renewed at the highest levels," he said later. "And with no indication of any concern or issue that needed to be cleared up."

Zelikow said later that if there had been a criminal investigation, he suspected it was an effort by the CIA to play "hardball" with him over his long-standing disputes with the agency over how he and the commission had tried to push previously classified information onto the public record. The CIA, he suspected, had tried "to criminalize this dispute and target me in the process."

When staff members later heard rumors of the Justice Department investigation in 2004, they thought there was no little irony that Zelikow was under investigation for just the sort of infraction that had led to his decision to dismiss Dana Lesemann, the former Justice Department lawyer, in such a brutal fashion the year before. In a sense, the allegations against Zelikow were more serious. Lesemann, unlike Zelikow, had never been accused of doing anything that threatened to expose classified information outside the commission's offices. She was alleged to have obtained, prematurely, a copy of a classified document that she would eventually be allowed to see anyway.

CIA officials would later say that, whatever their differences with

Zelikow, they had no choice but to refer the issue to the Justice Department because the complaint was not coming from within the CIA; it was coming from within the 9/11 commission itself. The CIA had received a written complaint from at least one commission staff member—the identity of the staff member remains secret—about Zelikow's purported carelessness with classified documents.

Marcus kept the information about the Justice Department's investigation mostly to himself. He and others on the commission's staff understood that if word of the investigation leaked to reporters in the final weeks of the commission's work, it might do irreparable damage to the panel's credibility. The commission's critics at the White House and on Capitol Hill would have delighted in a scandal that focused on potential security violations by the commission—just the sort of scandal that Kean and Hamilton had warned against in the first weeks of the investigation.

It was another irony about Zelikow. Just as some members of the commission's staff worried that he was suppressing information from the commission's final report, especially when it might do damage to his friends in the Bush administration, others on the staff worried that he was pushing too much sensitive, classified information into the final report that might embarrass the Bush and Clinton administrations alike. In a sense, it was more evidence that Zelikow's instincts as a historian could overwhelm any other motivation, partisan or otherwise.

The handling of classified information had been a subject of angry disputes between Zelikow and some of the intelligence specialists on his staff throughout the commission's investigation, especially Doug MacEachin, the former CIA analyst, as well as with Marcus.

MacEachin, Marcus, and others believed that Zelikow had taken it upon himself to declassify information without seeking the permission of the agencies that had provided the information to the commission in the first place. As he wrote staff statements during the investigation and then drafted chapters for the final report, MacEachin would flag individual sentences and paragraphs that contained classified information as "ORIGINATOR CONTROLLED," suggesting that the material could not be released publicly without the permission of the CIA, the NSA, or whatever other agency had provided it.

But Zelikow wanted to do things in reverse. He wanted the commission to operate under the assumption that it—or, rather, *he*—knew best what could be declassified. Throughout the investigation, he wanted the commission's written reports—initially, the staff statements that were released at the public hearings, and then the final report—to be written with the assumption that everything in them could be made public. If they contained information that the White House or the CIA considered too classified to be revealed, they would have their chance to object when they reviewed the reports before they were released.

Zelikow knew too well that if the assumption in the process was that the material in the commission's reports was classified, the government could hold up their release—or edit it to the point where the reports were incomprehensible. That explained many of the problems faced by the joint congressional investigation that had investigated the 9/11 attacks; its final report was riddled with blacked-out passages, including the notorious twenty-eight pages about Saudi Arabia that were never made public.

The White House, CIA, and other intelligence agencies pushed back from the start. Who was Zelikow to decide what material might or might not "harm the nation's security"? they asked. Declassifying information was their job, not his. But Zelikow had the support of the commissioners, especially Kean and Hamilton, who thought that Zelikow had come up with an ingenious strategy to prevent the final report from being unnecessarily censored by the administration. "Looking back, I believe our view of the correct approach was vindicated," Zelikow said later. "No one has credibly alleged that there were any leaks of genuinely classified information from the commission."

At the White House, maybe in all of Washington, there were days in 2003 and 2004 when no one was angrier with Zelikow than John B. Bellinger III, Rice's in-house counsel at the NSC. Bellinger was a throwback to a time when the people who held influential White House jobs like his were invariably the cream of the Ivy League—Princeton and Harvard Law School in Bellinger's case, by way of St. Alban's, the preppiest of Washington prep schools. He was a good match for Rice. Like her, Bellinger was poised and articulate, effortlessly charming, as good at a Washington dinner party as he was in a tricky diplomatic negotiation. But he repeatedly lost his button-downed cool with Zelikow.

Often he found himself screaming down a telephone line at Zelikow, furious with Zelikow's endless demands of the White House for more classified documents or additional interviews. Zelikow was at his most bombastic and obnoxious in dealing with Bellinger. "Philip was relentless," Bellinger said later.

Before joining Rice at the NSC, Bellinger had been at the Justice Department in the Clinton administration, handling national security cases for Janet Reno; that meant that his loyalties to the Bush White House were sometimes called into question, mostly in jest. He was a frequent target of abuse for David Addington, Cheney's counselor, who would accuse Bellinger of defending a "liberal" legal viewpoint, the ultimate insult in the vice president's office.

So Bellinger thought he had a perspective on Zelikow that others in the White House might lack. "And I really don't think the fix was in" between Zelikow and the White House, he said. While it was certainly true that Zelikow and Rice were friends, Bellinger believed that Zelikow had developed a rocky relationship with the White House because "he recognized that his personal reputation was at stake here and that he had to bend over backwards to show to everyone—the families, the press, the commissioners, particularly the Democratic commissioners—that he was being tough on the White House. And he *was* being tough on the White House."

It was not clear how the Justice Department's criminal division concluded its investigation of Zelikow, or even how seriously it was treated within the department. CIA officials say that Zelikow's allegation that the agency was playing "hardball" was disproved by the simple fact that, if the agency's supporters had really wanted to play hardball, information about the inquiry would have found its way to the commission's many critics on Capitol Hill or in the press, creating a firestorm for the commission as well as for Zelikow. Several members of the 9/11 commission said later they had never heard anything about a criminal investigation of Zelikow, then or since.

— 58 —

OFFICE OF THE CHIEF OF STAFF
The White House
JULY 2004

A ndy Card was beginning to like what he was hearing. The final report began arriving at the White House in pieces in late June. As each chapter was finished, it had to be forwarded to the White House for a declassification review by a special team of intelligence specialists that Card had assembled. So as the day of the report's release approached, Card was hearing back from the team. It was almost all good news for the White House.

After all the worrying about Dick Clarke's allegations against Rice and Bush, about the August 6 PDB, about Ashcroft, about the subpoena threats, about Kean's loyalty to the GOP, Card could see that the commission's final report posed no threat to Bush's reelection. The report would show that several government agencies, notably the FBI and CIA, had failed in their responsibilities before 9/11. But the report did not single out individuals for blame. Certainly not George Bush. The he-said, she-said material about Clarke and Rice did not seem to do any serious harm to Rice.

The feelings of relief were not universally held in the White House. Dick Cheney and his counsel, David Addington, were outraged by the commission's timeline on Cheney's actions on September 11—and the clear suggestion that Cheney had issued an unconstitutional shoot-down order that morning without Bush's knowledge or approval.

Kean learned about Cheney's outrage a few days before the report's release when he was pulled aside for a phone call. It was Cheney, who made it clear he was angry. He was demanding that the sections be rewritten to remove the insinuation.

"Governor, this is not true, just not fair," Cheney told Kean, according to other commissioners who later heard Kean describe the call.

Cheney said he thought it was startling that the commission did not accept the word of the president of the United States and the vice president. "The president has told you, I have told you, that the president issued the order. I was following his directions."

The truth, Kean knew, was that the staff did not believe what Bush and Cheney were saying. Kean ended the call by promising the vice president that he would ask the staff to give the material about the shoot-down another review before publication. But no major changes were made.

To the surprise of some of the commissioners and the staff, there was no similar protest from Cheney or anyone else in the White House over the commission's conclusion that there was no significant alliance between al-Qaeda and Iraq. After the earlier blowup with Cheney over Iraq, the staff had gone back and reviewed everything the commission had in its files about the ties between Osama bin Laden and Saddam Hussein. At the end of it, the staff was more convinced than ever that there had been no serious collaboration between the terrorists and the Iraqis, no matter how much the administration wanted to cling to the idea to justify the war.

To satisfy the administration, the report was rewritten to include every bit of evidence the staff could find to demonstrate links between al-Qaeda and Iraq in the 1990s, but the conclusion remained solid. The final report declared that intelligence reports about al-Qaeda and Iraq "describe friendly contacts and indicate common themes in both sides' hatred of the United States. But to date, we have seen no evidence that these or the earlier contacts ever developed into a collaborative operational relationship. Nor have we seen evidence indicating that Iraq cooperated with Al-Qaeda in developing or carrying out any attacks against the United States." The report included a special subchapter, entitled "Atta's Alleged Trip to Prague," that debunked the idea of the Prague meeting.

DAN MARCUS was proud of the report. It was a capstone to a career in the law and in government. He knew his own obituary would likely open with the words "Daniel Marcus, general counsel of the commission that investigated the 9/11 attacks..." He knew he was returning to a happy retirement, teaching constitutional law part-time at the American University Law School and writing occasional law review articles about his newfound status as one of the nation's premier experts on questions of executive privilege.

Marcus could see all the flaws in the commission's final report, especially its lack of accountability. But he could also see that if the commission had been run by someone who was Zelikow's political polar opposite—a harshly partisan Democrat, someone determined to do damage to Bush—it would still have been forced to make many of the same sorts of compromises to reach unanimity.

"We did pull our punches on the conclusions because we wanted to have a unanimous report," he said. "There was this implicit threat, occasionally made explicit on both sides of the aisle on the commission, that by God, if you get explicit in criticizing Bush on this, we're going to insist on being explicit in criticizing Clinton, and vice versa."

Still, as a proud Democrat, Marcus had to admit something to himself, and it was a little painful. He understood that the commission had just helped reelect George Bush.

Bush was seeking a second term that November on the basis of his decisiveness in dealing with al-Qaeda and other terrorist threats around the globe. Voters were being asked to believe that the terrorist threat was as dire as ever and that the Iraq war had been made necessary because of it. The commission's report did not make the accusation that the White House had most had feared most: that Bush and his administration had mishandled terrorist threats before 9/11. And it had reached the conclusion that the White House had most wanted the public to hear and understand: that there was every reason to fear another catastrophic terrorist attack within American borders. "The report, by reminding everybody about 9/11 and the terrorist threat, reelected him," Marcus said.

KEAN AND HAMILTON were about to get another taste of the partisan games they both so loathed. They had known for months about the criminal investigation of Sandy Berger and the allegations that he had stolen classified documents from the National Archives during his review of files that were supposed to be shared with the 9/11 commission. They had both gotten phone calls earlier that year from Alberto Gonzales to advise them of the inquiry. He asked them to keep the information secret, since the investigation might not be completed for weeks or months. They had done as they were asked.

But on July 19, three days before the commission issued its final report, news of the Berger investigation leaked. The assumption on the commission and among its staff was that it was a leak from the White House, eager to suggest that Berger's acts had deprived the 9/11 commission of information that might have embarrassed him and the Clinton administration. The office of House Speaker Dennis Hastert rushed out a statement to reporters:

> What information could be so embarrassing that a man with decades of experience in handling classified documents would risk being caught pilfering our nation's most sensitive secrets? Did these documents detail simple negligence or did they contain something more sinister? Was this a bungled attempt to rewrite history and keep critical information from the 9/11 Commission and potentially put their report under a cloud?

Berger immediately announced that he was stepping down as an adviser to John Kerry's presidential campaign. The following April, he pleaded guilty to a misdemeanor count of "unauthorized removal and retention of classified material" and of mishandling classified documents. Under the plea bargain, the Justice Department asked the court to impose a $10,000 fine; the charges carried up to a year in prison, but prosecutors did not request jail time. The judge in the case, Deborah A. Robinson, rejected the Justice Department's proposal as too lenient. She fined Berger $50,000 and ordered him to give up his security clearance for three years. "My actions...were wrong. They were foolish. I deeply regret them, and I have every day since," Berger told Robinson. "I let considerations of personal convenience override clear rules of handling classified material."

THE DAY of the report's release, Thursday, July 22, was Washington at its summer worst—miserably hot and muggy—and reporters were sweating through their clothes as they found their way to the Andrew W. Mellon Auditorium downtown to attend the news conference at which the commission would release the report. Kean and Hamilton first went that morning to Capitol Hill, where they provided congressional leaders with copies of the final report and offered them a short briefing of its findings. It was protocol to give it to Congress first, since the commission was considered at least nominally a creation of the Congress. The Norton version came in at 567 pages, with a simple, elegant design for the cover:

red and blue type set on a white background. The commission's formal name remained the National Commission on Terrorist Attacks upon the United States, but the commissioners had always referred to themselves as the 9/11 commission, and that was the name that appeared on the title: *The 9/11 Commission Report.*

At 9:00 a.m., Kean and Hamilton arrived at the White House for a meeting with President Bush in the Oval Office. Bush asked Kean and Hamilton to join him in the Rose Garden, where reporters had gathered. "I want to thank these two gentlemen for serving their country so well and so admirably," said Bush. "They've done a really good job of learning about our country, learning about what went wrong prior to September eleventh, and making very solid, sound recommendations about how to move forward. I assured them that where government needs to act, we will."

The report was released to almost universal acclaim. For days afterward, Bush and Kerry tried to one up each other on the campaign in expressing enthusiasm for the commission's work. Bush eventually embraced the commission's central recommendation—creation of the job of director of national intelligence—and put John Negroponte, the veteran American diplomat who was Bush's ambassador to Iraq at the time, into the job. Although the DNI did not have the sweeping powers imagined by the commission, Negroponte was thought to be sufficiently close to Bush that he could force reform on the CIA and other spy agencies.

Andy Card did not begin reading the report himself until the day it was released. But when he did start paging through it, he was impressed by how engrossing it was. "The first part is a good read," he said. He went up to Bush later in the day. "It's not as bad as I thought it would be," he told the president. "It reads like a novel."

The report was hailed as much for the quality of the writing as for its findings. The historian Arthur Schlesinger Jr. called it a "tour de force." *Time* magazine called it one of "the most riveting, disturbing and revealing accounts of crime, espionage and the inner works of government ever written." In *The New Yorker* magazine, the novelist John Updike wrote that the King James Bible had been "our language's lone masterpiece produced by committee, until this year's '9/11 Commission Report.'" Both ABC and NBC announced plans for a television miniseries based on the report. The report rose to number one on *The New York Times* Best Seller List. It was nominated for a National Book Award.

———

THE COMMISSION failed to win the book award. But there was no short-age of honors and other rewards for the commissioners and the staff. The commissioners delighted in the accolades.

"This is one of the best things I've ever done," Jim Thompson said later to an interviewer at home in Chicago. "I've had, over the years, quite a bit of face recognition. But I've never experienced anything like this. People coming up to me in airports, in restaurants, to talk about the commission's work. And they always start by saying, 'Thank you. Thank you for doing this.' That's extremely gratifying."

Norton, which had initially planned a press run of 500,000 copies of the report, eventually printed more than 1.5 million. Although Norton was not required to reveal its profits from the book, it announced in 2005 that it planned to donate $600,000 of the profits to two universi-ties to support the study of terrorism and emergency preparedness.

Bush replaced George Tenet at the CIA with Representative Porter Goss, a Florida Republican who was chairman of the House Intelligence Committee and a former agency spy. Goss was considered a disaster in the job and resigned under White House pressure after less than two years. He was replaced by General Michael Hayden, the director of the National Security Agency. Negroponte stepped down as director of national intelligence after only twenty-two months and was named dep-uty secretary of state. He was replaced by John Michael McConnell, a retired Navy admiral who had also once run the NSA.

Despite Robert Mueller's promises for reform at the FBI, the bureau remained the target of withering criticism for its failures in terrorism investigations and for its outdated technology. Five months after the 9/11 commission released its report, Mueller announced that the FBI was abandoning a $170 million computer overhaul that was considered critical to its stepped-up efforts to track terrorists; the system was found to be riddled with technical problems. Despite Mueller's continued insis-tence that terrorism remained the bureau's number one priority, there was no stability in senior management at the FBI when it came to terror-ism investigations. In the five years after September 11, six people had moved through the job of counterterrorism chief at FBI headquarters.

The Saudi embassy in Washington was so pleased by the conclusions of the commission's final report that it posted large excerpts of the report on its website. "The 9/11 commission has confirmed what we have been saying all along," said the Saudi ambassador, Prince Bandar bin Sultan. "The clear statements by this independent, bipartisan commission have debunked the myths that have cast fear and doubt over Saudi Arabia."

Investigations by the Defense Department's inspector general and by the Senate Intelligence Committee disputed allegations by a group of military officers and contractors who reported in 2005 that a top-secret Pentagon data-mining program known as Able Danger had identified Mohammed Atta and other 9/11 hijackers long before the attacks and linked them to a terrorist cell inside the United States. The 9/11 commission was drawn into the dispute after it was disclosed that a navy captain who had overseen the Able Danger program visited the commission's offices on K Street in Washington in 2004 and urged it to investigate, only to be rebuffed by Dieter Snell. The commission later said it was aware of Able Danger but had uncovered nothing in its investigation to suggest that Atta and the other hijackers were known to the government before 9/11.

Several staff members of the commission said later that while they were convinced the rumors about Able Danger and Atta were untrue, they believed that other vital intelligence about the 9/11 attacks and about al-Qaeda did remain hidden in government files after the commission had shut its doors. They were alarmed especially about what the commission had missed with its frantic, last-minute search of the NSA's terrorism archives. To date, they said, those archives have never been thoroughly reviewed by outside investigators. "I never felt complacent and remain ready to believe that someone may, in the future, find evidence we missed or didn't know about," Zelikow acknowledged later when asked about the NSA files.

On november 2, 2004, President George W. Bush was elected to a second term, taking 51 percent of the vote to John Kerry's 48 percent. Even though its conclusions questioned the Bush administration's justification for the Iraq war, the 9/11 commission's final report was never a major issue on the campaign trail. Opinion polls showed that a key factor in Bush's victory was the perception that he was the more decisive leader in dealing with terrorist threats. Several of the most prominent of the 9/11 family activists, including some of the Jersey Girls, had campaigned actively for Kerry.

Within days of his reelection, President Bush moved to oust Secretary of State Colin Powell, who was perceived within the White House as insufficiently loyal to the president's agenda, especially the pursuit of the war in Iraq. Even before Powell was told of Bush's decision, Bush had approached National Security Adviser Condoleezza Rice about replacing him. With what she insists was reluctance, she accepted. She was confirmed by the Senate on January, 26, 2005, by a vote of 85–13, becoming the second woman, and the first black woman, to run the State Department. It was the largest number of "no" votes in the Senate for any secretary of state since 1825. The same day, the Senate Judiciary Committee voted even more sharply along partisan lines to approve White House counsel Alberto Gonzales as Bush's attorney general, replacing John Ashcroft.

Many of the Senate Democrats who voted against Rice's nomination said they were troubled by her role as an architect of the Iraq war, as well as by her failings before 9/11 to deal with terrorist threats. Senator Barbara Boxer, a California Democrat, said she voted against the nomination because she wanted "to hold Dr. Rice and the Bush administration accountable for their failures in Iraq and in the war on terrorism." Senator Robert C. Byrd, the West Virginia Democrat who was one of the most vocal opponents of the Iraq invasion, said Rice simply did not deserve to be promoted given her record before and after 9/11. "I cannot support higher responsibilities for those who helped set our great nation down the path of increasing isolation, enmity in the world, and a war that has no end," he said on the Senate floor.

Rice quickly set to work to put a new team in place at the State Department, to replace the Powell loyalists who had departed with him. On February 25, she announced that she had decided to reestablish the job of State Department counselor, a sort of all-purpose adviser who would have her ear at all times. The position, which had been a powerful one earlier in the history of the department, had been vacant for four years, and she found just the candidate for the job: Professor Philip Zelikow of the University of Virginia.

"Philip and I have worked together for years," Rice said in a press release. "I value his counsel and expertise. I appreciate his willingness to take on this assignment."

Zelikow told his new colleagues at the State Department that it was the sort of job he had always wanted.

— ACKNOWLEDGMENTS —

In a sense, I began work on this book in January 2003, when I was assigned the 9/11 commission as a beat for *The New York Times*. I was not sure I wanted the job. It is odd to think of it now, but it was not clear to anyone at the time that the 9/11 commission would be much of a story. Only a few weeks earlier, Henry Kissinger had resigned as chairman of the commission in a dispute over his apparent refusal to abide by federal ethics rules and reveal the names of his consulting clients. He was replaced by former governor Tom Kean of New Jersey: a successful state politician, to be sure—but Kean would be the first to admit that in terms of national celebrity and geopolitical expertise, he was no Henry Kissinger. Far from it. Kean had removed himself from the political stage for more than a decade; he had never worked in Washington or for the federal government and he seemed to take pride in that fact. Certainly it seemed that Kean and the commission's vice chairman, former Democratic congressman Lee Hamilton of Indiana, lacked the clout to get at the rest of the truth surrounding what happened on September 11. And was there much more to tell? The origins of the 9/11 plot and the history of the government's failures to deal with the al-Qaeda threat had already been well fleshed out in the joint House-Senate investigation of 9/11, or so it appeared; the congressional inquiry was beginning to wind down just as the 9/11 commission opened for business. In early 2003 the public's attention, and the attention of many of my colleagues, was turning to what seemed to be the imminent invasion of Iraq. That was the much bigger story.

But in the nearly two years that followed, the commission became one of the best assignments of my career. There were days when I got lost in the exciting twists and turns of a story that had elements of a well-paced Washington thriller: Before terrorists struck on American soil, what did the president know about the threat and when did he know it?

Would he be forced to divulge his super-secret daily intelligence memos to the public? Would his savvy and telegenic national security adviser agree to testify in public and under oath regarding the damning charges made against her by a whistleblowing aide? Who was this mysterious White House whisteblower and what did he claim to know about the president and his top aides? Why did a top White House aide in the previous administration try to steal classified documents from the National Archives, apparently stuffed in his pockets, maybe in his socks? Every so often, I took a deep breath and reminded myself how important all of this was—how much larger this story was than the day's twists and turns might sometimes suggest. All of my stories dealt in some way with the most important event of our time: September 11, 2001. For our generation, this was our Pearl Harbor; this was our equivalent to the Kennedy assassination; this was the horrifying moment that changed all of our lives. I had daily contact with many of the widows and widowers and mothers and fathers and daughters and sons of the people who died at the Twin Towers and the Pentagon and that lonely field in Pennsylvania. Better than anyone else, they reminded me why this was not just another blue-ribbon federal commission that deserved the occasional 700-word story in the *Times*. The 9/11 commission was the last, best hope to understand why September 11 happened—and if it had to happen.

This book would not have happened without the help of many people who took risks to talk to me about the 9/11 commission. That is especially true of several of the commission's former staff investigators. Many of the key sources in this book are men and women who were detailed temporarily to the staff of the commission and then returned to their careers elsewhere in the federal bureaucracy. Although they do not figure by name elsewhere in the book, I have real admiration for the work of Mark Bittinger, Daniel Byman, Sam Caspersen, Lance Cole, Steven Dunne, Alvin Felzenberg, Susan Ginsburg, Doug Greenburg, Barbara Grewe, Bonnie Jenkins, William Johnstone, Janice Kephart-Roberts, John Raidt, John Roth, Peter Rundlet, Kevin Scheid, and several others on the staff. Whether I talked to these people or not is secondary; they should be saluted for terrific work on the commission. Certainly their colleagues had admiration for them.

Among the commissioners, Governor Kean and Congressman Lee Hamilton deserve my special thanks. They are model public servants and exceptionally decent men. When I first considered writing a book about the 9/11 commission, I thought about trying to help the two of them write their own account of the investigation. I was too late: It turned out they were already at work on a book, and the result, *Without Precedent: The Inside Story of the 9/11 Commission,* was published in 2006 by Knopf and co-written by the very talented Benjamin Rhodes. Their book was invaluable to me in organizing this unofficial history of the commission, and I have retold a couple of that book's best stories.

I am grateful to my colleagues at *The New York Times* for all of their assistance on this project and on so many other reporting projects over my career there. I shared many bylines on stories during that period with generous colleagues who made me look good, including Lowell Bergman, Elizabeth Bumiller, Jeff Gerth, Carl Hulse, Douglas Jehl, David Johnston, Neil Lewis, Eric Lichtblau, Alison Mitchell, Robert Pear, James Risen, David Sanger, Eric Schmitt, Thom Shanker, Richard Stevenson, David Stout, Don Van Atta, Matt Wald, and the late Christopher Marquis and David Rosenbaum; Chris and David are greatly missed by their colleagues. On stories about the 9/11 commission, I had terrific backing from the editors of the Washington bureau of the *Times,* especially Richard Berke, Greg Brock, Jack Cushman, Adrianne Goodman, and Susan Keller, as well as our team of researchers, especially Barclay Walsh, Monica Borkowski, and Marjorie Goldsborough. The former Washington bureau chief, Philip Taubman, convinced me to take on the 9/11 commission as an assignment over those initial misgivings, and I'm thankful he talked me into it.

In working on this book, I have had several cheerleaders from within the *Times,* especially my friends Jan Battaile, Marion Burros, Lynette Clemetson, Linda Greenhouse, Jan Harland, and the late, great R.W. Apple Jr. The new Washington bureau chief, Dean Baquet, has impressed everyone with his extraordinary talents as both a newsman and as a manager; he was generous to give me additional leave to finish this book. He is the fitting successor to my first boss in journalism, the legendary James "Scotty" Reston of the *Times.* A week after my college graduation, I began my career at the *Times* as Scotty's clerk in the Washington bureau. Dean and Scotty are alike in many ways, and that is a tribute to them both. Everyone in the Washington bureau owes a debt to Maureen Dowd, who has demonstrated her bravery so often during the

Bush administration. In the bureau, we all miss William Safire, who was a remarkably generous colleague. I am grateful to the executive editor of the *Times,* Bill Keller, and managing editor Jill Abramson for recognizing the importance of stories about the 9/11 commission long before editors at other news organizations.

I thank my colleague Michael Gordon of the *Times* for his wise counsel on the book-writing business. He urged me to hire on his research assistant, Christopher Mann, and it may have been the best decision I made in reporting and writing this book. Christopher is the perfect reporting partner—smart, hard-working, imaginative, unflappable—who has a brilliant future wherever he ends up. I look forward to reading his books someday soon. Christopher also led me to the very talented Alexis Blanc, a graduate student at George Washington University, who gave up weeks of her time to assist me with research.

I have been blessed to be represented by Kathy Robbins of The Robbins Office; with this book, I have learned that Kathy is as talented an editor as she is an agent. She is spectacular. She also has surrounded herself with terrific colleagues, including Coralie Hunter and Kate Rizzo. The talented David Halpern of The Robbins Office has given me my early education in dealing with Hollywood.

Kathy immediately thought of Jonathan Karp to publish this book, and it became obvious why. Editor, publisher, marketer, diplomat, deadline-enforcer, psychotherapist—he can do it all, with grace and humor, all the while bouncing that cute little kid of his on his knee. Jon is the great future of American publishing. It is an honor to be among the authors of the first twelve of his Twelve books. I am grateful to Jon's many talented colleagues at Twelve and at Hachette, including Cary Goldstein and Nate Gray. Robert Castillo, the managing editor of New York operations for Hachette Book Group, makes everybody look good. Jon and Bob found a splendid copyeditor in Sona Vogel. Hachette provided me with the services of a fine lawyer, Kevin Goering, who proved to be a thoughtful editor as well.

I am grateful to my loving parents and the rest of my extended family in northern California for putting up with my long disappearances to get this book done—and, for that matter, to pursue a career in newspaper journalism for the past quarter-century far from home. I'll try to get home more often. And my thanks and love to Susan Howells for also putting up with my long silences in Washington. My friends Grace and Evan know who they are.

Edward B. MacMahon, the brilliant court-appointed defense lawyer for Zacarias Moussaoui, the French-born extremist who would later be described as "the 20th hijacker" of September 11, and Ed's crackerjack deputy, Michele Jenkins, gave me valuable insight over the years into the workings of the legal system in the aftermath of September 11. Moussaoui almost certainly does not realize it, and he would not express gratitude, but the fact that he is not on death row is due largely to the hard work of Ed and Michele.

Although I have told him he will not like much of this book, Bill Harlow, the former chief spokesman for the CIA, has still been hugely helpful to me. I hope Bill takes some solace from the fact that, because of his assistance, this book is doubtless more balanced in its presentation of the CIA and its officers than it would otherwise have been. The same is true of Mark Corallo, John Ashcroft's former spokesman at the Justice Department. Bill and Mark have always served their bosses well, yet I have never felt led astray by either of them; that is the highest compliment I can pay to men who hold jobs like theirs.

My many friends at Café 1612, Steam Café, and the Starbucks at the corner of U and New Hampshire, all in the Dupont Circle neighborhood of Washington, kept me fed and well-caffeinated during the long, otherwise lonely writing of this book in 2006 and 2007. The bulk of the text was written in those three places, mostly over cups of steaming coffee. There were days I talked to almost no one else.

If anyone is responsible for this book, ultimately, it is the families of the victims of the 9/11 attacks. The families were responsible for the creation of the commission, over the fierce opposition of the Bush White House and many in Congress; the families fought to try to keep the investigation honest, against incredible odds. They did much of the digging that produced scoops for me and raised important issues about the commission, its leadership and the conduct of the investigation. I cannot imagine their suffering. If the full truth is ever told about September 11, 2001, it will be their doing. It has not been told yet.

Washington D.C.
December 2007

— NOTES —

I don't like anonymous sources either. I have spent my career at a newspaper that is so wary of anonymous sources that the word "sources" is effectively banned. (The popular formulations at other papers—"according to sources" or "sources said"—do not appear in *The New York Times*.) But in any sort of reporting on the inner workings of the government, especially when it involves intelligence agencies and classified information, there is almost always a need to depend on sources who cannot be identified by name. This book is no exception. Whatever they are called, the anonymous sources cited in this book had good reason to keep their names out of print. After the 9/11 commission went out of business in August 2004, many members of its staff returned to jobs in the CIA, the Pentagon, or other government agencies in which they could lose their jobs, even be prosecuted, if it became known they had talked to a reporter without permission. That sort of fear among government officials has grown steadily worse in Washington in the years since 9/11. I feel honored that so many of the commission's staff members who now hold sensitive government jobs were willing to take the risk to speak to me, albeit with a promise of anonymity.

My first executive editor at the *Times,* the legendary A.M. Rosenthal, had a firm rule about anonymous pejorative quotations about an individual: He would not allow them into his newspaper. And I have tried, whenever possible, to follow that rule in this book. As often as possible, I have tried to use material from "on-the-record" sources, including almost all of the commissioners and several key members of the commission's staff. Nearly two-thirds of the eighty members of the commission's staff talked to me for this book, on or off the record.

I covered the 9/11 commission for the *Times* for twenty months, from the day of its first meeting in January 2003 until the day it closed its doors for the last time in August 2004. After that, I spent months covering the debate that followed in Congress and at the White House over how to respond to the commission's recommendations. I developed a close relationship with several of the ten commissioners; there are some commissioners I spoke to virtually every day. All but two of the ten commissioners—Republicans Fred Fielding and James Thompson—agreed to give me extensive on-the-record interviews for the book. Both Fielding and Thompson did grant interviews to Kirsten Lundberg of Harvard's Kennedy School of Government for her well-crafted 2005 history of the commission, which the Kennedy School uses for its case-study program; I have used quotations from Ms. Lundberg's report and I cite them in these notes. The commission's executive director, Philip D. Zelikow of the University of Virgina, declined face-to-face interviews for the book. But he did agree to an extensive e-mail exchange over several months that, to my surprise, proved very successful. I know he gave up many hours of his time to deal with my questions, and I appreciate that. Whatever his opinion of this book and of me, I have huge admiration for Dr. Zelikow's intellectual firepower and his talents as a writer and editor.

There is an attempt in this book to draw readers into the rooms where the 9/11 commission did its work: into the commission's offices in Washington and New York; the Oval Office, the Situation Room, and other offices at the White House; the director's suite of offices at CIA headquarters, the mayor's office at City Hall in New York, among them. That has required an attempt to reconstruct conversations of which I was not a part. In almost all cases and whenever possible, my sources for these reconstructions were the people who were part of these conversations. In all my years of reporting, I have never had an assignment in which so many of my sources have something close to photographic memories.

Material in several chapters of this book is drawn from the public record, especially that material dealing with the commission's public hearings. Although it is no longer updated, the commission's official website, www.9-11commission.gov, is still available online and is now managed by the National Archives. On behalf of reporters and researchers everywhere, I can only hope it is maintained in perpetuity. It is an invaluable resource and includes all of the commission's staff reports, hearing transcripts, and videos, as well as the commission's complete final report. All quotations from the commission's pubic hearings are taken from transcripts available at the website.

More detailed notes for the book, along with copies of the government documents referred to in the book, will be available at the website created for this book: www.thecommissionbook.com. The website will also include extended e-mail exchanges between myself and Dr. Zelikow in which he responded to my questions. He is obviously entitled to respond to criticisms made of his leadership of the commission.

Chapter 1. National Archives

The theft of documents from the National Archives by former national security adviser Samuel Berger has been well documented, both in Justice Department filings made as a result of Berger's criminal guilty plea and in separate reports by the inspector general at the National Archives and by the staff of the House Oversight and Government Reform Committee. Many of the quotations from National Archives staff members and from Berger were drawn from these reports. Several of Berger's friends and former colleagues, who to this day remain perplexed by his crimes but still admire his efforts in the Clinton White House to deal with terrorist threats, provided me with extensive help in describing his mind-set. Berger has been represented throughout his legal ordeal by one of Washington's best lawyers, Lanny A. Breuer, and he was helpful in getting at the truth of this story. It is widely believed in Washington legal circles that Mr. Breuer got his client an extraordinarily lenient deal from the Justice Department.

Chapter 2. 350 Park Avenue

The December 2002 meeting in Henry Kissinger's office was described to me by several of the 9/11 family members who were there, most notably Kristen Breitweiser and Lorie Van Auken, two of a group of 9/11 widows who became known as the Jersey Girls. Kristen's book, *Wake-Up Call*, recounts some of the most colorful details of the encounter with Kissinger, the accuracy of which was confirmed by Lorie and others. Andrew Card, the former White House chief of staff, offered me an extensive interview in 2006 about White House dealings with Kissinger and the commission. Two senior White House officials, speaking on condition of anonymity, provided me with an account of Karl Rove's involvement in the selection of a chairman for the 9/11 commission.

Chapter 3. Bedminster, N.J.

The commission's chairman, former New Jersey governor Thomas Kean, agreed to be interviewed, in phone and in person, repeatedly from 2003 to 2007, and his account of his initial contacts with the White House are drawn from these interviews and from his 2006 book, *Without Precedent*, written with Congressman Lee Hamilton and Ben Rhodes, Hamilton's very able deputy at the Wilson Center. Card's comments are drawn largely from my interview with him. The background on Kean and his political career is drawn largely from my interviews with him and from two books: *Governor Tom Kean*, a fascinating 2006 biography by the historian and political scientist Al Felzenberg, who served as the 9/11 commission's chief public spokesman; and Kean's 1988 memoir, *The Politics of Inclusion*. Kean's comments about the "eye-shade mentality" of Republican leaders in Washington were first reported in an article in *The Washington Post* by writer Dale Russakoff on September 1, 1995 ("Kean Blames GOP 'Radicals' as Reason Against Senate Race").

Chapter 4. Office of the Chief of Staff

Andy Card provided me with the detailed account of his work in the White House and his liaison work with the 9/11 commission. In January 2005, Mark Leibovich, then of *The Washington Post*, now of *The New York Times*, wrote a terrific profile of Card that included a reference to Card's "kitchen stove" memory technique for organizing the White House. The article, "Pressure Cooker: Andrew Card Has the Recipe for Chief of Staff Down Pat," was published in the *Post* on January 5, 2005.

Chapter 5. Office of the Majority Leader

Close friends and aides to former senator Tom Daschle provided me with extensive information about how congressional Democrats selected their party's members of the 9/11 commission. Howard Fineman of *Newsweek* was present in Daschle's office when Vice President Cheney called in January 2002 to complain about Senate plans for public hearings on 9/11 intelligence failures. Fineman wrote about it on *Newsweek*'s website on May 22, 2002, under the headline: "Living Politics: Washington Looks for a September 11 Scapegoat." Hamilton acknowledged his gullibilty in the Iran-Contra investigations in an interview with Stephen Engelberg of *The New York Times* that was excerpted in a profile of Hamilton published on May 11, 1989, in the paper's "Washington Talk" column.

Chapter 6. Office of the Chief of Staff

Much of the material in this chapter comes from interviews with Kean and Card, and from Kean's book, *Without Precedent*.

Chapter 7. Charlottesville, Va.

Much of this material comes from an extensive e-mail exchange with Zelikow in 2007. Mark Fabiani, the former Clinton White House official who was a college classmate of Zelikow's, confirmed information about his partnership with Zelikow on their college debate team. The controversy in Japan over Zelikow's comments there on the atomic bombs dropped on Hiroshima and Nagasaki was reported by the Associated Press in an article on July 17, 1992 ("About 50 Stage Sit-in to Protest U.S. Scholar's A-Bomb Remark"), as well as in articles in Japan's *Daily Yomiuri* newspaper and by the Kyodo news service. The controversy over Zelikow's transcripts for his Kennedy book was set off by an article in the *Atlantic Monthly* by Sheldon Stern, the former Kennedy Library official, that was published in the magazine on May 1, 2000 ("What JFK Really Said"). Zelikow's response to the article was published in the magazine on August 1, 2000. Card's comments on Zelikow come from my interview with him. In interviews, Hamilton told me about his initial contacts with Zelikow.

Chapter 8. J. Edgar Hoover FBI Building

Much of this material comes from current and former FBI officials who are close to FBI Director Robert Mueller. The information about Mueller's Vietnam war record and his Bronze Star citation comes from a profile of Mueller in *VFW Magazine* (October 2002); the article, "Vietnam Vet Tackles Terror as Head of FBI," was written by reporter Tom Nugent. Coleen Rowley's letter to Mueller was first published in its entirety on *Time* magazine's website, www.time.com, on May 26, 2002. Former acting FBI director Thomas Pickard provided me with an extensive interview regarding his dealings with Ashcroft and the 9/11 commission.

Chapter 9. Offices of the Select Committee on Intelligence

Much of this material comes from interviews with former senator Bob Graham and from his 2004 book, *Intelligence Matters*. Much of the material about Senator Warren Rudman comes from an interview with Rudman. The full report by the joint House-Senate committee on pre-9/11 intelligence failures is available at the website of the Senate Select Committee on Intelligence: http://intelligence.senate.gov/107351.pdf.

Chapter 10. Drew University

Much of this material comes from interviews or e-mail exchanges with Kean, Hamilton, Gorton, and Zelikow, as well as from Kean and Hamilton's *Without Precedent*. Zelikow's article in *Foreign Affairs* (written with Ashton Carter and John Deutch) was published in the magazine's November/December 2001 issue under the title "Catastrophic Terrorism: Tackling the New Danger." Zelikow's book with Condoleezza Rice, *Germany Unified and Europe Transformed: A Study in Statecraft,* was published in 1995 by Harvard University Press.

Chapter 11. Offices of the National Security Council

Much of this material comes from interviews with Clarke, Zelikow, Kean, and Card, as well as from Clarke's 2004 book, *Against All Enemies*. Daniel Benjamin's remarks about Dick Clarke's relationship with colleagues on the staff of the National Security Council are drawn from Benjamin's hugely informative 2002 book (written with Steven Simon), *The Age of Sacred Terror*.

Chapter 12. Woodrow Wilson International Center for Scholars

Much of this material comes from interviews with Kean, Hamilton, Ben-Veniste, and Cleland, as well as from Kean and Hamilton's book, *Without Precedent*. Kirsten Lundberg's 2005 history of the commission, "Piloting a Bipartisan Ship," prepared for the Kennedy School of Government at Harvard, was invaluable in determining the timeline of the commission's work.

Chapter 13. Office of the Counsel to the President

The description of Zelikow's interactions with Gonzales comes from interviews with Zelikow, Kean, and various White House officials who agreed to be interviewed on promise of anonymity. The material on Zelikow's meeting at the CIA comes from Mark Lowenthal and Winston Wiley, as well as from former senior aides to Tenet and other CIA officials who agreed to be interviewed on condition of anonymity. The physical description of the grounds of CIA headquarters comes in part from material available on the CIA website, www.cia.gov.

Chapter 14. U.S. Navy Command Center

The description of Zelikow's job interview with Kevin Shaeffer comes from interviews with Zelikow and other commission staff members, as well as a description of the scene from Kean and Hamilton's *Without Prejudice*. Shaeffer has given several interviews to news organizations about how he survived the September 11 attack on the Pentagon and his long recovery from his injuries. Some of the more illuminating interviews were given to the Navy's official news service ("9/11 Pentagon Survivor Addresses Ike Crew," September 12, 2006, by reporter Nathaniel Moger), the *Navy Times* newspaper ("Crawling Toward the Light," September 11, 2002, by reporter Bryant Jordan), and PBS *NewsHour* ("Recovering," September 11, 2003, by reporter Susan Dentzer). Zelikow's memo, dated March 2, 2003, and titled "What Do I Do Now?" was addressed to "All Incoming Staff." Much of the material about the commissioners' response to the structuring of the committee comes from interviews with Gorelick, Cleland, and Ben-Veniste. The description of Lorry Fenner's hiring and her concerns about the NSA Archives comes from interviews with several staff members, including Lloyd Salvetti and Douglas MacEachin. Ellie Hartz's comments about her late husband, John, are taken from an episode of the PBS program *Frontline* ("Sacred Ground," September 7, 2004). Emily Walker's comments come from interviews with her.

Chapter 15. K Street Offices of the 9/11 Commission

Much of this material is drawn from interviews with Zelikow, Kean, Hamilton, Gorelick, and Roemer. The material about Carol Elder Bruce's awkward job interview was offered to me in interviews with Bruce, Kean, and lawyers who are friends of Bruce's.

Chapter 16. City Hall

The confrontation between Zelikow and his team and Bloomberg's aides is described in *Without Precedent* and was confirmed in interviews and e-mails with Zelikow and other members of the staff. The scene at the New York hearings, including the last-minute search for a gavel and the need to rent water pitchers, is detailed in *Without Precedent*. I credit Ben Rhodes, who organized and wrote much of the book with Kean and Hamilton, with an eye for a good detail. The reaction of the families of the 9/11 victims was explained to me in interviews with Lorie Van Auken and others.

Chapter 17. K Street Offices of the 9/11 Commission

The material on Karen Heitkotter and Dana Lesemann was provided to me by several staff members who are familiar with their accounts. Zelikow and Daniel Marcus, the commission's general counsel, confirmed the information about Lesemann and the purported security breach.

Chapter 18. K Street Offices of the 9/11 Commission

The material in this chapter is drawn from interviews with Gorton, Ben-Veniste, and John Farmer, the team leader who oversaw the commission's investigation of the crisis in the skies on the morning of 9/11. Excerpts of the testimony from former transportation secretary Norman Mineta, the FAA's Cathal Flynn, and retired Air Force major general Larry K. Arnold are drawn from transcripts of the commission's hearings.

Chapter 19. Office of the Counsel to the President

The description of the commission's dealings with White House counsel Alberto Gonzales is drawn from interviews with Kean, Hamilton, and Marcus, as well as with current and former administration lawyers who worked with Gonzales. The material about Cleland is drawn from interviews with Cleland and several of the other commissioners.

Chapter 20. K Street Offices of the 9/11 Commission

The National Security Strategy of the United States, the September 2002 document that was written mostly by Zelikow, is available at the White House website: http://www.whitehouse.gov/nsc/nss.pdf. Zelikow's comments about Iraq were quoted by the Associated Press on June 14, 2002, in an article titled "Bush Lays Foundation for Potential Attack on Iraq," by reporter Ron Fournier. In their book *Hubris,* Michael Isikoff of *Newsweek* and David Corn of *The Nation* offer the best published profile anywhere of Laurie Mylroie, the influential American Enterprise Institute scholar. Zelikow confirmed in interviews that he had invited Mylroie to appear before the commission and described his reasoning for the invitation. Mylroie's book, *The War Against America,* was published in 2001 by ReganBooks. In an interview, Judith Yapfe of the National Defense University, described her appearance before the commission. In an interview, Lorie Van Auken described her encounter with Zelikow after Mylroie's testimony.

Chapter 21. Department of History

Alexis Albion's views on employment in the intelligence community were captured in a witty article, titled "Female Bonding," for *The Washington Post Book Review* on January 16, 2005. The description of Albion's role on the commission was provided in an interview with several commission staff members. The material about Rudy Rousseau's work at the CIA was provided by Rousseau in an interview. The material about Tenet was provided in interviews with Rousseau; Tenet's former chief of staff, John Moseman; and several other former senior officials at the CIA.

Chapter 22. Room 5026

The descriptions of Warren Bass's review of NSC documents and his interactions with Zelikow and Michael Hurley were provided in interviews with several members of the commission's staff, including Marcus, the general counsel. The description of room 5026 in the New Executive Office Building was provided by staff members and commissioners who visited the reading room. David Kay's harsh appraisal of Rice, first revealed publicly by Bob Woodward of *The Washington Post,* was repeated to me and expanded upon in interviews with Kay. The description of Len Hawley's hiring was provided in interviews with several commissioners and staff members. The description of Bass's questioning for his security clearance was reported in a profile of Bass by the alumni magazine of his Canadian alma mater, the *Queen's University Alumni Review Magazine,* in its November 2005 issue; the article, titled "Dr. Bass Goes to Washington," was written by Geoff Smith.

Chapter 23. Washington, D.C.

Much of the detail on the terrorist warnings reaching the White House in the spring and summer of 2001 is drawn from the commission's final report, especially from its extensive footnotes. Bush's comments in an interview with Bob Woodward were first published by *The Washington Post* in an article by Woodward and Dan Balz ("Bush and His Advisers Set Objectives, but Struggled With How to Achieve Them") on January 28, 2002. The material on Lorry Fenner and the NSA Archives was provided in interviews with several members of the commission's staff, including Salvetti and MacEachin.

Chapter 24. K Street Offices of the 9/11 Commission

Cleland provided much of this material in interviews. The material on the commission's relationship with Cleland and his resignation from the commission is drawn from interviews with Kean, Hamilton, Roemer, and Gorton, among others. The transcript of Kean's December 8, 2003, news conference, in which he discussed Cleland's departure, can be found on the commission's website. Cleland's description of Republican election tactics as "pure evil" was reported by the *Las Vegas Review-Journal* in an article on September 14, 2004; the article, titled "Kerry Should Take Cue from Cleland," was written by reporter John L. Smith. The description of the accident in which Cleland's Cadillac was destroyed was reported by *The Washington Post* in an article on July 3, 2002, titled "Political Veteran: Max Cleland Survived His Vietnam War Wounds. But He Has Yet to Recover From His Last Campaign Battle"; the article was written by Peter Carlson. The article revealing Bob Kerrey's involvement in the Vietnam massacre was published in *The New York Times Magazine* on April 29, 2001; written by reporter Gregory Vistica, the piece is titled "What Happened in Thanh Phong."

Chapter 25. Home of Lorie Van Auken

Lorie Van Auken, Kristen Breitweiser, and other family advocates were the source of much of the information about the deliberations that led to the call for Zelikow's ouster. In her book, *Wake-Up Call,* Breitweiser described her confrontation with Zelikow in the Washington coffee shop. In interviews, Kean and Zelikow described Zelikow's strained relationship with the family advocates. The article in the *Newark Star Ledger* about the confrontation between Kean and the families was published on February 12, 2004 ("Kean Feels the Wrath of Irate 9/11 Families") and was written by Bob Braun. Marcus, Zelikow, and other staff members described the sworn testimony taken by the commission from Zelikow. Marcus confirmed his conversation with Karen Heitkotter about Zelikow's phone logs.

Chapter 26. Office of Political Affairs

The description and size of Rove's office comes from a floor map and article published in *The Washington Post* on June 6, 2005. Rove's degree of interest in the 9/11 commission and its investigation was described to me in interviews with Card, other White House officials, and John Lehman. The relationship between the White House and Kean and Hamilton was described in interviews with Card, Kean, and Hamilton, among others. In an interview, Lehman described his dealings with the White House over allegations of ties between Iraq and al-Qaeda. Lehman described his showdown with Admiral Hyman G. Rickover in his memoir, *Command of the Seas,* which was published by Scribner.

Chapter 27. Offices of the Director of Central Intelligence

Kean and Hamilton describe the meeting with Tenet in *Without Precedent* and provided additional details about the encounter in interviews with me. The description of Dieter Snell comes from Kean, Hamilton, and other commissioners and staff members. Former senior CIA officials described Tenet's positions on the issue of the commission's access to terrorist detainees. The best timeline of the commission's negotiations over the detainees is contained in *Without Precedent.* The investigation by Michael Jacobson into the connections between two of the 9/11 hijackers and a group of Arab men in southern California was described by Senator Bob Graham in his book *Intelligence Matters.* Several staff members of the commission also described Jacobson's work on the issue. In an interview, Gorelick confirmed that she had gone to FBI Director Mueller to complain about the FBI's failures to cooperate with the investigation. In an interview, Lehman described his detailed concerns about the Saudi government and its possible connections to the 9/11 plot.

Chapter 28. K Street Offices of the 9/11 Commission

Michael Scheuer provided much of the material for this chapter through interviews and in e-mails. Several staff members described the nature of the commission's interviews with Scheuer. Clarke's comments about Scheuer were made in an article published in *Vanity Fair* magazine in a richly reported November 2004 article, titled "The Path to 9/11: Lost Warnings and Fatal Errors"; the article was written by Ned Zeman, David Wise, David Rose, and Brian Burrough.

Chapter 29. The Capitol

Much of this material is drawn from interviews with Roemer, Clarke, and Dan Marcus, the commission's general counsel. The description of Clarke's encounter with President Bush on September 12, 2001, is drawn from Clarke's book *Against All Enemies*.

Chapter 30. Offices of the 9/11 Commission

John Farmer's description of his frustrations with the investigation is drawn from interviews with Farmer and other members of his team, including John Azzarello. Miles Kara, a member of the team, provided a detailed chronology of the portion of the investigation involving the FAA and NORAD. Kean and Hamilton's *Without Precedent* also offer a valuable description of the work of Farmer's team. In interviews, Hamilton and Gorton described their meeting with Defense Secretary Donald Rumsfeld. They and Kean described how the vote was taken on the NORAD subpoena.

Chapter 31. CIA Headquarters

Valuable descriptions of the president's daily brief (the PDB) and its preparation are provided in both Kean and Hamilton's *Without Precedent* and in George Tenet's 2007 memoir, *At the Center of the Storm*. In several interviews, Kean described his thinking with regard to the PDBs. The CBS News story that revealed the existence of the August 6, 2001, PDB was reported by the network's national security correspondent, David Martin, on May 15, 2002. The "BUSH KNEW" headline was published by the *New York Post* on May 16, 2002. The article by Bob Woodward and Dan Eggen about the same PDB was published in *The Washington Post* on May 18, 2002 ("Aug. Memo Focused on Attacks in U.S.; Lack of Fresh Information Frustrated Bush"). The description of the commission's strategy in requesting the PDBs is offered in detail in *Without Precedent* and was confirmed in separate interviews with Kean, Hamilton, Zelikow, Marcus, and others from the commission. My article about Kean's threat to subpoena the PDBs was published in *The New York Times* on October 26, 2003 ("9/11 Commission Could Subpoena Oval Office Files"). The reaction by Roemer and Cleland to the commission's final agreement with the White House over the PDBs was explained to me in interviews with both men. Kristen Breitweiser made her comment to me about Zelikow in interviews.

Chapter 32. Room 5026

In interviews, Kean, Gorelick, and Zelikow provided me with details of their inspection of the PDBs and other documents. In interviews, Marcus described his attitude toward the possibility of issuing subpoenas to the White House. Zelikow's quotation about the perception of the value of the PDBs was drawn from Kirsten Lundberg's report on the commission for Harvard's Kennedy School. Much of the information about the detailed content of the SEIBs and of Richard Clarke's files is found in the final report of the 9/11 commission, especially in the report's detailed footnotes.

Chapter 33. Office of the Speaker

Much of the material about House Speaker Dennis Hastert's attitude toward the 9/11 commission was offered to me by his former press spokesman, John Feehery, and other former congressional officials who worked with Hastert. In interviews, Kean and Hamilton described their difficult meeting with Hastert and other Republican congressional leaders. In interviews, Slate Gorton described his frustration with his membership on the Senate Intelligence Committee.

Chapter 34. The Situation Room

In interviews, several members of the commission and its staff described the White House meeting with then-national security adviser Condoleezza Rice. Dan Marcus, who conducted much of the questioning of Rice, provided an especially valuable account of the session. The comments about Rice by Kean, Lehman, Gorton, Gorelick, Kerrey, Ben-Veniste, and Roemer were provided to me in interviews. Portions of Rice's comments to the commission in the private interview were published in the commission's final report. Ben-Veniste's "Jean-Paul Belmondo" quotation appeared in *Newsweek*'s October 4, 1976 edition ("Watergate Winners," by Eileen Keerdoja). The comic-book character Ben Vincent appeared in *The Incredible Hulk* issues 176–178 (Marvel Entertainment Inc.).

Chapter 35. 26 Federal Plaza

Much of this material was drawn from an extensive interview with former acting FBI director Thomas Pickard and from interviews with commission investigators who researched his allegations against former attorney general John Ashcroft. Portions of Pickard's comments from his private interview with the commission are reproduced in the panel's final report.

Chapter 36. K Street Offices of the 9/11 Commission

The description of former national security adviser Samuel Berger's private interview with the 9/11 commission is drawn from interviews with several commissioners and staff members. Portions of Berger's comments in the interview are cited by the commission in its final report. Much of the detail of Berger's thefts at the National Archives and the discovery of the thefts is documented in the reports of the inspector general of the National Archives and of the staff of the House Oversight and Government Reform Committee.

Chapter 37. Offices of the Director of Central Intelligence

The CIA's Rudy Rousseau gave me an extensive interview, which is responsible for much of the material in this chapter. Additional material was drawn from an interview with John Moseman, Tenet's former chief of staff at the CIA. The descriptions of the commission's initial private interviews with Tenet were drawn from interviews with Zelikow, Ben-Veniste, and several other commissioners and staff members. Zelikow's comment that "we just didn't believe" Tenet was first published in *The New Yorker* magazine, in a profile of a senior FBI counterterrorism official, published on November 8, 2004. The article, titled "Learning to Spy: Can Maureen Baginski Save the F.B.I.?" was written by Elsa Walsh. Former senior CIA officials provided me with an account of Tenet's attitude toward the commission and his conduct in the private interviews.

Chapter 38. Studios of NBC News

The comparison of *Meet the Press* with a confessional is from an October 31, 2005, profile of NBC News Washington Bureau chief Tim Russert by Todd Purdum, then of *The New York Times,* now of *Vanity Fair* magazine; the article is titled "TV Newsman Is His Own News in the Leak Case." The transcripts of the appearances of Kean and Hamilton, and of Vice President Cheney, on *Meet the Press* are available on the NBC News website: www.msnbc.msn.com. The description of the commission's investigation into the September 11, 2001, order to shoot down commercial planes was described in interviews with Dan Marcus, the general counsel; John Farmer, the leader of the team who led that part of the inquiry; and several other members of the commission's staff. The description of the White House logs that recorded communications on the day of the attacks is found in the commission's final report, especially in its footnotes.

Chapter 39. Federal Bureau of Investigation

Much of this material is drawn from interviews with the commission's staff investigators, including members of Team 6, which was responsible for studying the FBI's performance. Some of the most frightening details about the FBI's outdated technology were published in Amy Zegart's extraordinary book *Spying Blind: The CIA, the FBI and the Origins of 9/11.* Former FBI acting director Thomas Pickard's comments about the FBI's technology are drawn from his public testimony to the commission on April 13, 2004. Kean's and Zelikow's comments about the FBI were made to me in interviews. Freeh's best defense against the attacks on his tenure at the FBI on counterterrorism was made in his 2005 book, *My FBI,* and in his public testimony to the commission. Much of the material about Ashcroft's performance in 2001 was drawn from interviews with former senior Justice Department officials, including Mark Corallo, Ashcroft's former spokesman.

Chapter 40. K Street Offices of the 9/11 Commission

The description of the reaction of the commission's staff to Richard Clarke's book *Against All Enemies* was provided to me in interviews with Dan Marcus, the general counsel; Zelikow; and other members of the staff. Clarke told me in an interview about his decision to bar Zelikow from reading an advance copy of the book and about his reaction to the White House attacks. A partial transcript of Clarke's interview with CBS News for *60 Minutes* is available on the CBS News website, www.cbsnews.com. Rice made the comments about Clarke in interviews with ABC News and CNN. In an interview, Card described the White House reaction to Clarke's appearance on *60 Minutes.* The transcript of Cheney's interview with Rush Limbaugh is available on the

White House website: http://www.whitehouse.gov/news/releases/2004/03/200403
225.html. The columnist Robert Novak made his comment about Clarke on the CNN
program *Crossfire* on March 25, 2004; a transcript is available on the CNN website at:
http://transcripts.cnn.com/TRANSCRIPTS/0403/25/cf.00.html. The description
of Clarke as a "drama queen" was made by commentator Laura Ingraham on the radio
program *Imus in the Morning* on March 23, 2004.

Chapter 41. Office of the Counsel to the President

The description of the campaign by White House counsel Alberto Gonzales and
others in the White House to undermine Clarke's credibility was described to me by
former White House and Justice Department officials. The phone calls from Gonzales
to Fred Fielding were first reported by *The Washington Post* on April 1, 2004, in an article by reporters Dana Milbank and Dan Eggen ("Bush Counsel Called 9/11 Panelist
Before Clarke Testified"). The transcript of Richard Clarke's 2002 background briefing on the Bush administration's antiterrorism record is available on the Fox News
website at: http://www.foxnews.com/story/0,2933,115085,00.html. News of the
existence of the taped background interview with Clarke was first reported by reporter
Jim Angle of Fox. The *Time* magazine cover story, "The Secret History," was published in its August 4, 2002, issue and is available at the magazine's website: http://
www.time.com/time/covers/1101020812/story.html. The transcript of *The O'Reilly
Factor* for March 25, 2004, the day of Clarke's hearing, is available through Lexis-Nexis.
The Pew Research Center poll on the public's response to Clarke's testimony was cited
on National Public Radio on the program *Morning Edition* on March 26, 2004. Karen
Hughes made her comments about the decision to allow Rice to testify to my colleague
Elizabeth Bumiller of *The New York Times* for a March 31, 2004, article that she and I
wrote, ("Bush Allows Rice to Testify on 9/11 in a Public Session"). The description of
Ben-Veniste's April Fool's joke is found in Kean and Hamilton's *Without Precedent*.

Chapter 42. Room 216

The description of the reactions of Ben-Veniste, Kean, Hamilton, and Kerrey to
Rice's testimony was provided to me in interviews with those commissioners. The
encounter between Zelikow and Raj De, the staff investigator, was confirmed to me
by Zelikow. Dan Rather of CBS News made his comments about Rice during a special
report with live coverage of Rice's hearing on April 8, 2004. The article by Tom Shales
of *The Washington Post* about Rice's performance at the hearing was published on April 9,
2004 ("Cool, Calm Condoleezza Rice").

Chapter 43. 301 7th Street SW

The meeting with Clinton is detailed in Kean and Hamilton's *Without Precedent* and was described in subsequent interviews with several of the commissioners
who attended, including Kean, Hamilton, Lehman, Kerrey, and Gorton. The quote
from Republican commissioner Fred Fielding comes from *Without Precedent* and was
confirmed by Kean and others. Mayor Michael Bloomberg of New York referred to
the 9/11 commission as "ghoulish" on his WABC-AM radio program on November
21, 2003.

Chapter 44. Riyadh, Saudi Arabia

The confrontation with Fahad al-Thumairy, the Saudi diplomat, was described to me by staff members, including Raj De. The information about the Tunisian taxi driver, Qualid Benomrare, was revealed in the footnotes of the commission's final report. The material about Doug MacEachin, the commission's investigator, was provided to me by MacEachin and others on the commission. In interviews, Kerrey and Lehman described to me their reactions to the aftermath of the *Cole* bombing.

Chapter 45. K Street Offices of the 9/11 Commission

The material about Len Hawley is drawn from interviews with several of the commission's staff members. Scott Allan was interviewed about his staff statement and the staff debate over Zelikow's rewriting of the statement. Zelikow's role in the debate and his frustrations in running the investigation were explained to me in my e-mail interviews with him. The final version of "Diplomacy" staff statement is available at the commission's website: www.9–11commission.gov.

Chapter 46. Room 216

This material is drawn largely from interviews with Gorelick, Kean, Gorton, and Kerrey, as well as with Mark Corallo, Attorney General John Ashcroft's former spokesman, and other former senior Justice Department officials. My articles on Ashcroft appeared in the *Times* on April 6, 2004 ("9/11 Panel Plans Hard Questions About the F.B.I. and Justice Dept.") and April 13, 2004 ("9/11 Panel Is Said to Offer Harsh Review of Ashcroft," with my colleague Lowell Bergman). The full transcript of the public testimony by Ashcroft is available at the commission's website: www .9-11commisison.gov.

Chapter 47. Offices of the Law Firm of Wilmer Cutler & Pickering

The death threats against Gorelick were first reported by ABC News and CNN on April 17, 2004. The next day, a report by National Public Radio on the threats included the audio from Rush Limbaugh. The background material on Gorelick is from several sources, most notably a terrific profile of her written by my colleague Eric Schmitt of the *Times* that was published on February 1, 1994, titled "Washington at Work: Pentagon Lawyer Quietly Gets Notice As a Rising Star in the Administration." Gorelick's op-ed article was published in *The Washington Post* on April 18, 2004 ("The Truth About 'the Wall'"). The description of the commission's visit to Florida on April 28, 2004, is drawn from Kean and Hamilton's *Without Precedent,* as well as from interviews with Gorelick, Kean, Gorton, and Hamilton. In interviews, Card and Kean offered a similar account of their telephone call on the eve of the Oval Office meeting with Bush.

Chapter 48. The Roosevelt Room

This material is drawn largely from interviews with Card and with several of the commissioners, notably Kean, Hamilton, Gorelick, Gorton, Kerrey, Ben-Veniste, Lehman, and Roemer. The transcript of White House spokesman Scott McClellan's criticism of Ashcroft is available at the White House website: http://www.whitehouse

.gov/news/releases/2004/04/20040429-4.html. The *New York Post* headline about the meeting, "DEM DUO DISSES DUBYA," appeared on April 30, 2004.

Chapter 49. The New School

The comments by former New York City director of emergency operations Richard Sheirer were made at a commission hearing on May 18, 2004. The transcript is available at the commission's website: www.9–11commission.gov. John Farmer explained his preparations for the New York City hearings in an interview. The events of the hearing were also described to me by Lehman, Kean, and Hamilton. The joint comments by Kean and Hamilton about the Giuliani hearing as a "low point" were made in *Without Precedent* and in subsequent interviews.

Chapter 50. Offices of the Director of Central Intelligence

Much of the material about the 1998 Memorandum of Notification was provided to me in interviews with Zelikow and other commission staff members, as well as with former CIA officials. Roemer expressed his concern about Tenet's August 2001 briefings in interviews with me. Tenet's point of view was explained to me during interviews with several former CIA officials, including his former chief of staff, John Moseman, and Rudy Rousseau, who led the DCI Review Group.

Chapter 51. J. Edgar Hoover FBI Building

Much of this material is drawn from current and former associates of FBI Director Robert Mueller, as well as from interviews with Kean, Hamilton, Gorton, and Dan Marcus, the commission's general counsel. The description of Dame Eliza Manningham-Buller's private meeting with the commission was provided to me by several commissioners and commission staff members who were there. The detail about her performance as the fairy godmother in an Oxford student performance of *Cinderella* was drawn from a profile of her in *The Guardian* by reporter Richard Norton-Taylor ("Head of MI5 is Second Woman to Hold Post"); it was published on May 18, 2002.

Chapter 52. K Street Offices of the 9/11 Commission

The material about Lloyd Salvetti was provided to me in interviews with Salvetti. The description of the agency's museum is found at the CIA website: www.cia.gov. The material about Lorry Fenner and the NSA archives was provided to me in interviews with Salvetti, Doug MacEachin, and other staff members of the commission.

Chapter 53. K Street Offices of the 9/11 Commission

In interviews, Zelikow acknowledged his conversation over the secure telephone with the CIA (although he disputed the memory of others about what was discussed). The confrontation between Zelikow and Ben-Veniste was described to me in interviews with both men. Current and former CIA officials provided me with information about the views of Barbara S. and Dwayne B., the CIA analysts who helped write the August 6, 2001, PDB.

Chapter 54. K Street Offices of the 9/11 Commission

Much of this material is drawn from interviews with the commissioners and the panel's staff. President Bush's May 2003 speech aboard the aircraft carrier *Abraham Lincoln* is available at the White House website: http://www.whitehouse.gov/news/releases/2003/05/20030501-15.html. The initial Associated Press article on April 16 was written by reporter Hope Yen ("Sept. 11 panel: Bin Laden sought Saddam's help but Iraq rebuffed him"). The later version was written by Terence Hunt ("Sept. 11 Commission Undercuts Bush Argument for War in Iraq"). Large portions of the CNBC interview with Vice President Cheney can be found at the MSNBC website: http://www.msnbc.msn.com/id/5233810/%20. Bush's comments on the relationship between al-Qaeda and Iraq can be found at the White House website: http://www.whitehouse.gov/news/releases/2004/06/20040617-3.html. Hamilton's comments about the need to see Vice President Cheney's evidence were made in an interview with me that was published on June 19, 2004 ("Leaders of 9/11 Panel Ask Cheney for Reports That Would Support Iraq-Qaeda Ties"); the co-author of the article was Richard W. Stevenson.

Chapter 55. Harvard University

Much of this material is drawn from Ernest May's extraordinary account, published in *The New Republic* on May 23, 2005, of his involvement in the commission's investigation; the article is titled "When Government Writes History." May also responded to e-mailed questions. A copy of the outline prepared by Zelikow and May was provided to me by a commission staff member. Kean and Hamilton described their reaction to the outline in *Without Precedent*. The article by Richard Falkenrath was published in *International Security* magazine in its Winter 2004/2005 article, under the title "The 9/11 Commission Report: A Review Essay." The subsequent letter from May and Zelikow and the response from Falkenrath were published in the magazine's Spring 2005 issue.

Chapter 56. K Street Offices of the 9/11 Commission

This material is drawn from interviews with Zelikow and several members of the commission's staff, including Dan Marcus, the general counsel. The material on the history of W.W. Norton is drawn from the publisher's website: www.wwnorton.com. I wrote about Zelikow's ties to Norton and the publisher's selection by the 9/11 commission in an article in the *Times* on May 25, 2004, titled, "9/11 Panel Chooses Publisher for Report."

Chapter 57. K Street Offices of the 9/11 Commission

Much of this material is drawn from interviews with the commissioners, including Kean, Hamilton, and Gorton. The call between Card and Kean regarding George Tenet was described to me by both Card and Kean.

Chapter 58. Office of the Chief of Staff

Much of this material is drawn from interviews with Card, Kean, Hamilton, and Marcus. The description of the guilty plea and sentencing of former national security adviser Samuel Berger is drawn from several articles in *The New York Times* and *The Washington Post*.

The description of Kean's and Hamilton's actions on the day of the release of the report is drawn in part from *Without Precedent*. Arthur Schlesinger's praise for the report was reported by the *San Francisco Chronicle* in an article published on November 12, 2004, titled, "The 9/11 Commission Report is a Compelling Read. But Does it Deserve a Literary Award?" The reporter was Heidi Benson. John Updike's praise was published by *The New Yorker* in a book review in its November 1, 2004, edition. Commissioner James Thompson's comment about the reception for the commission's final report is drawn from a profile of Thompson in *Chicago Lawyer* magazine in its February 2005 issue; the article by reporter Jim Day is titled, "9/11 Report Marked a High Point in Thompson's Career." As of late 2007, portions of the 9/11 commission's final report remain posted at the website of the Saudi embassy in Washington: www.saudiembassy.net. Zelikow's comments about his concerns over the NSA archives were made to me in an e-mail exchange. Secretary of State Condoleezza Rice's announcement of Zelikow's appointment as her counselor can be found at the State Department's website: http://www.state.gov/r/pa/prs/ps/2005/42745.htm.

BIBLIOGRAPHY

Baer, Robert. *Sleeping with the Devil: How Washington Sold Our Soul for Saudi Crude.* Crown, 2003.

Bamford, James. *A Pretext for War: 9/11, Iraq and the Abuse of America's Intelligence Agencies.* Doubleday, 2004.

Benjamin, David, and Steven Simon. *The Age of Sacred Terror.* Random House, 2002.

Breitweiser, Kristen. *Wake-Up Call: The Political Education of a 9/11 Widow.* Warner Books, 2006.

Clarke, Richard A. *Against All Enemies: Inside America's War on Terror.* Free Press, 2004.

Coll, Steve. *Ghost Wars: The Secret History of the CIA, Afghanistan and Bin Laden, from the Soviet Invasion to Sept. 10, 2001.* Penguin Books, 2004.

Drumheller, Tyler (with Elaine Monaghan). *On the Brink: An Insider's Account of How the White House Compromised American Intelligence.* Carroll & Graf Publishers, 2006.

Dunbar, David, and Brad Reagan (editors). *Debunking 9/11 Myths: Why Conspiracy Theories Can't Stand Up to the Facts.* Hearst Books, 2006.

Dwyer, Jim, and Kevin Flynn. *102 Minutes: The Untold Story of the Fight to Survive inside the Twin Towers.* Times Books, 2005.

Felzenberg, Alvin S. *Governor Tom Kean: From the New Jersey Statehouse to the 9-11 Commission.* Rivergate Books, 2006.

Freeh, Louis J. (with Howard Means). *My FBI.* St. Martin's Press, 2005.

Gertz, Bill. *Breakdown: How America's Intelligence Failures Led to 9/11.* Regnery Publishing, 2002.

Graham, Bob (with Jeff Nussbaum). *Intelligence Matters: The CIA, the FBI, Saudi Arabia and the Failure of America's War on Terror.* Random House, 2004.

Gunaratna, Rohan. *Inside Al Qaeda: Global Network of Terror.* Columbia University Press, 2002.

Isikoff, Michael, and David Corn. *Hubris: The Inside Story of Spin, Scandal, and the Selling of the Iraq War.* Crown, 2006.

Kean, Thomas H. *The Politics of Inclusion.* Free Press, 1988.

Kean, Thomas, and Lee Hamilton (with Benjamin Rhodes). *Without Precedent: The Inside Story of the 9/11 Commission.* Alfred A. Knopf, 2006.

Kessler, Glenn. *The Confidante: Condoleezza Rice and the Creation of the Bush Legacy.* St. Martin's Press, 2007.

Lance, Peter. *Cover Up: What the Government Is Still Hiding About the War on Terror.* ReganBooks, 2004.

Lance, Peter. *1000 Years for Revenge: International Terrorism and the FBI*. ReganBooks, 2003.

Lundberg, Kirsten. *Piloting a Bipartisan Ship: Strategies and Tactics of the 9/11 Commission*. John F. Kennedy School of Government, 2005.

McDermott, Terry. *Perfect Soldiers: The Hijackers: Who They Were, Why They Did It*. Harper-Collins, 2005.

Miller, John, and Michael Stone (with Chris Mitchell). *The Cell: Inside the 9/11 Plot, and Why the FBI and the CIA Failed to Stop It*. Hyperion, 2002.

The National Commission on Terrorist Attacks upon the United States. *The 9/11 Commission Report: Final Report of the National Commission on Terrorist Attacks Upon the United States*. W. W. Norton, 2004.

Office of the Inspector General, National Archives and Records Administration. *Report of Investigation: Samuel R. Berger*. Washington, November 4, 2005.

Posner, Gerald. *Why America Slept: The Failure to Prevent 9/11*. Ballantine, 2003.

Scheuer, Michael (originally published as "Anonymous"). *Imperial Hubris: Why the West Is Losing the War on Terror*. Brassey's, 2004.

Scheuer, Michael (originally published as "Anonymous"). *Through Our Enemies' Eyes: Osama Bin Laden, Radical Islam and the Future of America*. Potomac Books, 2003.

Suskind, Ron. *The One Percent Doctrine: Deep Inside America's Pursuit of Its Enemies Since 9/11*. Simon & Schuster, 2006.

Suskind, Ron. *The Price of Loyalty: George W. Bush, the White House and the Education of Paul O'Neill*. Simon & Schuster, 2004.

Tenet, George (with Bill Harlow). *At the Center of the Storm*. HarperCollins, 2007.

Thompson, Paul, and the Center for Cooperative Research. *The Terror Timeline: Year by Year, Day by Day, Minute by Minute*. ReganBooks, 2004.

Unger, Craig. *House of Bush, House of Saud: The Secret Relationship Between the World's Two Most Powerful Dynasties*. Scribner, 2004.

United States House of Representatives Committee on Oversight and Government Reform (staff). *Sandy Berger's Theft of Classified Documents: Unanswered Questions*. Washington, January 9, 2007.

Weiss, Murray. *The Man Who Warned America: The Life and Death of John O'Neill, the FBI's Embattled Counterterrorism Warrior*. ReganBooks, 2003.

Woodward, Bob. *Bush at War*. Simon & Schuster, 2002.

Woodward, Bob. *Plan of Attack*. Simon & Schuster, 2004.

Woodward, Bob. *State of Denial*. Simon & Schuster, 2006.

Wright, Lawrence. *The Looming Tower: Al-Qaeda and the Road to 9/11*. Alfred A. Knopf, 2006.

Zegart, Amy B. *Spying Blind: The CIA, the FBI and the Origins of 9/11*. Princeton University Press, 2007.

Zelikow, Philip D., and Condoleezza Rice. *Germany Unified and Europe Transformed: A Study in Statecraft*. Harvard University Press, 1995.

— INDEX —

About the Author

Philip Shenon is an investigative reporter with *The New York Times,* based in Washington, D.C. He was the lead reporter on the investigation of the September 11 commission and has held several of the most important assignments of the Washington bureau, including chief Defense Department correspondent, diplomatic correspondent, congressional correspondent, and Justice Department correspondent. He has reported for the *Times* from scores of countries across six continents.

ABOUT TWELVE

TWELVE was established in August 2005 with the objective of publishing no more than one book per month. We strive to publish the singular book, by authors who have a unique perspective and compelling authority. Works that explain our culture; that illuminate, inspire, provoke, and entertain. We seek to establish communities of conversation surrounding our books. Talented authors deserve attention not only from publishers but from readers as well. To sell the book is only the beginning of our mission. To build avid audiences of readers who are enriched by these works—that is our ultimate purpose.

For more information about forthcoming TWELVE books, please go to www. twelvebooks.com.